Meetings, Expositions, Events, *and* Conventions

An Introduction to the Industry

Fifth Edition

George G. Fenich, PhD

 Pearson

330 Hudson Street, NY NY 10013

Dedicated in memory of Loretta Lowe, San Francisco MEEC industry veteran and faculty member at San Francisco State University

Vice President, Portfolio Management: Andrew Gilfillan
Portfolio Manager: Pamela Chirls
Editorial Assistant: Lara Dimmick
Senior Vice President, Marketing: David Gesell
Field Marketing Manager: Bob Nisbet
Product Marketing Coordinator: Elizabeth Mackenzie-Lamb
Director, Digital Studio and Content Production: Brian Hyland
Managing Producer: Cynthia Zonneveld
Manager, Rights Management: Johanna Burke
Operations Specialist: Deidra Headlee, LSCC Communications, Inc.

Creative Digital Lead: Mary Siener
Managing Producer, Digital Studio: Autumn Benson
Content Producer, Digital Studio: Maura Barclay
Full-Service Management and Composition: SPi Global
Full-Service Project Manager: Raja Natesan, SPi Global
Cover Design: Jessica Chernyak, StudioMontage
Cover Image: Anton Gvozdikov/123RF.com and Razihusin/Shutterstock
Printer/Binder: LSC Communications, Inc.
Cover Printer: Lehigh-Phoenix Color, Inc.
Text Font: Sabon LT Pro.

Credits and acknowledgements borrowed from other sources and reproduced, with permission, in this textbook appear on the appropriate page within text.

Library of Congress Cataloging-in-Publication Data

Names: Fenich, George G., author.
Title: Meetings, expositions, events, and conventions : an introduction to the industry / George G. Fenich, Ph.D.
Description: Fifth edition. | Boston : Pearson, 2018. | Includes index.
Identifiers: LCCN 2017056522| ISBN 9780134735900 | ISBN 0134735900
Subjects: LCSH: Hospitality industry. | Congresses and conventions. | Meetings.
Classification: LCC TX911.2 .F455 2018 | DDC 338.4/791—dc23 LC record available at https://lccn.loc.gov/2017056522

1 18

ISBN-10:   0-13-473590-0
ISBN-13: 978-0-13-473590-0

ABOUT THE AUTHOR

George G. Fenich, PhD, is a professor in the School of Hospitality Leadership at East Carolina University. Dr. Fenich worked in the hospitality industry for 15 years before joining academe. He teaches and researches in the area of conventions and meetings, has written over 75 academic articles, and has presented at over 200 conferences, including the International Council on Hotel Restaurant and Institutional Education; the Destination Marketing Association International; the Association for Convention Operations Management; the International Association of Assembly Managers; AHTMM in Istanbul, Taipei, and Mauritius; the International Conference on Meetings & Events held in Shanghai, China; the Professional Convention Management Association; IMEX, America and Frankfurt; among others. He is on the editorial board of six academic journals, including editor-in-chief for the *Journal of Convention and Event Tourism.* He is also the principal of the consulting firm Fenich & Associates LLC.

BRIEF CONTENTS

CONTENTS

PREFACE

The meetings, expositions, events, and conventions (MEEC, pronounced like *geese*) industry continues to grow and garner increasing attention from the hospitality industry, colleges and universities, and communities. This book gives a broad overview of this industry and is, thus, an introduction. It is not meant to provide a hands-on or step-by-step method for handling gatherings in the MEEC industry. The latter is addressed in two books by Fenich: *Planning and Management of Meetings, Expositions, Events, and Conventions* and *Production and Logistics in Meetings, Expositions, Events, and Conventions*. Both of the books are based on and aligned with the Meeting and Business Event Competency Standards (MBECS).

This book is being produced at this time for a number of reasons. One is the continued growth of this industry; in spite of the ebbs and flows of the economy, the MEEC segment of the hospitality industry remains resilient. Communities continue to build or expand MEEC venues unabated, and the private sector has also become a player in convention center construction and operation. People still feel a need for face-to-face meetings. The MEEC industry appears to be on a growth curve, and is of interest to many people.

Also, college faculties have indicated a need for a book such as this. I have been teaching an introductory MEEC course for many years and have found myself having to continually supplement the existing books to make them both current and more complete in addressing the various segments of the MEEC industry. Therefore, I began to contemplate the development of a book on the subject. Then, at a meeting of the Convention Special Interest Group at the International Council on Hotel, Restaurant, and Institutional Education (iCHRIE) Convention in 2001, the need for a new text was discussed. The members of this group all noted the need, and I volunteered to spearhead an effort to put together a new book using faculty and industry experts to write various chapters. This book is the culmination of that effort. The result is a text where some of the best and most notable people in the MEEC industry have made contributions; as you will see, there is a balance of educators and practitioners among the chapter contributors.

The approach to deciding on topics was unusual. Rather than have a list of topics or chapters based on people's willingness to contribute, a more scientific method was used. I reviewed existing books, both theoretical and practical, to ascertain which topics to cover. Topics that appeared in more than one text were compiled into a list. Then a number of meetings were held with educators, and the relative importance of topics was discussed, which led to the development of a comprehensive list of topics. This list was sent to educators and practitioners, who were asked to rank the importance of each topic as critically important, important, or not important. Results were used to pare down the list, and this iterative voting procedure (called the Delphi technique) was used to reach the decision as to what topics to include in this book. This fifth edition has not only updated material and statistics, but has also relied on feedback from adopters and reviewers to make improvements to the previous edition.

It should be noted that this industry is referred to in many ways: meetings and events, events, meeting planning, and others. A very common acronym, and one used extensively in Asia is "MICE," which stands for "meetings, incentives, conventions, events" and is pronounced as the plural of mouse. This acronym was purposely *not* chosen for the title of this text. The reason is that most programs of study deal with incentives or incentive travel very little, if at all. Furthermore, the incentive travel segment has evolved significantly in the past few years, moving away from trips that were strictly for pleasure (as a reward for performance) toward trips that have notable education and training components. Thus, they are now much more like sales training meetings, motivational meetings, or team building exercises, but on a more grandiose scale. Thus, this book deals with meetings, expositions, events, and conventions.

New in This Edition

- Case studies have been included at the end of each chapter and enable the student to apply the content in each chapter to real-life scenarios.
- All data has been updated to reflect the current state. This includes charts, tables and figures.
- The chapter on technology has been totally rewritten and updated, and artificial intelligence and big data have been added to the chapter.
- All-new chapters Chapter 13, Planning MEEC Events and Chapter 14, Producing MEEC Events are included.
- Chapter 15, International, features additional regions of the world, including Nigeria and Senegal and cities, including Kazan, Beijing, Sydney, and Rio De Janeiro.
- Chapter 16, Putting It All Together, is designed to tie all the other chapters together by providing an in-depth, detailed case study.
- The Glossary has been updated to include all key terms found in the chapters.

Meetings, Expositions, Events, and Conventions should be of interest to practitioners, educators, students, and the general public. It is the most up-to-date book on the MEEC industry, and will provide users with an overview of the industry. It is also comprehensive and covers a wider range of MEEC topics than any other book available. It can easily serve as the basis for an introductory college course on the subject, or for orientation sessions for new employees in the industry. It should meet the needs of anyone interested in knowing more about the MEEC industry.

Online Supplements Accompanying the Text

An online Instructor's Manual, PowerPoint slides, and TestGen are available to Instructors at www.pearsonhighered.com. Instructors can search for a text by author, title, ISBN, or by selecting the appropriate discipline from the pull-down menu at the top of the catalog home page. To access supplementary materials online, instructors need to request an instructor access code. Go to www.pearsonhighered.com, click the Instructor Resource Center link, and then click Register Today for an instructor access code. Within 48 hours after registering, you will receive a confirming email including an instructor access code. Once you have received your code, go to the site and log on for full instructions on downloading the materials you wish to use.

ACKNOWLEDGMENTS

I would like to thank Kathryn Hashimoto for her unabated support, patience, and encouragement; the chapter contributors for their work and insights; and students everywhere for their interest in the MEEC industry. Also, thank you to the educators in the MEEC field for helping to develop the concept for this book and for continuing their support through adoptions of this text. I would like to thank the reviewers of this edition for their thoughtful and insightful comments. They are Donald Brown, Ohio University; Jane Foreman, Hinds Community College; Tamoura Jones, Atlanta Technical College; Ara Karakashian, Hudson County Community College; Eric Olson, Iowa State University; Autumn Patti, Harrisburg Area Community College; Amy Slusser, Genesee Community College; David Smiley, Indiana University Bloomington; and Kate Sullivan, San Jose State University.

The success of this book is, in large part, a result of the efforts of the chapter contributors who are all experts in their particular area of the MEEC industry. They are:

Chapter 1: Introduction to the Meetings, Expositions, Events, and Conventions Industry (MEEC)

Karen Kotowski, CAE, CMP
Chief Executive Officer
Events Industry Council
Washington, DC

Kathryn Hashimoto, PhD, CMP, CHE
Professor Emeritus
School of Hospitality Leadership
East Carolina University
Greenville, NC

Chapter 2: Meeting, Exhibition, Event, and Convention Organizers and Sponsors

Kristin Malek, PhD
Assistant Professor
Kansas State University
Manhattan, KS

Chapter 3: Destination Marketing Organizations (DMOs)

Craig T. Davis
President and CEO
VisitPITTSBURGH
Pittsburgh, PA

Chapter 4: Meeting, Expositions, Event, and Convention Venues: An Examination of Facilities Used by Meeting and Even Professionals

Lisa Y. Thomas, PhD
Assistant Professor
School of Hospitality Leadership
DePaul University
Chicago, IL

Mary Jo Dolasinski
20-year industry veteran
Now on the faculty of DePaul University
Chicago, IL

Chapter 5: Exhibitions and Trade Shows

Amanda Cecil, PhD, CMP
Associate Professor
Indiana University (IUPUI)
Department of Tourism, Conventions and
  Event Management
Indianapolis, IN

Chapter 6: Service Contractors

Sandy Biback, CMP, CMM
CEO
Imagination + Meeting Planners, Inc.
Toronto, Canada

Chapter 7: Destination Management Companies
William R. Host, CMP
Associate Professor
School of Hospitality & Tourism
  Management
Roosevelt University
Chicago, IL

Chapter 8: Special Events Management
David Smiley, MS
Indiana University Bloomington
School of Public Health, RPTS
Bloomington, IN

Chapter 9: Food and Beverage
Donnell Bayot, PhD, CHE, CPCE, CFBE
Director of Academic Affairs
The International School of Hospitality
Las Vegas, NV

Gary L. McCreary, CPCE, CMP, CSEP
Vice President of Catering and Convention
  Operations at The Venetian/The Palazzo
  Resort Hotel & Casinos
Las Vegas, NV

Chapter 10: Legal Issues in the MEEC Industry
Tyra Hilliard, PhD, JD, CMP
Assistant Professor
College of Coastal Georgia
Tybee, GA

Chapter 11: Technology and the MEEC Professional
Jim Spellos, CEO
Meeting U.
Bayside, NY 11364

Kathryn Hashimoto, PhD
Professor Emeritus
School of Hospitality Leadership
East Carolina University
Greenville, NC

Chapter 12: Sustainable Meetings and Events
Michelle Millar, PhD
Associate Professor
School of Management/Department
  of Hospitality Management
University of San Francisco
San Francisco, CA

Chapter 13: Planning MEEC Gatherings
Amanda Cecil, PhD
Associate Professor
Indiana University
School of Physical Education and Tourism
  Management (PETM)
Department of Tourism, Conventions and
  Event Management (TCEM)
Indianapolis, IN

Chapter 14: Producing Meetings and Events
Amanda Cecil, PhD
Associate Professor
Indiana University
School of Physical Education and Tourism
  Management (PETM)
Department of Tourism, Conventions and
  Event Management (TCEM)
Indianapolis, IN

Chapter 15: International Aspects in MEEC
Mady Keup
Course Director
SKEMA Business School
France

Jenny Salsbury, CEO
IMC Convention Solutions
China

Dr. Chunlei Wang
Associate Professor
Department of Event Management
School of Tourism and Event Management
Shanghai University of International Busi-
  ness and Economics
Shanghai, China

Uwe P. Hermann
Faculty member and researcher
Department of Tourism Management
Tshwane University of Technology
Pretoria, South Africa

Chapter 16: Putting It All Together
M. T. Hickman, CMP, CSECP
Lead Faculty
Hospitality Exhibition and Event
  Management
Richland College
Dallas, TX

The Vancouver Convention Center is a unique venue.
David Wei/Alamy Stock Photo

CHAPTER 1

Introduction to the Meetings, Expositions, Events, and Conventions Industry

Chapter Objectives

- Define the foundational concepts relating to the meetings, exhibitions, events, and conventions industry.
- Outline the history of the events industry.
- Detail the evolution and maturation of the events industry.

- Articulate the ways in which ethical practices are important factors in the events industry.
- Discuss career definitions and opportunities for the meeting or events professional.
- Outline ongoing trends in the MEEC industry.

The meetings and events industry is a complex and multifaceted business and the professionals who support the planning and execution of events must bring a diverse set of skills and knowledge to the job.

1

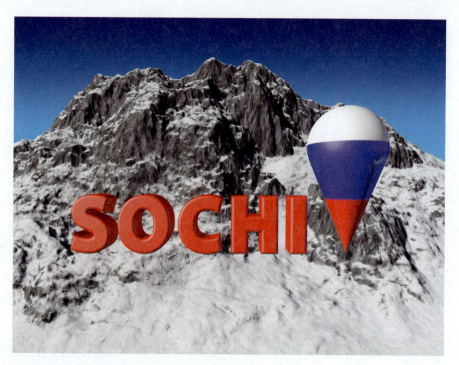

The Olympic Games are one of the many aspects of the MEEC industry.
rommma/Shutterstock

What Is the Meetings, Expositions, Events, and Conventions Industry?

The **meetings, expositions, events, and conventions (MEEC)** industry is large and touches virtually every aspect of the hospitality industry. MEEC includes business sectors, such as travel and hospitality, convention and visitors' bureaus, corporate meeting planning, event venues, equipment providers, and more. The types of events that are part of the industry include: sporting events, such as the Olympics and Super Bowl; Social events like family reunions and weddings; corporate events, such as sales meetings and strategic planning meetings; business events, such as trade shows, consumer shows, county fairs, and much more.

The global MEEC industry is set to reach $1.245 billion in 2023 which represents a 7.5 percent growth rate between 2017 and 2023. In the United States alone, more than 1.8 million events, conventions, and meetings occur each year with a combined total impact of almost $400 billion. The MEEC industry contributes more to the gross domestic product than the motion picture, spectator sports, performing arts, and sound recording industries. Almost two million people in the United States are employed in this industry, and the event planner profession is projected to grow by 33 percent over the next ten years. Being a MEEC planner has been identified as one of the best business jobs.

Performing poorly at any of the hundreds of potential failure points, or "moments of truth" in a meeting or event, can affect the ability of the event organizers to achieve the objectives of the event and meet the needs of the participants. Poor performance can have financial and reputational impacts for years to come. A good experience by each attendee will result in praises; on the other hand, a negative experience tends to spread to even more people.

Industry Terminology and Practice

We have always, generically, referred to gatherings of two or more people as meetings. This term could also encompass meetings that are called conventions, congresses, symposia, and so on, some of which could have tens of thousands of people in attendance. If one adds displays of materials or products to a meeting, the meeting then has a trade show or **exposition** or **exhibition** component. When sporting, social, or life-cycle activities are added, then a generic term that encompasses them all is events. Even broader, and more generic, is the term gathering. One must be conscious of how your stakeholders or target audience will interpret the name that is applied to a specific gathering.

The following list of terms is important for anyone involved in the MEEC industry to know. The terms were developed by the terminology panel of Accepted Practices Exchange, a part of the Events Industry Council, and are a small sample of the thousands of words that apply to this industry. The complete glossary of terms used in the MEEC industry can be found online at www.eventscouncil.org. Terms from the Events Industry Council are used throughout this book with their permission.

MEEC INDUSTRY TERMS

- **Assembly:** (1) A general or formal meeting of an organization attended by representatives of its membership for the purpose of deciding legislative direction, policy matters, and the election of internal committees; and for approving balance sheets, budgets, and so on. Consequently, an assembly usually observes certain rules of procedure for its meetings, mostly prescribed in its articles and bylaws. (2) The process of erecting display-component parts into a complete exhibit.

- **Break-Out Sessions:** Small group sessions, panels, workshops, or presentations offered concurrently within an event, formed to focus on specific subjects. Break-out sessions are separate from the general session, but within the meeting format, and formed to focus on specific subjects. These sessions can be arranged by basic, intermediate, or advanced information; or divided by interest areas or industry segment.

- **Clinic:** A workshop-type educational experience where attendees learn by doing.

- **Conference:** (1) A participatory meeting designed for discussion, fact-finding, problem solving, and consultation. (2) An event used by any organization to meet and exchange views, convey a message, open a debate, or for publicity of some area of opinion on a specific issue. No tradition, continuity, or periodicity is required to convene a conference. Although not generally limited in time, conferences are usually of short duration with specific objectives. Conferences are generally on a smaller scale than congresses. *See also*: Congress and Convention.

- **Congress:** (1) The regular coming together of large groups of individuals, generally to discuss a particular subject. A congress will often last several days and have several simultaneous sessions. The length of time between congresses is usually established in advance of the implementation stage, and can be either semiannual or annual. Most international or world congresses are of the former type, whereas national congresses are more frequently held annually. (2) The European term for a convention. *See also*: Conference and Convention.

- **Convention:** Gathering of delegates, representatives, and members of a membership or industry organization convened for a common purpose. Common features include educational sessions, committee meetings, social functions, and meetings to conduct the governance business of the organization. Conventions are typically recurring events with specific, established timing. *See also*: Meeting, Exhibition, Trade Show, and Consumer Show.

- **Event:** An organized occasion, such as a meeting, convention, exhibition, special event, gala dinner, social gathering, and so on. An event is often composed of several different yet related functions.

- **Exhibition:** An event at which products, services, or promotional materials are displayed to attendees visiting exhibits on the show floor. These events focus primarily on business-to-business (B2B) relationships (same as an Exposition or Trade Show).

- **Exposition:** *See* Exhibition.

- **Forum:** (1) An open discussion with an audience, panel, and moderator. A meeting, or part of a meeting, set aside for an open discussion by recognized participants on subjects of public interest.

- **Institute:** An in-depth instructional meeting providing intensive education on a subject.
- **Lecture:** An informative and instructional speech.
- **Meeting:** An event where the primary activity of the attendees is to attend educational sessions, participate in meetings/discussions, socialize, or attend other organized events. There is no exhibit component to this event.
- **Panel Discussion:** An instructional technique using a group of people chosen to discuss a topic in the presence of an audience.
- **Seminar:** (1) A lecture and dialogue allowing participants to share experiences in a particular field under the guidance of an expert discussion leader. (2) A meeting or series of meetings of 10 to 50 specialists who have different, specific skills but have a specific common interest, and come together for training or learning purposes. The work schedule of a seminar has the specific objective of enriching the skills of the participants.
- **Social Life-Cycle Events:** Events that mark the passage of time in a human life, such as weddings, bar and bat mitzvahs, anniversaries, and, today, even funerals.
- **Symposium:** A meeting of many experts in a particular field, during which papers are presented and discussed by specialists on particular subjects with a view to making recommendations concerning the problems under discussion.
- **Trade Show:** An exhibition of products and/or services held for members of a common or related industry that is not open to the general public. If it is open to the public, it is called a Consumer Show. Compare with Gate Show, Public Show, and Consumer Show. *See also*: Exhibition, Gate Show, Public Show, and Consumer Show.
- **Workshop:** (1) A meeting of several persons for intensive discussion. The workshop concept has been developed to compensate for diverging views in a discipline or on a subject. (2) An informal and public session of free discussion organized to take place between formal plenary sessions or commissions of a congress or of a conference, either on a subject chosen by the participants themselves or on a special problem suggested by the organizers. (3) A training session in which participants, often through exercises, develop skills and knowledge in a given field.

The Organizational Structure of the Hospitality Industry: How MEEC Fits in

MEEC is a part of, and encompasses, many elements of the hospitality and tourism industry. To understand how MEEC is related to the hospitality and service industry, one must understand the organization and structure of the tourism and hospitality industry itself.

There are five major divisions, or segments, of the tourism and hospitality industry: lodging, food and beverage, transportation, attractions, and entertainment.

The hospitality and tourism industry is multifaceted. The framework offered in the following list is meant to help provide a basic understanding of the industry, and is not intended to be an all-inclusive inventory.

Lodging

The lodging segment consists of all types of places where travelers may spend the night. These can include hotels, conference centers, resorts, motels, bed-and-breakfasts, Air BnB accommodations, and college dormitories. The important characteristics of this segment are that they are available to the public and charge a fee for usage.

Food and Beverage

Obviously, this segment contains two sub-segments: food service operations, and beverage operations. Food service operations can include the following: table service facilities that can be further broken down by price, such as high, medium, and low; by type of service, such as luxury, quick service, and so on; or by cuisine, such as American, East Asian, Italian, and others. Food service also embraces other types of operations including caterers and institutional operations (hospitals, schools, nursing homes, and so on). Beverage operations can also be broken down by price or type of service, and whether they serve alcoholic beverages or not.

Transportation

This segment includes any means or modality that people use to get from one place to another, including walking. The better-known elements include air, water, and ground transportation.

> *Air transportation:*   This sub-segment includes regularly scheduled airline carriers, such as Delta or Lufthansa, as well as charter air services that can involve jets, propeller aircraft, and helicopters.
>
> *Water transportation:*   This sub-segment includes cruise ships, paddle wheelers, charter operations, ferries, and water taxis. Cruise ships are a significant element since they not only provide transportation but lodging, food and beverage, entertainment, *and* meeting facilities.
>
> *Ground transportation:*   This sub-segment includes private automobiles, taxis, limousines, jitneys, buses, trains, cog railways, cable cars, monorails, horse-drawn vehicles, and even elephants and camels.

Attractions

This segment of the hospitality and tourism industry includes anything that attracts people to a destination. This segment can be further divided into natural and person-made attractions.

> *Natural attractions:*   This sub-segment includes national parks, mountains, seashores, lakes, forests, swamps, and rivers.
>
> *Person-made attractions:*   This sub-segment consists of things made or constructed by human beings, including buildings such as monuments, museums, theme parks, zoos, aquariums, and so on.

Entertainment

This includes anything that provides entertainment value for a guest, such as movie theaters, playhouses, orchestras, bands, and festivals.

Overlapping Industries

There are many overlaps between these categories, for example: A hotel may be an attraction in itself, such as the CityCenter in Las Vegas. Hotels often have food and beverage outlets, attractions, and entertainment. Furthermore, some of the businesses mentioned earlier cater to tourists, meeting attendees, and local residents alike. It would seem, then, that the meetings and events industry is involved with all segments of the hospitality and tourism industry.

Understanding the interactions and complexities of the hospitality and tourism industry helps explain why it is difficult to determine the size and scope of these industries. Until the late 1990s, the US government, using its North American Industry Classification System (NAICS) codes, did not even track many elements of these industries.

Because travel and tourism is not a single industry, producing a single product, it cannot be measured in its true form by a singular NAICS code. Travel and Tourism Satellite Accounts (TTSAs) are a relatively new economic statistical method to measure more accurately the impact of the travel and tourism industries on the US economy. Similarly, meetings and events cannot be measured by a single industry measure. The **Events Industry Council (EIC)** undertakes a research project every three or four years to measure the economic significance of the meetings and events industry.

History of the Industry

Gatherings, meetings, events, and conventions (of sorts) have been a part of people's lives since the earliest recorded history. Archeologists have found primitive ruins from ancient cultures that were used as meeting areas where citizens would gather to discuss common interests, such as government, war, hunting, or tribal celebrations. Once humans developed permanent settlements, each town or village had a public meeting area, often called a town square, where residents could meet, talk, and celebrate. Under the leadership of Alexander the Great, over half a million people traveled to Ephesus (now Turkey) to see exhibitions, which included acrobats, magicians, animal trainers, and jugglers. Andrew Young, the former US ambassador to the United Nations, said at a Meeting Professionals International (MPI) meeting in Atlanta in the mid-1990s that he was sure there would have been a meeting planner for the Last Supper, and certainly for the first Olympics. In Ancient Rome, organized meetings to discuss politics and decide the fate of the empire were held at the Forum. Ancient Rome also had the Colosseum, which was the site of major sporting events such as gladiatorial contests—someone had to organize them. Using excellent roadways, the Romans were able to establish trade markets to entice people to visit their cities. In Old England, there were fictional stories of King Arthur's Round Table, another example of a meeting that discussed the trials and tribulations of the day. Religious gatherings of various faiths and pilgrimages to Mecca are examples of religious meetings and festivals that began centuries ago. The Olympics began as an ancient sporting event that was organized as similar events are today. World's fairs and expositions are still another piece of the MEEC industry.

The First Continental Congress in Philadelphia is an example of a formal meeting; in this case, it was to decide the governance of the thirteen colonies. Political conventions have a long history in the United States and are part of the MEEC industry. Americans

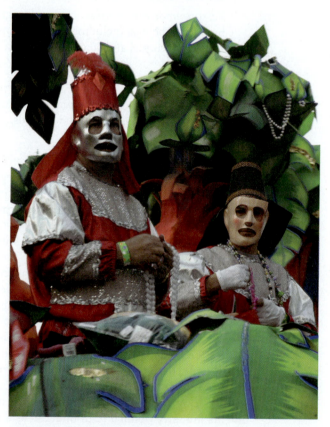

Mardi Gras in New Orleans.
Wendy Kaveney Photography/Shutterstock

have also made festivals and celebrations of every sort, such as Mardi Gras in New Orleans, a part of their lives since the early days of this country, and events like these can also be part of the MEEC industry.

Today, structures supporting the MEEC industry are integral parts of major cities. It is a well-known fact that in order to be considered a *world-class city*, a community must have a convention center and a stadium or arena for sports and events. All the largest cities have them, including New York; Washington, DC; Barcelona; Chicago; London; Moscow; Pretoria; and Hong Kong. These public facilities attract out-of-town attendees for conventions and events, and are an important economic driver for the community.

In spite of the long history of meetings, meeting planning as a recognized profession has only more recently been developed. The development of the first academic meeting-planning program in the United States was approved by the state of Colorado in September of 1976, and was implemented by Metropolitan State College (now University) in Denver. This initiative was closely followed by the meeting-planning program at Northeastern Oklahoma University in Tahlequah. In 1979, Patti Shock started hotel convention service management and meeting-planning classes at Georgia State University (GSU). In 1983, trade show classes were added with the financial support of the National Association of Exposition Managers (NAEM) (now the International Association of Exhibitions and Events, IAEE), and the International Association of Fairs and Expositions (IAFE). Today, there are almost 700 academic programs worldwide, and more than 150 in the United States alone that teach about MEEC.

One factor that contributed to the rapid development of both industry education and academic programs during the 1980s was the development and implementation of the **Certified Meeting Professional (CMP)** examination and designation by the Convention Liaison Council (now the Events Industry Council). This certification gives both status and credence to the person who achieves it. Additional certificate programs have followed, including the Certified Meeting Manager (CMM), Certified Destination Marketing Executive (CDME), Certified in Exhibition Management (CEM), and others.

The Events Industry Council (previously, the Convention Liaison Council) has lead its constituent organizations in the professionalizing of the industry through certification, best practice, and education since its founding in New York in 1949 by four organizations: the American Society of Association Executives (ASAE), American Hotel and Motel Association (AH&MA, now the American Hotel Lodging Association), Hospitality (then Hotel) Sales and Marketing Association International (HSMAI), and the International Association of Convention and Visitor Bureaus (IACVB, now Destinations International).

The basis of today's destination marketing organizations (DMO), which are also called convention and visitor bureaus (CVBs), was put forth in 1895 when journalist Milton Carmichael wrote in *The Detroit Journal* that local businessmen should get together to promote the city as a convention destination, as well as represent the city and its many hotels to bid for convention business. Shortly thereafter, the Detroit Convention and Businessmen's League was conceived to do just that. Carmichael was the head of the group that later evolved into the Detroit Metro CVB, which is now labeled *VisitDetroit*.

The role of CVBs (now referred to as Destination Marketing Organizations or DMOs) has changed over time. As in Detroit, most began by trying to attract only conventions and business meetings to their community. Later, they realized leisure visitors were an important source of business and added the "V," for visitors, to their name. Today, virtually every city in the United States and Canada, and many cities throughout the world, has a DMO or convention and visitors' association (CVA). The DMO (CVB, CVA) is a membership organization that helps promote tourism, meetings, and related business for their cities. In some international destinations, the DMO is a division of government. Many DMOs have now evolved to not only market but to help develop and manage tourism at their destinations. Most recently, the term DMO is being used in place of CVB. In this text, the terms are synonymous and interchangeable.

Evolution and Maturation of the MEEC Industry

(The following section is adapted from Fenich *Planning and Management of Meetings, Expositions, Events, and Conventions* 1st Edition.)

It can be said that events and meetings have been around since the dawn of time. In America, town hall forums were a type of meeting begun in the eighteenth century. While someone had to plan all of these events, there was neither formal training nor an established set of skills, standards, and abilities for those who organized those events. However, like other industries, such as law and accounting, as the industry evolved and matured there was an increasing need to formalize a set of competency standards to which professionals must adhere. Until very recently, no common set of **knowledge, skills, and abilities (KSAs)** existed for event professionals.

This dearth of standards changed in 2011 with the development of several competency standards, all of which building off a common platform—The Canadian Human Resources Council Competency Standards, the **Meetings and Business Events Competency Standards (MBECS)**, and the CMP International Standards. While all slightly different for their individual purposes, they all contain similar DNA: a similar set of knowledge, skills, and ability statements required of meetings and events professionals at the different levels of position or purpose.

MBECS

Using the MBECS as an example, the standards are divided into 12 domains or blocks with 33 skills and almost 100 sub-skills or sub-segments.

The domains and skills are listed in the following figure:

MBECS STANDARDS

A. STRATEGIC PLANNING
1. Manage Strategic Plan for Meeting or Event
2. Develop Sustainability Plan for Meeting or Event
3. Measure Value of Meeting or Business Event

B. PROJECT MANAGEMENT
4. Plan Meeting or Event
5. Manage Meeting or Event Project

C. RISK MANAGEMENT
6. Manage Risk Management Plan

D. FINANCIAL MANAGEMENT
7. Develop Financial Resources
8. Manage Budget
9. Manage Monetary Transactions

E. ADMINISTRATION
10. Perform Administrative Tasks

F. HUMAN RESOURCES
11. Manage Human Resource Plan
12. Acquire Staff and Volunteers
13. Train Staff and Volunteers
14. Manage Workforce Relations

G. STAKEHOLDER MANAGEMENT
15. Manage Stakeholder Relationships

H. MEETING OR EVENT DESIGN
16. Design Program
17. Engage Speakers and Performers
18. Coordinate Food and Beverage
19. Design Environment
20. Manage Technical Production
21. Develop a Plan for Managing the Movement of People

I. SITE MANAGEMENT
22. Select Site
23. Design Site Layout
24. Manage Meeting or Event Site
25. Manage On-site Communications

J. MARKETING
26. Manage Marketing Plan
27. Manage Marketing Materials
28. Manage Meeting or Event Merchandise
29. Promote Meeting or Event
30. Contribute to Public-Relations Activities
31. Manage Sales Activities

K. PROFESSIONALISM
32. Exhibit Professional Behavior

L. COMMUNICATIONS
33. Conduct Business Communications

These competencies represent all the KSAs an event professional needs to acquire, and be proficient in, during the course of their career. The **Certified Meeting Professional International Standards (CMP-IS)** have adapted these domains and skill statements for the purpose of defining the Certified Meeting Professional (CMP) Exam leading to the CMP credential. The development of these common standards marks a milestone in the MEEC industry. These standards, synopsized previously, represent the first time that the base of knowledge in the meetings and events industry has been codified, and has been a great advancement for the meeting-planning profession, and the individuals who work in the industry, as well as academics, students, and individuals who train the next generation of professionals.

Uses for Meetings and Events Professionals

Industry professionals can perform a personal-skills assessment of the standards and skills to discover those skills at which they are adept and at which they are not. The resulting gap analysis can help guide their professional and personal development. MBECS can also help plot career paths. Being able to provide an assessment that shows a broad mastery of the subject will enhance employability and mobility across sectors and countries, by allowing an industry professional to promote the attainment of this knowledge and associated skills to employers or clients.

Standards are of great value to employers and managers. The standards can aid in the development of job descriptions and job specifications. This leads to improvements in determining workforce requirements and producing worker solicitations. The standards can also help in developing a sequence of training for employees, as well as a basis for performance assessment and feedback.

Uses for the Academic Community

These standards provide an internationally accepted basis for developing courses of study and their requisite content. It is up to a given program or institution to determine how the content is delivered: in meeting/event specific courses, in business courses, in general education, or a combination. The significant advantage of using a standard like MBECS is that it is not prescriptive: one size does not fit all. Existing programs can benchmark themselves against the standards with resulting global recognition. The MBECS also provide a platform for dealing with governmental authorities and accrediting bodies. Using MBECS, a program can show the relevance of their course offerings and justify the content based on an international body of knowledge. Students can use the standards to develop their educational pathways and to validate their employability to recruiters. They could also use the standards to determine which educational programs best meet their learning needs. For academics, the standards can help delineate areas or topics in the meetings and events world that are in need of research.

Uses for Associations

First and foremost, standards provide recognition of the knowledge, skills, and abilities required by the industry. This can then help guide the development of program content and delivery that is consistent with international standards. They can also be used by the members of an association to determine their educational or professional development needs, and how the association can best fulfill those needs.

Accepted Practices Exchange

Throughout this book, you will hear about the Events Industry Council (formerly the Convention Industry Council) and its **Accepted Practices Exchange (APEX).**

The Events Industry Council is at the forefront of efforts to advance the meeting, convention, and exhibition industry. It represents a broad cross-section of the industry with more than 30 meetings- and events-related associations as members, representing more than 103,500 individuals, with more than 19,000 firms and properties involved in the meetings, conventions, and exhibitions industry. Formed in 1949, the council provides a forum for member organizations to advance the industry. The council facilitates this by enabling the exchange of information among members through the development of programs to promote professionalism within the industry and by educating the public on the industry's profound economic impact. By its nature, the council provides an impartial and inclusive forum for the APEX initiative and the development of accepted practices for the industry.

APEX brings together stakeholders in the development and implementation of industry-wide accepted practices to create and enhance efficiencies, as well as solve common problems and address industry issues. APEX also creates resources and tools to address these issues, such as education, white papers, and sample documents.

Some of the results of accepted practices implementation include:

- Time and cost savings
- Eased communication and sharing of data
- Enhanced customer service
- Streamlined systems and processes
- Less duplication of effort and increased operational efficiencies
- Better educated, more professional employees
- Solving common issues and problems

Ethics

The Professional Convention Management Association (PCMA), a widely recognized authority on convention and meeting management, published *PCMA's Principles of Professional and Ethical Conduct* in 2002.

Open and trusting relationships with your venues, facilities, vendors, and service providers will be priceless over time. Although practicing ethical behavior may not be a matter of law, violation of fair and equitable business practices can be considered illegal. There is a very long list of ethical issues, but a few of the easiest to violate, due to inexperience, are mentioned here.

Trouble Spots to Avoid

- Refrain from accepting or encouraging gifts or accepting promises of gifts from venues or service providers. This is particularly an issue prior to making decisions on sites, venues, vendors, and other service providers.
- Refrain from using travel points earned from airlines and hotels during business trips for personal travel.
- Refrain from conducting site inspections or accepting invitations to familiarization (FAM) trips sponsored to any location unless your group will seriously consider booking business there.
- Refrain from any activity that would discredit you or your organization.

What to Practice

- Full disclosure of any rebates, commissions, or incentives accepted for any reason.
- Notice to attendees that a rebate from registration fees will be used to offset an expense; a legitimate example would be a shuttle service expense.
- Fair and equitable negotiations in good times and bad.
- Confidentiality during the bidding process.
- Prompt and professional notification when site and vendor selections have been decided.
- Identify and address unethical behavior in others that could result in damages to your event, organization, or group. Ethics is not limited to your own personal behavior.

Suggested Industry Etiquette (Professional Courtesy)

- Be prepared, considerate, realistic, and factual in all verbal and written communications.
- Be cognizant of the value of everyone's time, and be timely with all.
- Meet your deadlines and keep your promises.
- Treat venues, facilities, vendors, and service providers as partners rather than subordinates. Everyone has a vested interest in your success.
- Understand the need for your event partners to make a reasonable profit.
- Maintain a calm and courteous demeanor under pressure.
- Work diligently toward agreement and solutions that will be mutually beneficial.
- Don't criticize. Seek resolutions.
- Make every effort to engage in respectful communications with everyone and in every circumstance.
- Resort to confrontation only when there is absolutely no other alternative to fixing an immediate problem.
- Approach working relationships as long term rather than one-time-only, as it is likely you will work with the same service provider companies in other locations, or you will rely on their referrals if they do not provide service where your event will be located.
- Share the glory. When your event is successful, praise your partners and the staff who helped produce it.

What Does a Meeting or Event Professional Do?

When asked about a typical day in the life of a meeting planner, there are few, if any, who could say that any day is typical, whether they work in an organization or operate an external planning company. The job of a planner is ideal for those who love to multitask, who have broad interests, who enjoy problem solving, and who care passionately about building community through meetings.

Doug Heath, Certified Association Executive (CAE), CMP, and the second executive director of MPI, said many years ago that meeting planners must be more than coffee-cup counters. When Heath said that, it was a time when most meeting planners were concerned only with logistics—ensuring the provision of room sets, coffee and refreshment breaks, meals, and audiovisual setup.

Today, the jobs of an event professional are strategic. Planners are charged with supporting the work toward an organization's bottom line. In order to do this, both when planning, and during a meeting or event, a planner may do any or all of the following, and more:

- Define meeting/event goals and objectives, and develop session content and design.
- Develop a request for proposal (RFP) based on the meeting/event objectives, audience profile, budget, and program (see Appendix of this book for examples).
- Send the RFP to national sales offices of hotel and conference center companies, to DMOs, and to external meeting-planning companies.
- Prepare and manage a budget and expenditures, which can range from a few hundred dollars into the hundreds of millions.
- Negotiate contracts with a facility or multiple facilities, transportation providers, decorators, speakers, entertainers, and all the vendors and venues that will support a meeting/event.
- Market the meeting/event electronically and in print, and track results.
- Invite and manage the needs (travel, lodging, registration, room setup, and audiovisual) for all speakers, trainers, and facilitators involved in delivery of information and knowledge for the meeting/event.

- Invite, manage contracts and manage the needs of entertainers.
- Design food and beverage events, and negotiate contracts for these events. To do so, an event professional must know the audience (age of participants, gender, abilities, allergies, geographic location, and more), the timing for the programs, the budget, and the prices, including labor costs and taxes.
- Prepare a crisis management plan in conjunction with other staff, facilities, vendors, and emergency personnel.
- Register participants, or manage a registration company, ensuring data are accurately entered and processed securely.
- Manage the multitude of changes that happen from the first conceptualization of a meeting or event to the execution and follow-up.
- Monitor industry and business publications for changes in management companies or hotel ownership, as well as for hotel foreclosures, facility and other strikes, and other issues.
- Calm others' nerves and remain calm.

Careers in and around the MEEC Industry

The MEEC industry is a vibrant, dynamic, and exciting part of the hospitality industry. Many careers in MEEC involve multiple aspects of the hospitality industry. For example, someone who works in convention or group sales in a facility must interface with, be knowledgeable about, and manage people who work with guest rooms, front desk, food and beverage, catering, and all of the meeting facilities.

The MEEC industry is a sub-segment of the hospitality industry, which itself is part of the larger services industry. It encompasses many areas of the hospitality industry. Thus, readers are challenged to conceptualize their personal ideal job and then determine how and where in the MEEC industry they could be employed doing what they dream of.

Some of the careers in MEEC are included in the following figure:

- *Event Planner:* Plans special events like the Olympics, the Super Bowl in football, the Final Four in basketball, festivals, and gala celebrations.
- *Wedding Planner:* A wedding planner is a type of event planner who assists parties in selecting the site, décor, photographer, and other needed vendors, and is often there on the day of the event to ensure smooth operations.
- *Meeting Planner:* Organizes meetings and other gatherings for companies, corporations, and associations. These gatherings can include a small, board of directors meeting, a stockholders' meeting, new product introductions and training, educational seminars, and regional or national conventions. Corporate Meeting/Event Planners fall into this category.
- *Exhibition Managers:* Organizes and manages trade shows.
- *Hotel or Conference Center Sales:* The majority of sales and conventions, or catering service positions in hotels and conference centers deal with groups, and MEEC covers most of these groups.
- *Restaurant Sales:* While most people think of restaurants attracting walk-in clientele, many rely heavily on the MEEC industry for business. Food and beverage (F&B) venues employ significant numbers of people on their group sales staff. In New Orleans, Arnaud's and Emeril's, for example, have group or convention sales teams.
- *Entertainment/Sporting Venue Sales and Services:* Although these places primarily attract individual patrons, most also devote much time and effort to selling, providing space for, and producing events for groups. These off-site venues are often good alternatives for experiential learning.
- *Destination Management:* **Destination Management Companies (DMCs)** function as the local experts for companies and associations, organizing gatherings and events, arranging and supervising transportation, and securing entertainers. People employed for DMCs usually work in either sales or production.
- *Hotels:* Hotels are one of the primary locations where MEEC events are held, using ballrooms, meeting rooms, break-out rooms, and so on, for their gatherings along with sleeping rooms and F&B for their attendees. The hotel departments that deal with the MEEC industry are sales, catering, and convention services.

A Smiling Wedding Planner Sets Up the Wedding Reception Venue by Organizing the Table's Flower Decorations before the Formal Function Begins.
Ryan Jorgense-Jorgo/Shutterstock

- ***Convention Centers:*** These venues include dedicated facilities, such as McCormick Place in Chicago, the Jacob K. Javits Convention Center in New York, the Congress Center Messe in Frankfurt, Germany, and the Canton Fair in Guangzhou, China—the world's biggest convention center.

- ***Multipurpose Venues:*** Like the Superdome in New Orleans or the Astrodome in Houston. With these venues, careers are found in either sales or operations.

- ***Exposition Services Contractors:*** If you like to build things or have thought about being an engineer or architect, you should consider being an exposition services contractor (ESC). ESCs design and erect the booths, backdrops, staging, and so on for exhibitions, meetings, and conventions. The decorations and backdrops for your school prom may have been done by an ESC. Again, career paths exist in sales and production and, increasingly, in design of sustainable/ green products and services.

- ***Destination Marketing Organizations (Convention and Visitor Bureaus):*** DMOs serve to represent a wide range of MEEC companies and to market the destination to business and leisure travelers. DMOs have many departments and careers, including convention sales, tourism sales, housing bureaus, convention services, marketing, research, and member services.

Some of the most important aspects of working in MEEC are business acumen (financial and people management, legalities and risk management, sales and marketing, and ethical practices), envisioning (what can be) and executing ideas into reality, and having knowledge of adult learning techniques. In addition to having knowledge and ability for preparing and delivering virtual and face-to-face meetings, industry professionals must know more about sustainability and going green for meetings and events.

It is often said that MEEC is a relationship industry, that is, it is one built on who you know and with whom you do business. As in many industries, we depend on those we know to help us learn and grow, and to provide accurate information. These relationships are built over time and always with the understanding that, first and foremost, ethical business practices will be the most important aspect of how we relate.

Think for just a moment about all the individuals and businesses involved in the execution of a single meeting or event. They could include the following:

The Meeting Sponsor

- Association or corporation sponsor
- Meeting planner
- Executive director or chief executive officer
- Staff specialists in departments that include marketing, governance and government affairs, education/professional development/training, membership, information technology, and accreditation
- Others who staff call centers, copy materials, process registrations, manage human resources, control purchasing, and more
- Board of directors
- Committees
- Sponsors

The Facility

- Owners
- Executive staff, including but not limited to: the general manager, revenue manager, resident or hotel manager, directors of sales, marketing, convention services, catering, housekeeping, engineering, maintenance, purchasing, human resources, food and beverage, front office operations, social responsibility, and security
- The thousands of other full- and part-time, year-round, and seasonal staff: groundskeepers, animal handlers, housekeepers, food servers (for banquets, room service, and the outlets), maintenance, security, and engineering

The Destination

- DMO/CVB (president, directors of sales, marketing, convention services, membership, registration, social responsibility, and all support staff)
- Restaurants
- Attractions
- Off-site venues
- Theaters (movie and legitimate)
- Copy and printing companies
- Transportation (buses, airport shuttles, taxicabs, and limousines)
- Airport concessions
- Doctors, medical personnel, and emergency workers
- Pharmacies
- Florists
- Destination management companies
- Audiovisual suppliers
- General services contractors
- Specialty services contractors
- Dry cleaners and tailors
- City, county, and state employees
- IT division and telecommunications department

All Others Who Provide Services for Meetings

- Talent (entertainers, disc jockeys, bands, and magicians)
- Education (speakers, trainers, and facilitators)
- Sound and lighting
- Transportation (air, rail, car, boat, and travel agencies)
- Printing
- Shipping
- Promotional products
- Off-property food and beverage
- Translators for those who speak American Sign Language and other languages
- Americans with Disabilities Act equipment
- Carpentry
- National sales (hotels and conference centers)
- Third-party or independent meeting planners

Even the president of the United States and Congress impacts our industry by determining trade regulations, travel restrictions, security issues, who needs a visa, and whether or not our country goes to war.

Is there anyone who does not have some influence on the meetings and events industry? A case can be made that every person has an impact, in some way, on each and every meeting—even those meetings of two or three that take place in an office or restaurant. Take a few minutes and add to the jobs or functions previously listed that might affect a meeting, and then think again. Also, create a career pathway for at least one of the careers noted previously.

Which Career Is Right for You?

The following are some of the career planning questions you might ask yourself to determine if this may be the right profession for you:

- Do you like to plan parties, work events, or just your day, down to the last detail, ensuring everything is locked in?
- Do you have, and regularly update, a date book or Outlook calendar that includes everything you need to do for weeks or even months into the future?
- Has any of the activities or skills outlined in this chapter struck a chord, and made you say, "this sounds like me" or "I have that ability or strength" and I want to be part of that?
- Do you ask good questions, rarely taking anything as a given? Do you think about contingencies or what if "x" happened? How would I adjust?

If you answered "yes" to some of these questions, you may just have the aptitude to be a good meeting professional.

Trends and Best Practices

The following are ten trends in the meetings and events industry.

1. *Meetings Are Experiences:* Meetings and events today aren't just face-to-face gatherings for the sole purpose of exchanging business information. Rather, they're enriching, one-of-a-kind experiences that attendees will treasure forever. Event professionals are increasingly creating these distinctive experiences in a variety of ways, oftentimes by simply choosing unique or unexpected venues that offer a "WOW factor." Another way to create memorable experiences is by engaging all five senses in what are referred to as multisensory events. Meals are also part of the attendee experience, and in the years ahead, food and beverage offerings will be increasingly tailored, either to reflect the event theme or to serve as special events in and of themselves.

2. *Content Will Condense:* Attendees' available time and attention spans are ever shrinking. Meeting schedules are shrinking as attendees' time is more and more consumed by business and family pressures. Content must be concise and it must have hard-hitting, take-home value. Event attendees want to be engaged for the short time they are at our meetings, and then they want to go home.

3. *Attendees Want a Sense of Place:* There is growing popularity in incorporating local elements into the meeting or event, giving attendees a taste of the locale they're in, such as offering attendees samples of the regional cuisine. Another way for attendees to experience a destination is to engage in local volunteer efforts or *voluntourism*, which can be included as part of the meeting's program (inclusion), and also plays into the growing interest in and importance of sustainability and corporate social responsibility (CSR).

4. *Attention to Diversity Will Become Even More Important:* With various generations—all with different work ethics and characteristics—working alongside each other, and issues related to gender equity and racial diversity still being addressed, companies continue to examine their recruitment and talent development strategies, approaching them with more awareness and creative solutions.

5. *Mobile Technology Is Here to Stay:* Having an event website, app, and social media presence used to be nice to have; today, they are required. Other than corporate meetings, all events must have an app. For cost-saving reasons, as well as sustainability reasons, most meetings no longer have printed programs, or there are a very limited number of printed programs. All of the event information is posted on the app. Not only do they allow for on the fly changes, posting of speaker handouts and bios (again, less printed documents), but they also allow for engaging the attendee before, during, and after the event. Mobile technology allows event professionals to not only push information out to attendees, but also get information from attendees to help them craft their programs on the front end, and to make adjustments during the event to provide more value. As a result, access to reliable, universal Wi-Fi will be increasingly expected with sufficient bandwidth.

6. *Technology Will Get More Connected:* The MEEC industry will continue to work toward greater connectivity, with the boundaries between online and offline further blurring the term hybrid, as every event moves toward such multifaceted experiences.

7. *Social Media's Dominance Will Deepen:* Social media will play a more measurable part in marketing and communication strategies all across the MEEC industry.

8. *Consolidation in the Hospitality Industry Will Continue:* Recently, we saw two of the largest hotel companies, Marriott and Starwood, merge into *the* largest hotel company in the world. This trend will only continue, even among the smaller hotel companies. It is hard to imagine that the US government will allow more consolidation in the US airline industry, but who knows. Most thought it would block the American/US Airways merger. Travelers lament the lack of competition in airline choice, let alone the deterioration of service and comfort. This is an unfortunate trend that will continue.

9. *The Importance of Meetings Will Get Noticed:* Meetings not only drive local and national economies (as demonstrated by the Events Industry Council's *Economic Significance Study of Meetings to the US Economy*), they also drive business results. An industry coalition called *Meetings Mean Business* promotes not only the economic benefit of meetings, but also tells the story of how meetings drive business forward.

10. *Face-to-Face Is Here to Stay:* Some prognosticators have predicted that technology and virtual gatherings will spell the demise of face-to-face. This is not the case. Human beings are social animals—they have an innate need to physically interact with one another. Technology is, and will continue to be, used to enhance and supplement face-to-face gatherings, especially before and after an event.

For meeting/event professionals, meetings/events never truly end. No matter how we define an event, each is a matter of intense planning and execution, evaluation, follow-up, and starting over. The role of a MEEC professional is critical in ensuring outcomes that contribute to a sound economy.

The success of the industry for individuals who currently work in, or who will choose to work in, MEEC depends on what we do now and how we anticipate and plan for the future. Those who choose to stay in or join this industry must have critical thinking skills and the willingness to consider the impact of all local and worldwide events on one's own meetings and events. Event professionals will need to know more about changing demographics in order to accommodate the needs of broader audiences; adult learning techniques to incorporate experiential learning and technology into face-to-face or virtual presentations, or for blended learning; nutrition and food allergies to ensure healthy and safe participants; climate change to understand its impact on sustainability, the availability of food and water, and the bottom line; current events and projections about world population shifts; and the worldwide economy and its impact on availability of products and services, including safety and security; and so on. The list is even lengthier than those stated.

In order to succeed, the meeting/event professional needs to be curious, informed, and customer focused. They will be planning experiences, not just meetings. They will change how spaces are used in facilities; how content is derived and delivered; and how participants are engaged. Those who succeed will enhance what they learn in classes and sessions by looking outside the industry for information.

Summary

In this chapter, you have been introduced to the world of MEEC. As we have seen, MEEC is multifaceted and exciting, and offers diverse career opportunities. MEEC is also very large and incorporates many aspects of the hospitality industry. It has tremendous economic impact. You are now prepared to continue with the remaining chapters in this book. They expand on and provide more details about the concepts and practices of MEEC that this first chapter only touches on.

CASE STUDY

The Big Day

Picture this: The sun rises above the horizon, releasing rays of blue and pink light that whisk across the ocean and spill onto the beautifully manicured greens of the resort hotel's championship golf course. Against the backdrop of the crashing surf and pleas of hungry gulls, you can also hear the sounds of morning stirring at the resort hotel. Car doors slamming, muffled voices sharing greetings and farewells, china and silver clashing, and the squeaking wheels of fully laden carts, each heading off to its appointed area under the guiding hand of one of many hotel staff who have arrived before most guests are awake.

Today is a big day. The Association of Amalgamated Professionals (AAP) will open its 35th Annual Congress with an evening reception, and, before the day is done, 1,900 guests and hundreds of vendors will have descended on this resort hotel. Since there were growing concerns about the image conveyed by using apparently glitzy venues, the venue eliminated the word resort from its name. This was done after the contract was signed.

Todd Cliver, Convention Services Manager for the hotel, convenes a last-minute meeting for the hotel's team handling the Annual Congress. Todd has worked tirelessly for nearly nine months, when the account was turned over from the Sales and Marketing Department of the hotel, coordinating all of the plans, wants, and needs of his client,

(Continued)

the association's Senior Meeting Manager, Barbara Tain. Today represents the culmination of hundreds of emails, phone calls, videoconferences, and personal meetings between Todd and Barbara. Todd interacted with every department in the hotel. Barbara worked closely with AAP staff and volunteers, worked with other vendors, and supervised AAP support staff for the AAP's 35th Annual Congress.

Donna Miller, Director of Sales and Marketing, whose department was responsible for contracting this—the largest meeting the hotel will have ever managed—reports on her client's last-minute changes and concerns, all meticulously logged since her client, Barbara Tain, arrived two days ago. David Stern, Front Desk Manager, recaps the latest report on expected room occupancy and on the timing and numbers of anticipated arrivals. Throughout the day, he will continue to check with his staff to ensure that there will be adequate (and contracted) numbers of front desk clerks to support the check-in flow, bell staff to manage the deluge of luggage and golf clubs, and door staff, valet parkers, concierge and guest services staff, and housekeeping services.

David Fenner, Director of Catering, provides his final status report, commenting on the readiness of the kitchen and banquet staff to serve the equivalent of almost 12,000 meals and untold gallons of juice, milk, coffee, tea, soda, and alcoholic beverages over the next three days. In addition, the hotel's outlets (restaurants and lounges) expect a much higher than average volume and have planned for supplies and personnel accordingly.

Other hotel staff members report to the Director of Sales and the Convention Services Manager. These include those involved with recreation (golf, tennis, health club, and pool), maintenance, security, and accounting. Even the animal handlers, who work with the parrots, an attraction for guests as they enter the property, want to ensure there are only healthy, well-behaved birds to greet the guests.

This one convention has already impacted, and will impact, every area of the hotel's operations. Armed with all this information, Todd leaves for his final preconference meeting (pre-con) with Barbara Tain.

Meanwhile, on the other side of the country, Jane Lever steps onto Concourse B of the Philadelphia International Airport, her airline-boarding pass, e-ticket receipt with its special meeting-discount price, and a US government-issued photo ID firmly in her grasp. She has checked her luggage, making sure it is locked with only the TSA-approved locks for a possible security search. She scans the bank of monitors for her flight information. Before her day ends, she will have touched down at two other airports, eaten one airline snack, grabbed a candy bar on her way through a change of planes at another airport, made numerous cell phone calls, bought a newspaper and a few magazines, and paid for a taxi to the hotel. Around the country, 1,899 other professionals, just like Jane, will do the same thing and travel to the same place for the same purpose—a **meeting**.

In the hotel's destination city, Kathy Sykes, the Owner and President of Skylark Destination Management Company (DMC), is already at her office reviewing final arrangements for ground transportation for VIPs and off-site events, event theme preparations, and entertainment for the AAP meeting. Kathy has already received two complaints from the manager of the headliner rock star booked for tonight's reception: The entertainer wants only chilled glasses for his orange juice, which he expects to be freshly squeezed in his suite, and can only get dressed if he is provided with navy blue towels for his after-shower rubdown. Kathy, of course, will ensure compliance with these requests; she wants to avoid any problems before tonight's event.

With a thunderstorm threatening for tomorrow afternoon, Kathy's mind is also already racing about alternatives for the golf tournament. She knows the golfers can play in the rain, but a thunderstorm would endanger their safety.

Jack Ardulosky, a Senior Technical Engineer for an audiovisual company, pulls into the hotel's delivery area while completing his mental checklist for final site review, satellite link integrity, picture clarity, and sound quality. With three global broadcasts and webcasts, he will have little room for error. He sees the florist unloading the last of the fresh floral arrangements and makes a note to himself that leaves and petals can cause just as much of a viewing obstruction as meeting room columns. He scans the area around him for a parking spot since not much is available with all the trucks and vans unloading the trade show booths. Jack notices the rising ambient temperature and expects a long, hot day. He will feel better if he can find parking in the shade, even if he must walk a greater distance.

Barbara Tain, the Senior Meeting Manager for the association, wipes the beginning of fatigue from her eyes—she has already been on site for two days, and her constant checking of details has not allowed her to sleep as well as she would have liked—and continues her walk-through of the registration area, information center, and cyber café, en route to a meeting with Todd Cliver and David Fenner, ensuring the meeting space will be appropriately set for delivery of the education critical to the meeting's objectives. Having eaten just a few bites of her breakfast during a meeting with association executives and key committee members, she will still be late to her meeting with Cliver and Fenner because of last-minute details and concerns from the meeting with association staff and volunteers.

Only half glancing at the space around her, she again reviews her lengthy checklist: speaker and trainer arrivals and needs, **banquet event orders (BEOs)**, transportation schedules, badges, staffing, centerpiece design and delivery, phone and data lines, computers and printers, Wi-Fi bandwidth, exhibitor booth setup, VIP procedures, concerns about tomorrow's weather, special check-in processes, audiovisual equipment, opening production rehearsal times and needs, PowerPoint files, handouts, arrangements for participants with disabilities including those who have specified food allergies, and amenities for VIPs—her mind is crowded with details.

With all this and more going through her mind, her most dominant thought is, "What could go wrong over the next three days: weather; delayed arrivals; delayed departures; the illness, or worse, death, of a participant, vendor, or speaker; or a natural disaster like an earthquake? How prepared am I? Is the hotel, our vendors, and off-site venues ready to respond quickly and effectively?" The fact is, although it is almost never apparent to a meeting participant, some things may not proceed as planned. The meeting planner and CSM are never more important than at that moment when a crisis must be anticipated and then averted.

It Is Opening Day at Last, and Everything Is in Motion

It is the end of the first day of the AAP's 35th Annual Congress, which Barbara Tain refers to as the Annual or Annual Meeting, and so far all has gone well.

Barbara will have had formal, prescheduled meetings with Todd Clive. Barbara will also have spoken with Todd and many others who work for the hotel via radio (walkie-talkie) and/or mobile device, as well as by chance and scheduled meetings. These talks include a review of banquet checks with various departments, one of which will include accounting. Barbara will have talked with those on the AAP staff and in volunteer leadership, and with outside vendors.

She will also check the weather many times on her smart phone, television, radio, and, if there is one, the newspaper. Barbara will have eaten on the run, tried to find a few minutes to check office voice mail and email, and, through it all, kept a smile on her face, even while her feet hurt.

At the end of the day, she will review her notes and check room sets for the next morning's sessions and crawl into bed for a few hours of sleep before it all begins again.

When the final curtain closes on the AAP's 35th Annual Congress, Barbara Tain will be one of the last to leave the hotel. Before leaving for the airport to fly home, she will review all the master account charges, conduct a post-convention (post-con) meeting with the property staff and her vendors, and make notes for next year's meeting. Once back in the office, she'll work with the vendor companies that conducted the evaluations, review all the bills, and ensure timely payment, and write thank you notes.

Face-to-face meetings will continue because there is a need for human interaction. These meetings and events will succeed because they are enhanced by virtual audiences who add to the energy and diversity prior to, during, and after the meeting or event. (Think Twitter and the hashtags being used now for meetings, and envision even greater involvement in the future.)

You've thus far decided to read this text and to learn about this dynamic industry. *You* are the future; you bring to it your experiences and insights. Observe, learn, and take action to keep MEEC moving forward.

Key Words and Terms

For definitions, see the Glossary

Accepted Practices Exchange (APEX)
banquet event orders (BEOs)
Certified Meeting Professional (CMP)
Certified Meeting Professional
  International Standards (CMP-IS)
conference
convention

Destination Management Companies
  (DMCs)
Events Industry Council (EIC)
exhibition
exposition
knowledge, skills, and abilities
  (KSAs)

Meetings and Business Events
  Competency Standards (MBECS)
meetings, expositions, events, and
  conventions (MEEC)
meeting

Review and Discussion Questions

1. What are meetings?
2. Describe some events from the past that were meetings.
3. Describe some current aspects of MEEC industry jobs.
4. Who attends meetings?
5. What can be accomplished by convening or attending a meeting?
6. What are five key jobs in a facility (hotel, resort, or conference center) that contribute to the successful outcome of a meeting?

7. What is the CIC?
8. What is APEX, and what is its impact?
9. What is the impact of meetings on the US economy?
10. What is MBECS?
11. What is the future of electronic meetings?
12. Create your own career pathway in the MEEC Industry.
13. Create a list of situations in the MEEC industry where ethics would come into play.

About the Chapter Contributors

Karen Kotowski, CAE, CMP, is the CEO of the Events Industry Council, a federation of more than 30 associations in the meetings, conventions, events, and exhibitions industry. The council administers the Certified Meeting Professional (CMP) credential, develops best practices through its APEX Initiative, promotes sustainable meetings practices, and conducts research on the economic impact of meetings and events.

Kathryn Hashimoto, PhD, is a faculty member in the School of Hospitality Leadership at East Carolina University. She has theoretical expertise in marketing and consumer behavior with operational expertise in meetings/events and casino management.

Previous Edition Chapter Contributor

Joan L. Eisenstodt, president of Washington, DC–based Eisenstodt Associates, LLC.

Industry Associations are significant organizers of expos and trade shows such as the E3 Electronic Expo organized by The Entertainment Software Association (ESA).
logoboom/Shutterstock

CHAPTER 2

Meeting, Exhibition, Event, and Convention Organizers and Sponsors

Chapter Objectives

- Understand the major types of organizations that hold gatherings, and differentiate the types of meetings and the planning required for each.

- Identify the associations that support the professional development of those responsible for producing gatherings.

- Outline the major trends facing MEEC organizers and sponsors.

This chapter focuses on explaining the entities that organize and sponsor different types of gatherings. Each of these segments creates gatherings to satisfy its unique needs and target attendee population. Whether the organization is a nonprofit association or a corporation, a government agency or a private company that produces exhibitions, it has goals that may require a MEEC gathering to commemorate an event. The purpose of this chapter is to identify who these organizing/sponsoring organizations are, the types of gatherings they hold, how much time they must have to plan an event, who their attendees are, and how they build attendance. The people who play a major role in producing the gatherings are identified, as are the professional associations who provide them with support and professional development.

Who Holds Gatherings?

The three most significant entities that organize and sponsor MEEC gatherings are (1) corporations, (2) associations, and (3) the government. Other organizations who arrange gatherings are also discussed here.

Corporations

Although there are numerous kinds of corporations, for the purposes of this chapter the term **corporations** will refer to legally chartered enterprises that conduct business on behalf of their owners with the purpose of making a profit and increasing its value. These include public corporations that sell stock on the open market, and have a board of directors who oversee the affairs of the corporation on behalf of the shareholders (or owners) who elected them. Private corporations have the same fundamental purposes as public corporations, but their stock is not sold on the open market.

Virtually all businesses have needs that require them to plan and execute gatherings. Publicly held companies have a legal requirement to hold an annual shareholders meeting. Many companies hold press conferences or a ribbon-cutting ceremony. Organizations also have continuing needs to train personnel in matters of company policy and procedures, and to further develop new policies and procedures to improve their effectiveness. Client groups may be brought together to capture their opinions in a focus group, or to introduce them to a new product or service. Incentive meetings are held to reward top producers within a corporation. Executive retreats may be held to improve communication or to develop long-term business plans. Gatherings are also held to honor employees (for promotion or retirement), to celebrate holidays, and to build overall morale within the organization. Companies may also be involved with a sporting event or entertaining clients in VIP areas at major sporting events, such as the US Open or the Super Bowl.

Many corporate meetings are booked as needed, typically less than six months before the meeting will take place, and are normally held at a hotel when exhibit space is not needed. When a corporation decides to hold a gathering, it determines what the budget will be, where the gathering will be held, and who will attend. Since the corporation typically pays for all expenses associated with attending the meeting, the corporation is in complete control. The decision to hold a corporate meeting is typically made by persons in positions of key responsibility within the corporate hierarchy. Officers and senior managers in the sales and marketing area may call for a meeting of their regional sales managers to develop sales strategies for new product lines; or senior financial managers and controllers may call a meeting of their dispersed staffs to discuss budgets for next year. Most of the attendees of a corporate gathering or event are members of the corporate family or are persons who have a close business relationship with the company. Attendance by corporate personnel is usually mandatory.

In terms of marketing, while the purpose of corporate meetings should be carefully crafted, attendance at these meetings is mandatory for most of the attendees. Therefore, sending invitations or notices to those who will attend constitutes the majority of promotional activity. Company websites are normally updated with the information regarding the meeting, its theme, and objectives. The company should create excitement prior to the meeting so attendees arrive eager to learn, listen, and enjoy their time out of the office. Even though it may be a command performance, this does not lessen the need to make the meeting informative, productive, and enjoyable for those attending.

Types of Corporate Gatherings and Events—Their Purposes and Objectives

Corporations have a variety of needs that can be satisfied by scheduling a gathering. What follows should not be viewed as a comprehensive list, but rather as an indication of the types of gatherings sponsored by corporations:

Stockholder Meetings   Voting shareholders of a corporation are invited to attend the company's stockholders meeting. This is an annual meeting that is usually held in the city where the company is headquartered, although there has been an emerging trend to move it to different locations to be more accessible to the stockholders. Attendees are presented with reports on the state of the corporation and can vote on issues of corporate significance. While most stockholders do not attend this meeting, they do participate in the governance of the corporation by filing a proxy statement in which they identify how they want their shares voted. According to *Meetings & Conventions magazine*, the average stockholder meeting has 79 attendees, lasts 1.7 days, and is planned with 5.2 months lead time.

Board Meetings   The board of directors is the governing body of a corporation and typically meets several times a year, usually in the city where the corporation is located. While a board meeting may be held in the corporate headquarters, these meetings may require lodging, dinners, and related activities, which are often held at local hotels and other types of venues.

Management Meetings   There are numerous reasons for a company to hold management meetings. Every major division of a corporation may have a need to bring its decision makers and other important personnel together to develop plans, review performance, or improve their processes. While some of these meetings may occur on a scheduled basis, others may be called spontaneously to solve problems and address situations that require immediate attention. According to *Meetings & Conventions magazine*, the average management meeting has 42 attendees, lasts 2.2 days, and is planned with 3.5 months lead time.

Training Meetings   As companies undergo change, it may be necessary to hold training meetings to bring managers and key employees up-to-date on improved methods of job performance or to gain skills needed to operate new systems and equipment. Companies may also use training meetings to introduce new managers to corporate procedures and culture. Some of these meetings may be held on a regularly scheduled basis, while others may be held when conditions dictate. According to *Meetings & Conventions magazine*, the average training meeting has 73 attendees, lasts 2.5 days, and is planned with 3.7 months lead time.

Sales Training and Product Launches   Sales training and product launches are a specific type of training meeting. These events are often held to upgrade the performance of the sales staff, distributors, and retailers, and to introduce new products and services to distribution networks and the general public. These events are designed to educate and motivate those who have a significant impact on the success of the corporation.

Professional and Technical Training   Professional and technical training are another specific type of training meeting. These meetings may be held to bring managers and others up-to-date on issues relevant to their role within the company and to enhance the knowledge of their service providers. For example, a company may have a meeting of its unit and regional controllers to discuss changes in tax law and company policies.

Incentive Trips   Many corporations offer **incentive trips** to reward their top performers based on certain criteria. At these meetings, there is a large amount of time spent on fun activities that the employees see as rewarding them for a job well done, such as a golf tournament, sightseeing tours, and outdoor adventures. However, there is a trend towards incorporating more business related sessions into incentive trips, thus making them more akin to conferences. Those winning these trips may be employees, distributors, and/or customers. Companies may bring together these top performers with their corporate leadership

Corporations organize a significant number of MEEC events, such as this Shaklee company meeting.
dycj-Imaginechina/AP Images

to create a more synergistic organization. While these trips are often to exciting and glamorous destinations, an emerging trend is to schedule several activities for the participants to provide an added value to the sponsoring corporation. According to *Meetings & Conventions magazine*, the average incentive trip has 130 attendees, lasts 5.0 days, and is planned with 8.2 months lead time.

Public Shows   **Public shows** (also called consumer shows) are gatherings where businesses sell their products directly to the general public. This is often in the form of trade shows where exhibitors display products that the locals will have an interest in and would be excited to attend. This is the reason they are called public shows. Examples of these types of events are boat shows, car shows, winter sport shows, and art shows. There is normally a fee for each attendee to get into the event. Corporations that sell the types of goods on display at a public show own and sponsor these events. To attract the public to attend, the organizers use social media, local radio and television stations, newspapers, and, often, local billboards to announce the event. Rarely are there educational sessions associated with these types of events.

Department and/or Individuals Responsible for Organizing and Planning

Corporate planners are really a hybrid group. Many of the people who plan corporate meetings have responsibilities beyond, or in addition to, the planning of meetings. Corporate planners spend about three-quarters of their time planning meetings. While about half of these meeting planners have meeting planner/convention management titles, the remaining majority have job titles that do not identify their meeting planning responsibilities (executive or management, 27 percent; general administration or management, 20 percent; sales and marketing, 14 percent; and other, 21 percent).

Therefore, at smaller corporations, since the typical meeting planner's job title does not specifically indicate meetings as part of their responsibilities, it should be no surprise that the majority do not work in a meeting-planning department. They tend to work in the departments that hold the meetings (sales and marketing, human resources, or finance) and have assumed meeting-planning responsibility at the request of their supervisors. For larger corporations, like Microsoft, Coca-Cola, Exxon-Mobile, and Cisco, meeting planning departments are large, as these organizations have many large and small meetings throughout the year.

Many corporate meeting planners join associations to support their professional development. These planners are members of these organizations so they can always be on the cutting edge of their profession, and they are well respected within their organizations. The associations that they most often join include Meeting Professionals International (MPI), Professional Convention Management Association (PCMA), the Society for Incentive Travel Excellence, and the Association of Insurance and Financial Services Conference Planners. Of the corporate meeting planners who have earned professional certifications, 32 percent were Certified Meeting Professionals (CMP) and 11 percent were Certified Meeting Managers (CMM).

CORPORATE MEETING PLANNING

Mary Jo Blythe, CMP
President, Masterplan, Inc.

Corporate meetings range from small VIP board of directors' meetings to large sales meetings, customer incentive meetings, and lower tiered staff training meetings. One common thread between them is that they are always paid for (hosted) by the corporation. The funds come from a department or individual budget, thus creating a VIP(s) host(s) at the meeting. This VIP(s) usually expects special treatment, and it is the planner's job to ensure that the VIP(s) is taken care of well.

The planner must also embrace the corporate culture and ensure that it is depicted in all aspects of the meeting, from hotel selection to airport transportation, to menu choices and social activities. Flashy companies will have flashy meetings, and conservative companies will have conservative meetings. The planner is the ultimate controller of this element, and it is the planner's job to make sure that all entities hired to help execute the event are aware of this culture, and what is expected from management and attendees.

The meeting objectives will typically include motivation, training, camaraderie, brainstorming, and reviewing goals. There is also quite often an emphasis on the social events at a corporate meeting. Although perceived as recreation, the opportunity for sidebar conversations and networking at non-meeting functions will often impact future corporate decisions. Social events should be strategically planned to ensure that the proper people are sitting together at dinner, or assigned to the same foursome at the golf outing.

Corporate meetings, although a category of their own, can be as diverse as corporations themselves. Paying special attention to your VIPs, embracing the corporate culture, and knowing your objectives get the corporate meeting off to a successful start.

Associations

In the United States, 315,000 association meetings and events occur each year, which are attended by 60 million people. Spending in this category is anticipated to grow at about four percent per year. This is a segment of the industry that cannot be ignored. The term **association** is defined as a group of people organized for certain common purposes, whether that be for professional, industry, educational, scientific, or social reasons. This definition of the word is true in MEEC as well. Gatherings, such as annual conventions, topical conferences, world congresses, and topical workshops and seminars are held for the benefit of the association's membership. Internally, meetings, such as board of directors' meetings, committee meetings, and leadership development workshops, need to be held for the betterment of the association. Many associations have an affiliated exhibition held in conjunction with their annual convention, at which products or services of interest to the attendees are displayed by various vendors. Besides providing value to the members of the association and potential recognition for the association, these gatherings also generate a significant revenue stream for the organization. According to *PCMA Convene Magazine 26nd Annual Meetings Market Survey* (February 2017), associations derive 32 percent of their organization's income from conventions, exhibitions, and meetings.

Although 60 percent of all national meetings and trade shows have an average attendance of 300 or less, the average attendance of all conventions is approximately 1,500 people ("Recent Meetings Market Report" by *Meetings & Conventions* magazine). Association meetings, especially conventions, can range from several hundred to tens of thousands of attendees. Two thirds of conventions are held in conjunction with a trade show or exhibit. The average convention has 265 exhibitors and requires approximately 56,000 square feet of exhibit space. This size issue can eliminate many smaller cities and venues from being selected as the location for these events. This limited availability of size-appropriate venues can create increased demand by larger associations for big cities and venues that can accommodate their meetings/events. It also creates increased competition among the larger destinations to capture the larger associations' business. This business means big dollars to the cities and venues, and can have a big economic impact on the city as a whole. To adjust to these supply and demand factors, larger associations typically book their major gatherings five to ten years, or even more, ahead of the scheduled date to ensure that they have the space needed for their event. Small associations have a broader selection of locations, including second tier cities that can accommodate their gatherings and, therefore, require less lead time to secure needed accommodations and facilities. However, unlike corporations, associations with smaller meetings still tend to book their meeting locations at a minimum of one year before the meeting date.

The decision-making process for association meetings is rather complex and goes through several distinct stages. Once it is decided that a meeting will be held (usually by the board of directors or as stated in the association's constitution or bylaws), the objectives of the meeting are first to be established. No planning of any meeting should begin until these objectives are established. The next step is to decide on the location where the meeting will be held. Some organizations rotate their meetings through their geographic regions, thereby dispersing hosting opportunities and responsibilities throughout their total membership. The specific city to host the meeting is sometimes decided by the association's board of directors, and at other times is dictated by the executive director based on the report of site visitations by the association's own meeting planner or by a contract meeting management provider. This report will give a summary of reasons why a destination is being recommended: hotel prices, convention center prices, available **air lift** (number of daily flights and quantity of seats) into the city, weather expected at the time of the meeting, availability of enough hotel rooms in the city, cost per attendee to visit the city, history of the meeting being held in the same city in the past, labor rates in the city, and overall ease of doing business in the city.

Once the choice has been narrowed down to a specific city, the meeting planner, based on site visits and inspections, will locate a venue (e.g., hotel and/or convention center) that is both available on the desired dates and well suited to the needs of the meeting. Typically, the meeting planner makes the recommendation to the association's board and leadership and, if approved, negotiates the financial and meeting details with the facility. This results in a contract that is eventually signed by both the venue and the association's senior staff person (usually the executive director or chief financial officer).

According to *CVENT*, the top cities that hosted meetings include:

United States	Europe	Asia Pacific
1. Orlando	1. London	1. Singapore
2. Chicago	2. Barcelona	2. Sydney
3. Las Vegas	3. Amsterdam	3. Kuala Lumpur
4. Atlanta	4. Paris	4. Bangkok
5. San Diego	5. Berlin	5. Hong Kong

ASSOCIATION MEETING PLANNING

Susan Reichbart, CMP
Director, Conferences, and Meetings (Retired)
College and University Professional Association for Human Resources

Associations offer their members opportunities to enhance their professional development at conferences, seminars, and workshops. These events may combine structured educational sessions of several hours or days with informal networking events, such as receptions, golf tournaments, and dinners. These activities encourage collegiality and allow members to exchange information in a relaxed social setting.

Associations encourage their members to become involved so that meetings *for* members are planned with input *from* members. The meeting planner works with member committees from the initial planning stage through the final production of the event. Committee members can suggest program topics and speakers that their colleagues will find appealing and, at best, compelling. Local committee members may suggest local venues for social events, tourist attractions and tours, entertainment options, and golf courses for a conference tournament. One particularly enterprising volunteer once researched local options and put together a comprehensive notebook rivaling those found at hotel concierge desks. Working under the supervision of the meeting planner, volunteers perform a myriad of duties during the event, such as giving out badges to preregistered attendees at registration, monitoring recreational events, and hosting social events—all duties that save the association the cost of hiring temporary staff. Member assistance is a value-added and integral part of planning that helps ensure an event's appeal and success.

Association events are a source of revenue for associations. The greater the number of paid attendees, the greater the revenue, and the more lucrative the event is to the association. However, since members must pay registration fees and spend additional funds for travel and lodging, the association must provide programs that its members will find too valuable to miss. The meeting planner develops a marketing strategy that promotes benefits to entice members and prospects to attend. The marketing plan may feature keynote speakers, concurrent session programs, an appealing location, and exciting social and recreational events. This information may be posted on the association's website, highlighted in newsletters, mailed in comprehensive preliminary programs, posted on social media, and sent as email blasts. In addition to promoting all facets of the event to members and prospects, additional marketing emphasis may be directed at targeted groups, such as past attendees.

Association meeting planners work with their member committees to develop worthwhile programs and then design effective marketing plans to maximize participation. The combined focus results in events that are beneficial to members and the association.

Types of Associations

As defined by the leading association for association planners, the Professional Convention Management Association (PCMA) has segmented the association category into four types: professional, medical or health, trade, and SMERF.

Professional   A professional association is an association where membership is comprised of persons from the same industry. Membership exists at the individual level and each person is responsible for paying his/her own membership dues. According to *PCMA Convene Magazine 26nd Annual Meetings Market Survey* (February 2017), professional associations comprise 47 percent of all associations.

Medical or Health   This is an association where membership is comprised of persons specifically from a medical or health area. According to *PCMA*, this segment encompasses 28 percent of all associations.

Trade   This is an association where membership is comprised of organizations from the same industry. Membership exists at the company level, and individuals employed by the member company become members by extension. According to *PCMA*, this segment encompasses 18 percent of all associations.

SMERFs   This term refers to small associations with members who join for Social, Military, Educational, Religious, and Fraternal reasons. Educational groups could include universities, for profit education groups, or high schools. Fraternal groups could include Kiwanis, Elks, or university fraternities and sororities. Persons attending these meetings tend to pay their own expenses; accordingly, this category tends to be very price sensitive. According to *PCMA*, this segment encompasses six percent of all associations.

Any of these association segments can take place at a local, state, regional, national, or international level, which is dictated by where the association members are located. Additionally, in the United States, any of these categories can have a special tax-exempt status granted by the Internal Revenue Service. Although tax-exempt associations do not have a profit motive, these associations need to be run efficiently and must have their revenues exceed expenses. Since all revenues are used to support the mission of the organization, excess funds (like profits in the corporate world) are allowed to stay with the organization, tax-free. On average, associations derive one-third of their annual operating revenues from excess revenue (profits) derived from their annual meeting/convention.

Types of Association Gatherings and Events—Their Purposes and Objectives

Conventions   According to the accepted practices exchange (APEX), a convention is a gathering of an industry organization convened for a common purpose. Common features include educational sessions, committee meetings, social functions, and meetings to conduct the governance business of the organization. Many conventions have an exhibition (or trade show), which may be a major source of revenue for the association. Exhibitors pay to participate in these events because these events offer them an opportunity to show their products and services to a well-targeted group of potential buyers at a much lower cost than making individual sales trips to meet with the association members individually. Conventions are supported, in part, by **sponsors**: companies or entities that will benefit from exposure to attendees at the convention.

Board Meetings   The association's board of directors typically meets several times a year to provide collective advice and direction to the association. These meetings are usually the smallest association meetings held. Oftentimes these will be held face-to-face.

Committee Meetings   Many association committees will hold their own smaller meetings to discuss the affairs related to their purpose (e.g., government relations, convention host committee, national conference program committee, and publications committee). Depending on the committee, these are oftentimes conference calls.

Regional Conferences   Organizations with a regional structure often schedule one or more events each year to bring together members who are in the same geographic area.

Training Meetings   Associations often offer their members opportunities to upgrade their professional skills and knowledge through meetings targeted to specific topics. Many professions require continuing education (e.g., continuing medical education for different medical specialties). Members will earn **continuing education units/credits** (**CEU**) by attending training meetings. Some associations offer training meetings to develop the leadership potential of the association's elected national and regional officers.

Educational Seminars   Association meetings led by experts that allow the participants to share their views and experiences.

Marketing and Attendance

One major difference between association and corporate gatherings is that attendance at association meetings is voluntary, not mandatory. Since attendance at association meetings is voluntary, the meetings must offer appealing programs to draw members to the events.

Another difference is that many of the attendees are personally responsible for their own registration cost, transportation, hotel, and related expenses. In some instances, employers may fund the attendance of employees at industry and professional association events that are work related and are seen as having an educational value for the employee.

The marketing of association meetings is critical to their success. All good association marketing should begin with an understanding of who the members are and their needs. This focus should be brought into the development of all meetings. In today's business world, attendees are reluctant to spend too much time out of the office in order to attend a meeting. It is the association's job to plan a robust program that entices the attendee and gives him or her a true and valuable reason to travel to a meeting. Many attendees must prove the value of the meeting to their boss to get permission to attend. Good marketing material is crucial to demonstrate this value.

If the meeting provides genuine opportunities for the members to satisfy their needs, the promotional aspect of marketing the meeting becomes much less intense. Since the primary group of attendees is members of the association, the key elements of marketing include providing advance notification of the date and location of the upcoming meeting, along with information about the planned content, speakers, and special activities. Later, detailed registration information and a preliminary program will need to be provided.

The vehicle for communicating this information to members has traditionally been through direct mail and notices or advertisements in the association newsletter and magazine. Today, this has changed as technology and cost considerations have moved many associations toward the use of electronic media to communicate with their members. There has been a rapid growth in the use of emails and social media to promote a meeting that emphasizes that recipients should visit the association's website to seek out details. Promoting and marketing next year's meeting or convention at the current year's event is also recommended so that attendees can block these dates on their calendars and can begin to create excitement one year in advance.

To expand the number of attendees at the gathering, many associations send promotional materials and notices to non-members who have been targeted as sharing an interest in the meeting's purpose. Since the non-member fee to attend the meeting is usually higher than the member fee, this effort, if successful, could result in attracting new members to the organization and can raise additional revenue for the association.

Department and/or Individuals Responsible for Organizing and Planning

According to *PCMA Convene Magazine 26nd Annual Meetings Market Survey* (February 2017), 80 percent of the respondents said that meeting planning was their primary job responsibility. The person in charge is most likely to hold the position of manager (41 percent) or director (28 percent). Three percent are vice presidents and eight percent are CEOs. They tend to be more experienced, with an average of 15 years of work experience in the meetings field. Seventy-seven percent of respondents have at least ten years of meeting management experience, and more than two-fifths (42 percent) have 20-plus experience. More than half of the respondents (63 percent) have earned an undergraduate degree (with 19 percent having earned a post-graduate degree). According to the *Convene 2016 Salary Survey*, 91 percent of meeting planners have earned the CMP designation, 6 percent have earned the CMM, and 5 percent have earned their Certified Association Executive (CAE) certificate.

Association meeting planners join professional associations in greater numbers than their corporate counterparts. Those associations include the PCMA, the American Society of Association Executives (ASAE), the Center for Association Leadership, MPI, and the Religious Conference Management Association. There are also many local organizations for meeting planners that provide support and professional development opportunities.

Table 2-1 provides characteristics of the major sponsors and organizers of meetings and conventions.

TABLE 2-1

Comparison

	Corporation	Association	Government
Definition	Legally chartered enterprises that conduct business on behalf of their owners with the purpose of making a profit and increasing its value	A group of people organized for certain common purposes, whether that be for professional, industry, educational, scientific, or social reasons	Subdivisions of federal, state, or local government
Purpose	Training, team building, and incentives	Primarily educational and networking with some trade show components	Primarily training and educational
Decision Makers	Centralized (typically leaders in the corporate hierarchy)	Decentralized (oftentimes committee decision)	Managers who decide to have the meeting and fund it from their departmental budget
Attendees	Members of the corporation or have a close business relationship with the company	Members of, or people interested in, that particular industry	Government employees and, depending on the event, the general public
Spouse Attendance	Rare	Common	Rare
Attendance	Mandatory	Voluntary	Mandatory for personnel; voluntary for public
Size	Varies by company; typically less than ten to one thousand	Several hundred to tens of thousands	Varies by event
Marketing	Minimal; invitation or notice to all attendees	Crucial; often includes mailers, magazines, and electronic marketing	Internally, similar to corporate; when the public is invited, similar to association
Location and Site Selection	Convenience, service, and security are valued	Seek attractive locations to help build attendance; amenities and nearby attractions are important	Convenience, service, and security are valued
Lead Time	Less than six months	Large associations—five to ten years or more; Smaller associations—minimum one year	Less than three to four months
Payment	Corporation pays for everything	Attendee pays for travel, hotel, and registration; registration and sponsorships cover cost of the conference	Funding is awarded through legislative process; department allocates meeting budget
Planner	Corporate planner, most likely a part of someone's job, could be any department in the company	Association planner and board, or outsourced to association management company	Similar to corporate planners who are spread throughout the agency; will outsource an independent planner if outside of their internal capabilities
Professional Associations	Meeting Professional International (MPI), Professional Convention Management Association (PCMA), Society of Incentive and Travel Executives (SITE), and the Association of Insurance and Financial Services Conference Planners	Professional Convention Management Association (PCMA), the American Society of Association Executives (ASAE), Meeting Professionals International (MPI), the Center for Association Leadership, and the Religious Conference Management Association	Society of Government Meeting Professionals (SGMP), Professional Convention Management Association (PCMA), and Meeting Professionals International (MPI). If responsible for organizing exhibitions—International Association of Exhibitions and Events (IAEE).

Government

Government entities at all levels find it necessary to hold gatherings since they have continuing needs to communicate and interact with many constituent bodies. These meetings may involve the attendance of world leaders, with large groups of protestors and supporters, or a small group of elected local officials holding a legislative retreat. Different than corporate and association meetings, government meetings are subject to various rules. The federal government and many state governments have established **per diem rates** that set limits on the amount of money a government attendee can spend per day for lodging and meals. Facilities where federal meetings are held must be able to accommodate persons with certain physical limitations, as per the Americans with Disabilities Act, and they must meet fire safety certifications. Since the list of per diem rate tables is so extensive, it is recommended that those in need of the current federal domestic per diem rates go to the General Services Administration (GSA) website at www.gsa.gov/.

Managers at government agencies are typically those who identify the need to hold a meeting and have the responsibility to provide funding through their departmental budget process or to locate other sources of funding. Meetings, like other parts of an agency's budget, are very dependent on funding provided through the legislative process. Accordingly, as political interest in an agency's mission grows or diminishes, the budget will increase or decrease, as will its ability to sponsor gatherings. Public backlash and policies by the US government can severely curtail off-site meetings by employees of government agencies, which has happened in the past.

Government meetings have characteristics typical of both corporate and association meetings. The purpose of many government meetings is the training of government workers. On the federal level, many of these meetings are replicated in several areas of the country to minimize travel expenses for the employees of an agency's branch offices. Other government meetings may involve both agency employees and those in the general public who may have an interest in the topic of the meeting. Meetings, such as those to discuss prescription drug proposals or the future of social security, are likely to go on the road to gather input from the public. Attendance by employees at government meetings would generally be mandatory, while attendance by the general public would be voluntary. Mandatory attendance by government employees requires only that sufficient notice be provided so that participants can adjust their schedules in order to attend. Attracting voluntary attendees may require additional promotion.

There has been some movement by government agencies to hold virtual meetings with the goal of reducing costs.

Security

There is no segment of the MEEC industry more attuned to safety and security than government. They work on a regular basis with the Department of Homeland Security in the United States since many of their attendees are high-profile leaders. Although this list is in no way comprehensive, the following are some suggestions for implementing security:

- Plan and prepare
- Refine the pre-convention meeting to emphasize security issues
- Be sure there is coordination of all parties involved
- Establish a security team and its decision makers
- Provide education on security for attendees
- Be proactive rather than reactive
- Stay informed and alert to incidents

Department and/or Individuals Responsible for Organizing and Planning

Government meeting planners resemble their corporate counterparts, as they are located throughout their agencies. While some government meeting planners devote all their work time to planning meetings, others handle meetings as one of their extra assigned duties.

Many government agencies hire meeting management companies or independent meeting planners to handle meetings that fall beyond their internal capabilities. In the Washington, DC area, there are several meeting-planning companies that specialize in managing government meetings. There are very strict guidelines within the government as to what a government-meeting planner can provide to the attendees in terms of food and beverage, and outside activities. It is imperative that the government-meeting planner study these regulations and be prepared at any time to go through a financial audit at the conclusion of the meeting.

Meeting planners who work for the government and/or independent meeting management companies are likely to join associations to support their professional development. These organizations will help the government-meeting planner learn and understand the strict financial guidelines described earlier. Regulations change yearly, and staying on top of these changes is crucial for the planner's success. These associations include the Society of Government Meeting Professionals (SGMP) and its local or regional chapters, the PCMA, and MPI. Those who have responsibility for organizing exhibitions are likely to join the International Association of Exhibitions and Events (IAEE).

GOVERNMENT MEETINGS ARE DIFFERENT FROM A US PERSPECTIVE

Meetings for the government have characteristics that set them apart from other types of meetings. They are different from any other type of conference. Why is this so? Because these meetings are bound by government regulations and operating policies that do not apply to other types of meetings.

First, consider rates for sleeping rooms. To save the government money, the GSA Office of Government-Wide Policy sets per diem rates for lodging, meals, and incidental expenses for individual travelers for all locations in the continental United States. In most cities, these rates are below those charged to conference groups, which take up a larger amount of a hotel's inventory of rooms than transient travelers. To offset this problem, GSA allows government-meeting organizers to negotiate a rate up to 25 percent above the lodging allowance. Also, GSA's Federal Premier Lodging Program offers government travelers guaranteed rooms at guaranteed rates and enters into contractual relationships with hotels in the top 70 US travel markets. Additionally, meetings may only be held in properties that comply with the Hotel and Motel Fire Safety Act of 1990. Government regulations regarding travel are located at www.gsa.gov.

Federal procurement policies also distinguish the government meeting. Bids for meeting supplies and services must be obtained from *at least* three vendors for all but the smallest purchases. Additionally, government-meeting planners usually are not the people who commit federal funds. All purchases must be approved and contracted for by a federal procurement official. In some cases, meeting planners have been trained by their agencies in procurement practices, so they are able to commit a limited amount of money (e.g., $2,500, $10,000, or $25,000). But private-sector meeting suppliers should be forewarned to determine who has the authority to commit funds and sign contracts.

Hotel contracts are not considered official by the government. A hotel contract may be attached to the paperwork submitted to the procurement official, but, in all cases, the government contract—not that of the private sector—is the prevailing authority. This applies to all procurements for meeting services. Funds *must* be approved before the service is rendered, not after. In addition, the government *must* be able to cancel a contract without liquidated damages if funding for an event is withdrawn, if there are furloughs or closures of government facilities, or if other government actions make it inadvisable to hold the meeting. The government cannot pay for services not received. Furthermore, the government cannot indemnify or hold harmless anyone who is not a government employee conducting official business.

Other characteristics that make government meetings unique include the following:

- *There is a short turn-around time for planning government meetings.* While associations plan their conferences with many years of lead time, most government meetings are planned only months—or even weeks—before the event. This is true for large, multifaceted meetings as well as small gatherings.

- *Government meetings do not fit a particular mold.* They may be elaborate international conferences for high-ranking dignitaries or small scientific conclaves for 8 to 12 researchers. Some meetings may be held only once and, therefore, have no history.

- *Government meetings often require a disproportionately large amount of function space relative to the number of sleeping room nights booked.* This may be because only a small percentage of attendees are coming from out of town.

- *Policies for meetings can vary from agency to agency.* Some agencies collect registration fees to cover expenses. Others will not allow appropriated fees to pay for lunches; collections often must be made on-site from attendees. In addition, as GSA allows each agency to implement the "up to 25 percent" allowance as they see fit, government lodging allowances may vary from agency to agency.

- *Government meetings frequently bring together representatives from the Uniformed Services and non–Department of Defense agencies.* Often, these groups share software applications designed for their *own* purposes, such as encrypted messaging and global directory systems that list only those who "need to know" the information. Frequently, such meetings are classified and are required to be held in a secure facility, whether at a government building or a public facility secured by trained personnel.

  Government-sponsored meetings are far more complicated than most private-sector conferences because they are often planned by people who are not full-time meeting planners. They may be budget analysts, public affairs officers, scientists, secretaries, or administrative officers. And, as government meetings are perceived to provide less revenue for a hotel, they may be assigned to junior members of the hotel sales staff.

  All government-meeting organizers are bound by a code of ethics that prohibits them from accepting anything from a vendor that is valued at more than $50. Those who work with the government should realize this and not put the planner in a compromising position.

  Thankfully, there is an organization that specializes in providing education and resources to government planners and suppliers—the Society of Government Meeting Planners (SGMP).

Other Organizations Arranging Gatherings

Political Organizations

Aside from their subject matter, political events do not differ much from non-political events, with primary differences being in security, press, and venue management. Political events could include major conventions and special events, such as inaugurations, trade shows, fundraising events, and local events. Oftentimes, conventions tend to be significantly larger than non-political conventions, which can create challenges for crowd control. Since attendees are highly passionate about their cause, and political speakers can be very polarizing, specialized security agencies are utilized; and disruptive guests are handled in a much harsher fashion, which could result in formalized legal action. The press is a known presence; and dedicated space, such as press boxes, press risers, and a room for multiple cameras, is expected.

The inauguration of US President Obama was a complicated and highly secure government event.
Alex Wong/Getty Images

Labor Unions

The labor union market has seen a steep decline in private sector union membership, going from 24.3 percent in 1973 to 6.6 percent in 2014. Despite this, there are still over 150 unions in the United States that hold meetings regularly, such as The Teamsters, Service Employees International, and the Pipe Fitters Union. Union meetings are typically held every other year, and are only held at unionized properties. They tend to be large because all members attend. Oftentimes, prominent political speakers are featured in the meeting. National conventions typically have sponsored functions, social programs, high-spouse attendance, and high-per-person expenditures.

Entities That Help Organize Gatherings

There are many categories of organizations that are key players in aiding corporations, associations, government and other entities in producing their meetings and events. They include exhibition and meeting management companies.

Exhibition Management Companies

There are several companies that are in the business of owning and managing trade shows and expositions. These companies both develop and produce shows that profit their companies, as well as produce events for sponsoring corporations, associations, or government clients. While trade shows and expositions are both events at which products and services are displayed for potential buyers, the **trade show** or exhibition is generally not open to the public, while expositions are usually open to the public and charge an admission fee. Depending on the nature of the exposition, the attendees vary greatly. For exhibitions, the market is well defined by the trade or profession. For public shows, the attendees are basically defined by their interests and geographic proximity to the show location.

The companies who operate these exhibitions are profit-making enterprises that have found areas of economic interest that attract, according to the purpose of the exhibition, either the general public (e.g., an auto, boat, home, or garden show) or members of a specific industry (e.g., high-technology communications networking). Exhibitions provide the opportunity for face-to-face marketing. The owners and senior managers of company-owned shows decide where, when, and how often they will produce their shows. The decision is driven by the profit motive. Offering too many shows could lead to a cannibalization of the market, whereas offering too few shows creates an opportunity for competition to enter the market with their own show. Larger exhibition management companies manage several exhibitions within a given year. They will divide their staff by the various shows so that their time can be dedicated to getting to know the event, growing it, marketing it, and eventually producing it on-site. When the exhibition management company is smaller, all staff members most likely will work as one team on the exhibition. The associations that support the exhibition management industry include the International Association of Exhibitions and Events (IAEE) for the production side of the business. Other related associations include the Exhibit Designers and Producers Association, the Exposition Services and Contractors Association, and the Healthcare Convention and Exhibitor Association.

Some associations hire **exhibition management companies** to manage all or part of their exhibitions. For their efforts, the companies are paid for the services they provide. Among the largest exhibition management companies are Reed Exhibitions, which organizes over 500 events in 41 countries, and Emerald Expositions, which markets and produces over 50 shows. Their shows serve a wide variety of industries, domestically and globally, including aerospace, art and entertainment, electronics, hospitality, security, sport and health, and travel. Other exhibition management companies include International Gem and Jewelry Inc., Cygnus Expositions, and National Event Management Inc.

An exhibition management company is really a marketing company, because it is creating the environment in which need-satisfying exchanges can occur. Their focus is on selling exhibit space, producing an event that will keep the exhibitors happy and returning year after year, and building buyer attendance. Exhibition management companies have a need to market to two distinctly different yet inextricably linked publics. One group that must be targeted is exhibitors who need to reach potential buyers of their products and services. The others are members of the trade or general public who have a need or desire to view, discuss, and purchase the products and services presented by the exhibitors. The trade group only needs to be informed of the dates and location of the exhibition/trade show. Direct mail, email, and posting the trade show on social media outlets may be all that is needed for an established show. Shows appealing to the general public require extensive media advertising (newspaper, radio, social media, and television) to communicate the specifics within the geographic region. Promotional efforts like the distribution of discount coupons are common. In both cases, it is essential that the marketing effort results in a high volume of traffic at the exhibition to satisfy the needs of the exhibitors.

Association Management Companies

As the name of this category implies, this type of company is contracted by an association to assume full or partial responsibility for the management of the association based on its needs. A designated person in the association management company is identified as the main contact for the association and interacts with the board of directors and members to fulfill the association's mission. If the association is small and has limited financial resources, the contact person will most likely serve in this capacity for two or more associations. Since these organizations manage more than one association, association management companies were formerly known as multi-management companies. Confusion as to whom they targeted their services to necessitated this change.

Other employees of the association management company support the main contact and provide services as contracted (such as membership, finance, publications, government relations, and meeting management services). With this type of arrangement, the association office is typically located within the offices of the association management company. Examples of these types of companies include SmithBucklin & Associates and the Association Management Group.

Meeting Management Companies

These companies, also known as **third parties**, operate on a contractual basis. This is like an association management company, but meeting management companies limit their services to providing either selected or comprehensive meeting management services. They may manage all aspects of the meeting or may be focused on meeting planning services (pre-meeting as well as on-site support), city and venue research (also called **sourcing** in the industry), hotel negotiations and contracting, exhibit and sponsorship sales, on-site exhibit floor management, providing registration and housing services, providing lead retrieval equipment/platforms and meeting apps, marketing services, providing virtual meeting platforms, or any combination of these. In many instances, these companies make a large portion of their money from collecting a ten percent commission on each hotel room night booked at the hotel in return for bringing the booking to the property. A full-service third party will use some of these commissions to offset the fee charged to the client for other services provided. The meetings that these companies assist with may be held at convention centers, conference centers, special venue facilities, or hotels. Examples of meeting management companies include Conference Direct, Meeting Management Group, and Experient Inc.

Independent Meeting Managers

Experienced meeting professionals often use their expertise and contacts to set up their own business of managing meetings, or parts of meetings, for almost any entity that has a need; an association, several associations, corporations, individuals, and so on. An independent meeting manager may be called to plan and run a wedding, run a golf tournament that is an integral part of a gathering, to provide on-site management, or to act in a similar way as a full-service meeting management firm and handle all logistics for a meeting. There are also times when an independent is hired to handle crises in a meetings department at an organization. Personnel changes in the meetings department shortly before a meeting may require hiring a competent professional to pull the meeting together and bring it to a successful conclusion. The independent model works well for planners who have worked full time for an organization, gained significant knowledge and respect in the industry, and want to go out on their own and determine their own schedule. Independents are paid on a contract basis and can pick and choose for whom they want to work.

The segment of the industry that individuals are associated with will dictate the type of entity that they would likely join to support their professional development. Many will join PCMA or MPI. Others will choose to join organizations like the International Live Events Association (formerly the International Special Events Society), the National Association of Catering Executives, or the Association of Bridal Consultants.

Professional Congress Organizers

Outside the United States, the term Professional Congress Organizer (PCO) is used to designate a meeting management company. In international destinations, a congress is defined as a conference or convention. According to the Convention Industry Council (CIC) APEX Glossary, a PCO is a local supplier who can arrange, manage, and/or plan any function or service for an event. PCOs are very similar to destination management companies in the United States.

When sponsoring organizations from North America hold international events, they often engage the services of a PCO from the host region to assist them with local logistics. Some countries actually require that a domestic company be contracted to handle the meeting.

Trends and Best Practices

Experts believe that the face-to-face meeting business will never go out of style. Although technology now allows people to join communities online and interact more frequently, human nature dictates that people enjoy meeting with each other, and need to get together to exchange ideas and to network.

Meetings are also being influenced by emerging technologies and changing business needs. Some of those changing patterns are:

- *Budgetary constraints:* Meetings/events must show value to those organizations that sponsor them and for the individual attendee. Meeting planners are being scrutinized and forced to rethink how they plan meetings and where they spend money.
- *Shortening meetings:* Some sponsoring organizations have clipped off a day or half day from their meetings to reduce lodging and meal expenses for their participants.
- *Changing the frequency of annual meetings:* Some associations are considering holding their major meeting every other year, and focusing on regional gatherings that attendees can drive to at a lower cost.
- *Creating more value for their members:* Some associations are streaming live video of keynote speakers to non-attending members, who in turn will see the enhanced value of their memberships.
- *Increasing the interactivity of meeting sessions:* Social media has been introduced to encourage greater involvement of attendees. The term **gamification** has emerged in the meetings industry, which involves the use of technology to help engage attendees during a meeting. Examples include the use of smartphones as voting devices in a meeting room or for polling attendees. Another example is having Twitter feeds on a large screen in the front of a meeting room, which gives instant feedback to the speaker and is highly interactive in today's meetings.
- *Merging of sponsoring organizations:* Organizations with compatible missions, goals, and objectives, as well as some overlapping members and exhibitors, are

combining their strengths into a single joint meeting. This helps reduce costs to the organizations, as well as allows attendees to attend one single meeting instead of feeling obliged to attend two within one year. The educational track of joint meetings in many instances brings a more robust program and a greater return on investment (ROI) to an attendee. Many attendees must justify to their employers why they want to attend a meeting, and the educational and networking value is one that attendees point to in many cases.

- *Virtual conferences:* Technology has evolved to allow meetings of all sizes to occur via the Internet, thereby eliminating the need for participants to get on a plane and check into a hotel. This type of event, often with limited objectives, serves to complement more traditional face-to-face gatherings. Organizations also believe that if an attendee receives great value from attending a virtual meeting, they might get excited and think that the face-to-face meeting would also be a great personal benefit as well. This is one way to help an organization increase their attendance numbers at their face-to-face meetings.

- *Virtual trade shows:* A wider range of potential buyers can view innovations in their fields. Today's advanced technology allows a virtual attendee to feel like they are walking the aisles at a live trade show. Virtual trade shows can also complement a live trade show where attendees and non-attendees can view the displays and communicate with representatives working the show.

- *Outsourcing:* Some organizations have downsized, or even eliminated their meeting-planning departments as a cost-saving measure. The responsibilities are transferred to independent meeting planners or meeting management companies: entities to which the sponsor or organizer has no long-term commitment.

- *Focus on ROI:* Many organizations, whether they are corporations or associations, are increasingly concerned about the ROI of their meetings and events. They are taking a hard look at costs and benefits with the goal of decreasing the former and increasing the latter. Post-event evaluations are more and more important.

- *Limiting government meetings/events:* The US federal government has come out with laws that limit the number of meetings a government employee can attend in a year. This law is of great concern to associations because many of their members are government employees, and they offer great value to these members. This is a trend that will be monitored over the years to come.

Summary

The types of organizations that sponsor gatherings are as diverse as the types of gatherings held and the people who attend them. Most of the US population will participate in these gatherings at least once in their lives. For many of them, attending a meeting, convention, exhibition, or other event will be a regular occurrence. The gatherings attended reflect the personal and professional interests of the attendees.

People seeking meeting-planning career opportunities with sponsoring organizations will have to use targeting techniques to locate them, although these positions do exist throughout the nation. The greatest number of these positions can be found in locations where the organizations are headquartered. The metropolitan Washington, DC area is considered to be the meetings capital of the world, with several thousand associations located in and around the city. The federal government, also physically located in Washington, DC, employs many people in the meetings profession as they organize and hold hundreds of meetings each year. In addition to governmental state agencies, state capitals are home to many state and regional associations, all of which have many meetings of their own that are held annually.

Major corporations tend to be located in large cities. Although many may be in smaller cities and towns, their meetings are typically planned from corporate headquarters.

Employment opportunities with organizations and facilities that host gatherings are in both major cities and small towns. An organization will select a meeting/event location for its proximity to access by its attendees (near a major airport or an interstate highway).

With baby boomers (the largest age group in the US population) approaching retirement age, it is anticipated that there will be an increasing number of employment opportunities in the coming years on both the planner and supplier sides of the meeting, exposition, event, and convention industry.

CASE STUDY

Conference Marketing in a Competitive Marketplace

One of the main differences between corporate events and association events is the guaranteed attendee base. Typically, in corporate events, there is a set group of people who must attend (such as a sales meeting or corporate training). Association meetings are not required and, therefore, the organization advertises to the relevant professional community at large to secure attendees. Therefore, marketing is extremely important for these types of events.

The Engineering Association of America is a nonprofit association of members who are professional engineers. This association is the longest running association focused in engineering, but has recently faced sharp competition over the past decade from conferences focusing on specific segments of engineering (mechanical, electrical, etc.) and niche conferences (Women in Engineering, etc). Due to this competition, conference attendance has decreased by over 35 percent in the past five years. You have just been hired as the new Director of Marketing.

1. What is the first thing you would do now that you are hired?
2. When should the association begin to market its annual meeting?
3. What kind of marketing should the association do for potential attendees? What kind of marketing should be done for existing attendees?
4. What kind of marketing should be done for sponsors? What kind of marketing should be done for exhibitors?
5. What new conference experiences could you integrate onsite to generate excitement and positive word of mouth?
6. For this particular group, which social media outlets would you focus on? Why?

Key Words and Terms

For definitions, see the Glossary.

air lift
association
continuing education
   units/credits (CEU)
corporation

exhibition management
   companie
gamification
incentive trip
per diem rate

public show
sourcing
sponsor
third partie
trade show

Review and Discussion Questions

1. Identify the type of sponsoring organization that holds the greatest number of gatherings, and the type that generates the greatest economic benefit.

2. Which type or types of sponsoring organizations have the greatest marketing challenges to ensure the success of their gatherings?

3. What changes are occurring with incentive trips to provide more value for the corporation sponsoring the gathering?

4. How do not-for-profit associations differ from for-profit organizations?

5. What types of organizations comprise the category of associations known as SMERFs, and what similarities do they share with each other?

6. How do government procurement officers view meeting contracts from their hotel suppliers?

7. Distinguish between the trade show and the exposition.

8. What efficiencies do association management companies bring to the management and operation of small associations?

About the Chapter Contributor

Kristin Malek, PhD, CMP, CHE. Dr. K, as she is known by her students, has over ten years in hospitality and event management experience. She began her career in the restaurant industry where she developed a love for hospitality. After moving quickly into an assistant store manager role, she switched over to the retail side, and then into hotels. While working for an architectural engineering firm as a designer, she was put in charge of planning all the office trainings and company social events. She quickly realized her love of event planning and decided to go back to school.

After completing internships and contract work in event management, she went on to receive her master's degree in International Hospitality and Tourism Management from the University of South Carolina and her PhD in Hospitality Administration from the University of Nevada, Las Vegas. Dr. K served as the Executive Director of Events for a third-party planning company in Las Vegas where she oversaw the medical association meeting market. In this role, she managed association events greater than one million dollars and led a team of staff and hospitality management interns. She was recognized by *Meetings Today* magazine as a Top 20 Meetings Industry Trendsetter for 2016 and serves as the 2017 PCMA Faculty chair for the meetings and events industry.

Currently, Dr. K works at Kansas State University teaching event management classes at undergraduate and graduate levels.

Contact Information:

Kansas State University
107 Justin Hall, 1324 Lovers Lane, Manhattan, KS 66503
785-532-2208, kristinmalek@ksu.edu

Previous Edition Chapter Contributors

The contributors for previous editions of the chapter were:

Nancy DeBrosse, Senior Vice President at Experient
Howard E. Reichbart, Emeritus from Northern Virginia Community College.

DMOs provide visitors insights regarding the attractions and services available in their destination.
George G. Fenich

CHAPTER 3

Destination Marketing Organizations

Chapter Objectives

- Articulate the roles and functions of a destination marketing organization.
- Outline the needs and opportunities a DMO can meet for a meeting professional.
- Illustrate the convention marketing and sales activities expected of a DMO.
- Describe the tools and associations available through Destination International.
- Discuss trends in the field of designation market organizations.

If a destination were merely a place, a dot on a map, a bump in the road, or just another stop along the way, then the destination would not matter. However, destinations matter. They are called destinations for a reason: People want or need to go there and visit. In many instances, people go to great lengths to get to a destination. They are drawn to certain destinations. For a few, they may be the realization of a lifelong dream. By boat, car, plane, or train, they go. Why? Because contrary to the wise, old proverb, it is not about the journey but the destination. And the reasons for making the journey are as varied as the people traveling. Whether for business, a convention/meeting, or leisure, they come because of the expectation of an enjoyable experience. In short, the destination must provide experiences unique enough to compel someone to travel to it and spend their time and money there.

Travel and tourism enhances the quality of life for a local community by providing jobs and by bringing in tax dollars for cultural and sporting venues, which cater to both tourists and locals. Tourism creates jobs at the local level in a multitude of ways. Convention facilities are often rented by groups that cater to local residents. Popular examples include: Home and Garden Shows, Boat Shows, Car Shows, Golf Shows, Comic Book Expositions, and almost any show one can imagine. If sold aggressively, convention centers and similar venues can optimize their space 12 months a year.

The Role and Function of Destination Marketing Organizations

What Is a Destination Marketing Organization?

A **destination marketing organization (DMO)** is often called a national tourism board, state or provincial tourism office, or convention and visitor bureau (CVB). They are often not-for-profit organizations, government entities, or a hybrid and are charged with representing a specific destination and helping the long-term economic development of communities through a travel and tourism strategy. The DMO in each city, county, state, region, or country has a responsibility to market its destination to potential visitors. This includes leisure and business travelers along with meeting/event planners who might hold meetings, conventions, and trade shows at their destination. DMOs also service those groups who hold meetings at their destination with meeting preparations. DMOs entice and influence visitors to enjoy all the historic, cultural, and recreational opportunities that the destination has to offer. In most instances, the DMO is the only entity charged with selling and marketing the destination brand and, therefore, serves everyone.

A DMO does not typically organize meetings, events, and conventions. However, it assists meeting planners in learning about the destination and area attractions to make the best possible use of all the services and facilities the destination has to offer. The history of DMOs stretches back to 1895 when a group of businessmen in Detroit put a full-time salesman on the road to invite conventions to their city. His function expanded, and the organization for which he worked was called a Convention Bureau. Today, DMOs operate throughout the world and are charged with the responsibility of bringing new revenue to the community they represent by attracting visitor dollars.

Initially, DMOs existed to sell and service conventions. As the years passed, more and more of these organizations became involved in the promotion of tourism. What was originally called Convention Bureaus expanded their scope to include tourism, and was then called CVBs. This evolution and expansion of roles and functions continues today. Many CVBs are interchangeably using the term DMO to better reflect their activities in selling and promoting their destinations to their wide range of customers.

The Purpose of a DMO

DMOs assist in the long-term economic development of their local communities. Some DMOs are membership based, bringing together local businesses that rely on tourism and meetings for revenue. DMOs serve as the official contact point for their destination. Some DMOs are departments of local government, not unlike the library or highway department. This structure is most common outside the United States where DMOs may be quasi-autonomous nongovernmental organizations (QUANGO) or may function as a division of local government called an authority. Many within the United States fall under the government tax structure of a not-for-profit organization and are classified as either 501(c)(3) or 501(c)(6).

For visitors, DMOs are like a key to the city. DMOs are an unbiased resource and are experts about their destination. They are a one-stop shop for local tourism interests, and save visitors and meeting professionals' time and energy. DMOs provide a full range of information about a destination, and they do not charge for their services.

For conventions, they are often the intermediary between the sponsoring organization and hospitality businesses. As such, the DMO may coordinate site visits, the dissemination and collection of **requests for proposals (RFPs)**, and the development of collateral material. Some DMOs will also find funding to help attract large conventions, and may, in some cases, provide direct financial assistance to present the most attractive proposal to the customer—if the business is valuable enough to justify the subsidy. Usually, cities compete against each other to attract business, which can mean millions of dollars to the local economy for just one event. On balance, the best financial deal usually wins the business, if the competing cities' facilities are similar.

A cornerstone value of most DMOs is to offer unbiased information about a destination's services and facilities. The goal is to outsell their competition by successfully matching the customers' specific meeting needs with the facilities and services offered in the community. For example, a group of students might be budget-conscious and, therefore, most interested in economy-priced hotels and lower-cost meeting facilities. Conversely, corporate groups tend to be attracted to the finest hotels and venues the community has to offer. A DMO's job is to determine the customer's needs and budget, and provide options they will ultimately be willing to purchase. The DMO works to bring the business to the entire community and represents all equally.

If DMOs Do Not Charge for Their Services, How Do They Make Money?

DMOs do not charge their clients—the leisure visitor, the business traveler, and the meeting planner—for services rendered. Instead, most DMOs are funded through a combination of a share of hotel occupancy taxes, membership dues, and, sometimes, through a tourism improvement district (TID). In the United States, an improvement district is an area specifically designated in the community where any incremental increase in property taxes generated is earmarked for a specific purpose, in this case, the DMO. These can come in many forms. For example, if hotels, restaurants, and other hospitality venues are added, expanded, or improved, the DMO benefits financially. The underlying concept is that these new facilities are a direct result of the marketing and promotion efforts of the DMO. Another derivation of a TID is when the hotels within a district charge an additional user fee on every occupied room night; the collected revenue oftentimes goes to the DMO for marketing purposes. If the DMO is a government agency, then funding comes from the local government.

MEMPHIS CONVENTION AND VISITORS BUREAU

Memphis has more than 60 tourist attractions, including Graceland, Beale Street, and the Memphis Pyramid, plus restaurants, theaters, and art museums. The Memphis Convention and Visitors Bureau takes advantage of these iconic attractions to market the city to visitors around the world.

In addition to leisure attractions, the Memphis Cook Convention Center attracts over 500,000 visitors annually to conventions, trade shows, and performing arts. Despite all that Memphis has to offer, the Convention Center was last renovated in 2003 and was in need of additional renovation projects. Unfortunately, the money to update the convention center just wasn't there.

To remain competitive and fund improvements to the Convention Center, the bureau, hoteliers, and the city worked together to form the first tourism improvement district in Tennessee. They were able to leverage their commitment and worked with the city to simultaneously dedicate new bed tax funds for center improvements.

The Memphis TID began January 1, 2016, assessing $2.00 per occupied room per night to fund destination marketing programs. The district raised $5.3 million in annual TID funding.

Used with permission by Civitas Advisors

Attracting Leisure Travelers

While hotels, attractions, and organizations have a role in marketing a destination, the DMO is the primary tourism marketer of most destinations. Its primary objectives are to promote the destination and to drive overnight guests. It leverages the community's assets and unique qualities to compel people to visit. It also leads the community in the creation of a destination brand and marketing plan.

DMOs will often group the community's attractions to market to specific demographics. For example, if the destination has a zoo, children's museum, and amusement park, the DMO will market to families and provide examples of itineraries to create enjoyable family vacations. So too, they may use their city's many shopping venues, spas, and local restaurants to sell a "girls getaway" weekend. DMOs may also market sporting events and craft beer festivals to other demographics. In short, DMOs use the most attractive grouping of destination assets to attract the largest number of leisure visitors—visitors who will spend money and return again.

It's All About Marketing

While some cities have built a reputation as tourist cities, such as Las Vegas and Orlando, most cities have to educate potential visitors as to the reasons why they should plan a trip.

A DMO must decide the most effective way to reach their audience and will often purchase a combination of marketing products based on their overall ad budget, and research of the buying habits of their target customers. They may use traditional channels, such as television, radio, newspaper, and magazines; or purchase digital ads on websites like Facebook or any of the limitless offerings available to reach customers.

DMOs use public relations activities to project positive stories about the destination. An effective tactic is to invite travel press for a complimentary visit to their community and to experience it. The DMO will invite the travel writer for an experience (usually lasting three days) in their community with the intention that the journalist or blogger will write positive stories about his or her experience. This unbiased, third-party endorsement of the destination is extremely effective in piquing the interest of loyal readers, as travel writers are considered credible sources for travel information.

Website

The most effective marketing tool for any DMO is a smart and comprehensive website that features the best attractions and facilities the destination has to offer. The best websites feature great photos, videos, and blogs that relay compelling experiences about the community. Known as storytelling, the most effective blogs feature engaging experiences and memorable events that make the destination attractive; they feature food, communities, nature, and interactions with real people.

What a DMO Can Do for Meeting Professionals

What Meeting Planners Need to Know about DMOs

Many people are not aware of the existence of DMOs, and, therefore, they do not realize the wealth of information and resources they provide on a complimentary basis. The best analogy to describe what a DMO does for meeting professionals is to think of their role as being similar to a realtor. They find potential prospects (meeting planners) to purchase the goods and services available to them in the destination. They act as an agent for both the buyer and seller to remove the barriers to a sale.

A DMO has many responsibilities. Most importantly, it serves as *the* official point of contact for convention and meeting planners. In most cases where a convention center is present, the DMO controls the bookings of the center 18 months and beyond the date of a potential event. It encourages groups to hold meetings at their destination and assists groups with meeting preparations. DMOs also provide promotional materials, giveaways, and video teasers to encourage attendance and establish room blocks (hotel rooms set aside for a group), among other things.

Meeting planners can access a range of services, packages, and value-added extras through a DMO. Before going into the specifics of what a DMO can do for a meeting planner, let us examine a few common misconceptions about DMOs.

> *Misconception 1:*   DMOs solely book hotel rooms and convention space.
> *Fact:*   DMOs represent the gamut of visitor-related businesses, from restaurants and retail to rental cars and racetracks. Therefore, they are responsible for introducing planners to the range of meeting-related products and services the city has to offer.

> *Misconception 2:*   DMOs only work with large groups.
> *Fact:*   More than two-thirds of the average DMOs' efforts are devoted to meetings of fewer than 200 people. In fact, larger DMOs often have staff members specifically dedicated to small meetings, group tours, leisure tourists, and transient business travel.

> *Misconception 3:*   DMOs own and/or run the convention center.
> *Fact:*   Only ten percent of DMOs run the convention center in their locations, such as the Las Vegas Convention and Visitor Authority. Nevertheless, DMOs work closely with local convention centers and can assist planners in obtaining what they need from convention center staff.

> *Misconception 4:*   Planners must pay DMOs for their services.
> *Fact:*   In truth, most services of a DMO are free.

Some may question the need to work through a DMO when planning a meeting, particularly in cases where the bulk of an event takes place at one hotel or only at the convention center. However, the DMO can help a planner work with those entities and can help fill out the convention schedule (including spouse tours and pre- and post-tours) with off-site activities. Since the DMO is an objective resource, it can efficiently direct

---

A BUSINESS CASE FOR DMOS

How DMOs Provide Return on Investment to Their Communities

Based on the budget and the needs of each community, DMOs are charged with creating and effectively selling the destination brand to potential visitors. They are the sales, marketing, and public relations firm for the entire community.

As in every business, DMOs must constantly prove their worth to their stakeholders (hotels, attractions, members, and government). DMOs are trusted to invest the revenue they receive, in most cases through tax dollars, and are under scrutiny to show a substantial return on investment. To do this, most DMOs report in their annual meeting how they measure against key performance indicators (KPIs).

Examples of KPIs (numbers of) include:

Communications: media contacts, press releases, media coverage, press tours, and media impressions

Convention sales: trade shows attended, familiarization tours conducted, sales calls, site inspections, leads sent, definite bookings, definite room nights, definite convention attendance, and lost opportunities

Services: citywide events, welcome booth referrals, planning bulletins, registrar hours, site visits, housings, reservations processed, and room nights processed

Marketing: web statistics, social media statistics, tracked visitors, inquiries, retail revenue, visitor satisfaction, advertising spent, and ad value gained

The KPIs that receive the most attention tend to be those associated with total industry economic impact, jobs, and local taxes paid by out of town visitors.

planners to the products and services that will work best to accommodate the needs and budgets of their attendees.

DMOs make planning and implementing a meeting less time-consuming and more streamlined by providing direct access to the services they require. The DMO knows the inner-workings of their destination, and gives meeting planners access to a range of services, packages, and value-added extras. Before a meeting begins, DMO sales managers can help locate meeting space, check hotel availability, and arrange for site inspections. DMOs can also link planners with suppliers, from motor coach companies and caterers to off-site entertainment venues, which can help meet the prerequisites of any event. A DMO can act as a liaison between the planner and community officials, thus clearing the way for special permits, street closures, and so on. The DMO can offer suggestions about how meeting attendees can maximize their free time, along with developing companion programs and pre- and post-convention tours.

2015 DMO ORGANIZATIONAL AND FINANCIAL PROFILE STUDY

Executive Summary

The 2015 DMO Organizational and Financial Profile Study is the most comprehensive benchmark study on DMO structures and organizational practices in the destination marketing sector today. This biennial survey of DMOs produces a series of core organizational metrics for peer comparison and to assist in the development, strategies and management of all DMOs. A total of 246 DMOs from the United States, Canada, and Bermuda participated in the 2015 program.

This study is made available by the Destination Marketing Association International (DMAI), which protects and advances the success of official destination marketing organizations worldwide. DMAI thanks all of the respondents for their invaluable contribution to this study.

The following Executive Summary content provides some key highlights at an industry-wide level. More detailed results and summary findings of the 2015 survey are presented in the main body of this report.

2015 DMO INDUSTRY AVERAGES
Annual Budget

$2.89M	$2.91M	$3.00M	$3.31M	$3.39M
2011	2012	2013	2014	2015

DMO budgets on average continue an upward trend since 2011, reaching their highest level at $3.39 million in 2015. Significant growth in average DMO budgets was recorded between 2013 and 2014.

Funding / Revenue

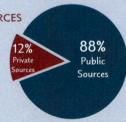

TOP 5 PRIVATE REVENUE SOURCES
1. Advertising Revenue
2. Membership Dues
3. Partnership Revenue
4. Corporate Sponsorships
5. Event Hosting

12% Private Sources / 88% Public Sources

TOP 5 PUBLIC FUNDING SOURCES
1. Hotel Room Tax
2. TID/Marketing District Assessment/ Voluntary Marketing Fee
3. Other Country/City/State/Province Tax Fund Sources
4. Special Restaurant Tax
5. Other National Tax Funds

HOTEL ROOM TAX

13.1%
average taxes and fees on hotel rooms

Most DMOs surveyed continue to receive the vast majority of their funding from public sources. Smaller (less than $1 million) and mid-sized ($1 million to $5 million) budget DMOs reported receiving approximately 90 percentage of their total funding from public sources. More than 87 percentage of DMOs reported receiving hotel room tax revenue, by far the leading source of public investment. Tourism Improvement District/Marketing District/Voluntary Assessments are rapidly growing as a revenue source, with 14 percentage of DMOs receiving these funds.

Advertising revenue is the most prevalent form of private source revenue reported by DMOs generally in 2015 (19%), with membership dues representing 16 percentage of revenues on average. Approximately 39 percentage of DMOs have dues-paying members, with the percentage increasing to nearly 60 percentage for the larger DMOs (greater than $5 million). Partnership revenue accounted for 12 percentage of private source funding received by DMOs generally.

Annual Budget Allocations

For 2015, reporting DMOs allocated just over half of their budget to specific marketing/promotions programs, with 37 percentage invested in personnel costs, and just over 11 percentage in administrative/general expenses. These broad allocations varied by DMO budget size – marketing/promotions programs generally increased as a percentage of overall expenses as DMO budgets grew, while personnel costs generally decreased as an overall percentage as DMO budgets rose. Administrative/general expenses fluctuated a little, yet were generally consistent in the range of 10%—12% of overall expenses regardless of DMO budget category.

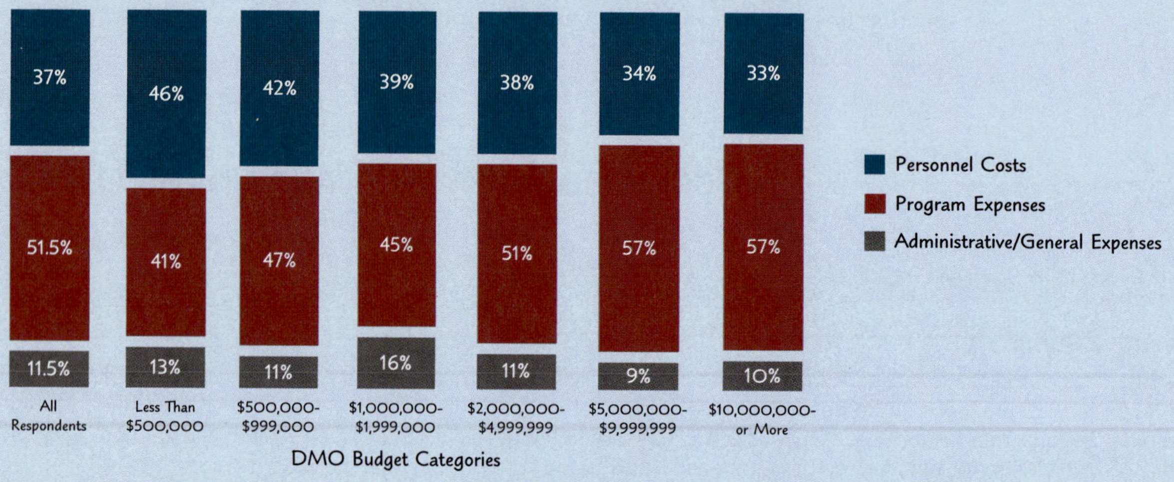

Overall Staff Size → Staff Size by DMO Budget Category

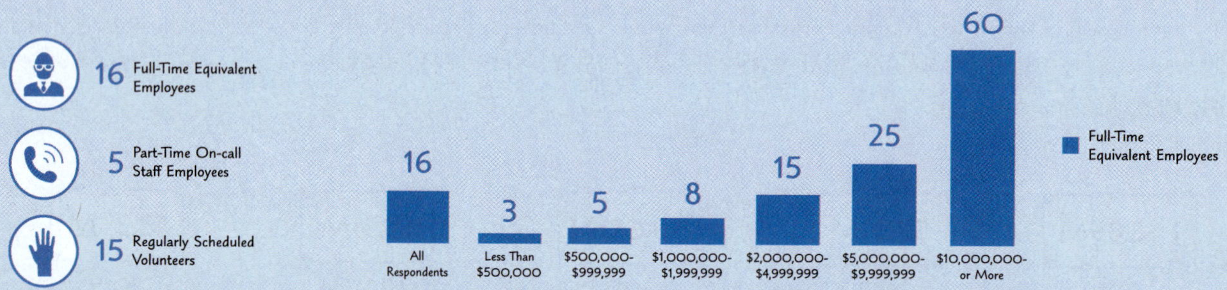

More than one-third of DMO survey respondents added full-time staff in 2015. Only 8 percentage reported a decrease, predominantly among the mid-sized DMOs. For the 2015 fiscal year, the median number of full-time equivalent employees among all reporting DMOs was 16.

Staff Composition

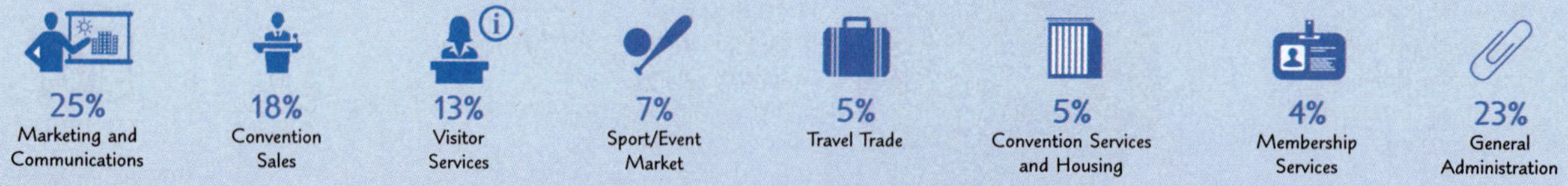

DMOs overall continue to deploy a staffing strategy that focuses on targeted marketing, business development, and visitor servicing efforts for their respective destinations. Of note, DMOs are increasingly dedicating more specialized staff to the sport/event market. The sport/event market now joins destination-level marketing and communications, convention sales, visitor servicing, and travel trade support as a core visitor market development activity specifically assigned to DMO staff.

Marketing / Promotions Program Allocations

Market Sector Spending

| 51% Leisure Market | 23% Meetings and Conventions | 12% Sport/Event Market |

| 8% Travel Trade | 6% Other Market Sectors |

Online versus Offline Spending

2013   2014   2015

ONLINE/DIGITAL ACTIVITIES

31%   35%   39%

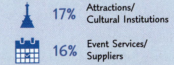

ONLINE/TRADITIONAL ACTIVITIES

69%   65%   61%

Geographic Markets

91% Domestic Market

91% International Market

On an individual basis, DMO respondents report a variety of marketing/promotions efforts that directly reflect their destination profile as a leisure destination, a business market destination, or a combination of both. Among all DMOs reporting on average, the largest program spending is generally focused on the leisure (direct consumer) market, followed by the meetings and conventions sector, the sport/event market, and then the travel trade sector.

Marketing/promotions budgets overall are increasingly being allocated to online/digital activities, with continued spending reductions generally reported for offline/traditional activities. In 2015, 39 percentage of budgeted spending by reporting DMOs overall is now dedicated to online/digital marketing and engagement strategies, with a new low of 61 percentage allocated to offline/traditional marketing and promotions.

On an overall basis, responding DMOs report that they are directing the vast majority (91%) of their marketing/promotions program budgets to their domestic markets in 2015.

DMO Membership Profile

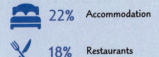

39% of DMOs have dues-paying members

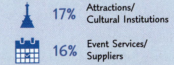

522 members on average

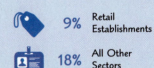

89% membership retention rate

Thirty-nine percent of DMOs have dues-paying members currently, recording an 89 percentage member retention rate going into the 2015 fiscal year.

Membership by Industry Sector

22% Accommodation

18% Restaurants

17% Attractions/ Cultural Institutions

16% Event Services/ Suppliers

9% Retail Establishments

18% All Other Sectors

Membership representation by sector has remained relatively consistent in recent years, with the largest membership base still generally found in the accommodation sector, followed by restaurants, attractions/institutions, event services/suppliers and retail establishments.

Destination Performance Averages

2.4M Overnight Visitors Annually

$466M Spent by Overnight Visitors Annually

13,285 Jobs Supported by Tourism

Individual DMOs responding to the survey reported a variety of specific destination performance statistics that reflect their unique scale of operations, the characteristics of the destination they represent, and the composition of the markets they serve and specifically target. Yet, on an overall industry basis and as an average among all DMOs surveyed (median value), DMOs were directly involved in generating more than 2.4 million overnight visitors and $466 million in direct overnight visitor spending for the communities and destinations they served in 2014. This general level of business activity assisted in supporting more than 13,000 jobs in tourism as a community/destination average.

DMO Departments and Staff

Although departments, job titles, and responsibilities vary from one DMO to another, most with convention facilities have the following:

- President and CEO/Executive Director
- Vice President of Convention Sales
- Vice President of Convention Services
- Vice President of Marketing
- Vice President of Finance
- Vice President of Communications
- Vice President of Membership

Within each department, there are staff members who support the work of the Vice President, including Directors, Managers, Coordinators, and Assistants. Some DMOs are more leisure focused and, therefore, have more staff support for marketing and public relations functions, while others with large convention facilities will also assign a larger amount of staff to selling and servicing conventions. Some destinations have Research Directors, Community Relations Directors, or Government Relations Directors.

DMOs are very interested in engaging students in and out of college for careers in the field. Many offer a wide array of internships, primarily to college students. In many instances, these interns are the first considered for entry-level positions within the organization. Make sure to check DMO websites for internship opportunities, which may exist year round.

Activities of DMOs Relative to Convention Marketing and Sales

Professionals who work in a DMO serve as the sales representative for their destination. There is an entire process that a DMO undertakes with meeting professionals in order to bring a meeting to its destination.

Sales Processes

DMOs want to attract their share of this lucrative market and hire professional salespeople to sell their destinations. They use various sales strategies and tactics to attract conventions, trade shows, meetings, and events. There are numerous industry events where DMO salespeople can meet potential planners to discuss their meeting requirements. An example of some of the larger not-for-profit industry shows are as follows:

- American Bus Association
- American Society of Association Executives
- Destinations International Destinations Showcase
- International Travel Association
- National Association of Sports Commissions
- National Coalition of Black Meeting Planners
- NCAA Convention
- Professional Conference Management Association Annual Meeting
- Religious Conference Management Association

The largest for-profit trade show in the US as well as Germany is organized by a company called IMEX, which is based in London, England. Each of their shows attracts approximately 10,000 attendees.

There are numerous local, regional, and national expositions in which DMOs may choose to participate, based on the best match for their community with the type of customer who would typically attend an event. For example, a destination that does not have sporting facilities would not typically benefit from attending the NCAA Convention.

Most industry events offer the DMO the opportunity to participate in a multi-day trade show, as well as many educational and networking events. The goal is to build personal relationships with existing and new customers to further the process of selling their destination.

DMOs exhibit at industry shows to promote their destination.
Horacio Villalobos/Corbis/Getty Images

DMO sales professionals also use traditional sales solicitation tactics (phone, email, and post) to find new meeting-planner customers. In this information age, the DMO salesperson can access customer lists and market intelligence that can streamline their efforts.

Site Review and Leads Process

Determining if a site or location can accommodate a meeting's requirements is critical. The DMO is the central information source for advice, on-site selection, transportation, and available local services, all with no cost or obligation to the meeting or event manager. DMO representatives have the knowledge and information to provide up-to-date data about the area, as well as future planned developments.

Regardless of the meeting size, the DMO can serve as the first stop in the site review process. When a meeting planner contacts a DMO, a DMO sales manager will be assigned to assist in securing the necessary information and facts to produce a successful meeting. The DMO sales contact will gather information about preferred dates for the event and find out what facilities are available, if there are adequate sleeping rooms and meeting rooms, and whether convention facilities are available for the entire time period, including time for exhibitors to move in and out.

In order to represent all their constituents, most DMOs have a leads process, wherein the sales contact circulates meeting specifications to facilities and lodging entities that can accommodate the requirements. Basic information required by the DMO is indicated on the convention lead sheet and distributed electronically.

The lead distribution may also be limited by establishing certain parameters, such as specifying a location downtown or near the airport. In cases as this, the lead would be forwarded only to properties that meet the requirements identified by the customer. For example, quantity of rooms, square feet of meeting space, off-site venues for meal functions, nearby sporting facilities, or any customer requirement from big to small. If a meeting planner is familiar with the destination's properties, he or she may express interest in certain facilities by name. Then, only those facilities receive the lead.

The DMO sales contact will request that the receiving property send the information directly to the meeting planner, or the sales contact may gather the information, compile it into a package, and send it to the meeting planner. In the United States, federal antitrust laws prohibit DMOs from discussing pricing policies with hotels under consideration. All pricing discussions must take place between the meeting planner and the prospective property. A DMO sales contact may relate to a property that a meeting planner is looking for a specific price range for room rates, but cannot negotiate on the meeting planner's behalf.

CONVENTION LEAD SHEET

The convention lead sheet used by DMOs will usually contain the following information:

- Name of the DMO sales contact
- Distribution date of the convention lead sheet
- Name of the meeting planner and title
- Name of the group or organization
- Address information for the group or organization
- Email, telephone number, and fax number of the meeting planner
- Total number of room nights anticipated
- Peak room nights, and day of peak
- Dates for the event or meeting
- Decision date
- Total anticipated attendance
- Occupancy pattern
  - Day
  - Date
  - Rooms
- Meeting space requirements
  - Exhibit space
  - Food functions
- History
- Competing cities
- Bedroom rate history
- Bedroom pickup history
- Meeting rotation pattern (south, north, east, west, or central)
- Decision steps
- Additional information
- Name of person who prepared the sheet and date of preparation

Many times during the sales process, the DMO sales professional interacts with the customer to ensure that the destination has provided the most attractive offer in terms of available venues, services, and cost. Some DMOs and destination venues will create specific money reserves to offer financial incentives to assist the customer in offsetting the cost of their event. These incentives are a very powerful motivator to some groups in deciding to choose one destination over another.

The lead process takes place in advance of the event. For an association, the average horizon, or time between looking at a destination and the event taking place, varies. However, with large groups and large cities, the horizon can be years and even decades in advance. For example, the Morial Convention Center in New Orleans regularly garners commitments from large groups as much as 25 years in advance of the event itself.

The DMO sales manager will communicate with the meeting planner and the facilities to ensure that all information is disseminated, received, and understood. Any additional questions will be answered, and the meeting planner will be encouraged to visit the city and visit venues/hotels being considered. The DMO can also be of significant assistance during a personal site review by arranging site inspections.

Site Inspections

A site inspection is a physical review of proposed venues and services prior to the actual program. A site inspection may be required at any point in the sales process. A site inspection by the planner may occur prior to the proposal, after the proposal, or once it is contracted for space. A site inspection occurring prior to the proposal is a part of the information-gathering visit by the client. Often this is hosted by the DMO. A site inspection by the planner that occurs after the proposal has been submitted, yet prior to the customer's decision, is used to address questions regarding the execution of the submitted proposal. Finally, a site inspection visit by the planner occurring after the contract has been signed is often the first step in the finalization of a program or event. Site inspections can vary in time and detail.

These inspections must be carefully planned and orchestrated to show a customer the venues and services offered as well meet the destination team, which includes community contacts. The site inspection can often be the most critical step in winning a customer's business, as this is when the DMO has an opportunity to develop a relationship with the customer and gain their confidence. Many programs have been won or lost over a seemingly simple lunch conversation during a site inspection.

DMO Services for Meeting Professionals

There are multiple general services that DMOs provide meeting professionals. One category of services might be referred to as connecting the planner and attendee to the destination. In doing so, the DMO might provide hotel room counts and meeting space statistics, as well as a central database of other meetings to help planners avoid conflicts and/or space shortages. The DMOs can help with meeting facility availability—information on the availability of hotels, convention centers, and other meeting facilities—as well as help connect planners to their local transportation network offering shuttle service, ground transportation, and airline information. Furthermore, DMOs can provide access to special venues, as most DMOs have ties to city departments and personnel are well connected with local government officials. Whether an official letter of welcome from the mayor is needed, or a road needs to be blocked for a street party, a DMO can pave the way. DMOs can also help meeting attendees maximize their free time through the creation of pre- and post-conference activities, spouse tours, and special evening events. Lastly, DMOs are a liaison in destination government and/or community relations—a local resource regarding legislative, regulatory, and municipal issues that may affect a meeting or the meetings industry.

A second category of service could be labeled information. DMOs can offer unbiased information about a wide range of destination services and facilities. They can serve as a vast information database and provide one-stop shopping, thus, saving planners time, energy, and money in the development of a meeting. DMOs can also act as a liaison between the planner and the community. For example, DMOs are aware of community events with which a meeting may beneficially coincide (like festivals or sporting events). Lastly, DMOs provide destination information—information on local events, activities, sights, attractions, and restaurants—and assistance with tours and event planning.

A third category of service is assistance with the meeting or event. Here, DMOs can assist in the creation of collateral material and with on-site logistics and registration. Furthermore, DMOs can develop pre- and post-conference activities, spouse tours, and special events; and assist with site inspections, familiarization tours, and site selection. DMOs can also provide speakers and local educational opportunities. Lastly, DMOs can provide help in securing auxiliary services: production companies, catering, security, and so on.

The Changing Scope of DMO Responsibilities

A DMO wants clients to be happy, and will work to match the meeting planner with the perfect setting and services for their meeting.

DMOs have traditionally focused on success in driving hotel occupancy and the number of meetings and conventions held at their destination. But the rapid growth in global tourism has caused, in some communities, a significant change in the ratio of visitors-to-locals. And, as tourism grows, residents in many destinations are beginning to ask: At what point does growing tourist arrivals begin to detract from their quality of life?

There has been a recent shift in the roles of DMOs to transition from full-time marketers to destination managers. DMOs are working to foster stronger connections with governments and planning authorities to ensure that tourism has a seat at the table. Creating a tourism master plan is a good start, as it represents a long-term development framework for tourism (10–20 years) with an emphasis on policy and strategy, planning, institutional strengthening, legislation and regulation, product development, and diversification.

DMOs are increasingly being asked to work as a community partner to help strengthen the destination's tourism infrastructure. For example, many DMOs work with the local airport authorities to increase air lift, or work with hotel developers to build the type of property that would best enhance the city's assets.

Amateur and professional sports have become increasingly popular through the years, and many DMOs have added Sports Development Departments, or created Sports Commissions to capture this business. Every sport has a youth component, and destinations have found success in attracting sports tournaments to their communities. An advantage of youth sports groups is that they have their tournaments on weekends and in the summer, thus, complementing the typical Monday to Thursday schedule of conventions. Baseball diamonds, swimming pools, soccer fields, and ice arenas are examples of the types of venues being offered for teams willing to travel to compete. Locals benefit as they can also use these facilities. Hotels, local restaurants, and attractions benefit from this lucrative business as well.

Many DMOs hire a full-time research director to gather a wide variety of relevant tourism industry data, such as:

- Hotel occupancy, average daily rate, and revenue per available room
- Number of local tourism jobs
- Local and state taxes paid by the tourism industry
- Total direct spending relating to tourism
- Impact studies of groups, festivals, and sporting events
- Satisfaction studies of travelers to the destination

These statistics are curated and presented to local community partners, governments, and stakeholders and can effectively prove the worth of the work being done by the DMO in relation to the entire local tourism effort.

Destinations International

As the global trade association for official DMOs, **Destinations International (DI)** protects and advances the success of destination marketing worldwide.

DI's membership includes over 600 official DMOs with more than 4,100 staff members in over 15 countries that command more than $2 billion in annual budgets. Membership is open to all official DMOs recognized by their respective governments from the smallest town to the largest country, including convention and visitor bureaus, regional tourism boards, state and provincial tourism offices, and national tourism boards.

DI provides members with information, resources, research, networking opportunities, professional development, and certification programs. The following are the characteristics of DI:

Our Cause
DI protects and advances the success of destination marketing organizations worldwide.

Our Mission
DI advocates for the professionalism, effectiveness, and significance of destination marketing organizations worldwide.

Our Promise
DI is the passionate advocate and definitive resource for official destination marketing organizations and professionals worldwide.

Our Values
DI is committed to the following core values: innovation, transparency, responsiveness, and inclusiveness.

DI actively promotes DMOs worldwide, highlighting the value of using a DMO's services to the media and general public.

DI Professional Development Offerings

DI provides professional development to DMOs and their employees via an annual convention, forums, summits, sales academy, and certification.

Certified Destination Management Executive

DI has a certification program that is the equivalent of the CMP designation in the meeting professional community.

Recognized by the DMO industry as its highest educational achievement, the **Certified Destination Management Executive (CDME)** program is delivered under the auspices of Purdue University and DI. The CDME program is an advanced educational program for veteran and career-minded DMO executives who are looking for senior-level professional development courses. The main goal of the CDME program is to prepare senior executives and managers of DMOs for increasing change and competition.

The focus of the program is on vision, leadership, productivity, and implementation of business strategies. The outcomes of the program are demonstrating the value of a destination team and improving personal performance through effective organizational and industry leadership.

PDM Program

Although Professional in Destination Management (PDM) is not a designation, like CDME, it is recognized throughout the industry as a highly valuable skills package needed for the destination management career. DMO professionals who participate in the PDM Certificate Program acquire the necessary knowledge and skills to be more effective and successful destination management professionals.

Accreditation

In fall 2006, DI launched the Destination Marketing Accreditation Program (DMAP), starting initially with a beta test followed by a full program rollout. Currently utilized by the US Chamber of Commerce, the healthcare industry, and institutions of higher education, accreditation programs are becoming increasingly popular with organizations that wish to define standards of performance for their member constituents and measure their compliance. DI research shows that 93 percent of DMO executives say their organization would seek accreditation if an acceptable program were developed by the association. DMAP aims to provide a good method that assures staff, volunteer leadership, and external stakeholders that their DMO is following proper practices and performing at an acceptable level for the industry.

DI Research

DI's research arm, the Destination & Travel Foundation, provides destination management professionals with access to insightful, comprehensive, and industry-specific information that they can use to enhance the effectiveness of their DMO's day-to-day operations and in their business planning. DI offers a wealth of research and resources that provide statistical data and information essential for calculating economic impact, budgeting and strategic planning, marketing and promotion, and educating stakeholders. The following outlines the research and resources of DI:

> *DMO Compensation and Benefits Survey:* This report, conducted biannually, provides a baseline for more than 45 job position compensation levels, as well as for benefits packages offered to DMO employees in the United States and Canada.

DMO Organizational and Financial Profile: This survey, the most comprehensive of its type for DMOs, provides standards for a variety of operations while also allowing DMOs to compare their operations with their peers. Also conducted every two years, the report includes information on DMO funding sources, available facilities, tax rates, budgets, staff structure, expense categories, and reserves.

Event Impact Calculator

The DMAI Event Impact Calculator is the official industry standard for measuring the economic value of an event and calculating its return on investment to local taxes.

The Event Impact Calculator measures the economic value of an event and calculates its return on investment to local taxes. Armed with this information, DMOs are better prepared to make the case to policymakers for the ongoing development and growth of the meetings sector.

Updated annually, the calculator draws on ten different data sources to provide an industry-wide standard that is also:

Credible: With minimal user inputs, DMOs can produce impact analysis based on the latest survey and economic data available.

Localized: Each DMO receives access to a model that is uniquely developed for their destination.

Comprehensive: The calculator measures the direct impact of events on businesses, employment, income, and taxes.

DestinationNEXT

Commissioned by the Destination and Travel Foundation, **DestinationNEXT** is designed to provide DMOs with practical actions and strategies for improving their performance and attainment of future goals.

DestinationNEXT sets out to answer the question of what tomorrow's DMO will look like and how today's DMO leaders get their organization on a path that preserves tourism benefits, secures marketplace position, and engages their community interests.

Destination & Travel Foundation

The Destination & Travel Foundation was created in 1993 to enhance and complement DI and the destination management profession through research, education, visioning, and developing resources and partnerships for these efforts. The DI Foundation integrated with the US Travel Association's Foundation in 2009 to become the Destination & Travel Foundation.

The foundation is classified as a charitable organization under Section 501(c)(3) of the US Internal Revenue Service Code. Therefore, donations to the foundation are tax deductible as charitable contributions.

ASSOCIATION OF AUSTRALIAN CONVENTION BUREAUX

The Association of Australian Convention Bureaux Inc. (AACB) consists of 17 city and regional bureaus and is dedicated to marketing each specific region as a convention destination. The destinations are marketed to local, national, and international markets. The bureaus also recognize their responsibility to promote Australia.

The role of the AACB is as follows:

- To market its member destination as a leading location for meetings and business events
- To be the main vehicle in obtaining meetings and business events for the destination
- To create incentive travel rewards programs for corporate meetings, special events, and exhibitions.

- To derive the highest numbers of attendees by increasing marketing and promotions for events that the destination has won

- To exchange ideas, develop networking, and trade contracts

The responsibilities of the AACB are to provide measurable benefits for its stakeholders through a range of sophisticated sales and destination marketing activities, and to coordinate advisory services.

AACB has its offices in South Wales, Australia.

Trends

The role and function of DMOs will continue to expand. Many are now involved in managing the destination. They are helping to guide the community in tourism development and policy, building infrastructure, planning and expanding convention centers, attracting hotel developers, and more.

Some consider DMO to stand for destination marketing organization, while others consider it to stand for destination management organization. Furthermore, some experts in the field have suggested that an even better and more descriptive term would be Destination Marketing and Management Organizations (DMMOs).

DMMOS

The following is a synopsis of a presentation by Chris Fair of Resonance Consultancy at the European Cities Marketing Meeting in Gdansk, February 22–25, 2017

The transformation of the destination marketing organization is so profound that the organization's name itself needs to change. How should the DMMOs evolve into the future?

At this point in time, DMOs have an important choice to make as they consider how to lead their destination's success. Destination Marketing Organizations have been traditionally focused on and measured by their success in driving hotel occupancy, and the number of meetings and conventions held at a destination. But the rapid growth in global tourism has caused the ratio of visitors-to-locals to change significantly in cities from around the globe. As tourism grows, residents in many cities and destinations are beginning to ask at what point growing tourist arrivals begin to detract from *their* local quality of life. Savannah, Georgia has commissioned a research study to investigate exactly this issue. Perceptions of tourism can change quickly from being a nice addition to the local economy to a threat to the local quality of life. DMOs can go from being perceived as community boosters to community detractors. Those DMOs that don't address this issue can quickly find themselves on the wrong side of this conversation.

As destination marketing organizations think about evolving into destination marketing *and management* organizations, they need to look at all aspects of a destination's needs and overall development. DMOs currently have very little influence on city planning, policy, and programming. One step in becoming a DMMO is to foster stronger connections with government and planning authorities to make sure that tourism has a seat at the table. Creating a *Tourism Master Plan* in partnership with the city can be a good first step in this regard. DI helps a DMO do this through their *DestinationNext* initiative. Another step is developing the roles and responsibilities within the organization, with appropriate funding to support them, to ensure that the recommendations within the plan are implemented and monitored over time. Lastly, DMOs can play a more significant role in managing the guest experience within the destination. This goes beyond staffing a visitor center, and should consider how tourism affects the experience of locals as well.

DMOs often evaluate visitor satisfaction with the destination, but they do not often engage with residents. Evolving into a DMMO means the organization needs to spend as much time communicating with residents, monitoring and measuring resident satisfaction, as they do with visitors.

Not many industries have been more disrupted by technology than travel, and DMOs' approach to marketing has changed significantly as a result. But little attention has been paid to leveraging technology as a marketing channel and how technology can be used to enhance and manage visitors' experiences once they arrive at the destination. DMMOs should be modifying their existing digital channels or creating separate websites, apps, and booking systems for visitors to access upon arrival so they can better manage their own experiences. At the same time, the DMMO needs to deepen their connection to, and knowledge of, the visitors on the ground.

DMOs need to expand their roles within cities or destinations, and position themselves as the stewards and managers of the city's brand. This applies not only to tourism, but also for talent attraction and investment as well. No other organization in a destination has the funding or expertise to do it, and by assuming that role, a DMO can expand its value proposition to the community it serves.

The process of building a shared vision with the community that establishes strategic direction requires considering where you want to go. Then, you need to create a plan that articulates how you'll get there. Of course, the plan is just the first step. Implementing it is the hardest part and that takes budget and staff to do so. Some DMOs have created special administrative positions within their organizations to accomplish this. Two of these titles are Chief Experience Officer and Vice-President of Destination Development.

DMOs help visitors focus on aspects of the destination that will fulfill their wants and needs.
flavia raddavero/Alamy Stock Photo

The trend of putting destination marketing, tourism services, and convention center operation under one umbrella is likely to continue. This helps to make sales and delivery of the tourism product, especially with large citywide conventions, more efficient and seamless.

DMOs will continue to educate the community and stakeholders about the importance and value of face-to-face meetings.

DMOs are likely to see continued threats to their budgets. Politicians often try to divert funding away from DMOs to more visible endeavors, such as schools. Therefore, DMOs will look for ways in which to diversify their funding.

The greatest increase in the number and scope of DMOs will likely take place in developing regions such as China and Africa.

How to find out more about DMOS: Visit www.destinationmarketing.org, the official website of the DI.

VIENNA CONVENTION BUREAU—ABOUT US

The Vienna Convention Bureau is your neutral partner. Our job is to promote Vienna as Central Europe's leading conference city. We offer our services free of charge to any national or international organizer of meetings, conventions, and incentives.

The Vienna Convention Bureau was set up in 1969 as a department of the Vienna Tourist Board with financial support from the Vienna City Council and the Vienna Chamber of Commerce. Additional funding comes from sponsors. In order to hold its corner in today's networked global markets, the Vienna Convention Bureau belongs to a number of international convention and meeting industry associations.

A team of 11 conference specialists, headed up by Christian Mutschlechner, acquires convention, meeting, and incentive business from around the globe and play a key role in maintaining Vienna's international reputation as a recognized destination.

Conferences, corporate meetings, and incentives play an important part in Vienna's tourist industry and account for 12.3 percent of all overnight stays. Outstanding conference facilities, excellent conference support services, and cultural appeal help ensure that Vienna ranks among the leading destinations for international meetings.

Courtesy of the Vienna Convention Bureau

Summary

DMOs are an integral part of the meetings, conventions, and travel industry. For over 100 years, DMOs have been working diligently to bring meetings and conventions to their destinations and to service these meetings with a variety of free services. Over the years, DMOs have gone from being destination marketers to destination managers, becoming involved in every aspect of their destinations and, therefore, enriching the experience for all visitors.

The DI is the professional association for DMO employees, and it has been providing a wealth of member services to DMOs since 1914.

CASE STUDY   PITTSBURGH IS UNEXPECTEDLY CHOSEN TO HOST THE G-20 SUMMIT

In 2009, the G-20 Summit (an international forum for the governments and central bank governors from 20 major economies) was scheduled to take place in Washington, DC, but, for an unexpected reason, the city was unable to host it. Pittsburgh learned in May of that year that they were chosen to host this prestigious worldwide event.

In just four short months, VisitPITTSBURGH and their community partners (City, County, and Chamber of Commerce) worked as a coalition to ready the community to welcome 30 international delegations. Their Convention Services team called out to the community to find native speaking immigrants from all nations, and asked them to volunteer

in each host hotel to be on hand for translation, and most importantly, to be a welcoming representative from Pittsburgh. Most wore traditional ethnic dress and engaged the guests every day during their stay.

VisitPITTSBURGH also spearheaded cross-cultural training for the entire community, and produced a booklet of phrases, customs, and courtesies for all of their visiting nations.

The Pittsburgh Summit was a huge success for the community and proved to the world that a second-tier city could execute an important and complex conference of international note.

Key Words and Terms

For definitions, see Glossary.

Certified Destination Management Executive (CDME)
DestinationNEXT

Destinations International (DI)
destination marketing organization (DMO)

requests for proposals (RFPs)

Review and Discussion Questions

1. Define the role and function of a destination marketing organization.

2. Name the different ways that DMOs can be funded.

3. Name two things that a DMO does for meeting professionals.

4. Name two things that the DI does for meeting professionals.

5. What can the DI do for DMOs?

Internet Sites for Reference

www.destinationmarketing.org

www.empowermint.com

About the Chapter Contributor

Craig Davis is the President and CEO of VisitPITTSBURGH. He is a tourism industry veteran, having worked in convention services, catering, and sales senior management for Hilton International and Starwood Hotels in Canada and the United States. Craig joined VisitPITTSBURGH in 2000 as the Vice President of Convention Sales and was promoted to CEO in 2012.

He has held executive committee positions in both the association and foundation boards of Destinations International Association.

Contact Information:

VisitPITTSBURGH
Fifth Avenue Place
Suite 2800
120 fifth Avenue
Pittsburgh, PA 15222
craig.davis@visitpittsburgh.com

Previous Chapter Contributor

Karen M. Gonzales, CMP.

Cruise ships are sometimes used for meetings and conventions.
David Wingate/Alamy Stock Photo

CHAPTER 4

Meeting, Expositions, Event, and Convention Venues: An Examination of Facilities Used by Meeting and Event Professionals

Chapter Objectives

- Discuss the physical characteristics and financial structure of hotels.
- Identify the types of events best suited to a convention center and the reasons behind that solution.

- Discuss the space, functions, consortiums, and financing involved in using conference centers for events.
- Identify the similarities, differences, and benefits of cruise ships and other event venue options.

- Articulate the benefits of specific-use facilities as event venues.
- Outline the appeal and uses of colleges and universities as event venues.
- Cover the unique needs and uses that differentiate retreat facilities from other kinds of venues.

- Discuss the increasing need for unique and unusual venues.
- Illustrate the typical needs and obstacles specific to an outdoor event.

Meeting planners and event professionals work in a variety of facilities. (Throughout this chapter the terms meeting planner, event professional, planner, and professional are interchangeable.) These facilities range in size from **hotel** suites that hold a handful of people to major convention centers and outdoor festival sites that accommodate tens of thousands. Any location where two or more people gather is a meeting/event site. Whether it is a multimillion-square-foot convention center or a street corner under a light pole, people will find a place to gather. The event professional's job is to match the event and the venue. Thus, the planner must determine two things about the group: (1) Who are they? and (2) Why are they here? Most events and meetings are appropriate only for a limited range of facilities. For an event to succeed, the characteristics of the event must be properly matched to the facility in which it is held. Whether the venue is the conference room at the end of a suite of offices, or the flight deck of an active aircraft carrier, the goal of the meeting must fit with the choice of venue for the meeting to work.

Thus, the planner must appropriately research the group and the facilities that may fit the group's needs, understand the needs and expectations of the group, communicate the benefits offered by a facility that meet the needs of the group, and verify the arrangements between the group and the venues. Before selecting a meeting venue, the planner must complete a needs analysis. See Chapter 12 on Planning MEEC events for a more detailed explanation of needs analysis.

To properly exploit the tremendous range of available facilities, a meeting planner must be familiar with both the physical characteristics of the venue and its financial structure. The combined impact of these two factors determines a meeting planner's relationship with the facility's management, and both parties' relative negotiating positions. Many other features of a facility are relevant to the success or failure of any meeting/event, but an understanding of the significance of the facility's physical form and its financial structure is vital for a meeting planner to effectively use the facility to support the meeting.

The vast majority of meetings take place in conference rooms or offices on the meeting participants' property. Typically, one room in a suite of offices is designated as a conference room, and a handful of colleagues gather to address a current issue. Whether scheduled or impromptu, these meetings rarely involve a full-time meeting planner. Yet, these meetings are often organized by an employee who has meeting-planning tasks included as part of their job description. As these meetings become larger and involve more people, the person who has had the position of scheduling these on-property meetings frequently plans meetings that take place outside of the company's office.

Hotels

"Today's meetings have moved beyond dates, rates, and space and organizations are looking for a value-added approach,"

Elliot L. Ferguson,
President and CEO, Destination DC

Physical Characteristics

Meeting Room Spaces

Hotels have traditionally been the go-to location for corporate events. Any hotel that has at least one small **boardroom** is part of the meeting and events world. At one end of the meeting room spectrum is the smaller meeting room, which is often a boardroom that is typically focused on a small number of attendees and has a dedicated table and chairs. At the other end of the meeting room spectrum are the large ballrooms that are typically more formal and elegantly appointed, with some ballrooms able to handle several thousand guests. Because of their size and scope, ballrooms are generally planned as part of the initial construction of the facility. A common floor plan provides larger divisions flanked by smaller ones accessible from the side corridors. It is not uncommon for the ceiling to be lower in the smaller divisions than in the larger ones. This is not always obvious from printed floor plans.

In addition to boardrooms and ballrooms, larger hotels also have **break-out rooms**. The size and number of the break-out rooms can vary from hotels that have one small break-out room to ones that have thousands of square feet of break-out room space. Break-out rooms tend to be decorated and equipped like a smaller version of a ballroom, and serve identical functions for smaller numbers of people.

Event planners are challenging hotels to rethink ballroom and break-out room configurations as the demand for traditional classroom sessions and meals are decreasing. Instead, meeting planners and attendees are looking for unique ways to engage, maximize, and create interactive meetings. Creative and welcoming spaces, with a higher level of customization and personalization, are key.

Meeting planners are looking at spaces today that were not traditionally part of the event-planning scene. Hotels are now competing with many other venues in their market for the same meeting/event business. This has challenged them to look at their space differently and innovate. Gone are the days of just using sliding doors or air walls to subdivide a giant ballroom. Meeting planner and attendee expectations have forced hotels to focus on specific and dedicated rooms designed for different objectives, like small group conversations, attendee reflection spaces, informal gatherings, and formal presentations. It is not uncommon to see meeting rooms that look homey and relaxing. Boring meeting rooms and boardrooms are giving way to rooms that can accommodate all the necessary technology, speaker needs, thought sessions, team sessions, and social breakouts. To emphasize their flexibility, some hotels have even gone so far as to change the names of their ballrooms and meeting rooms, showing that they are different.

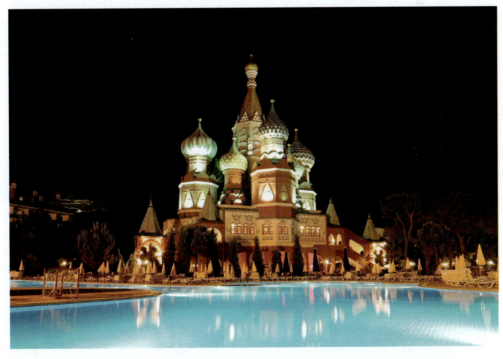

Many hotels have magnificent pools that can be used for events and receptions. This one is at a Kremlin-style hotel in Antalya, Turkey.
slava296/Shutterstock

Other Hotel Meeting Spaces

Many hotels have public spaces that can also be used for meetings and events. Pools, patios, atriums, lobbies, lawns, and gardens can all be used as meeting/event locations. For example, many of the resort hotels in Las Vegas have magnificent outdoor patios and pool areas that are regularly used for events.

In addition to utilizing outdoor venues, the use of **pre-function space**, such as corridors or lobbies adjacent to meeting rooms, may also provide a location for ancillary meeting or event needs. More hotel venues are creating small areas within the pre-function space where two or three attendees can connect, check emails, or make phone calls before an event or during a break. Refreshment breaks, registration desks, mobile charging stations, and cocktail receptions may also be situated in these pre-function areas to provide necessary services without compromising valuable meeting rooms.

As meeting planners and attendees require more experiential events, just like with break-out rooms and ball rooms, the more unique, interesting, and creative a hotel can be with non-traditional space the more competitive the hotel will be against its competition. Tables 4-1 and 4-2 show the hotels with the largest meeting spaces.

Financial Structure

Hotels tend to be owned by major branded hotel companies, or are owned and franchised by real estate investment companies that hire hotel management companies to manage the facility in accordance with their corporate brand guidelines. For most hotels, meetings and events are not necessarily their primary business. The primary business of almost all hotels is the sale of sleeping room nights. In the past, the meeting space in a hotel business was often a loss leader, whose primary purpose was to fill what would otherwise be empty sleeping rooms, especially on **shoulder** nights when the hotel didn't have its core corporate business. Today, while filling sleeping rooms is still very important, meetings, events, and food and beverage (F&B) are playing a more significant role in the profit and loss equation. For example, the Marriott Marquis in New York City's catering department generates annual revenue in the tens of millions of dollars. There are now many hotels that derive significant revenue from their extensive meeting spaces.

Other revenue streams from which hotels may generate significant income include restaurants, bars, and branded coffee kiosks, which are frequented by convention attendees. A smaller percentage of revenue is also the result of **concessionaires** at pools, beaches, or spas. This dynamic changes somewhat when the hotel is associated with a theme park or casino. Casinos can be moneymaking machines and may have a significant impact on a planner's ability to negotiate. Hotels associated with theme parks have a similar effect.

TABLE 4-1

Hotels with the Largest Meeting Space

	Hotel	Destination	Total Meeting Space (Sq Ft)	Hotel Rooms
1	The Venetian & The Palazzo	Las Vegas, NV	2,250,000	7,094
2	Mandalay Bay Resort & Casino	Las Vegas, NV	2,100,000	3,215
3	Marina Bay Sands Resort & Casino	Singapore	1,300,000	2,561
4	Rosen Shingle Creek Resort	Orlando, FL	445,000	1,501
5	Gaylord Palms Resort Convention Center	Kissimmee, FL	400,000	1,416
6	Marriott Orlando World Center Resort	Orlando, FL	399,214	2,004
7	Hilton Anatole	Dallas, TX	286,654	1,606
8	Caesars Palace Las Vegas	Las Vegas, NV	240,000	3,793
9	Sheraton Hotel Walt Disney World Dolphin	Lake Buena Vista, FL	238,792	1,509
10	Hilton Orlando Orange County Convention Center	Orlando, FL	225,000	1,417

Data Summarized from STR Global's Hotel Census Database

TABLE 4-2

Largest Meeting Space for Global Convention City Hotels

Hotel	City	Total Meeting Space (Sq Ft)	Hotel Rooms
The Venetian Macao Resort Hotel	Macau, SAR, China	199,132	2,905
Marriott Washington Wardman Park	Washington, DC	193,169	1,152
Hyatt Regency New Orleans	New Orleans	155,644	1,193
Hilton Chicago	Chicago	155,385	1,544
Hilton New York Midtown	New York	151,000	1,929
Hotel New Otani Tokyo	Tokyo, Japan	139,480	1,533
Estrel Hotel	Berlin, Germany	122,181	1,125
Novotel Sydney Rooty Hill	Sydney, Australia	93,602	164
Beijing Yanqi Lake Intl Convention & Exhibition Center	Beijing, China	85,500	66
Hotel Queen Mary	Long Beach, CA	81,826	346
JW Marriott Los Angeles LA Live	Los Angeles, CA	77,000	878
Grand Cevahir Hotel & Convention Center	Istanbul, Turkey	71,311	323
Novotel London West	London, England	69,408	630
Hilton Frankfurt Hotel	Frankfurt, Germany	66,193	342
Marriott Rive Gauche Hotel & Conference Center	Paris, France	51,667	757
Grand Hilton Seoul Hotel	Seoul, South Korea	50,289	396
JW Marriott Marquis Hotel Dubai	Dubai, UAE	48,125	1,608

Data Summarized from STR Global's Hotel Census Database

Negotiating Your Event

When entering the negotiation phase, the major discussion points for the meeting planner and venue to negotiate are sleeping room rates, F&B menus and costs, meeting space costs, and audiovisual (AV) and technology costs. While there may be other smaller concessions, like negotiating parking, transportation, or additional hotel services, these should only be discussed once the main points are agreed upon.

Room Rates

When booking rooms for transient or corporate hotel guest segments, a hotel typically works directly with the guest staying in that room. When booking meetings and events, the hotel's main customer is the meeting planner. Their needs and preferences are an important part of the sales and negotiation equation. Conventional wisdom suggests that meeting planners do not pay for meeting space in hotels. However, meeting space is expensive for hotels. The interest paid on the investment capital needed to build the hotel, and the staff and materials required to clean, maintain, and operate the meeting rooms are some of the most significant costs related to a meeting space. These costs must be funded from somewhere. Most often, these costs are covered by requiring a meeting or event to commit to using a minimum number of sleeping rooms for a minimum number of nights. This is often referred to as a room block.

Sleeping room rates are often negotiated by the size of the block of rooms the meeting planner needs for the event. Usually the bigger the block, the lower the rate. Complimentary rooms are typically associated with the room block. The industry norm is one complimentary room for every 50 rooms blocked. This could be a negotiating point to get additional complimentary rooms by negotiating the ratio to one for every 30 rooms blocked. Typically, room blocks are also linked to meeting space availability. By linking sleeping room use with meeting space availability, it lowers the cost of the meeting, but has become a challenge for hotels based on how accurate the projection of sleeping rooms is.

Before going into the negotiation, meeting planners should do an online search of rates offered on sites like Expedia, Booking.com, and Trip Advisor for that specific hotel.

Given the popularity of Internet travel booking sites, many planners are realizing that their attendees are going to these sites and booking lower rates than the negotiated rate. These rooms are not included in the contracted room block and are causing the planner to pay **attrition** penalties for not meeting their room block numbers. There are clauses that can be added to the contract that address this issue, but they should be discussed with an attorney familiar with these issues. The planner's goal in this process is to get credit for every room night the hotel sells as a result of the meeting or event. This one issue may be the toughest part of any hotel negotiation. To avoid attrition, some associations require their attendees to book in the room block, or face paying a significantly higher registration fee.

Food and Beverage

Another significant source of revenue for most hotels is food and beverage (F&B). The restaurants and bars in a hotel are generally designed to handle the hotel's regular transient guests, which is likely a mix of business travelers and tourists. Many meeting planners and hotels realize that there are certain times during the meeting or event where the hotel will receive increased business in their outlets from the attendees. An example would be attendees congregating in the hotel bar before and after a meeting or event in the ballroom. During the negotiation, this ancillary business should be included as part of the F&B spend discussion.

Hotel banquet catering departments have the responsibility to create menus and to meet the catering requirements of the meeting or event. The scope and quality of hotels' banquet departments vary as much as the quality of the sleeping rooms. In a reaction to the reluctance of some meeting planners to agree to elevated sleeping room rates to guarantee meeting space, some hotels have linked banquet revenue with meeting space. Thus, a meeting planner who meets a threshold of spending in the catering department gets a break in the meeting room cost.

Other Revenue Generating Departments

Hotels derive revenue from a variety of other non-meeting services as well. These services are also a part of the negotiation process between the meeting planner and the hotel. These types of services can enhance a meeting or event, but can also add significant costs. When negotiating with the hotel, meeting planners need to understand what the added costs to the meeting or event are. Golf courses, spas, equestrian centers, and beaches all provide revenue to the hotel. Corporate meetings or conventions often plan a golf tournament for attendees.

Hotels often contract with exclusive vendors to provide services within the hotel. Service contractors, musicians/entertainment, disc jockeys, florists, and bus companies can all be contracted to the hotel as exclusive vendors of their specialized services. Commissions paid back to the hotel can be as high as 40 percent. Some hotels charge attrition on those services as well. The hotel's theory is that the hotel and the vendor have made an investment in the facility and equipment for the meeting planner's benefit. Should the planner elect not to use these services, the services should be paid for anyway because they were available. This is particularly common with AV services. Hotels often require planners to use the in-house AV department or an exclusive vendor. If a planner insists on using an outside company, they may have to pay a hefty fee. It is especially important to discuss these expectations early in the negotiating process to avoid confusion later. The negotiated size of the projected commission may be the determining factor.

Hotels attached to theme parks are a special case. It is not uncommon for a theme park–based hotel to include an estimate of how much money the attendees or their families will spend in the attached entertainment facilities when they decide whether or not to take a particular piece of business. Clauses relating the number of theme park passes purchased to the availability of meeting room space can appear in some contracts at these hotels. Meetings planned with sufficient free time to allow the attendees to visit the theme parks may have an easier time contracting their desired meeting space. Receptions and meal functions for meeting attendees often take place in the theme park.

If the hotel is attached to a casino, it is possible for the hotel to derive more revenue from the casino than it does from the sleeping rooms. In recent years, casino hotels have come to realize that convention attendees are good business: They come during the week and, thus, are synergistic with the typical gambler who comes on the weekend; they do not need comps or other enticements to come as gamblers do; they will pay a higher price for their hotel rooms; and they often gamble as much when not in meetings as other casino patrons. All the hotels constructed in gaming destinations over the past decade have included significant meeting and event space. The prices charged for the sleeping rooms are fixed in advance of the guests' arrival. The potential revenue derived from the casino is limited only by the availability of credit on the guests' accounts. Meetings then can become a means to bring guests to the casino, where they potentially spend more money gambling than they will on other activities. On the other hand, if a group fails to spend enough time and money in the casino during their meeting, the sales department may not offer reduced hotel room rates or other reduced-price concessions with the group in the future.

Local Meetings and Events

Some meetings and events do not involve sleeping rooms, and many hotels are reluctant to deal with them. However, the demand for venues to hold local social events are great enough that hotels do market to them. For the planner of a **local event** to get complimentarymeeting space, a minimum amount of catering revenue would need to be guaranteed. In addition to catering revenue, hotels can also receive revenue from commissions paid by other support vendors for the privilege of working in the hotel, such as **Exposition Service Contractors (ESC)**, AV, the disc jockey, the florist, the limo service, and entertainers, among others. These revenue streams are calculated in the decision to accept a piece of *social business* once all other higher revenue opportunities have been exhausted. Since a planner of a social event may overestimate F&B projections, attrition on catering revenue projections is becoming more common.

Seasonality

Seasonality and fluctuating occupancy levels can have a significant impact on the cost of using a facility. A hotel with a severe seasonal variation can have an off-season price that is as little as half of its peak-season price. By paying attention to a facility's seasonal occupancy patterns, meeting planners can find some true bargains. A common misconception among meeting attendees is that the incredibly cheap rate that they pay to use an exclusive resort is due to their planner's negotiating prowess, when it is more likely that the great rate is because of the planner's choice of a venue with extreme seasonal variations.

Aside from the typical considerations when booking meeting space in hotels, such as the size of the space available, attrition penalties for sleeping rooms and/or catering, and seasonality, planners must be aware of move-in/move-out schedules and other groups that are in-house. Depending on the size and scope of a meeting or event, it may take anywhere from a few hours to a week to set up (or tear down) the physical aspect of an event, particularly if there is an exhibition component. This time is essentially a lost opportunity for the hotel, because rather than booking another group, which could generate money, the space is unavailable. Hotels may charge a rental fee for the space itself to gain back some of that lost revenue, but there is no opportunity to make additional profit through catering or other revenue centers. Planners must keep this in mind and expect to negotiate move-in/move-out dates because hotels prefer to utilize their meeting space as efficiently as possible. In addition, hotels often host meetings for several different groups at any given time. In many cases this is a non-issue, but when a corporation is promoting a new product launch or discussing proprietary information, they generally prefer their competitors not be in the same facility.

Coordinating space is also important when groups may have conflicting behavior. For instance, a significant conflict could arise if a professional organization giving a certification exam was placed in a meeting room adjacent to a daylong band rehearsal, or if a convention alcohol provider is booked at the same time as a religious convention. These are considerations planners must be cognizant of during the negotiating and contracting process to ensure the planning and execution of their event is successful.

Meeting planners negotiating with hotels need to consider the entire financial package their business will bring to the facility. The more closely aligned the meeting's financial structure is to the needs of the hotel, the better the deal the meeting planner can get for the meeting or event. The entire financial package includes not just the revenue from the event itself, but also the revenue from the sleeping rooms, restaurants, bars, and exclusive vendors. When negotiating with any meeting or event venue, meeting planners are not only negotiating based on what they will use, but also based on what is available whether they use it or not. The availability and cost of specific amenities often drives the attendee expectations of the venue. It is important that planners match the level of their attendee expectations with the level of service provided by the hotel at a cost the meeting planner feels is reasonable.

INDUSTRY SPOTLIGHT: A PASSION FOR HOSPITALITY!

Interview with Tim Obert, General Manager, Hyatt Regency McCormick Place

The Hyatt Regency McCormick Place is a 1,258-room hotel with 43,500 square feet of function space, and 6,600 square feet of pre-function space. It is conveniently attached via a skybridge to the McCormick Place: the largest convention center in the United States. It is also conveniently located near Chicago's museum campus, which holds the Field Museum, the Shedd Aquarium and Oceanarium, Adler Planetarium, and Soldier Field. It is also near the Chicago White Sox Baseball Stadium and the world-famous shopping on Michigan Avenue, also called the Magnificent Mile.

Tim Obert's career with Hyatt began at Hyatt Regency Waikiki when he joined their corporate management-training program upon graduation from college. The Hyatt Regency Waikiki is in the middle of all the action on Waikiki, Oahu's famous beach. Many associations and corporate conferences include the Hawaiian Islands as an important conference destination as part of their geographic rotation. The Hawaiian Islands are highly desired destinations by attendees due to their beautiful scenery, delicious food, and the welcoming hospitality of the Hawaiian people.

Upon completion of the management-training program, Mr. Obert was promoted in the hotel to Assistant Executive Housekeeper, and then Director of Bell Services. Over the course of 15 years, Mr. Obert held a variety of management positions in Hyatt properties located in Hollywood, Phoenix, Boston, and Chicago. In addition to hotel operation positions, Mr. Obert served as the Vice President of Revenue Management for the 119 North American full-service Hyatt Properties. Before returning to Chicago to manage the Hyatt Regency McCormick Place, Mr. Obert spent five years as the managing partner for The Beach House Restaurant, his family's restaurant on the Island of Kauai. Known for its stunning sunsets and delicious seafood, it is ranked one of the top ten restaurants in the world with an oceanfront view, making it a popular spot for weddings and corporate special events.

Do you have a favorite Hyatt hotel or memorable experience?

I enjoyed each of the Hyatt locations because I embraced each new destination when I lived there, as they each hold a special memory at that point in time. I enjoy working in the hospitality industry because I've had the opportunity to live in beautiful places and move to a new destination for my next career opportunity. In addition, every hotel had great role models that shared their expertise with me, which has given me a strong work ethic. A career highlight was opening a new hotel, where I had the opportunity to learn from the best and brightest managers at Hyatt who were sent to ensure the opening was a success. The experience taught me to roll with the moment, refocus, and find a way to make it happen when things didn't go as planned.

What recommendation do you have for students who are interested in pursuing a career in the event management field?

Become experts at creating relationships, and understand how hotels work, from guest experience to the foundations of revenue management. In a convention hotel, there are two types of event managers. First, are event planners who focus on large citywide events. They are knowledgeable on all aspects of planning a large-scale event. They understand each destination's uniqueness from the destinations' seasonality, hotel pricing range, special event venues, iconic menus of the region, and understanding the parameters of working within the city's union labor guidelines. The relationships they build with their key destinations help them plan their large-scale events that can be two or more years in the future. For example, these event planners may focus on planning aspects that are in conjunction with a major event, such as the VIP corporate parties for the Super Bowl. Or with the VIPs for a large entertainment company in conjunction with the Chicago Comic & Entertainment Expo (C2E2), which is an annual fan-based exhibition that celebrates the historic and ongoing contribution of comics to art and pop-culture.

The second type is the event planner who focuses on certain types of events, such as corporate meetings or consumer events (e.g., weddings and birthdays). The planner knows everything about each venue's event space, menus, preferred vendors, and labor guidelines. They also understand the destination's seasonality and the hotel pricing. Their expertise helps a client narrow down the hotel choice to the one that will fulfill the event experience the client wants to accomplish. The event planner's detailed knowledge also helps ensure the best value for their clients.

Since you have experience running hotels and a popular restaurant for events, what are the differences between holding a meeting or an event in a restaurant versus a hotel?

It's about the experience and engagement levels that you and your client want to accomplish. Is it to educate the attendees? Is it for a meeting to accomplish specific goals? Is it a celebration? How engaged do you want the attendees in the event?

If it is a several day conference, planning an event off-property, such as a nearby museum or famous landmark, can help incorporate the theme and message of the conference in a new location. Holding an event on a beautiful beach can also be a wonderful opportunity to celebrate a successful year of sales or an important life milestone.

What types of activities are necessary to prepare front line employees when a citywide event is in town?

At convention hotels, like the Hyatt McCormick Place, these large events are what they look forward to. C2E2 is one citywide event they love. How can you not have fun checking Wonder Woman into her room or serving her a drink? Our team really gets into it and has fun with our guests. In addition, they know how important these large-scale events are to the city, to bring tourism demand to Chicago, which means the entire city is busy thanks to event attendees.

Convention Centers

"Bookings will be higher for convention centers that can offer an authentic experience of their cities."

Barbara Palmer,
PCMA, 2016.

Conventional wisdom has it that convention centers are huge. Many are huge, and the biggest continue to get bigger. Convention centers are designed to handle larger events than could be supported in a hotel. Several convention centers feature over a million square feet of meeting and exhibit space. Their very size is both their strength and their weakness. Convention centers are meeting facilities without sleeping rooms, and are often little more than large bare buildings with exposed roof beams. Others are mammoth architectural marvels involving magnificent feats of engineering and awe-inspiring vistas. Table 4-3 lists the ten largest convention centers in the world, and Table 4-4 lists the largest convention centers in the United States.

Compared to hotels, convention centers are more likely to devote most of their space to **exhibit halls** and utilitarian spaces than to plush ballrooms. Common to these exhibit halls are trade shows. While hotel lobbies are designed to be comfortable and inviting, convention center lobbies are designed to facilitate the uninterrupted flow of several thousand attendees. This difference in design philosophy is evident in every phase of a convention center's operation.

While discussions about convention centers in the past typically involved the number of meeting rooms and the amount of available square footage, flexibility of the space is becoming more important. Customization of the space, adaptability, and integrating

TABLE 4-3
Largest Convention Centers in the World

	Name	City	Total Exhibition and Meeting Space Square Meters	Square Footage
1	National Exhibition and Convention Center	Shanghai, China	500,000	5,382,000
2	Messegelände Hannover	Hannover, Germany	448,900	5,300,000
3	Messegelände Frankfurt	Frankfurt, Germany	366,637	3,946,500
4	Fiera Milano	Milan, Italy	345,000	3,713,550
5	China Import & Export Fair Complex	Guangzhou, China	340,000	3,659,750
6	Koelnmesse	Cologne, Germany	284,000	3,057,000
7	Messe Düsseldorf	Dusseldorf, Germany	262,000	2,820,150
8	Paris Nord Villepinte	Paris, France	242,082	2,605,750
9	McCormick Place	Chicago	241,500	2,600,000
10	Fira Barcelona—Gran Via	Barcelona, Spain	240,000	2,584,000

TABLE 4-4
Largest Convention Centers in the United States

	Convention Center Name	City	Total Exhibition and Meeting Space in Square Footage
1	McCormick Place	Chicago, IL	2,600,000
2	Sands Expo & Convention Center	Las Vegas, NV	2,250,000
3	Las Vegas Convention Center	Las Vegas, NV	2,180,000
4	Orange County Convention Center	Orlando, FL	2,100,000
5	Mandalay Bay Convention Center	Las Vegas, NV	2,100,000
6	George R. Brown Convention Center	Houston, TX	1,800,000
7	Georgia World Congress	Atlanta, GA	1,400,000
8	Anaheim Convention Center	Anaheim, CA	1,280,000
9	I-X Center	Cleveland, OH	1,230,000
10	Kentucky Exposition Center	Louisville, KY	1,200,000
11	New Orleans Morial Convention Center	New Orleans, LA	1,100,000
12	Kay Bailey Hutchison Convention Center Dallas	Dallas, TX	1,019,000
13	The Moscone Center	San Francisco, CA	956,225
14	Jacob K. Javits Convention Center	New York City, NY	943,204
15	Donald E. Stephens Convention Center	Rosemont, IL	932,000
16	Walter E. Washington Convention Center	Washington DC, MD	901,000
17	Los Angeles Convention Center	Los Angeles, CA	867,000

local flavor are now essential parts of the discussion. Meeting planners and attendees are challenging the traditional approach to convention center space and trade show floors. Different configurations, different uses of space, and an expectation that all spaces be more engaging, relevant, and entertaining are the central focus. Creating hubs, education centers, interactive spaces, and tech centers are the new normal.

Just as hotels have a variety of space sizes, convention centers also have a variety of spaces. In the typical hotel, the ballrooms are the largest meeting spaces, followed by the break-out rooms. In a convention center, the exhibit halls tend to be the largest spaces, followed by the carpeted ballrooms, and then the break-out and meeting rooms. It would not be unusual for the pre-function spaces in a convention center to be larger than the

Inside a Convention Center.
George G. Fenich

break-out rooms attached to them, which is unlike a typical hotel, where the pre-function spaces tend to be smaller. Also, convention centers generally do not have spas, swimming pools, exercise rooms, saunas, restaurants, or bars. Another key difference between hotels and convention centers is that, while a hotel is open around the clock, convention centers can, and do, lock the doors at night, and the staff goes home when nothing is scheduled. In a hotel, someone is on duty at all times, whereas if someone is required to be available at odd hours at a convention center, that person must be scheduled in advance. Meeting planners using a convention center may need to plan in more detail than the meeting planner who holds the same meeting in a hotel.

With well over 400 convention centers in the United States alone, and more being built, meeting planners are looking for convention centers that offer unique features. Differentiating is key to the success of a given convention center. Meeting planners are making two choices when selecting a convention center: space and destination. In addition, each year, several convention centers expand, making the total exhibition and meeting space offered in each center a moving target.

Convention centers of the past have often been described as utilitarian and, occasionally, "cold" when compared to hotels. Newer convention centers have added more artistic design elements like sculptures and paintings. Many existing convention centers have been investing in complete remodels to meet future meeting needs. Common to both hotels and convention centers is the challenge of being flexible and able to create different environments based on the needs of the meeting planner and the attendee. One trend in convention centers is incorporating physical elements that engage the attendee by leveraging existing space and turning it into a new concept. An example would be a wellness stairwell to encourage attendees to take the stairs between the floors of an event. Choosing the stairs instead of the elevator is a quick way for people to add physical activity to their day.

Another trend in event space and meeting rooms are pop-up meeting rooms that can be set up or moved at a moment's notice. As meeting planners and attendees expect venues to be more flexible, the idea of pop-up meeting rooms for last minute meetings, executive sessions, conference calls, etc. will become a more significant part of negotiations. One strategy that marketers are using is promoting surrounding restaurants, local tours, museums, and natural resources. Some convention centers have added services to help meeting planners create events in the local market as part of their convention center meeting and event experience.

A Wellness Staircase Used by Convention Delegates to Exercise.
Hemis/Alamy Stock Photo

A pop-up meeting room in an exhibit hall of Messe Frankfurt.
George G. Fenich

Financial Structure

Unlike a hotel, which is most likely part of a corporation, most convention centers are owned by government entities. Governments want their investments in convention centers to pay off, and are putting more pressure on convention center profitability. Often, professional management for the convention center is contracted to a private company that specializes in managing such facilities. Many convention centers are actively supported by their local Destination Marketing Organizations (DMOs) and Convention and Visitor's Bureaus (CVBs), with some DMOs/CVBs even operating them. As with everything that concerns government, the management of these facilities is ultimately accountable to the taxpayers. One controversial issue among convention center managers is whether public- or private-sector companies can do a better job of managing these facilities. There are strongly held opinions on both sides of the issue. Even with all the discussion, one thing is still true: The quality of a planner's event is as dependent on the planner's relationship with the individuals running the facility, as how well the event is planned; especially in a convention center, the more thorough the planning, the more successful the event. There are some convention centers that are privately owned and operated, such as the Sands Convention Center in Las Vegas.

One overlooked fact that sets convention centers apart from many other types of facilities concerns the portion of their budget spent on energy. It is not unusual for a convention center to spend more money on utilities than it does on its full-time staff. This is not a reflection of the staffing levels, but rather an indication of how expensive it is to keep a large facility properly climate controlled. Hotels have significant energy bills as well, but unlike a convention center, they are not trying to climate control huge spaces with high ceilings and massive doors that stay open all day. In newly constructed convention centers, the green movement is at the forefront. Ceilings are being made of transparent materials and windows are being included to let natural sunlight come in, thus, reducing costs of lighting. Thermal heat pumps are being installed to reduce heating costs. Runoff water and "brown water" is being recycled and used for irrigation.

How does a convention center make money? They are not expected to make a profit in the conventional sense, but are expected to at least cover costs. Generally, the intent of the government for building a convention center is for it to be an economic driver for the whole community. Therefore, the facility can take events that benefit the community as a whole with less concern for driving the demand for sleeping room nights in the surrounding hotels. This is part of the reason why convention centers, unlike hotels, will take events, such as local consumer shows, that generate no sleeping room nights. However, the convention center may be funded in part by some kind of hotel sleeping room tax.

Negotiating for Your Event

Convention centers charge for everything they provide on a pay-per-use basis. Every square foot of the building has a price attached to it. Room rental, by the square foot per day, is the center's biggest single revenue source. Every chair, every table, and every service provided by the convention center has a price. F&B, catering services, and concessions are typically provided by an outside vendor who then pays the convention center a percentage. Unlike hotels that often put together packages, which include a total price for rooms, F&B, and other services, the convention center cost is specifically itemized. This itemized approach is the convention center's way of charging for services used, and not charging for what is not needed.

With attendees now accustomed to personalizing everything in their lives, they are bringing those same expectations to meetings. Convention centers and catering companies need to work together to accommodate their customers. In addition to catering, there are other vendors involved with convention centers. The financial arrangements between the vendors and the convention center vary. Some may pay a commission or a percentage based on their revenue. Others may not pay in cash but in the form of equipment, which is owned by the vendor and is installed in the building. For example, in many buildings, the facility does not own the soft drink vending equipment. The soft drink company with exclusive rights in the facility owns and services the equipment in return for a specified level of product sales.

Like a hotel, a convention center has relationships with vendors for services it does not provide internally. Such services might include parking, buses, AV, power, data–telecom, and florists. One ongoing debate in the convention center industry is whether it should have exclusive vendors, forcing meeting planners to use them if they use the convention center, or preferred vendors that the convention center recommends from which meeting planners can choose from.

Traditionally, catering was the only exclusive service, but in some facilities power, rigging, AV equipment, security, and telecom can also be exclusive vendors to the facility. Some of these relationships are the result of governmental regulations, and others are an attempt to avoid liability lawsuits. In contrast, some convention centers allow procurement of vendors that are not on the recommended list, but will then charge an additional fee to the meeting planner for using a non-recommended vendor.

Given the political climate in which most convention centers operate, combined with the size and scope of the events they support, pricing is fairly transparent. Typically, costs, services offered, and specifics on the size and scope of the facility are all either in print or on their website. With all this information readily available, it becomes the planner's responsibility to access the information, and not the facility's responsibility to guide a novice planner through the process.

Conference Centers

A **conference** is a meeting with an agenda and set objectives designed for consultation, education, fact-finding, problem solving, and/or information exchange. Conferences have a broad spectrum of reasons for meeting, which can include auditing, budgeting, marketing and sales forecasting, product launches, strategic planning, team-building, and/or training. Conferences are usually of a shorter duration and on a smaller scale than a convention.

Meeting Room Spaces

Because of a conference's wide variety of uses and goals, **conference center** facilities are designed to accommodate the multiple needs of the many organizations that use their facilities. Key conference center design factors include meeting rooms, refreshment areas, restrooms, secluded seating alcoves, and an on-site business center with the conference center's staff. Conference centers are designed specifically for conference activities, with acoustics, wall surfaces, lighting, and color schemes designed to enhance attendee productivity and comfort.

Conference center meeting rooms are specifically designed to enhance learning, and are often arranged in a classroom-style learning environment. The chairs are selected for comfort and alertness, such as ergonomic executive-style chairs. Tables are heavy and stable with smooth surfaces for note taking with additional room for laptops and other meeting materials. They often have electrical outlets for charging computers and smartphones. Conference centers are also known for their in-house inventory of AV technology and full-time media technicians. This results in better equipment quality and faster response time.

Conference centers provide outstanding service to accommodate their wide range of clientele who depend on an ideal meeting environment. When an organization books conference center space, a conference-meeting manager is dedicated to an organization with the full responsibility of their meeting. The conference meeting manager is involved in every aspect of the meeting, from coordinating program details, providing attentive service during the meeting, and administering the post-convention evaluation. This process provides a seamless service experience for the organization and attendees. Some conference centers are part of a corporate office complex and are used exclusively by a single corporation.

Associations and Consortiums

The **International Association of Conference Centers (IACC)** has developed a specific set of guidelines to ensure that their IACC conference centers provide a high quality and consistent conference meeting facilities around the globe. These IACC guidelines ensure that conference center meeting rooms have the required lighting, technology, and sound barrier standards that organizations depend on to provide the ideal learning environment. The IACC guidelines guarantee that the facility is ideal for intense, group learning environments, and is managed by event professionals who have obtained certain meeting planning certifications. Some conference centers have overnight guest rooms, known as **residential** conference centers, while non-residential conference centers do not have guest rooms. The IACC also has guidelines for conference center guest rooms, such as requiring a hard, writing-surface workspace with internet connectivity. Several major corporations run conference centers, including Aramark, Dolce, Hilton, Marriott, and Sodexo. The IACC website provides a list of their global conference centers with facility details and the services provided, making the initial search process simple for planners.

There are also other associations and consortiums that focus on conference centers. A consortium is an association, partnership, or union that is created by its members to expand their services to their regional, national, and international clients. Consortium members typically pay an annual fee that is then used to market their consortium, which in turn brings customers to the individual members. Consortiums, like associations, typically have guidelines that all their members must follow to provide a high-quality, consistent product and service. Some conference facilities may belong to several associations and consortiums to maximize their marketing efforts.

Venues of Excellence is the United Kingdom's largest consortium of dedicated conference venues, which share the highest possible standards for conference facilities and service quality. Their standards criteria include guidelines for conference rooms, lodging, and other services offered by each facility to ensure that organizations and their attendees have a successful conference.

The Historic Conference Centres of Europe (HCCE) presents a rich variety of professionally run conference centers, equipped with state-of-the-art technology in uniquely historic buildings in Europe. Each center has retained its character, yet has been adapted to hold the demanding and innovative functions required for conferences. Like IACC and Venues of Excellence, HCCE is a recognized quality seal in the meetings, conference, and exhibition industry.

Food and Beverage

The flexible dining and high-service levels experienced in conference center restaurants and bars are created to give attendees a high-quality experience. Menus are developed according to the dining environment that attendees need, including a wide variety of menus, such as international cuisine, vibrant networking lunches, and formal award dinners.

Negotiating Your Event

The major discussion points for the meeting planner and the conference center venue to negotiate are the meeting space costs, sleeping room rates (if selecting a residential conference center), F&B menus and costs, and AV and technology options.

Many conference centers have a pricing strategy called the **complete meeting package**, which means that whatever the facility owns, the planner may use at no additional charge. This puts the facility's entire inventory of easels, projectors, microphones, and sound systems at the planner's immediate disposal. For the planner, this is a flexible way to work, eliminating the need to schedule AV companies to provide the conference's technology needs and having to buy supplies at the last minute.

Attrition takes on a new meaning in a conference center. It is not unusual for a conference center to charge a planner a fixed price for up to a certain number of delegates. If some of the delegates do not come to the event, the planner is still responsible for the full amount of the contract. This fee is not based on the ability of the facility to resell the rooms. It is based on 100 percent of the negotiated facility fee regardless how much of the facility was used. Although the planner's tasks on-site are less intense than in a convention center, the planner's ability to predict room night use is very critical.

Cruise Ships

In a sense, cruise ships are floating hybrids of hotels, conference centers, and full-service resorts. Cruise ships are often overlooked as meeting venues, but they can provide a satisfying meeting experience. The quality of the planning for a cruise event has a greater impact on the success of the meeting than it does with any other type of venue. A ship moves by its own itinerary. Ensuring that all attendees' transportation arrives in time to properly accommodate the ship's schedule is key. Unlike a building, once the ship leaves port, latecomers are left behind, and getting to the next port of call is at their own additional expense.

A meeting held while the ship is under way will have a different attendance pattern than the same meeting held when the ship is in port. Schedule planning coordinated with the ship's itinerary can have a significant impact on a meeting's attendance. Many cruise lines have well-developed children's programs, which allow adults to participate in their meetings without being concerned where their children are or what they are doing. The

Cruise ships have meeting rooms that resemble those in hotels.
George G. Fenich

children's programs on many ships are better developed and provide more opportunities than in many major resorts. Also, meeting attendees are a *captive audience* while the ship is sailing and less likely to miss meetings.

Negotiating Your Event

In addition to finding creative uses for purpose-built facilities on existing ships, new ships are being designed and constructed with the MEEC industry in mind. Group bookings can be as small as a group of 16 guests and as large as chartering a ship for over 5,000 guests. A cruise program bring about significant savings as most of the event costs are included in the cruise fare, specifically, the accommodations, meals, entertainment, onboard activities, fitness facilities, meeting space, AV equipment, and coffee breaks. A reserved section of the ship's main dining room is also confirmed for each group.

Royal Caribbean International has dedicated, purposely built, meeting facilities on all their ships. The seating capacities and event space configurations vary depending on the ship. Conference center rooms can accommodate 18 to 400 guests, and can be configured to suit the needs of any meeting setup. A variety of room configurations including theater, classroom, boardroom, card room, or mini trade show setup can be chosen. Their conference facilities include LCD projectors, overhead projectors, slide projectors, screens, TVs, DVD players, flipcharts, laser pointers, microphones, and podiums. A tech fee only applies if a group needs a technician to operate the equipment. Prepaid Wi-Fi packages can be included in a group package so that everyone can stay connected, including sharing their favorite moments on social media. Each ship has dedicated onboard group coordinators available to assist through all stages of the program, including the post-convention report. In many ways, this is no different than working with a conference center.

There are a multitude of venues to facilitate group events. Many of the ships features were incorporated into a ship's design to attract large groups. For example, the cruise ship's ice skating rink can be converted into a large event space for a reception, general session, or meeting. The theaters, lounges, and outdoor spaces give planners the perfect venue for creating a spectacular evening reception under the stars.

For events that require the ultimate in privacy and customization for 3,000 to 5,500 guests, chartering an entire cruise ship is the answer. Ships are typically booked one to two years prior to the event. Chartering a smaller vessel is also an option with European barges that hold 12 to 20 passengers, or yachts for groups of around 100 attendees. Since the ship is solely for your group during the charter period, almost all aspects of the cruise can be modified. The ship's dining times, daily activities, and entertainment can be customized to better support the event's objectives. With just one group onboard, the company logo can be freely displayed throughout the ship, whether it is incorporating it on room keys or desserts, thus, creating a feeling of prestige and brand loyalty for everyone aboard the ship. The guests have exclusive use of all onboard facilities and function space, which results in the ability to create a VIP experience with unique opportunities for attendees to learn, connect, and form relationships. Whether it is a large corporation's annual event or a poker cruise where entire dining rooms are turned into poker tournaments, chartering a ship may be the perfect venue.

Seasonality

There are multiple factors that will increase or decrease the group or charter cruise price. First, as a general industry rule, the newer the ship is, the more expensive the pricing is. Second, pricing is more attractive during non-peak travel seasons, which typically includes the months of January, September, October, and early December. Peak demand begins in May and runs through August, along with cruises that occur during major holiday periods, such as Christmas and New Year's Eve. High demand cruises, particularly those to Alaska, Bermuda, and Europe, may also have a higher price. Finally, the type of stateroom selected for your group impacts the per guest price, from the least expensive inside cabin that does not have views to the outside, all the way up to a wide variety of suites. Of course, when an entire ship is chartered, all guest cabins are included in the combined price.

Specific Use Facilities

Theaters, amphitheaters, arenas, stadiums, and **sports facilities** can also be a great choice for large meetings and events. Spectacular and impressive events can be planned for any facility designed for public assembly. Entertainment venues range in size from huge outdoor stadiums to smaller, more intimate venues. Planners who wish to use these venues can be successful if they are careful to remember that entertainment, not meetings, is the venue's primary business. Furthermore, services considered standard in a hotel or convention center may not exist at an entertainment venue.

Financial Structure

Most of these facilities are focused on events for the general (ticket-buying) public, and a closed event for an invited audience can be a welcome change for their staff. Even though

Busch Stadium was an unusual venue for a reception for the MPI Annual Convention.
George G. Fenich

the front-office staff might welcome the meeting planner, the planner needs to carefully determine whether sufficient house and technical staff is available to support the event. Entertainment events generally occur on evenings and weekends; therefore, staff is frequently composed of part-time employees, or, in the case of those who are available during the day, retirees. The availability and demographics of the staff may or may not be an issue for any given event, but it should be discussed with the facility management prior to signing a contract.

Like convention centers, the larger arenas and amphitheaters are often owned by government agencies or are public–private partnerships. Like convention centers, there is a significant amount of planning required when using these venues. Depending on the facility's public events schedule, long rehearsal and setup times may not be feasible. For example, if it's a facility with a resident sports team, meeting planners will have to work around the team's practice sessions and games schedules, or have their event in the off-season.

Finances in a special use facility can be a hybrid between the practices of the convention center and those of a conference center. There is generally a fixed fee for the use of the facility and a specific subset of its equipment and services. Normal cleanup, comparable to a public event, would likely be included in the facility rental fee. The facility may require a minimum level of staff for which there would be an hourly charge based on a minimum number of hours. All other labor, equipment, and services would be exactly like a convention center on a bill-per-item system.

Considerations for Your Event

Among the specific use facilities, theaters can be ideal meeting facilities. They come equipped with comfortable chairs arranged in sweeping curved rows for maximum comfort. They have lighting positions and sound systems built-in, and staff members who know how to use them. If attendees are local, they probably know where the theater is and do not need directions. The stages are designed for acoustics and the seats are arranged to enhance visibility.

One issue for meeting planners to consider is how customized they need the theater to be. Moving existing equipment and adding equipment can be costly. There may also be additional charges for returning equipment back to its original location.

Another issue with using the in-house equipment has to do with reliability. Many theaters, particularly educational and community theaters, are not funded to the point where their equipment can be considered properly maintained or reliable. A lighting designer, unsure of the condition of the installed equipment, would likely import his or her own rather than take a risk.

When considering catering, additional planning and costs must be considered. In many of the arenas, stadiums, and amphitheaters, they often have well-developed concessions operation, but may not have more traditional types of catering. In some theaters, catering may not be an option at all. Menu selection may be challenging, depending on the scope of the meeting. Kitchen equipment for a concessions environment may not be capable of supporting the menu needs of a meeting or event, therefore, forcing the planner to contract with an off-site caterer.

Colleges and Universities

From quaint, private college galleries to Big Ten stadiums, college and university venues offer diverse meeting spaces for events of any size and budget.

There are many examples of university programs that have excellent reputations as meeting venues, including several that have well-known hospitality and tourism programs. Purdue University offers first-class conference and meeting spaces, lodging accommodations, and dining services year-round. Its Midwestern location, beautiful campus, and top-notch conference center and coordination service make it a prime spot for corporate, religious, association, and fraternal events. Another option is the UMass Amherst Hotel and Conference Center. Situated in the scenic Pioneer Valley, this venue offers full-service, year-round conference and hotel accommodations, plus summer residence hall availability. It has 32 meeting spaces, with the largest room accommodating 10,000 guests. The University of Nebraska, Lincoln has one of the largest summer conference operations of its kind in the United States. The university can accommodate up to 5,500 guests with full service meeting, dining, and overnight lodging options, and offers 200 meeting spaces. Oregon State University Conference Center is a beautiful, historic campus located in the charming city of Corvallis, in the heart of the picturesque Willamette Valley wine region and located on the west bank of the Willamette River. The university provides event attendees with state-of-the-art technology and fine event spaces, dining, catering options, and overnight stays for up to 2,000 people.

Considerations for Your Event

Universities have plenty of lodging space during non-classroom periods, such as summer breaks. But the facilities have significant differences from convention hotels or conference centers. College dorm rooms have single beds instead of doubles or queens. Most college beds are extra-long so standard linen does not fit, so using the college's linen service is recommended to provide bed linen and towels. While some dorm rooms are singles, the majority are double occupancy. The process of arranging and processing roommate assignments can be a full-time job. If the meeting is large, it might be a good idea to hire an intern for this task. Another lodging difference is that dorms generally have bathrooms shared among several rooms. While that might be appropriate for groups of high school and college athletes, it would likely not be comfortable for a meeting of professionals such as doctors or accountants. Newer and renovated dorms have elevators, but many older dorms still do not have elevator access to upper floors. Considerable savings can be realized using college campuses, particularly if the college's athletic facilities are part of the meeting plan; however, not all meetings work well in this environment.

Food and Beverage

University food service is a huge business, often run by large corporations. This means excellent chefs with extensive backgrounds from top restaurants are now running a campus food service, making it on par with any hotel or large convention center. These university chefs create custom menus for events, but outside staffing companies will be needed for the wait staff to give attendees the requisite level of service.

Some universities and colleges have academic programs in hospitality, food service, and/or cuisine. They may have food labs with multiple cooking and preparation stations. These can be ideal places for food-oriented meetings, non-meeting activities, or team building. While some colleges are well equipped for major meetings, the staff may not be as adept at responding to immediate meeting needs as expected at a full-time meeting facility. The planner using an academic facility needs to investigate and coordinate with multiple members of the institution's organizational structure.

College art museums and student centers may provide interesting and exciting locations for meetings. Art museums provide especially interesting opportunities for conversations that can enhance a networking event. All the delegates at the event will probably have opinions about the art, motivating strangers to converse. The art centers and theaters at universities have a unique attribute that many planners and the general public frequently overlook. Unlike the staff in the majority of meeting and special event venues, the venue is not just a job, it is a passion. The people who run these facilities on a daily basis take great pride in, and care deeply about, the condition of the building and its contents. Any planner who intends to use one of these facilities must understand the sensitivities involved. Equally important, they must convey this message to their own staff.

Consortiums

A great place to start searching for a college or university that may be an ideal venue for an event is to start with Unique Venues, a marketing and membership organization. The organization was started by a University of Nevada, Las Vegas Harrah Hotel graduate in the 1980s who began helping colleges and universities market their facilities to event planners. Unique Venues represent thousands of non-traditional venues in the United States, Canada, United Kingdom, and Ireland. Their non-traditional venues include colleges and universities, arenas and stadiums, camps and retreat centers, conference and business centers, and many other unique spaces to hold events.

Retreat Facilities

Retreat facilities can help relieve workplace pressures in a relaxing and inspiring environment. Retreat facilities are more likely to be owned by a family or closely held corporation than the other facilities. Not-for-profit entities, charitable organizations, or religious groups own many of the retreat facilities.

In addition to the classroom learning typical of a conference center, retreat facilities often specialize in unique extracurricular learning opportunities. Some retreat facilities are at dude ranches; others are cabins in the woods where nature is part of the lesson plan; while some are attached to religious organizations where a spiritual message is incorporated into the program. Many planners, out of fear that their delegates may not appreciate the opportunities presented by the unique environment, can unjustly overlook retreat facilities.

Retreat centers are an ideal setting for hard-working corporate or nonprofit teams to discover new synergies and create lasting memories. Corporate retreats take on the atmosphere of their relaxed setting. A mountain lodge, an ocean-side hideaway, or dude ranch can make the ideal setting for strategic planning, leadership training, and team-building sessions. Retreat venues are surprisingly affordable, customizable conference services with refreshing and motivating facilities.

A SPECIAL RETREAT FACILITY

An example of a retreat facility that can be used for meetings, workshops, and special events is the Sanctuary Resort in Thailand. Located on a beach on a small island in the Gulf of Thailand, The Sanctuary Resort, Spa & Wellness Center is located on a remote tropical island beach on Ko Pha Ngan. The Sanctuary offers a truly unique and supportive environment for attendees to learn, share, and grow together. Attendees' free time can include exploring the nearby gardens, enjoying the beach, taking a yoga class, or unwinding with a spa treatment.

A wide variety of food options are available, including an extensive menu of Thai and western food, seafood, vegetarian, and raw food choices. The facilities available include unique, secluded hall spaces, such as the intimate Tea Temple, Prana Hall with the soothing sound of a gentle waterfall running underneath, and Zen Hall nestled among the tree tops overlooking the ocean.

A wide selection of individual and group accommodations is available. Their large Zorba group accommodation space is set in their gardens on three levels. On the top floor is a 16-bed dormitory space with each bed having a lockable privacy box and shelf space. On the second level, there are four private rooms, and a private room with two king-size beds on the first floor. The Sanctuary also has exotic and romantic accommodations inspired by traditional Thai architecture in their luxurious garden rooms and unique jungle houses. Many of these houses are designed to give guests the feeling of living under the stars, while still having all the comforts, such as king size beds, hot water showers, bar fridge, kitchenettes, and lounge chairs and hammocks for complete relaxation.

The Sanctuary is also a unique venue for weddings. They are well known for their Traditional Buddhist wedding ceremony where the couple is married in front of nine Buddhist monks. The monks offer prayers and chants to bless the occasion while the abbot ties a sacred white string around the couples' wrists and sprinkles holy water over their heads with a leafy branch. Guests are encouraged to also tie string around the couple's wrists as a symbol of binding and unity. The Thai Love Lantern ceremony and a wide variety of entertainment and dining options can also be included in the celebration to make it a day to remember.

Unusual Venues

Unique venues have become more in demand for the purposes of holding MEEC gatherings. Organizations want their events to stand out from competitors, or to show their appreciation for their memberships. The desire to host events that are larger than life that feature unexpected experiences provide the wow factor that creates a lasting memory with attendees.

Some venues unaccustomed to this kind of business are now courting groups based upon increased interest and demand. Examples include the Ngala Private Animal Reserve in Naples, Florida, and the Maryland Zoo. Because of interest from group businesses, both facilities have constructed venues on their properties for specific meetings and events rentals. The PCMA annual convention has rented out and taken over SeaWorld in Orlando, Universal Orlando, an aircraft carrier in San Diego, the entire Gaslamp District in San Diego, the Museum of Science and Industry in Chicago, and Faneuil Hall in Boston: all for the exclusive use of their convention attendees.

Restaurants have always been a popular venue to host events, and due to increasing demand, many restaurants have private rooms for hosting these important events. If a group is staying at a hotel or conference center, many planners include a meal or two off-premise at a restaurant that showcases the local cuisine. Many restaurants have a group sales manager who can arrange for a seamless group dining experience, such as those at Maggiano's Little Italy. The group sales manager's contact information can be found on most restaurant's websites along with sample group menus and prices.

There are multiple options for organizations to host their MEEC events when they have a membership to a private club, such as a city club or country club. These members-only facilities require the member to organize and pay for the event, but the attendees do not need to be a member. Their facilities run from historic urban club with luxurious conference facilities and elegant dining rooms to country clubs with sprawling golf courses, spa facilities, and multiple dining options.

Members of the military have access to several military organizations, such as the Navy Lodge, Inns of the Corp, and the Air Force Inn. The hotel-style lodges include overnight accommodations and conference facilities for active and retired military to host meetings and events. Locations are primarily available throughout the United States, typically near a military base, although there are multiple global locations.

New unique venues continue to be imagined. Breakwater Chicago is a football-field-sized floating vessel in the planning stages for Lake Michigan. Breakwater will include several pools, three restaurants, and a nightclub, perfect for hosting large and small events. There will be boat docks for the water taxi service to bring guests out to the floating venue. Breakwater's design plans are centered around a multi-part sustainability plan to use renewable energy sources, follow LEED standards, and include an underwater garden to help filter and absorb dangerous nutrients from runoff into the Great Lake's water.

In addition to utilizing unusual venues for meetings and receptions, these locations have become increasingly popular with weddings. Destination weddings occur when a couple chooses to hold their wedding in a location where neither individual resides. For instance, a couple may elect to hold their wedding in Paris or Bali, as opposed to their hometown. In many cases these destination weddings take place in an unusual venue, in a famous restaurant, or on a sugar-sand beach. Beaches, botanical gardens, castles, sailboats, or theme parks are some of the many facilities that may be used for a destination wedding. Walt Disney World in Florida plays host to more than 2,500 weddings each year, some of which actually take place in Cinderella's castle in the Magic Kingdom (yes, there is a career opportunity to be a princess and be paid for it). In short, almost any venue may be used to host an event if the planner is willing to be a little creative.

Associations and Consortiums

There are multiple associations and consortiums that event planners can contact to find unique venues in most parts of the world. For example, the Westminster Collection is a consortium of unique venues in central London. Their event venues include townhouses, private members' clubs, famous attractions, historic institutes, and museums. One celebrated venue is the House of Commons, home to the UK government. It offers a historic backdrop for an event venue that is experienced in hosting glittering state occasions and other high-profile events. It is available on Saturdays and time periods when the House is not in session. Westminster Abbey is another extraordinary venue in their collection with a thousand years of royal history; it is the coronation church where monarchs have been crowned amid great splendor.

INDUSTRY SPOTLIGHT

Experiencing unique venues is an aspect of YeYoon Kim's job. Ms. Kim, a hotel management graduate from the University of Nevada, Las Vegas who also studied at the École hôtelière de Lausanne, Switzerland, plans membership chapter events for a global association. Her job takes her around the world to interact with local chapter leaders and increase learning opportunities for association volunteers.

For a conference in Philadelphia, Pennsylvania, an evening event was held at the National Constitution Center after public access to the museum had ended. A museum representative customized the tour and presented to their organization's membership, incorporating part of the museum's collection that reinforced some of their meeting's key goals. Afterwards, the members were given the chance to walk through the museum at their own pace, giving their global members the opportunity to experience the history of the US Constitution.

Another conference evening included the association buying out the Lucky Strike bowling alley for the night for their membership, with an open bar and light bites. Teams were formed for bowling competitions, giving the members a chance to network over some friendly competition.

During one of the association's conferences in Adelaide, Australia, members bonded during the first day on a pedal-powered pub called the HandleBar. This two-hour tour required the group to pedal together as a team while they toured the town and stopped at local pubs to try the local food, wine, and beers. As their 16-passenger pedal pub passed by, they received waives and cheers from the locals. A year later, the attendees still rave about how it was the perfect icebreaker for the start of the conference. A conference reception included an evening at The Wine Center, which showcased the wines made in each wine-producing region. Attendees enjoyed local wines paired with Australian appetizers while mingling with wine makers who shared knowledge about their wines. The members are thrilled with the VIP treatment they receive, no matter where their conference is held. For Ms. Kim, every conference and meeting is a great adventure and a wonderful learning experience.

Outdoor Events

For many, holding an event outdoors is the ideal venue. However, many of these venues do not have support equipment permanently in place. Therefore, virtually everything needed for the event must be brought in. These venues also have little or no staff. Public parks can be beautiful venues except that they are open to the public, making them difficult for a private event. If the event is a public event like an art show, a public park with its regular traffic can be an ideal location. But if the event is more private, especially if it involves alcohol, a public park may not be an option.

Outdoor sports arenas might be seen as easy venues as they come with bleachers and restrooms, yet they also present their own challenges. The irrigation systems for the landscaping at professional or competition fields are fragile enough that driving heavy loads over them can break the piping beneath the surface. Some venues prohibit anything heavier than a golf cart or building a stage unless it is properly padded with plywood sheeting. Pushing heavy supplies across the grass is not likely to be approved by a venue's head of grounds either. Similar restrictions can also be found for golf courses and resorts with substantial landscaping.

Outdoor Venue Challenges

In addition to all the normal concerns a planner needs to organize for an event, the planner using these facilities also needs to provide all the support services normally considered the responsibility of an event facility. Such services could include portable restrooms, parking, and trash removal, yet most outdoor venues share a general lack of support and equipment. All of them have heightened challenges with logistics and catering. Access to a venue can be an issue if roads flood in the rainy season or are impassable in the winter. Even if the road is substantial enough to support delivery trucks, it is necessary to determine if there is a dock where supplies can be unloaded, or whether a forklift is needed. If a forklift is needed, the planner must determine who supplies the driver as well as any other pertinent logistical questions.

Outdoor Tents

Tents are routinely used to create meeting venues. Tents fall into three categories: pole, frame, and clear span. An open-sided pole or **frame tent** set up on the grass is one of the simplest of all meeting venues. It requires little advance planning beyond making sure the tent rental people can get set up in time. Adding tent sides and air-conditioning can reduce the impact of weather. The tent may require a floor so that rain drainage flows under the floor and not over the feet of the people in the tent.

Clear span tents have a strong roof structure, and it is possible to hang lighting from its beams by using special clamps. If lighting is to be hung in a clear span tent, the lighting should be hung before the floor is put in, since many of the tent floors will not support the scissor lifts used by the lighting and décor people during setup. To hang lighting in a **pole tent** requires special brackets to attach the lights to the poles, if the poles are sturdy enough to support them. Therefore, for a pole tent, supporting the lighting from the floor on boom stands or truss towers may be a better plan. Since the purpose of the tent is to create a meeting space where none previously existed, other support services such as power, water, and restrooms may also not exist and will have to be brought in.

Outdoor Venue Permits

A challenge that frequently catches planners by surprise is obtaining permits. Many local governments require permits to use parks or even private property for special events. Failure to procure the proper permits can lead to an event being shut down at the last moment. Not only must the police and fire department be notified, but in many places the building code office must be notified as well. Tents must usually be inspected by the fire department. In some areas, generators are under the purview of the fire department; in others, there is a special office that deals with electrical issues. This office may be part of the Building and Zoning department or may be part of a designated special events office. A one-time-use liquor license may also be required.

Trends

There are a number of trends with regard to meeting and event venues. One of those is the mass utilization of unique venues. Planners are always looking for the newest and freshest ideas to make their events stand out from the competition, and the choice of venue is perhaps the most obvious method for accomplishing that. Attendees also expect to be wowed, and not see the same cookie-cutter event format year after year. Rather than holding an opening reception for attendees in a convention center hall, the planner can use unexpected venues to keep the attendees guessing and prevent them from getting bored. One year the opening event could be held at Mardi Gras World in New Orleans, the next year at the Cowboys Stadium in Dallas, and the following year at the Seattle Space Needle. In each location the attendees will have a different experience and leave feeling that their event was one of a kind.

The size and composition of convention centers are also seeing some significant changes. Convention center space in the United States continues to increase with many second- and third-tier cities building new centers and/or building additions to current facilities. Even though the MEEC industry is continually growing, the mass construction of convention centers will likely slow down because demand has not caught up to the available supply yet. However, some centers have moved toward adding space, which can easily double as business and entertainment venues. This trend may see more growth in lieu of building larger facilities.

Summary

Recommendations for Working with All Venues

When choosing a venue for a MEEC event, a planner should view the facilities offered through the eyes and expectations of the event attendees. Who are the attendees? What are the goals of the event? A facility without lodging might be a good fit if all the attendees are local. A remote venue might be a good option for a conference if attendees have a tendency to slip away midday when

they should be in sessions. A review of the event's *history* is important in determining what venue is the best option for the planned MEEC event.

Research and Understand Venue Options

Obtaining accurate information on the venue options is essential to planning successful meetings/events. Detailed and thorough research is the first step in the process.

This first step is much easier now than it has been, and promises to become even easier, as the Internet and websites provide planners with powerful resources to plan their events. Many of the best meeting facilities have extensive websites with detailed information. Some venues have 360-degree visual imaging that allows a planner to remotely view the facility.

A planner needs to determine whether to use the venue's technology or preferred vendor, rent it from another vendor, or buy their own equipment if their needs are very basic. Planners need to evaluate the proper use of their time. Is their time well-spent hauling a large plastic case through airport security, or is it better spent attending to details, such as ensuring the coffee is refreshed and lunch is ready on time? Many planners see their jobs in terms of cost containment. While that is surely part of the job, helping guarantee the success of the meeting is a more appropriate goal. Sometimes a penny saved is not a penny earned. Sometimes it is a pound lost in a missed opportunity. The planner's job is to know the difference.

Weather is an issue for all events, but particularly for outdoor venues. When planning an outdoor function, an indoor backup plan or contingency plan is vital to the success of the event. A professional planner should always recognize the potential for weather to have an impact on the event and, therefore, put the necessary plans in place for the worst-case scenario.

Communication and Verification

Once the event planner has done the research and feels a venue is a good fit, then, and only then, should the planner call the facility's sales department to start a dialogue. The most important component of working with any facility is the development of an open, honest, and trusting relationship with all parties involved. Unfortunately,

there are facilities that will take advantage of that relationship, just as there are planners who do not deal honestly with their suppliers. Despite the risks involved, the attempt must be made, because the success of every event depends on the interaction between the planner and all the other parties. This relationship begins with understanding what each of the participants brings to the relationship and what each needs.

Communication begins with a set of requirements. The more accurate the requirements are, the better. It is important to note, however, that accurate and detailed are not the same thing. In a contract, the hotel needs to know how many people are coming, but they may not need the names until relatively close to the event. Accurate and timely listings of requirements are the first step in developing a successful relationship. Verification of the documentation returned by the venue is the other half of this communication. Not only should the planner provide requirements, but the venue should also reply and acknowledge that it understands the requirements and how it will fulfill each requirement as appropriate.

An excellent resource to use when planning an event and determining what services are needed from the venue is a needs analysis. Go to the Event Industry Council's website and download their RFP workbook from their APEX (Accepted Practices Exchange) tab. By following this template, which follows industry standards, event planners can ensure that they are including all the details necessary for their event to be a success.

The key to working with any venue is fourfold: research, understand, communicate, and verify; research, understand, communicate, and verify; and repeat until done! This chapter provides information that can be used by meeting planners to research and understand, the first two steps of the event planning process. The remaining steps are what separates the best planners from the rest.

CASE STUDY

Was Adding Exhibit Space Worth It?

John is the owner of XYZ Resorts and Hotel, which has three all-inclusive properties located throughout Jamaica. All three resorts have hotels on the island's north coast on Montego Bay, Negril, and Ochos Rios. Being that his resorts and hotels are in the most beautiful and luxurious parts of Jamaica, John is pretty much guaranteed high-travel volumes almost year-round. Even with those factors helping John, he is now suffering from low sales due to the economy and other local resorts offering exhibit space that he does not have. John is now perplexed with the decision of

whether to add exhibit space to his resorts and hotels, and how to boost sales.

After extensive thought and research, John finally made the decision to add exhibit space to his resorts and hotels. The Ochos Rios property is one in which John put the most significant investments, creating almost 10,000 square meters of convention space, banquet facilities, and an exhibition center accommodating up to 2,500 people for receptions or 1,200 for banquets. John didn't stop there, the Ochos Rios property also included two separate ballrooms

(Continued)

and several additional meeting rooms, designed with break-out sessions and smaller gatherings in mind. The other two resorts received renovations that included new black rattan furniture in all guest rooms, bedspreads, and flat-screen televisions. To be sure that money was saved, John, being a builder by trade, oversaw all construction work and renovations.

To ensure that the new exhibit, convention, and banquet spaces would be sold, John hired Robin to be the new group sales manager of the North American region. As new sales manager Robin wanted to work with agents to secure the best rates as possible for groups. She steered groups that wanted shorter stays to the resort 15 minutes from the airport, and those groups who wanted longer stays to the resort furthest from the airport and closer to attractions. To

increase sales of the new found space, Karen implemented more packages for ceremonies and agents, and introduced nightly entertainment, full service spas, and specialty fine dining restaurants.

Needless to say, sales increased and the exhibit, banquet, and convention space generated more business for the XYZ Resort and Hotels. Robin feels that, because the company had fallen off on groups and off the radar for a while, it was very smart for the owner, John, to have poured a lot of money into the hotels to get back into the market.

1. Do you feel that it was a good decision for John to pour money into the hotels and hiring a new sales manager?

2. What would you have done differently?

Produced by George G. Fenich from East Carolina University

Key Words and Terms

For definitions, see Glossary.

amphitheaters	conference center	pole tent
attrition	Exposition Service Contractors (ESC)	pre-function space
boardroom	exhibit hall	residential
break-out rooms	frame tent	seasonality
clear span tents	hotel	shoulder
complete meeting package	International Association of	sports facilities
concessionaires	Conference Centers (IACC)	stadium
conference	local event	theater

Review and Discussion Questions

1. Compare and contrast a hotel's meeting space and a convention center's meeting space. Include in the comparison, the differences and/or similarities of the meeting room spaces, the financial structure, and food and beverage options.

2. What are the differences between a conference center and a convention center? Include a comparison of the meeting room spaces, the financial structure, and food and beverage options.

3. How is a cruise ship similar to a hotel, convention center, and conference center? How is it different from each of these venues?

4. What are the benefits of using a college or university as a venue? What are the challenges? Does your college or university have a conference center that they market to the general public?

5. How is the financial structure of a hotel different from that of other facilities? What is a hotel's biggest source of revenue? What is a convention center's biggest revenue source?

6. Why is seasonality important to a planner when selecting a venue?

7. What are some commonly used event space layouts? Go online and find a venue meeting-planning guide to find what different room options are available, and how many guests can be held in the rooms based on the room layouts.

8. What are the benefits of using a retreat or unique venue to participants? Find one that is appealing to you. Explain what benefits this venue would bring to an event that you would plan.

9. What should be a planner's greatest concern about an outdoor event? What should a planner do about it?

10. What is the name and location of the nearest convention center near you? How much total meeting space do they have? What is one of the largest conventions or expositions that they hold each year?

About the Chapter Contributors

Lisa Y. Thomas is an assistant professor at the School of Hospitality Leadership at DePaul University. Dr. Thomas has over 20 years experience in sales and marketing management positions with top hospitality brands. One career focus was to motivate industry sales by holding frequent special events, conventions, and trade shows to introduce clients to resorts, ships, and/or destinations. Her research interests include how special events are emerging as a strategic tool to increase revenue for resorts, and how hotels utilize large citywide conferences and festivals to increase key performance metrics.

After 20+ years in the hospitality industry, **Mary Jo Dolasinski** recently joined the School of Hospitality Leadership in the Driehaus College of Business at DePaul University faculty as an Assistant Professor. Dr. Dolasinski has served as a keynote speaker, authored several books, and developed over 100 training programs.

Previous Edition Chapter Contributors

Kathryn Hashimoto, East Carolina University
Kelly Virginia Phelan, Texas Tech University (now with University of Queensland)
Bob Cherny, Paradise Light and Sound

A large exhibition of jet aircraft.
Capture 11 Photography/Shutterstock

CHAPTER 5

Exhibitions and Trade Shows

Chapter Objectives

- Define the different types of exhibitions.
- Identify the key players of exhibition management.
- Categorize the components of exhibition planning.
- Identify the role of the exhibitor and fundamentals of exhibit planning.

With tens of thousands of exhibitions worldwide, the evolution of exhibitions and trade shows has turned into a thriving, ever-changing industry. This chapter provides an overview of the history and the current state of the exhibition industry from the perspective of the show organizer and the exhibit manager.

History

Trade fairs began in biblical times such as the one in Tyre in Palestine. They became popular in Medieval Europe and the Middle East. These fairs served as an opportunity for craftsmen and farmers to bring their products to the center of the town or city to sell their goods as a means of survival. This was the beginning of the public trade fair and featured handmade crafts, agricultural products, and other specialties. Germany, France, and Ireland have the first recorded history of organizing the earliest organized fairs, such as the Leipzig Fair in 1165, the 1215 Dublin Fair, Cologne's biannual fair starting in 1259, and Frankfurt's Book Fair in 1445. These types of trade fairs continued through the Renaissance period until the beginning of the Industrial Revolution when goods began being mass-produced.

Eventually, businesses realized the value of meeting, sharing information, and providing previews of their products to potential customers. This part of the industry blossomed in the late 1800s, with many facilities being built strictly for world-class exhibitions. This buyer–seller format was termed an **exhibition** and typically took place in a large city at a facility built specifically for the exhibition. For example, the Crystal Palace in London was opened for the *Great Industrial Exhibition of All Nations* featuring 13,000 exhibits from all over the world and attracted more than six million attendees. In the United States, facilities were opened in Chicago (the World's Fair: Columbian Exposition) and Philadelphia (the Centennial Exposition) to commemorate the industrial advances of participating countries. In 1895, Detroit started the first joint effort to attract exhibition business, and in 1914 the National Association of Convention Bureaus (now Destinations International—DI) was formed.

In the early and mid-twentieth century, trade associations grew and saw the potential of exhibitions being held in conjunction with their annual meetings as a way to stimulate communication in the industry and expand their revenues from the annual meeting. The twentieth century brought exciting and trying times to the exhibition industry, with notable pauses in progress during World War I, World War II, and the Great Depression. To increase the awareness and value of exhibitions, a group of industry professionals created the National Association of Exposition Managers, which is now named the International Association of Exhibitions and Events (IAEE), in 1978 and has members sponsoring, hosting, and organizing exhibits worldwide.

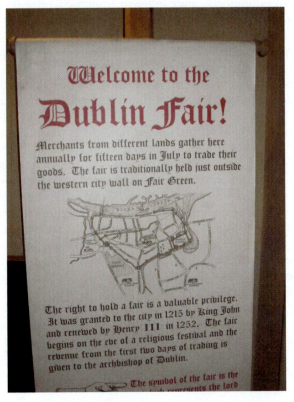

This replica of a pie stall from the Dublin Fair of 1215 is not so different than food vendors at festivals today.
George G. Fenich

THE CURRENT STATE OF THE EXHIBITION INDUSTRY

The exhibitions industry continues to be resilient and its growth always slightly trails economic recoveries of global sectors. Exhibitions are an integral part of the overall sales and marketing budgets and strategies for corporations and associations. Face-to-face interaction definitely enhances and augments the availability of information via the Internet and other valuable resources. Significant progress has been made by the exhibitions and meetings industry in focusing on demonstrating its value, measuring return on investments, and justifying participation and attendance at trade and consumer shows.

According to the Center for Exhibition Industry Research (CEIR), the exhibition industry's independent research organization, forecasts for 2017 and beyond call for a steady growth that will tie directly into global economic growth realities. CEIR measures four metrics: net square feet sold, attendance, exhibitor participation, and overall growth. The estimated direct spending for the global exhibitions industry is over $200 billion. The aggressive expansion of exhibition and convention centers around the world will initially create increased over supply of inventory. It will take many years to grow the demand for new exhibitions that will be directly tied to the vitality and growth of the global economy. Additional information is available via two websites: The International Association of Exhibitions and Events, www.iaee.com; and The Center for Exhibition Industry Research, www.ceir.org.

Authored by: David DuBois, CMP, CAE, FASAE, CTA, President and CEO
International Association of Exhibitions and Events, Dallas, Texas, USA

Types of Shows and Exhibitions

Trade Shows or Business-to-Business Shows

Business-to-business (**B2B**) exhibitions, also known as trade fairs or trade shows, are private events and are not open to the public. The definition of a trade fair has become close enough to that of a trade show that the terms are used interchangeably. The term trade fair is more often used outside the United States than trade show. Trade fairs are discussed in more detail in Chapter 15, International Perspectives in MEEC. Although the historical definition of exhibition is quite different from today, this term has also evolved to mean a trade show or trade fair. The term exposition has also evolved to be similar in meaning to a trade show. An association meeting may include an exposition, or expo, as the trade show segment of the association's annual gathering. In this chapter, we refer to trade shows, expositions, and exhibitions interchangeably.

The exhibitor is usually a manufacturer or distributor of products or services that are specific or complementary to those industries represented by the sponsor or organizer. Often, attendance is restricted to buyers from the industry, and business credentials are required for registration. Educational programs may or may not be a part of the exhibition program; although, in recent years, educational programs have expanded as a method of attracting attendees. Sponsorship or management of the exhibition is usually either under the auspices of a trade association, or more recently come under the sponsorship of a management company. Some exhibitions are the result of initiatives by companies and are fully intended to be profit-making ventures. Usually, exhibitions are annual events, although some occur more frequently, and others less frequently. Major organizations may also have regional exhibitions that are smaller than their standard national or international event. Attendees and exhibitors may come from all over the country or world; therefore, hotel rooms and transportation may be considered in selecting the show's location.

Many organizations are considering moving to a **hosted buyer** exhibition format. At these events, attendees are pre-qualified as having the buying influence and/or the authority to make a purchasing decision. These attendees have all or most of their travel expenses covered by the show's management company or exhibitors/sponsors. The exhibition organizer, in return, schedules meetings between these attendees and suppliers to conduct business.

A common form of marketing to potential B2B exhibitors is advertising in trade publications or targeted electronic communication. Until recently, well-established exhibitions had little trouble marketing to potential exhibitors. The exhibit halls were full, and waiting lists of exhibitors were commonplace. However, the past few years have seen many companies downsizing their exhibit space or opting to exhibit at fewer shows. Management companies have now placed a renewed focus on marketing to potential exhibitors. Exhibitions are now in competition for exhibitors, and exhibition management companies are working hard to retain existing exhibitors and attract new ones.

Ray Bloom, the Founder of IMEX.
The IMEX Group

In 1988, when Ray Bloom, now the Chairman of the IMEX Group, booked space in Geneva's PalExpo for his first non-UK trade show, he became concerned that his target audience of incentive travel buyers might not make the cross-border trip. He turned uneasiness into positive action, however, when he decided to ask industry trade publications whether they would like to host the top buyers from their readership, paying for their travel and hotel costs. Every publication he approached (with whom he had built former relationships) agreed to the proposal, and suddenly there was a whole new momentum for his event and a brand-new way to make a trade show work.

What started with a handful of trade media intermediaries in Europe has grown to include a global list of over 3,500 intermediaries for IMEX in Frankfurt, and over 25,000 intermediaries for IMEX in America. Intermediaries can include hotel chains, representation and destination marketing companies, airlines, trade publications, trade associations, and more.

Not only does this three-pronged relationship create a unique experience for the hosted buyer, but intermediaries are also able to expand their networks, develop new or strengthened business relationships, bring new value to their top clients and prospects, and explore new business opportunities and partnerships. "As a business model, once you can guarantee that the very best buyers are going to be at your show, then you have a compelling proposition for exhibitors. One follows the other," says Bloom.

To qualify for a place on the IMEX hosted programs, buyers must be responsible for planning, organizing, recommending, or making financial decisions for corporate meetings, conferences, seminars, exhibitions, road shows, association meetings, or incentive travel programs. In order CHANGE MADE to qualify, buyers need to place business with two global events in the preceding 12 months. Given the immense size of the US home market, however, IMEX America also reserves a few hosted buyer places for high-level buyers who place business outside their home state, but not necessarily internationally.

Hosted buyers meeting with suppliers.
Maksym Poriechkin/Shutterstock

In return, IMEX hosted buyers receive complimentary travel and accommodations, one-stop shopping to domestic and global destinations and suppliers, and world-class education and networking. Hosted buyers are asked to schedule up to eight appointments per day using the exclusive IMEX online scheduling tool, which gives them full freedom of choice of who they choose to meet with. Furthermore, these meetings can be individual appointments, open-stand presentations, or group appointments, which give hosted buyers even more freedom. This is a win–win for all, as many hosted buyers report getting a full year's worth of business done during the three day IMEX shows.

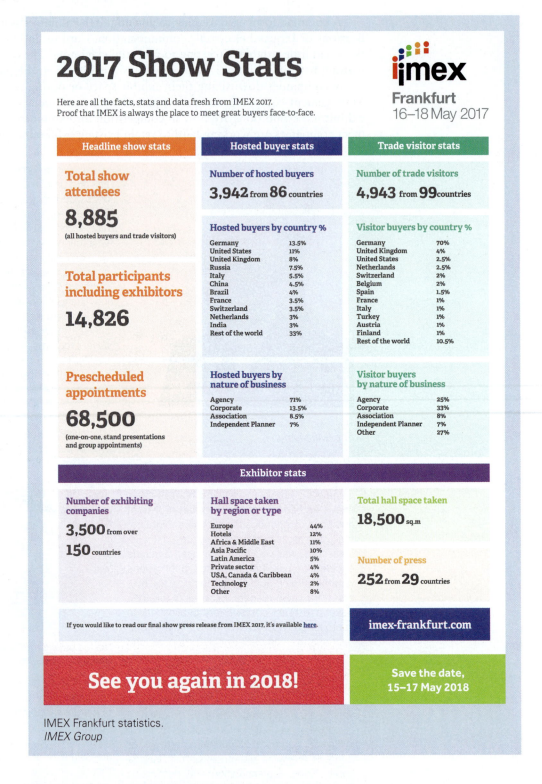

2017 Show Stats

Here are all the facts, stats and data fresh from IMEX 2017.
Proof that IMEX is always the place to meet great buyers face-to-face.

imex
Frankfurt
16–18 May 2017

Headline show stats	Hosted buyer stats	Trade visitor stats

Total show attendees

8,885

(all hosted buyers and trade visitors)

Number of hosted buyers

3,942 from **86** countries

Number of trade visitors

4,943 from **99** countries

Total participants including exhibitors

14,826

Hosted buyers by country %

Germany	13.5%
United States	11%
United Kingdom	8%
Russia	7.5%
Italy	5.5%
China	4.5%
Brazil	4%
France	3.5%
Switzerland	3.5%
Netherlands	3%
India	3%
Rest of the world	33%

Visitor buyers by country %

Germany	70%
United Kingdom	4%
United States	2.5%
Netherlands	2.5%
Switzerland	2%
Belgium	2%
Spain	1.5%
France	1%
Italy	1%
Turkey	1%
Austria	1%
Finland	1%
Rest of the world	10.5%

Prescheduled appointments

68,500

(one-on-one, stand presentations and group appointments)

Hosted buyers by nature of business

Agency	71%
Corporate	13.5%
Association	8.5%
Independent Planner	7%

Visitor buyers by nature of business

Agency	25%
Corporate	33%
Association	8%
Independent Planner	7%
Other	27%

Exhibitor stats

Number of exhibiting companies

3,500 from over **150** countries

Hall space taken by region or type

Europe	44%
Hotels	12%
Africa & Middle East	11%
Asia Pacific	10%
Latin America	5%
Private sector	4%
USA, Canada & Caribbean	4%
Technology	2%
Other	8%

Total hall space taken

18,500 sq.m

Number of press

252 from **29** countries

If you would like to read our final show press release from IMEX 2017, it's available here.

imex-frankfurt.com

See you again in 2018!

Save the date, 15–17 May 2018

IMEX Frankfurt statistics.
IMEX Group

Consumer Show or Business-to-Consumer Shows

Business-to-Consumer (B2C) public shows, or simply consumer shows, are exhibitions that are open to the public and offer a wide variety of products for sale. This type of show is used by a consumer-based industry to bring their goods directly to their market's end user. Show management may or may not charge an admission fee. Shows open to the public are typically held on weekends. Consumer shows are often regional in nature, with exhibitors traveling from city to city with their displays and products. They also provide excellent opportunities for companies to brand or test market new products.

Summary of Characteristics—B2B and B2C					
Show Type	**Attendee**	**Registration or Admission**	**Marketing**	**Show Days**	**Location**
B2B Show	International and national	Preregistration, qualified buyers	Targeted electronic communications	Business week (Monday–Friday)	Large markets with significant meeting space, hotel, and transportation
B2C Show	Regional or local	Ticket purchase on-site, general public	Newspaper, regional magazines, billboards, social media, and TV advertising	Weekends (Friday–Sunday)	Large or secondary markets with large parking areas

Public exhibitions also require promotion to be successful. Typically, public shows are marketed through advertisements in trade or local public media. Advertisements may offer discounts for purchasing early tickets or may promote special events or speakers that will attract the largest number of attendees. Promoting public exhibitions is a daunting task because the potential attending audience is so large that it requires a significant expense to reach them through print, radio, social media, and television advertising. Producers must be confident that their investment in promotion will result in reaching the attendance objectives. Producers must also be attentive to other events that may be occurring during the exhibition time period that can affect attendance. Many B2C shows feature local and national celebrities to draw additional attention to the exhibition.

Common types of consumer shows include home and garden, travel-related, and sports-specific shows. Some examples include:

- *The Central Florida Home and Garden Show*, hosted each spring, features hundreds of exhibitors showcasing remodeling, home improvement, and outdoor gardening ideas.
- *The Kansas Sports, Boat and Travel Show* has been one of the most popular shows in the Heartland. It features exhibits on ATVs, hunting, fishing, camping, and the freedom of traveling in an RV. Tickets for the February event cost $7 for adults.
- *The Michigan Golf Show* hosts more than 350 exhibitors with great deals on every aspect of the golf game. This weekend show will cost adult golf lovers around $12.

Consolidation Shows
(Also Called Combined or Mixed Shows)

Consolidation shows are open to both industry buyers and the general public. Exhibitors are manufactures or distributors. Hours may differ based on the type of attendee, allowing trade professionals to preview the show prior to the consumer buyers. Consumer electronics and automobile industries, which have diverse audience needs, use this format to accommodate the varied industry buyers and retail consumers.

Exhibition Management: Key Players

Regardless of the exhibition type, there are three key players that ensure that the components of the show come together to accomplish the objectives of each stakeholder—the exhibition organizer, the facility manager, and the general service contractor.

Exhibition Organizer

The exhibition management company (organizer) may be a trade association, a company subcontracted to the trade association, or a separate company organizing the show as a profit-making venture. The exhibition management staff member in charge of the entire exhibit area is called the exhibit manager, and is responsible for all aspects of managing the show. Think of exhibition management as the "systems integrator" responsible for implementing the show, marketing it to buyers and sellers, and gathering together all the resources needed for success.

The exhibition management company must also consider the types of programs offered in addition to the event itself. Exhibition programs have evolved to encompass additional programs that serve to boost attendance. Additional programs to consider include:

- Educational programs
- Entertainment programs
- Availability of exhibitor demonstrations and educational/training programs
- Special sections on the show floor for emerging companies, new exhibitors, or new technologies
- Celebrity or industry-leader speakers
- Meal programs
- Continuing education units or certifications for educational programs
- Spouse and children programs
- Internet access and email centers

Facility Manager

Facilities are also needed to conduct the exhibition. Facilities range from small hotels with limited meeting space to large convention centers. Facilities also include adjacent lodging and entertainment facilities, which are used by the exhibitors and visitors. The facility manager, typically known as a convention service manager or event manager, will assist the show manager in arranging the show's logistical details. Exhibition organizers consider many variables when selecting facilities, including the size of the facility, the services available at the venue (telecommunications, dining, setup, and teardown times), cost, availability of service contractors, preferences of exhibitors and attendees, logistical considerations (airline services, local transportation, parking), and lodging and entertainment in the area.

Meeting and convention facilities have kept pace with the growth of the industry. From small, regional facilities to mega convention centers located in major cities, destinations have understood the benefits of attracting exhibitions and conventions to their area. Hotels and non-traditional venues are also investing in larger exhibit areas and expanding their meeting space. Many fair grounds, sports centers, large parking lots, museums, nightclubs, and community centers are being used for expositions. These options must be considered as alternatives to convention centers and large hotels for smaller exhibitions.

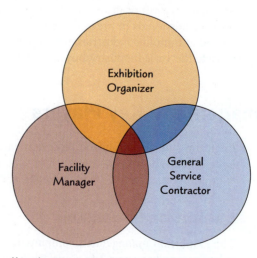

Key players.
Chart produced by George G. Fenich, Ph.D

General Service Contractor

The general service contractor, also known as an official exhibit service contractor or decorator, provides products and services to the **exhibition management company** and the show's exhibitors. Their services are often key to the success of a show. Once selected, the general service contractor will provide the exhibition management and exhibitors with a list of services supplied by the contractor or other subcontractors. Types of services the general service contractors provide include:

- Floor plan development and design,
- Aisle carpet and signage,
- Custom and modular booths,
- Freight handling and shipping,
- Storage and warehousing,
- Installation, maintenance, and dismantling labor,
- Lighting, electronics, and plumbing,
- Telecommunication and computer requests,
- Sound and audiovisual, and
- Coordination with specialty contractors.

Arranging and managing these services for a large show can be quite complex for the exhibition management company and exhibitors. Convention centers, management companies, and even exhibitors have become accustomed to working with various arrangements and companies. Because service contractors operate in a very competitive environment, they have learned that customer service, fair pricing, and responsiveness to customer needs are important. This enables organizers and exhibitors a level of comfort by being able to rely on service contractors to take care of the problems that arise with organizing a successful show.

The general service contractor, in conjunction with the exhibition management company, usually develops an exhibitor service manual that encompasses all the details that an exhibitor needs in order to plan and implement an exhibit program for the show. It also includes the forms needed to order services from the service contractors, and the rules and regulations of the exhibition management company, convention center or hotel, and the local government.

Despite the controls and organization put in place by the exhibition management company and service contractors, disputes arise. When this occurs, it is important to get all concerned parties involved in achieving a successful resolution. The show manager is responsible for compliance of exhibitors, attendees, and service contractors to the show rules. See Chapter 6 for more information on service contractors.

Knowledge, Skills, and Abilities of an Exhibition Manager

The world of event management has changed tremendously in the last few years, especially as newer technologies make things better. Different kinds of event software help to make the event run smoothly. If an exhibition or trade show manager uses technology prudently, he or she can gain an edge over his or her competitors.

One of the most important Knowledge, Skills, and Abilities (KSAs) is having great interpersonal skills. An event manager must work with a team and others outside the team to ensure the event is a success. This means that the manager should have the ability to both speak and listen without any issues. It is important that the event manager understands what the client needs, and then find ways to fulfill those needs or come up with different options. Having interpersonal skills is a necessity; and managers who possess this skill can manage their team and communicate effectively. It is these people who often make great event managers.

Another KSA is having a keen eye for details. It is the small things that matter. A good exhibition manager will always delve into things, look at minute details, and try to get everything right. A person with a keen sense of observation will prevent small things from blowing up and turning into big issues. Attention to detail allows a person to ensure that everything is properly organized and in place for the event.

To be successful, an event manager must possess excellent leadership skills. They will have an innate quality for leading people and this is what shows that they were born to be an event manager. Outstanding leadership skills help guide teams toward end goals, and this is why the team's events are a roaring success.

A person cannot be an effective exhibition manager without superior organizational skills. Everything in an event must be seamlessly choreographed, so that each step of the event goes off smoothly. However, while organizational skills can be learned, mastering them is difficult.

The world of exhibitions and trade shows is quite hectic and frenzied. Thus, a manager must have good time management skills. The multitasking abilities of a manager are an indication that they are tailor-made to be an event manager. They must have the ability to prioritize things at work, allowing them to be more productive and achieve more within a limited time period.

Nothing is fixed or static when organizing events. Everything is in a state of flux and things can change at a drop of a hat. Hence, an event manager should be flexible to take these changes in stride and work accordingly. They need to be ready to face any sort of situation and be able to think on their feet. If they have always been flexible where work is concerned, they are in a position to be a successful event manager.

To be a successful event manager, one needs to do things differently. This requires innovation and creativity. If the exhibition manager is the kind of person who always thinks out-of-the-box, they are destined to be a successful event manager. This means that problems and challenges are not an issue for them as they have an innate ability to resolve them creatively.

Event management has changed tremendously with the availability of technology, so managers need to be well versed in using it. This will help get things done faster and make event managers more efficient and productive. Today, event managers have access to a wide range of event management software that makes their work easier, such as event ticketing software, venue management software, floor plan software, and more.

Considerations in Managing a Show

Location

Exhibition managers consider a number of variables when deciding on the location of a show. It is no secret that the city and venue selected to host an exhibition has a major effect on attendance. Thus, a balance must be attained between location, cost, and the ideal attendance level. Many organizations that conduct annual meetings and expositions stay in the same city year after year, and, thus, can negotiate the best agreements with the local convention centers and hotels, and still retain the optimum attendance levels. Typically, these are association meetings that have strong educational programs and are held at a desirable site.

However, other organizations or exhibition management companies prefer to move their exhibition from city to city each year. This strategy may help attract additional visitors. Different locations allow a new and varied local attendance base to attend inexpensively, as well as attract out-of-town visitors, who may be interested in additional local tourist offerings.

Organizations and exhibition management companies often survey their membership or potential attendees to assess their preferences on location. The success of convention centers in cities like Las Vegas, Chicago, Frankfurt in Germany, and Guangzhou in China is indicative of organizations paying attention to the needs and desires of their members and potential audience. Expansion of convention facilities in each of these cities indicates that these destinations value the revenue generated by large B2B and B2C shows.

Hotel facilities are also a factor to be considered when determining the location of an exhibition. Are the local facilities adequate for the projected attendance? Are the negotiated

Trade show booth in Germany
George G. Fenich

room rates within the budget of the typical attendee or exhibitor? What is the proximity to the exhibition site, and will local transportation need to be provided? What is the potential for labor problems to arise in the host city or at host hotels? Do the convention center and local hotels comply with government requirements?

In addition, the largest exhibitions often require substantial parking facilities and/or dedicated local ground transportation to assist visitors and exhibitors in getting from their hotels to the show site. Managers are now looking at a variety of parking and public transportation options for their ground transportation needs, such as trolleys, subways, or even bicycles, as they select meeting sites and venues. With increasing concerns about sustainability, ground transportation is becoming a key factor in the decision to select or not select a city for an event.

When determining whether dedicated ground transportation is required, consider that safety is often the key decision point. Even if hotels are within walking distance from the convention center, the conditions of the city between the hotels and the center may dictate that it is in your best interests to provide transportation. For example, in New Orleans there are many hotels within walking distance of the convention center, but in the summer, when temperature and humidity are both in the 90s, the meeting organizer is better off providing transportation. When choosing ground transportation providers, be sure to take into account experience, availability, special services, insurance, the condition of the vehicles, labor contracts, and cost.

Housing and transportation are essential elements for success for any B2B exhibition attracting a national or international audience. A large part of any organizer's time is spent negotiating room blocks in the host city and airline and car rental discounts for attendees and exhibitors. Recently, the trend has moved toward outsourcing housing and transportation arrangements to local convention and visitor bureaus or third-party housing vendors. Regardless of how housing and transportation issues are handled, the expectation is that they will be transparent to the attendee or exhibitor.

Exhibition organizers must also consider the food and beverage needs and preferences of the attendees and exhibitors. Food options can span from using a concessionaire serving items such as sandwiches, pizza, drinks, and snacks, to a sophisticated caterer offering a variety of salads, entrees, and desserts. Again, food and beverage service requires much thought around budget, offerings, space to service and seat guests, and so on.

Another selection factor is the weather. Unlike B2B exhibitions with many people coming from outside the city, B2C exhibitions rely on the local and regional population for attendance. Local and regional tourists will not venture out to a public show in the midst of a serious snowstorm or rainstorm. Thus, one episode of bad weather can drastically affect the bottom line of a show producer. The National Western Stock Show, held in Denver each January, is a good example of this. Years with extreme cold and snow greatly reduced the event's attendance. During years of unseasonably mild weather, attendance skyrocketed. The solution for the National Western Stock Show has been to extend the show to a sixteen-day period, ensuring that there will be good and bad days. This has led to a more consistent overall attendance figure from year to year.

Shipping and Storage

Once the location is chosen, the booths and other show materials need to be transported to the site. While airfreight may sometimes be used, over-the-road freight by truck is the most common method. Charges are typically per hundred pounds, and are based on the distance the freight must travel.

Since an exhibitor cannot afford for the freight shipment to arrive late for an exhibition, extra time is allowed for transit. Thus, the exhibitor must arrange for temporary storage of the materials at the destination, prior to the move-in date for the exhibition. One must also consider storage of the freight containers while the show is open. When the show closes, the whole process is reversed. Some exposition service contractors, such as GES of Freeman, have separate divisions of their company that deal with shipping and storage.

Marketing and Promotion

Without exhibitors, the exhibition will not be successful, and, in turn, without attendees, exhibitors will not participate or return. Exhibition managers focus their attention on marketing and promotion programs that will fill the exhibition hall with both exhibitors and attendees. Regardless of the type of exhibition, attendance is the key to success. It is primarily the responsibility of the exhibition management company to target and market to the right audience. This is typically done through direct mail, advertising in trade publications, social media, the show management's website, and e-marketing.

Exhibition management companies and service companies also offer additional marketing opportunities for exhibitors to consider. Exhibitors want to invest in a show because their potential customers are in attendance. Based on their objectives for the show, exhibitors can choose to invest in several programs such as:

- *General Sponsorships:*   These programs usually involve the company's name or logo being included or printed in the show's promotional materials or being posted in a prominent place in the exhibit hall.

- *Special Event Sponsorship:*   Special events are often conducted during the exhibition, such as receptions, press conferences, or entertainment. Companies who sponsor these events have their name or logo mentioned prominently in promotional materials and throughout the event.

- *Advertising in the Show Daily:*   Large shows usually have a daily newspaper available to all exhibitors and attendees each morning. It reviews the previous day's events and previews what is coming up. Exhibitors can advertise in the show daily.

- *Advertising in the Show Directory:*   Almost all exhibitions provide attendees with a show directory containing information about the show and exhibitors. Advertising opportunities also exist for this show directory.

- *Promotional Items Sponsorship:*   Management companies may offer sponsorship opportunities to companies for badge holders, tote bags, and other promotional items given to registered attendees. These items are given the acronym *SWAG*, which stands for stuff we all get.

Management companies (for B2B shows) must provide a convention program that has additional information beyond the exhibit hall to help attract visitors. Often, educational programs are provided as an incentive, or prominent industry leaders are hired to give keynote addresses that attract visitors. Contests, gifts, discount programs, and other tools to attract visitors are commonplace. Exhibitors are also involved in helping boost attendance at shows. Usually, they are given a number of free passes to the show, which can be passed on to their best customers. Exhibitors are also encouraged to sponsor or conduct special events and to promote them to their customer base.

Technology

Advances in technology have made managing the show, as well as the exhibition itself, easier and more productive (for more information, see Chapter 12 on technology).

- Gamification is now used in exhibits to motivate and reward attendees for engaging with exhibitors and one another. Game design is a new way to participate in a fun non-traditional way, or learn about the products or services of the exhibitors. Many shows offer prizes for attendees completing the game.
- The Internet has had a great impact on how exhibitions are marketed to potential visitors. Most shows have sites that allow attendees to register online (B2B shows) and purchase tickets in advance (B2C shows). Attendees can view exhibitor lists, review educational programs, and even make their travel arrangements online. They can also view interactive floor plans, and select educational programs and/or special events to efficiently plan their time.
- Lead retrieval systems are a great benefit to exhibitors. Systems are in place that enable the exhibit staff to swipe an attendee's card or bar-coded badge and capture all of that individual's contact information, saving many hours of entering business card data.
- The use of **radio frequency identification (RFID)** is now being used by convention and exhibition managers to track attendees' movement and behavior. This advanced technology is beneficial for data acquisition, lead retrieval, and reporting, but raises many issues regarding privacy and use of personal information.
- Many organizations are now introducing the option of participating in their exhibitions *virtually* to save attendees travel time and costs.
- Technology is also used to promote a company's products. Many companies now give visitors inexpensive flash drives or provide website links instead of bulky brochures. This electronic format can contain much more information and more elaborate presentations, which the potential customer can view at his or her leisure.

Risk and Crisis Management

Organizing and exhibiting at a show can be a risky business. If things are not done correctly, the show can quickly become a colossal failure. Both exhibition organizers and exhibitors need to have a risk management program. A risk management plan does the following:

- Identifies all potential risks for the exhibition management and the exhibitors.
- Quantifies each risk to determine the effect it would have if it were to occur.
- Provides an assessment of each risk to determine which risks to ignore, which to avoid, and which to mitigate.
- Provides risk avoidance steps to prevent the risk from occurring.
- Provides risk mitigation steps to minimize potential costs if the risk occurs.

Always keep in mind that an exhibition is a business venture that should be given every chance to succeed. Knowing how to apply risk management principles will help ensure success.

Crisis management has also become critical to exhibition organizers. A crisis is different from a risk in that it poses a critical situation that may cause danger to visitors or exhibitors. Examples of recent crises include the tsunami in Japan, the flooding in

Nashville, or the volcanic ash cloud that paralyzed travel to Europe. Exhibitions that were scheduled during these incidents were either canceled or curtailed midway through the schedule. Organizing companies suffered deep losses for these events.

Every exhibition organizer should have a crisis management plan that addresses the prevention, control, and reporting of emergency situations. The plan should address the more likely types of emergencies, such as fire, food-borne illness, demonstrations, bomb threats, terrorism, and natural disasters. It should contain all procedures to be followed in the event of an emergency situation.

Consider having a crisis management team who is well versed in assessing the potential for a crisis, taking actions to prevent emergencies, and taking control should a situation occur. The crisis management team should be represented in the site selection process.

More detail on these processes can be found in Chapter 12 in this book: Legal Issues in the MEEC Industry.

Exhibitor Perspective

If exhibitors were not successful from a business perspective, exhibitions would not exist. Exhibiting at shows is often a key part of a company's integrated marketing strategy. Companies invest a significant portion of their marketing budget into exhibitions and must see a positive return on their investment. This section of the chapter looks at the issues that face exhibiting companies.

Why Exhibit?

An exhibit booth is constructed to showcase products/services and to convey a message. It is important for a company to understand and analyze the benefits of exhibiting at a show prior to beginning the planning. Exhibiting is the only marketing medium that allows the potential buyer to experience a product or service, and, therefore, more money is spent on participating in exhibits than on traditional advertising or individual sales travel.

Additional reasons that companies participate in an exhibition include the following:

- Live marketing
- Branding of their name in the industry
- Annual presentation of products to industry analysts
- New product rollout
- Opportunities to meet with potential and existing customers
- Opportunities to learn about customer needs
- Opportunities to meet with trade media
- Opportunities to learn about changes in industry trends and competitor products

Exhibit Design Principles

Although exhibit design may be limited by the rules established by the exhibit management company, the constraints of the facility, or the business culture of the host country, there are some general principles that can be discussed. These principles include selecting the right layout of the exhibit to meet your purposes, selecting the right size for your company's budget and purposes, and making proper use of signage, lighting, and personnel. Exhibits and the space they occupy are a significant corporate investment, and attention must be given to each of these factors.

Exhibit size is a major consideration, if only because of cost. The cost of a standard booth can vary greatly based on the industry, show location, and venue. The more space an exhibit occupies, the more it costs in space rental, materials, labor for setup, additional staff, and maintenance. Therefore, be sure to balance the costs with the benefits of having a larger exhibit. A larger exhibit typically means being noticed by visitors, and it creates a better impression if done well. It gives the impression that the company is in a

TOP REASONS EXHIBITORS FAIL

1. Did not understand that every show is different
2. No SMART objectives were set for the show:
   Specific
   Measurable
   Achievable
   Relevant
   Time-constrained
3. Failure to differentiate your company from your competitors
4. No formal marketing or promotional plan created or shared
5. Logical planning was poor
6. Did not give attendees any reason to visit your booth space
7. Staff was not trained to sell your product or service
8. Exhibiting for all the wrong reasons—did not ensure that the right buyers would be there
9. Did not know how to measure return on investment
10. Did not do any post-show follow-up with leads generated at the show

Source: Amanda Cecil (class notes and materials)

solid financial situation and is a leader in the industry. However, the space must be used well, and convey the messages that the company desires to impart to potential customers.

Companies that participate in a large number of shows will have exhibits that range in size from very small (for less important or more specialized shows) to very large (for their most important exhibitions). For example, Xerox, a company that exhibits at a variety of shows each year, has very large exhibits for information technology shows, but also smaller peninsular or in-line exhibits for specialized shows or smaller, regional shows. Some companies even have two or three exhibits at the same show: a large one promoting the main theme and message they want to communicate, and smaller exhibits in other halls to promote specialized products or services.

Space assignments are often based on a priority points system in which the exhibition management company awards points based on desired space size, total dollars spent in exhibit space, number of years involved, and participation in sponsorship and advertising programs. From the organizer's perspective, this type of arrangement helps retain exhibitors and gives favor to the loyal, highest-paying exhibitors.

When selecting space, the company's exhibit manager should consider the following:

- Traffic patterns within the exhibit hall
- Location of entrances
- Location of food facilities and restrooms
- Location of industry leaders
- Location of competitors

Exhibit layout is also linked to the objectives a company establishes for the exhibition. If a company's main objective is to meet as many people as possible and establish its brand in the industry, a large open exhibit is appropriate. This type of layout encourages people to enter the exhibit, and it facilitates a large amount of traffic flow. There will be a few parts of the exhibit that will require visitors to stay for a period of time, such as at product demonstrations. It is the responsibility of the exhibit manager to notify the show management company if the company is hosting any celebrities, giving a loud presentation from a stage, or is hosting any special events in the booth that would draw an unusually large crowd.

Another type of layout may even purposely discourage people from entering, and parts of the exhibit may be by invitation only. Why would a company do this? If their purpose during the show is to only meet with serious buyers or existing customers, it is

A standard trade show booth.
George G. Fenich

important to limit visitors to only those falling in these categories. Therefore, this exhibit layout is set up to minimize traffic through the exhibit. Another strategy is to create a closing room within the booth space to meet with prospective buyers privately.

Most exhibition floor plans in the United States are based on a ten-by-ten-foot grid or an eight-by-ten-foot grid. This is known as the **standard booth**.

Typically, standard booths are set up side-by-side and back-to-back with an aisle running in front of the booth. Standard booths may also be used to line the inside walls of the exhibit area. Companies may combine standard booths to create an **in-line exhibit** using multiple standard booths to give greater length to the exhibit.

Island booths are created by grouping standard booths together into blocks of four, nine, or larger configurations. Island booths have aisles on four sides and can be an excellent format for medium-sized companies. **Peninsula booths** are made up of four or more standard booths back-to-back with aisles on only three sides.

Multilevel exhibits are often used by large companies to expand their exhibit space without taking up more floor space. The upper floor may be used for special purposes, such as meeting areas, private demonstration areas, or hospitality stations. Exhibitors using multilevel exhibits must be aware of each convention center's unique regulations for this type of exhibit.

As mentioned earlier, exhibitors must be aware of the location of food facilities, restrooms, entrances, and other special event areas. Each of these factors affects the traffic flow in the aisles, and can either hinder or help an exhibit. Although many companies strive to be directly in front of an entrance for exposure, it may create more problems than expected because of the large amount of traffic. The exhibit staff may have difficulty discerning between serious visitors to the exhibit and those just trying to get in or out of the exhibit hall. Food service areas may create unexpected lines at meal times that spill into an exhibit area, essentially making that area useless for that time.

Small exhibitors face a different set of problems. If they have an in-line exhibit, their options are limited in how the exhibit is organized. If they want to maximize interactions with visitors, they may "open" the exhibit by ensuring that there are no tables or other obstructions between the aisle and their staff. If, on the other hand, they want to focus interaction on serious potential customers, their approach may be to block off the inside of the exhibit as much as possible and have meeting areas within the exhibit.

Two story trade show booth.
George G. Fenich

Many people who pass by or through an exhibit only read the signs that the company is displaying. Signage, therefore, is important in planning an exhibit. Signs must communicate the messages that the company wants to convey clearly and quickly to visitors. Detailed itemizations of equipment specifications on signs are almost always ignored. Signs should instead focus on selling points and benefits to the user.

Lighting technology has come a long way in the past 20 years. Today, many companies use pinpoint lighting to focus visitors' attention on their products and signage. Color lighting is often used to accentuate certain parts of an exhibit to communicate a mood for the visitor. Lighting is also important for areas that will be used for discussions or meetings with potential customers.

Staffing the Exhibit

The most important part of any exhibit is the staff. A company may have an attractive, open, inviting, and informative exhibit space, but if the staff members are untrained, communicate poorly, and do not dress professionally, the exhibit will communicate the wrong message to attendees about the company and its products or services. Therefore, it is important that, whether for a large or small exhibit, the staff is well prepared and trained to promote the company, and represent the product or service professionally.

Staff must be trained to meet and greet. It is important that visitors are greeted warmly and made to feel welcome to the exhibit. Staff must also "qualify" visitors to determine if they are potential customers or not. By asking the right questions and listening to visitors, they can easily determine whether to spend more time with them, pass them to another staff member, or politely move them through the exhibit. Time is important, especially during the busy times at a show. Qualifying visitors is an important step in focusing your staff's time.

Many companies provide product demonstrations or even elaborate productions about their products or services at the booth. This aspect must be well managed and focus the visitors' attention on the main messages the company wants to communicate.

Exhibit staff must also be used wisely. All areas of the exhibit must be covered, and the right people must be in the right places. For large exhibits, greeters should be used to staff the outside of the exhibit. These people will direct visitors to the areas of their interest after initially greeting them. Technical staff may be stationed with the products displayed so that they are able to provide answers to the more detailed questions that a visitor may present. Corporate executives may roam the exhibit or cluster near meeting areas to enable staff to find them when needed. Often, serious customers want to be introduced to senior executives, and those executives need to be available.

Small exhibits have a special set of staff problems. Usually, the main problem they face is having enough staff to cover the busy times of the show, or having too much staff for the exhibit size. Again, it is important that the right people are used to staff the exhibit and that staff assignments are planned according to the show's busiest times.

Measuring Return on Investment

In these economic times, companies must select the shows with the right buyers in attendance. Far too often a company analyzes its **return on investment** (**ROI**) and cannot understand why a particular exhibition was not a success. Perhaps it exhibited at the show for years, and their return has dropped recently. This may possibly be due to not noticing a change in the show's theme and audience; it may no longer be an appropriate venue for the company.

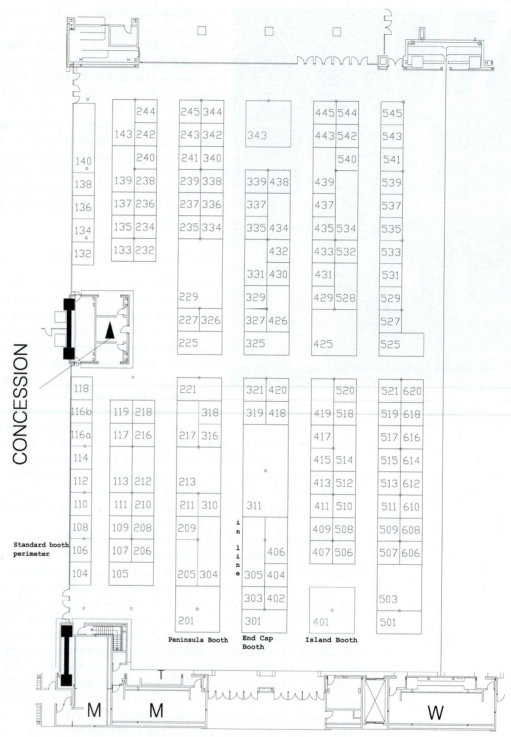

Floor plan.
Courtesy of Fern Exposition Services, LLC

Calculating ROI for each show is more critical than justifying whether or not a company is participating in the right shows, or using the right strategy and planning techniques. Often, however, determining ROI is ignored because "we can't tell whether a sale was derived from a show lead or not" or "we don't have the data to be accurate." Avoid these excuses by determining actual expenses and revenue generated by the exhibit leads.

When calculating ROI, establish all the expenses that are a part of the show. Typical expenses include:

- Space rental
- Service contractor services (electrical, computer, etc.)
- Personnel travel, including hotel and meals
- Personnel time for non-marketing personnel
- Customer entertainment
- Preshow mailings
- Freight charges
- Photography
- Brochure printing and shipment
- Promotional items
- Training
- Post-show communications

A simple method to determine revenue from the exhibition is to set a time limit on business that was the result of leads from the show. It is easy to maintain the lead list and determine which resulted in actual business; after a period of time, however, the business may very well be the result of other activities and not participation at the show. Thus, one simple formula for measuring show ROI is subtracting expenses (listed previously) from revenue generated from the buyers at the show.

Other methods of measuring ROI include evaluating results versus objectives:

- Cost per lead (total investment divided by the total number of leads)
- Percentage of the sales goal achieved (leads gathered divided by the leads identified in objectives)
- Percentage of leads converted to sales (number of sales divided by the leads generated)

Therefore, it is important that an exhibitor continually evaluates the show program and ensures that he or she is exhibiting at the right shows in order to meet his or her potential customers. Exhibitors can use a variety of tools to measure success. Examples of these include lead retrieval data, in-booth and post-event surveys, media clips, and RFID sales tracking.

ROI

A company exhibited at a show and collected 400 qualified leads and spent a total of $75,000 to exhibit. In the next six months, the company tracked its sales from the show and found it generated 100 new sales, totaling $175,000 in new business. The following list shows the calculations of ROI based on the company's objectives for participation in the show.

Leads generated: 400 qualified leads

Total cost to exhibit: $75,000

Sales resulting from the show: 100 new sales

Revenue resulting in show sales: $175,000

Target number of leads to gather from show: 700 qualified leads

ROI Calculations

Revenue–Expenses: $175,000; $75,000 = $100,000

Total cost per lead: $75,000/400 leads = $187.50 per lead

Percentage of goal achieved: = 700/400 leads = 57%

Percentage of leads converted to sales: 100/400 leads: 25%

The chart that follows shows a range of convention center space available to show organizers.

Convention Center Size		
Center	Square Feet of Exhibit Space	Meeting Rooms
McCormick Place (Chicago, IL)	2.6 million	114
Orange County Convention Center (Orlando, FL)	2.1 million	94
Las Vegas Convention Center (NV)	2.0 million	103
OK Indiana Convention Center (Indianapolis, IN)	66,600	48
Cox Convention Center (Oklahoma City, OK)	742,07	71
	137,125	21

Source: George G. Fenich

Trends and Best Practices

Exhibitions have been around and will continue to be around for many decades to come. However, as the times and economic conditions change, the exhibition industry must adapt in order to both survive and thrive.

- Attendance at future shows may be reduced, but it appears that the buying power of the attendee is greater. Many companies and organizations are not sending multiple representatives to shows and conferences, but are sending the decision makers.

- Technology will continue to push the exhibition industry to explore new ways of conducting business. Virtual shows will advance and continue to be a supplement to, not a replacement of, the face-to-face event. The human factor is still important in business. However, significant information is now available online, and attendees are researching companies and their products and services prior to attending the exhibition.

- With information readily available for attendees, exhibitors will have to be creative in their booth design and activities to draw attendees into their space. The use of the booth space, décor, signage, and displays will become even more important as attendees select vendors to engage with at the show site.

- Like associations, organizations and private media firms may be forced to merge shows or events as exhibitors may only be able to participate in a limited number of B2B and B2C exhibitions during this tough economic time. This trend allows for creative business agreements, bigger and better shows, and the opportunity to be innovative in event planning.

- Some exhibitions are being downsized or even phased out and replaced with hosted buyer. This is an attractive format for both exhibition attendees and exhibitors. More and more show management organizations are seriously considering this hosted buyer format in place of the traditional trade show program.

Summary

Exhibitions provide businesses with the opportunity to sell products and services to other businesses (B2B) or directly to the consumer (B2C). The exhibition organizer, the facility manager, the general contractor, and other suppliers must communicate and work together to service the show's exhibitors. Coordinating an exhibition requires the exhibition organizer to select a show venue and appropriate suppliers, to promote and market the show, to consider risks to the event, and to organize all logistics, including move in/out, shipping, technology, and many others.

Each individual booth also requires significant coordination. Exhibitors should carefully select the exhibitions they choose to participate in and establish clear goals and objectives for each show. Planning for the exhibit operation includes staffing the booth appropriately, determining the physical layout of the space, and designing strategies to engage with booth visitors. These exhibiting opportunities are business ventures and companies need to collect qualified leads. Following the show, the sales team should follow up with sales prospects, and the company should evaluate its ROI from each exhibition.

CASE STUDY NAMM

National Association of Music Merchants

Setting the Standard to Go Green

For more than 30 years, the National Association of Music Merchants (NAMM) and Freeman have collaborated on The NAMM Show, an annual event that attracts more than 99,000 attendees and 1,620 exhibitors. During this time, the event has evolved to meet the diverse needs of the music merchant community.

In recent years, the community has become increasingly interested in ways to reduce the event's environmental impact. NAMM approached us to look for ways that The NAMM Show could reduce waste, increase recycling, and reuse event materials to divert waste from local landfills.

Working across several departments, we created a green event plan, the five Rs (Rethink, Reduce, Reuse, Recycle, and Repurpose), to outline the sustainability efforts that would take place before, during, and after the show. The plan, which can be adapted to any size event in any industry, is now the standard for all Freeman clients who are interested in improving their sustainability efforts.

Our green event plan template included an environmental purchasing policy (e.g., preference for products containing post-consumer recycled content); a pack in, pack out policy for exhibitors, encouraging exhibitors to ship only the promotional materials needed and to send remainders back to their offices (instead of disposing of them on the show floor); and an online exhibitor kit, which reduced the amount of paper used and the amount of energy needed to deliver the kits.

Setting a New Sustainable Standard

To measure the outcomes of the plan, we provided NAMM with a post-show environmental performance report that included data to measure the sustainability of the event and to provide benchmarks for future events. The categories tracked included the fuel used for transport and show management freight; propane usage by forklifts and boom lifts; use and reuse of carpet, graphics, and other materials (e.g., table-top vinyl, Visqueen); and staff air travel.

The Loft Restaurant and Lounge is a popular networking area on the show floor that features comfortable seating areas, newsstands, charging stations, and food and beverages. In designing the area, we utilized several sustainability and waste diversion best practices, including thinking through the life-cycle of the materials used and potential reuse or disposal plans.

Measurable, Repeatable Success

Since its inception, our green event plan template has guided NAMM and Freeman to find innovative ways to produce an environmentally friendly event that still meets the needs of The NAMM Show's attendees and exhibitors.

We innovated in many different ways, including printing interior signage on honeycomb, a direct print high-quality corrugated cardboard that is 100 percent recyclable. Carpet in The Loft is made of 50 percent recycled content and is returned to inventory for future use before eventually being recycled. Aluminum extrusions for media racks and charging stations contain 85 percent recycled content and are returned to inventory for future use before eventually being recycled. And mesh banners used on the exterior of the event venue are undated and can be used multiple times.

The Freeman green event plan allows us to tap into their staff expertise and experience from other events. It is a solid foundation to build event sustainability goals now and in the future.

1. What do you think of what was done at NAMM?
2. What else could you think to do?
3. What would you NOT do?

Case study provided by Freeman

Key Words and Terms

For definitions, see Glossary.

Business-to-business (B2B)
Business-to-Consumer (B2C)
exhibition
exhibition management company
exposition

hosted buyer
in-line exhibit
island booths
multilevel exhibits
peninsula booths

public shows
radio frequency identification (RFID)
return on investment (ROI)
standard booth
trade fairs

Review and Discussion Questions

1. What is the difference between a B2B and B2C exhibition?

2. Give some examples of services that exhibition service contractors provide to exhibitors.

3. What attributes of an exhibit layout would a company want if its major objective were branding?

4. Describe the layout of a peninsula exhibit.

5. What kinds of additional marketing opportunities do management companies typically offer?

6. Why is risk management important to an exhibition management company? Why is it important to an exhibitor?

7. What factors are considered by an exhibition management company when determining the location of an exhibition?

8. What are the three phases of planning that a company exhibit manager must address?

References

Trade Publications

Convene

Exhibit Builder

Exhibitor

EXPO

Facility Manager

IdEAs

Meetings and Conventions

About the Chapter Contributor

Amanda Cecil, PhD, CMP, is an Associate Professor at Indiana University's Department of Tourism, Conventions, and Event Management in Indianapolis, Indiana, and teaches several courses in meeting and exhibition management. Prior to joining the faculty at IUPUI, Dr. Cecil was an exposition manager for Host Communications, Inc., an association and event management association.

Previous Edition Chapter Contributor

Ben McDonald, Vice President of Benchmark Learning, Inc.

Service contractors are responsible for erecting trade show booths, signage, carpet and more.
Tinxi/Shutterstock

CHAPTER 6

Service Contractors

Chapter Objectives

- Learn the definition of service contractors and their role in meetings, expositions, events, and conventions (MEEC).
- Understand the responsibilities of service contractors.
- Become knowledgeable about the evolution of service contractors.

- Understand the organization of a general services contracting company.
- Learn about specialty service contractors.
- Understand the relationship between service contractors and event organizers.
- Discover resources in the service contractor industry.

An event producer or show manager (or show organizer) may have all the tools at his or her fingertips to promote, sell, and execute a show or conference, but there are many pieces of knowledge, human resources, and equipment that he or she does not have. For example, while you might be a great cook, you do not make the frying pan or the spatula—you turn to experts for that. For exhibitions and events to be produced smoothly and efficiently, the producers and managers must rely on professional service contractors

107

to give the event/show manager and the exhibitors the tools necessary to be successful. These are called **service contractors**. This chapter discusses their various roles in the process, their relationship with the organizer, and their relationship with each other.

Definition of the General Services Contractor

Depending on where you are in the world, a person who manages a trade show is known as a service contractor, show manager, an event manager, or an event producer. It should also be noted that not all events and conferences have an exhibitor component. If you are going to be doing events/conferences/trade shows outside of the United States or Canada, be sure to use your network to find the appropriate company that will help you wade through the changes in the meanings of positions, cultural and business changes, language barriers, and much more. Remember, only the United States uses feet and inches. In Canada, because much of its business is from the United States, dimensions will be given in feet and inches, as well as in metric dimensions. Elsewhere in the world, be prepared for dimensions to be in metric only.

The following chart shows the relationship of metric measurement to United States customary units.

Inches	39.37007874
Feet	3.280839895
Yards	1.093613298
Miles	0.0006213711922
Nautical Miles	0.0005399568035
Light-years	1.056998307e-16
Centimeters	100
Meters	1
Kilometers	0.001

A service contractor is anyone who provides a product or service for the exhibitor or show/event management during the actual show or conference. Service contractors can be the florist, the electrical company, the registration company, a staffing agency, and just about every service you can think of. Some service contractors are hired by the show organizers to assist with their needs, and others are hired directly by the exhibitor.

A service contractor is an outside company used by clients to provide specific products or services (e.g., pipe and drape, exhibitor manuals, floor plans, dance floors, flags, and so on). Exhibitor manuals, floor plans, dance floor layouts, and so on are generally in electronic format and often include an app. MEEC service contractors and their roles have evolved over time. Historically, they were referred to as *decorators*. This is based on their earliest primary function as service contractors, which was to decorate the empty space of a convention center or hotel ballroom. This decorating function included pipe and drape, carpets, backdrops, booths, and furnishings.

The **general services contractor (GSC)** (also called the official show contractor or exposition services contractor) is hired by the show manager to handle the general duties necessary to produce the show on-site.

General Service Contractor: An organization that provides event management and exhibitors with a wide range of services, sometimes including, but not limited to, installation and dismantling, creating and hanging signage and banners, laying carpet, drayage, providing booth/stand furniture, and designing and building specific client booths.

The show may have a contractor appointed by show management whose definition is:

Official Contractor: An organization appointed by show management to provide services, such as setup and teardown of exhibit booths; and to oversee labor, drayage, and loading dock procedures. This is a type of general service contractor.

General Service Contractor Responsibilities

Over the years, service contractors have expanded the scope of their activities to match the growing sophistication of MEEC. Today, service contractors can be, and likely are, involved in every aspect of the event from move in, to running the show, to tear down, and move out. As a result, the service contractor provides an important interface between the event organizer and other MEEC suppliers, such as hotel convention services, the convention center, exhibitors, local labor, and unions. After taking careful measurements, service contractors work with the organizer to lay out trade show floors. Service contractors are also involved before the setup of the show by sending out exhibitor kits and other information, usually electronically.

GCSs are responsible for assisting the show organizer with graphic treatments for the entrance and all signage, putting up the pipe and drape or hard wall exhibits, placing aisle carpet, and creating all the official booths, such as association centers, registration, food and beverage areas, lounges, and special areas. More importantly, the GSC offers the show organizer a valuable service by hiring and managing the labor for a particular show. They have standing contracts with unions and tradespeople. They know how to hire enough labor to move a show in and out based on the requirements of the show. It is their responsibility to move the freight in and out of the facility, manage the flow of the trucks coming in and out of the facility, create the marshalling yard schedule, and store crates and boxes during the show. This is called **material handling** or **drayage**. Drayage is an outdated term, however, the reader may still see it from time to time. It is the same as material handling, the more common term.

It is important to understand that material handling may either be a separate services contract, or included with the general services contract for the show/exhibition.

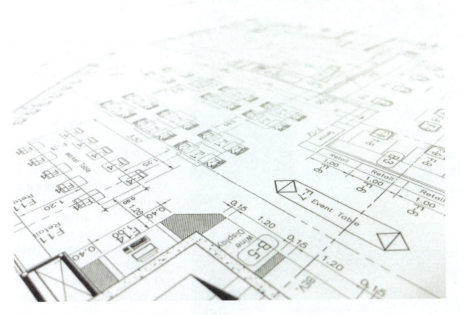

Trade show floor layout, metric measurements.
illiano/Shutterstock

MATERIAL HANDLING

Services performed by GSC include delivery of exhibit materials from the dock to the assigned space, removing empty crates, returning crates at the end of the event for re-crating, and delivering materials back to the dock for carrier loading. It is a two-way charge, incoming and outgoing. Sometimes referred to as drayage, material handling is the preferred term.

Drayage is a somewhat confusing term and can be traced back to medieval times. Drayage is the sum charge paid for the use of a dray or drays (a *dray* is a low, strong cart with detachable sides used for drawing heavy loads). Thus, *drayage* is the price paid for having trucks transport products. Today, the transport vehicle can be a truck or a plane, and the fee includes many aspects of the transportation service. Service contractors may charge for additional services like crating an exhibit in a box, using a forklift to get the box onto a small truck that takes the crate to a local warehouse or storage facility, and putting the crate onto an 18-wheeler for over-the-road transport. The reverse happens at the other end and ultimately leads to unloading at the convention center or event site. There, the service contractor supervises the unloading of the crate and delivery of it to the proper booth. After the crate is unpacked, the service contractor will arrange for storage of the empty crate until the show is over and the whole process is reversed. The price for drayage is based on the weight, not the size of the materials or crate. The fee is based on each one hundred pounds of weight, and thus is called *hundredweight*. A "bill of lading" is completed by the shipper and delineates what the package contains, who owns it, where it is going, and any special instructions. This is the official shipping document, and authorities at checkpoints, such as state or provincial borders, and especially national borders, may insist on examining it.

Many GSCs have expanded into specialty areas. Thus, GSCs today may provide audiovisual and other technological equipment, security, cleaning, and more. This is done for a number of reasons. One reason is that the GSCs are building on the relationship they have established with show organizers over years of interaction and rely on the marketing concept of relationship marketing. Provision of a wide range of services also gives the show organizer the advantage of one-stop shopping. By using a GSC that provides general and specialty services, the show/event organizer does not have to deal with a multitude of companies to produce the show. Also, providing an array of services allows the GSC to increase revenues and, it is hoped, profitability.

A note of caution if you are the show organizer—you must compare pricing for individual contractors versus putting all your eggs in one basket as described earlier. What is most cost/time efficient for your event/show?

GSCs not only serve the show organizer, but are also the official service contractor for exhibitors. Exhibitors can rent everything they need for their exhibit from the GSC, from a simple chair to a complete exhibit. Some GSCs will build a booth for exhibitors, store it, and ship it to other shows on behalf of the exhibitor.

The GSC adds value to his or her services by creating the **exhibitor service manual** (exhibitor services kit) along with the show organizer. Today, the manual is electronic and is often on a specific application for a particular event. This manual is a compilation of all the show information, such as dates, times, rules, and regulations for both the show manager and the city. Also included are all the forms necessary for an exhibitor to have a successful show. These forms typically include orders for carpet, furniture, utilities, setup and dismantling, and material handling. Some show organizers also include promotional opportunities to help exhibitors do pre-show and on-site promotion. The service manuals would be in an electronic format, included on a website, through cloud technology, or as an application, allowing exhibitors to order services and products from wherever they are. In some parts of the world, they may still be sent by mail or be hand delivered.

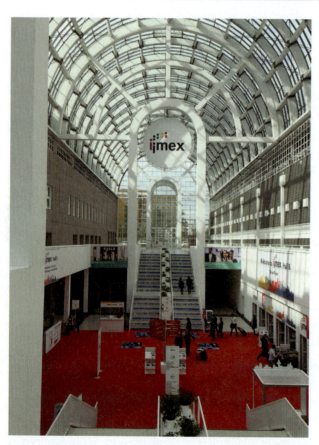

Signage is an important service.
George G. Fenich

On-site, the GSC works with both the show organizer and exhibitor to ensure a smooth move in and move out. He or she is often the conduit to a facility to make sure that the rules and regulations are observed. Many times, he or she solves the problems of the exhibitors by finding lost freight, repairing damaged booths or crates, and cleaning the carpets and booths in the evenings.

The services provided can include the following:

To the Show/Event Organizers:

- Account Management
- On-site coordination of the event
- Pipe and drape
- Entry areas
- Offices
- Registration areas
- Setup and dismantling of booths
- Planning, layout, and design of exhibit area
- Carpet
- Furniture
- Signs
- Graphics
- Backdrops
- Interface with labor and unions
- Cleaning

- Transportation services
- Material handling
- Customer service

To Exhibitors:

- Exhibit design and construction
- Booth setup and dismantling
- Carpet
- Furniture and accessories
- Signs/signage
- Interface with labor and unions
- Rigging
- Material handling
- Exhibitor kit
- Customs brokerage when dealing internationally

Labor/Trade Unions

Exhibition service managers, as well as show/event organizers, will make use of tradespeople in the community to help set up and tear down the show. Many of these tradespeople will be members of a trade union. An advantage of using members of a trade union is that the event organizer is assured that the worker has the requisite knowledge and skill to do the job assigned. A disadvantage of using trade union members is that they are restricted to only doing work in their *trade*; there are rigid regulations regarding the hours they can work; and the cost of using them is much higher than workers who are not members of a trade union.

Everyone involved in a show should be aware of the local laws and policies in the city, state/province, and country that the show/event is being held regarding the use of unionized personnel. The primary issue is whether the community is located in a right-to-work state/province. In these states/provinces, an individual working in a specific trade is *not* required to join the trade union representing that skill. Thus, show/event organizers and participants are free to hire whom they please, regardless of whether they are a union member. However, if the community is not in a right-to-work state/province, then people working in the trades such as electricians, plumbers, riggers, and porters must belong to the appropriate union. In these communities, there can be significant repercussions if the proper union members are not used. In some locales, an exhibitor cannot even carry their own materials from their automobile to the trade show booth: They must use a member of the porters' union. Prior to signing a contract, the event organizer should find out when union contracts are due for negotiations and learn whether past negotiations have been friendly or not. If a strike happened, how long was it before it was resolved? And, should a strike be in process, who manages the work that must be done to ensure that the conference/trade show setup and/or teardown is not jeopardized?

In the United States, the Taft-Hartley Act of 1947, also called the Labor Management Relations Act, gave states the right to enact right-to-work laws. This act restricts unions by prohibiting unfair labor practices, listing the rights of employers and employees who are union members, and so on.

THE CASE OF EXHIBITING IN A UNIONIZED CITY

Service contractors can play a pivotal role in dealing with unionized labor. This is especially problematic since (1) the unions and rules vary throughout the United States and other countries, and (2) local labor is essential for putting together an event or trade show. The following portrays one exhibitor's interaction with unionized labor in a city in the northeastern United States. The exhibit, in its crate, was transported to the convention center in a tractor-trailer; and according to local rules, the trailer had to be driven by a member of the Teamsters Union. On arrival at the convention center, the driver opened the back of the trailer but could do no more to facilitate the removal of the crate. Removing the crate required a forklift, and the forklift is considered a piece of heavy equipment, not a truck, and thus had to be operated by a member of the Heavy Equipment Operators Union. So, they waited for the forklift operator, who then moved the crate to the exhibit booth and placed it on the ground. At that point, the exhibitor was eager to get set up but could do nothing until a member of the Carpenters Union arrived to take the nails out of the crate: Wood and nails are a job for a union carpenter. The crate was opened, but the exhibitor was restricted from doing anything himself that a union member should do. Thus, he waited for a member of the Porters Union to come to take the exhibit contents out of the crate, which was then followed by a string of different union members who each did a separate, but distinct job and would not infringe on the responsibilities or activities of a different union. So, the exhibit frame that was made from pipes had to be assembled by someone from the Plumbers Union: only plumbers handle pipes. The products and cloth were assembled and laid out by a member of the Stage Hands Union: after all, an exhibit is part of a show. The sign over the booth required someone from the Heavy Equipment Operators Union to drive a bucket lift, while a member of the Riggers Union occupied the bucket to rig the sign. The exhibitor could not even plug his computer into the electrical outlet provided by show management—this had to be done by a member of the Electricians Union. The Internet and Wi-Fi had to be set up by a member of the Communications Workers Union, and the flowers had to be arranged by a member of the Agricultural Union. Of course, the cleaning people, security, and other service personnel had to be members of the appropriate union also. Furthermore, part of a supervisor's pay in each of these unions had to be paid by the exhibitor in proportion to the amount of time that the union spent at his booth. Further complicating matters, unless special fees are paid, there can be significant time lapses between when one union member finishes one particular job and when the next arrives. And—oh yes—if any union rule is violated or the exhibitor tries to do something himself, all the unions will boycott that booth and refuse to work. Obviously, a service contractor who is knowledgeable about local union rules and has established an ongoing relationship with local labor can be worth his or her weight in gold to an exhibitor or show organizer.

However, unions do serve a number of laudable purposes. They represent a class of workers, such as electricians, when negotiating with management over pay scales and working conditions. Thus, they carry more clout than any single worker could possibly have. Unions also set very specific guidelines regarding termination of an employee and will provide a union member with legal counsel if necessary. In addition, they help ensure that working conditions are safe and comfortable. Lastly, they work with government agencies to help establish guidelines for the construction trades.

Evolution of Service Contractors

Today, GSCs are evolving and changing to meet the needs of the client and the environment. One of the major changes has been increasing the scope of their work to center on meeting the needs of exhibitors. As is the case with the organizers of events, GSCs have come to the conclusion that it is the exhibitors who are the driving force of the trade show segment of MEEC. Furthermore, they have come to understand that exhibitors have more trade shows and vendors than ever to choose from, along with increased numbers of marketing channels through which to promote and distribute their products. Thus, both GSCs and show/event organizers are directing their attention to the needs of the exhibitor. Exhibitors are reacting to this effort by getting much more specific about their wants and needs, and they are also becoming much more discreet and selective when choosing a service contractor. Exhibitors spend huge amounts of money to participate in a trade show and, thus, want the best ROI they can get. In today's economic environment, exhibiting companies have to justify the expense of a trade show and are looking to service contractors to help with that justification, and to show the value added by participating in a face-to-face show.

In the long run, service contractors must deliver quality service and products to the user, whether it is the organizer or the exhibitor. Otherwise, both constituents will seek other marketing avenues and strategies. The status quo does not hold true any longer, and some companies have decided to forego trade shows in which they have participated for years. In lieu of exhibiting at an alternative trade show, some companies are developing their own private trade shows targeted toward specific markets or customers. Many are designing social media campaigns that eliminate some of the need to be face-to-face with customers.

Still another change for GSCs is that many facilities are now offering to do in-house what used to be the exclusive domain of GSCs. For example, many convention centers are now offering to provide utilities like electricity, water, steam, and gas, and may no longer allow GSCs to do this. These services are exclusive to the venue, and the show organizer must use the in-house services. Venues are also offering services like cleaning, security, audiovisual, Internet services, and room setups. This approach is cutting into the business and revenues of service contractors. Venues are creating exclusivity of product versus suggesting contractors, leaving the show/event organizer with no choice of which service contractor to use for specific services, such as those listed earlier.

The advent of **exhibitor-appointed contractors** (**EACs**), which are discussed later in this chapter, has cannibalized GSC business. This trend began in the mid-1980s, when the US courts ruled that service contractors could not have exclusive right to control and negotiate with organized labor. Thus, an EAC from out of the area had the legal right to compete with GSCs and set up a booth for an exhibitor. EACs are a subset of GSCs that, rather than work from one city or location, work for the exhibiting company and travel throughout the country setting up and dismantling their booths. Their success is based on the long-term relationship they have built with the client company, and is known as relationship marketing. Because the EAC works for the same company over many trade shows and events, the EAC is more knowledgeable about the client company's needs and can provide better service than the broader GSC.

This competition between GSCs and EACs has encouraged the GSCs to provide more specialized, streamlined, and efficient service to exhibiting companies. For example, one GSC now provides exhibiting companies with the same service representative before the trade show opens, during the show, and after the show for reconciliation and billing. This lets the customer deal with one source for the ordering of all services and products, a one-stop service desk, and a single master bill, representing every product and service used. This is analogous to an individual who gets a different credit card receipt for each transaction but a single, cumulative bill at the end of the month. Several service contractors have special programs for their best customers, which can provide special customer service representatives, who are available twenty-four hours a day, seven days a week; and private service centers that have a lounge, Wi-Fi, phone, copy services, and so forth. Many sales representatives of service contractors are equipped with cell phones, tablets, and so on so that they can go to a booth and provide on-the-spot service. Business transactions happen in real time, on the spot. A client uses their own tablet or smartphone and transacts most business requests, ascertains freight status, and prints forms like, shipping labels, invoice summaries, and order forms.

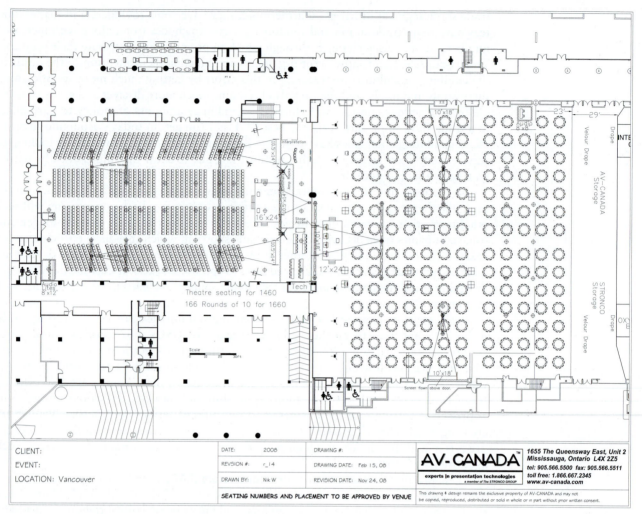

Floor plan for Vancouver Convention Center.
Produced by AV-CANADA: floor plan of Vancouver Convention Centre

GSCs are also expanding into the area of event marketing. This is also based on the desire by clients to do most of their business with someone or some company they know and trust—relationship marketing. The show/event organizer or association host may sponsor events, but corporations put on most events. As a result, many exhibitors are now responsible for corporate events outside the traditional trade show floor. GSCs, having developed a long-term relationship with the exhibitor, are now developing corporate event programs, multi-event exhibit programs, private trade shows, new product introductions, hospitality events for clients, multi-city touring exhibitions, and more non-traditional promotional materials.

Technology is also changing the way GSCs do business. As with many businesses, the computer, tablet, or smartphone are eliminating many activities traditionally done with pen and paper. This includes updating floor plans, tracking freight, and monitoring small package deliveries. For example, as little as 15 years ago, floor plans had to be drawn by hand using drafting instruments. A simple booth change, because it affects the entire show layout, could take a week or more to redraft. Now, thanks to computer technology, changes are almost instantaneous. GSCs have proprietary software that includes floor plans and artists' drawings for every major convention facility in the United States, Canada, and beyond. Clients can take a virtual tour of the venue, now often using 3D technology, and make floor plan changes immediately.

GSCs are also using technology to help them with material handling. Again, pen and paper is being replaced with computer technology, which allows faster and more accurate tracking of shipments of all sizes. Everything is online or in a mobile app so that when a truck enters or leaves a facility, it is in the computer system; and freight managers can go to the central computer to check the status of not only the vehicle but its contents as well. Global positioning systems on many trucks allow satellite tracking of its location. This technological monitoring happens on the trade show floor as well. An exhibitor can contact the GSC and know which crates are still on the truck and which have been delivered to the booth. Small packages, such as brochures, can be tracked in the same fashion. Even newer technology uses GPS tracking devices, placed by the exhibitor in each package or container, to track their location, in real time, from a smartphone.

Another technological innovation that has aided in the evolution of the role of GSCs is website development. They produce websites for show/event organizers that include interactive floor plans, exhibitor show information, booth reservation services, and as well as personal itineraries for show attendees, using social media and mobile applications.

Organization of a General Services Contracting Company

Service contractors are businesses, and, like most businesses, they are organized into functional areas. This means that there are different departments grouped by a common activity or function that support the mission of the company. The department that controls and directs the company can be called administration, and may include the general manager or chief executive officer, marketing, assistants, receptionists, and the like. Some of the other departments or divisions are as follows:

- *Sales:* Typically divided or broken up into national and local sales, or special events. Some companies also have a separate exhibitor sales department that takes over from national sales in dealing with exhibitors. Exhibitor sales will provide each exhibitor with an inventory of the supplies available and the cost of each item. Exhibitor sales also work to encourage exhibitors to upgrade (upsell) from standard to superior quality products at a higher price. Exhibitor sales typically will have an office and full-time presence at the trade show to facilitate interaction between production and exhibitors, and sell additional products and services on the trade show floor.

- *Logistics:* Handle planning, scheduling, shipping, labor relations, site inspection with show/event organizer, and preparation. This is the department that determines the flow and delivery of booth materials, with booths in the center of the hall being delivered before booths by the doors so that access is not blocked. This department may also work with the exhibit facility and lay out all the different-sized booths, aisles, food service areas, registration, and so on. Today a multitude of software exists to design exhibit floors and conference stages, and many companies have designed their own proprietary software.

- *Material Handling and Warehousing:* This includes transportation of materials, booths, exhibits, and so on, along with their temporary storage in the host city. Drayage may include air transport, and over-the-road tractor-trailer and local transportation.

- *Event Technology:* This includes technology, special effects, reports, and so on. This department oversees the planning and subsequent installation of the output of the production department.

- *Event Services:* This includes exhibitor kits, on-site coordination, and registration. The exhibitor kit tells exhibitors everything they need to know about the facility, capacities, rules, regulations, labor, and move-in and move-out times, along with the array of services provided by the service contractor. Today, this is largely handled using technology, and is saved electronically so changes can be made quickly, and everyone who needs it has access.

- *Production:* Woodworking, props, backdrops, signs, electrical, lighting, metal work, and so on. For example, at Freeman Decorating in New Orleans, clients regularly request backdrops that look like the French Quarter or a swamp. They are produced on large boards like those used in theater productions

- *Accounting and Finance:* Accounts receivable, accounts payable, payroll, and financial analysis.

Two of the largest US GSCs are Freeman Decorating and GES—Global Experience Specialists. You can learn more about these companies by using a search engine and viewing their websites.

The Freeman Companies are headquartered in Dallas, Texas, and they have offices in the United States, Canada, and the United Kingdom. Begun in 1927, they are a full-service contractor for expositions, conventions, special events, and corporate meetings. The company is privately held and owned by the Freeman family and company employees.

GES is headquartered in Las Vegas and has offices in 60 countries worldwide, including the United States, Canada, and the United Kingdom. GES is a wholly owned subsidiary of Viad Corporation.

The Stronco Group of Companies is an all-Canadian, privately owned company that was established in 1952. For more than 50 years, it has put on everything from trade shows and conventions to special performances, sporting events, and conferences. Stronco has grown to be the largest privately owned full-service contractor in the trade show and convention services industry in Canada. AV-Canada is a Canadian Company specializing in audiovisual, lighting, and staging. Both Stronco and AV-Canada bring their expertise to Canada and the United States. They are headquartered in Toronto, Canada.

Types of Service Contractors

Up to this point in the chapter, discussion has been about GSCs and how they interact with the individual exhibitor and the show/event manager. Now, the focus will broaden to all the potential service contractors that help to create a successful event.

Specialty Service Contractors

Specialty service contractors deal with a specific area of show/event production, whereas the GSC tends to be broad and generic. Specialty service contractors can either be official contractors (appointed by show/event management) or EACs (see the following). They provide all the services or equipment to complete the production, whether it is a special event/trade show/conference or general meeting, including:

- *Audiovisual:*   Services and supplies that enhance the exhibit/conference/special event through audiovisual technologies, possibly before and after the exhibit/conference/special event.
- *Business Services:*   Copying, printing, faxing, and other business services.
- *Catering:*   Food and beverage for show/event organizers at the conference/special event, and for individual exhibitors who may want to include food and beverage at their booth or private client event.
- *Cleaning Services:*   Cleaning of public areas of the conference/event, especially carpet along with booths, offices, and nonpublic areas.
- *Communications:*   Providing tablets, cell phones, and wired and wireless services.
- *Computers:*   Rental of computers and monitors.
- *Consulting:*   This can include pre-event planning, coordination, facilitation, layout and design of the trade show/event/conference, and booth design. They are often called third-party planners or independent consultants.
- *Décor:*   A basic décor company that can enhance staging, and the general décor theme. They can also provide florals and entertainment.
- *Electrical:*   Brings electrical power to the exhibits and any other areas where power may be required.
- *Entertainment Agency:*   Provides entertainment and acts as a liaison between the entertainer and show/event organizer.
- *Floral:*   Rental of plants, flowers, and props.

- *Freight:* Shipping of exhibit materials from the company to the show and back. There are various kinds of shippers: common carrier, van lines, and airfreight.
- *Furniture:* Rental of furniture for the exhibit, often fancier than in your home!
- *Internet Access and Telecommunications Equipment:* Rental of equipment and lines on the show floor or any other area required for the event/conference, including Wi-Fi and wired Internet access, ensuring enough bandwidth as required. Also included are cell phones, telephones, and walkie talkies.
- *Labor Planning and Supervision:* Expertise on local rules and regulations regarding what tradespeople to work with, union requirements, and supervision of workers on-site.
- *Lighting:* Design, rental, and lighting operators. This could be included as part of the audiovisual supplier's service.
- *Material Handling:* This includes over-the-road transportation of materials for the show, transfers, and delivery of materials from a local warehouse or depot to the show site, airfreight, and returns.
- *Moderator:* A specialist who manages the dialogue between virtual attendees, on-site attendees, and the presenter. Can be a part of the audiovisual team.
- *Producer:* A specialist who acts as a producer for the event, ensuring all production is designed and delivered without any errors or omissions. Can be a part of the audiovisual team.
- *Social Media Expert:* A team or person who is adapt at social media to enhance the reach of the exhibit, conference, or special event before, during, and after.
- *Staffing:* Temporary hiring of exhibit personnel, demonstration personnel, or registration.
- *Utilities:* Plumbing, air, gas, steam, and water for technical exhibits.
- *Photography:* For show/event organizers to provide publicity, and for individual exhibitors.
- *Postal and Package Services:* For both organizers and exhibitors.
- *Registration Company:* A company outsourced to manage the entire registration process for an event/conference or trade show. They manage all registration processes, including database, payment, badges, and, often, on-site staffing.
- *Security:* Security to watch the booth during closed hours and to control the entrances when the show is open, or for general security for an event/conference.
- *Speaker Bureaus:* Work with the show/event organizer to find ideal keynote speakers, entertainers, performers, and so on to open/close conference.
- *Translators:* Work with the show/event organizer to do simultaneous translation of speeches and presentations. They also work with exhibitors to provide communication between sales representatives and foreign attendees.

THE TRANSLATOR WHO KNEW TOO MUCH

A small American company decided that it wanted to exhibit at a trade show in Europe. One of the things it determined was that none of the sales managers who were going to staff their booth spoke any language except English. So, it was decided that a translator fluent in Spanish, Italian, and German would be hired. The translator worked so well that she was hired to provide services at another trade show a year later. At this second show, attendees asked many of the same questions asked at the first trade show. Since the questions were repetitive, the translator had learned the answers and would simply answer the attendee without translating and asking the sales managers. Response at this show was low, in spite of high attendance, and reactions to the products being displayed at the booth were poor. When the company manager did a post-show assessment, he uncovered the reason. The attendees got the impression that since a mere translator knew about the products, they must be very simplistic and not cutting edge. So, at all future trade shows, the translator was told to always translate, ask the sales managers, and never answer on her own!

Besides the standard needs listed earlier, each show has its own needs. A show in the food and beverage industry will have a contractor for ice and cold storage, while a show in the automotive industry might have a contractor who cleans cars.

Depending on the GSC, and what other suppliers are required, there may be times that all suppliers can be included in one-stop shopping with the GSC. Some examples of one-stop shopping are McCormick Place, Chicago; and the Metropolitan Toronto Convention Centre, Toronto. Many hotel chains also provide one-stop shopping, such as the Marriott (it is best to check with the specific hotel within the chain).

Exhibitor Appointed Service Contractors

As companies do more and more shows, their exhibits become more involved, and they often want one service supplier working with them throughout the year, or they have a favorite vendor who they have worked with in a city where they do many shows. This is particularly true with regard to the installation and dismantling of the exhibit. Most of the time, show/event organizers will allow this, assuming that a company meets the qualifications for insurance and licensing. This company is called an exhibitor-appointed contractor (EAC). As an EAC, they perform the same duties as a specialty contractor, but only for that exhibitor, not the show manager.

Some services may be provided only by the official service contractor and are called **exclusive services**. This decision is left up to the show/event manager who makes this decision based on the needs of the show, the rules and regulations of the facility, or to ensure a smooth move-in and teardown of the show. Can you imagine what would happen if every freight company and installation company tried to move its exhibitors' freight all at once? It would be chaos! So, material handling (drayage) is a service that is often handled as an exclusive service. Many facilities have very specific guidelines regarding the use of EACs. In some cases, the exhibitor must apply to the facility to use one.

This simple example of rigging was used to attract attention to a booth selling chairs.
George G. Fenich

The Relationship between Contractors and Event Organizers

One of the first actions that show/event organizers take when developing an event is to hire the GSC. This partnership develops as the show develops. GSCs will often recommend cities where a show should be held, the times of the year, and the facilities that fit the event. It is important to hire this company early on.

The process for hiring service contractors is through a **request for proposal** (**RFP**). The show organizer creates a list of questions and specifications for each show. Other areas of concern include knowledge of the industry and facility, other shows being handled in the same industry, size of the organization, and budget. Upon deciding which service contractor to use, accepting the proposed services by the organizer and the payment amounts by the service contractor, a legal contract is entered. This is a binding agreement. If either party fails to deliver on the terms of the contract, the case can be litigated.

As the show is developed, GSCs watch closely to suggest how marketing themes and association logos can be used in entrance treatments and signage so that, when a show goes live, it looks and feels the way the show organizer wants it. Color schemes, visual treatments, and types of materials all come from the mind of the GSC.

Specialty service contractors work with show organizers to help exhibitors save time and money. Reviewing the past history of a show can tell a service contractor what types of furniture, floral, and electrical services the exhibitors have used in the past. This permits the specialty contractors to offer money and time-saving tips to the show organizer and pass those savings on to the exhibitors. All of this creates a feeling of goodwill among exhibitors, who will continue to exhibit at the show.

After a time, the service contractor knows the show as well as the show organizer. This can be an added value to the show organizer because, as staff changes occur, the service contractor becomes a living historian of the show and its particular nuances.

Resources in the Service Contractor Industry

There are several national and international associations for individuals and companies in the service contractor industry. They can help the organizer find a services contractor in the city where the exhibit/conference/special event is taking place. To learn more about each association's mission, ethical principles, member responsibilities, contact information, and so on, go to their individual websites using a search engine. The following is a partial listing:

CEMA: Corporate Events Marketing Association.
HCEA: Healthcare Convention and Exhibitors Association.
ESCA: Exhibition Services & Contractors Association. Organization serving general and specialty contractors.
EDPA: Exhibit Designers and Producers Association. Organization serving companies engaged in the design, manufacture, transport, installation, and service of displays and exhibits primarily for the trade show industry.
EACA: Exhibitor-Appointed Contractors Association. Representing EACs and other individual show-floor professionals that provide exhibit services on the trade show floor.
IAEE: International Association of Exhibits and Events. An association of show organizers and the people who work for service contractors.
CAEM: Canadian Association of Exposition Management. A Canadian association of show organizers, and the people who work for service contractors.
NACS: National Association of Consumer Shows. An association of public (consumer) show organizers and the suppliers who support them.
EEAA: Exhibition and Event Association of Australia.
CEIR: Center for Exhibition Industry Research.
TSEA: Trade Show Exhibitors Association.

The example of ESCA indicates the professionalism that the various associations strive for. When looking for a show services contractor (or any contractor), be sure to check out the associations they belong to.

So, How Does It All Work?

Look at the organizational chart that follows (Figure 6-1), and you can see how the GSC interacts with the show/event organizer, the facility, the exhibitors, and the other contractors. Remember, exhibitions are like small cities, and the show organizer must provide everything a city does, from safety (security and registration) and a place to work (think of the exhibits as offices), to electricity, water, and transportation (shuttle buses). It must be done in a very short period of time, sometimes less than a week. Communication between everyone must function properly, and, often, it is the GSC who provides this conduit. The coordination of all the contractors is likely the responsibility of the GSC, who acts as the right hand of the show organizer.

Best Practices

Sustainability and corporate social responsibility (CSR) continue to be very important when deciding on a venue. Planners are becoming more aware of CSR and supply chains. Venues play a lead role in this by designing specific policies and procedures to ensure end users and service contractors meet requirements. The Metropolitan Toronto Convention Centre is an excellent example of being able to design a carbon neutral event with clients. Contractors can play a key role in the sustainability of exhibits/conferences/special events by reducing the carbon footprint; embracing the use of recyclable materials; using products that are locally produced; working with venues to meet its guidelines with respect to low lighting usage when full lighting is not required; and working with venues to ensure waste management policies are met.

Service contractors will develop relationships with organizers, planners, and sponsors as well as help produce meetings and events in multiple locations.

As technology improves, hybrid meetings will become more important when it can help to meet the objectives of the exhibit/conference/special event. This will require more specialized needs from audiovisual and/or technical service contractors, such as increased bandwidth. Specialized consultants, such as producers and moderators, ensure that the meeting is successful and that the attendee is engaged, whether the meeting takes place online, face-to-face, or is viewed afterwards from a recording.

3D technology is becoming mainstream and enables exhibitors to give participants a better view of their goods and services.

Robots will do more of the heavy lifting and moving around the floor, enticing participants to go to specific booths. Drones are already making their appearance. Rules, regulations, and policies will be put into place as their use become more prevalent. One

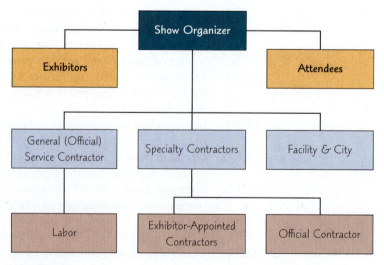

FIGURE 6-1

The relationship between the show organizer and service contractors.
Source: Sandy Biback

company has created robots that have two-way image capabilities—almost like robotic SKYPE. Participants can control movement remotely, see people and things in front of the robot, and transmit voice through the robot. It is almost as if the participant is actually at the show.

Show services continue to consolidate under the GSC umbrella.

Summary

Service contractors are the backbone of the exhibition/event/conference industry. Their support structure allows the show/event organizers and exhibitors to create an atmosphere that is smooth and efficient. Understanding the responsibilities of each contractor will allow a show/event organizer to offer exhibitors the best possible service, as well as creating a successful environment for buyers and sellers to do business in the exhibition format.

CASE STUDY

When you read this Case Study as it relates to The Distillery's Toronto Christmas Market, keep in mind the need to have contingency plans in place. Also, keep in mind the need to ensure that all your contractors become a part of your team and are brought in as early in the process as possible. Each contractor understands its specialty and can add to the success. Each contractor will also have contingency and risk plans in place that the event organizer can add to the overall plans of the particular event/conference.

The Relationship between Service Contractors and Show Organizers

Each year, since 2011, in a historic section of Toronto, Canada, known as The Distillery, the five-week Toronto Christmas Market takes place. In 2011, attendance was about 240,000. People came to enjoy food and beverage, caroling, and stage performances by well-known artists, as well as to purchase unusual gifts and enjoy the outdoor festival. In a short period of time, the Market has become a tourist destination and has a substantial economic impact for the shops of The Distillery and the City of Toronto.

By 2016, over 500,000 people attended, mostly on weekends. This has caused The Distillery District to look at traffic flow (people and transportation), safety, and more. To try to alleviate the large numbers on weekends, they now charge a minimal fee on weekends, with proceeds going to charity. This has also resulted in more security. After the terrorist attack in Brussels, The Distillery District immediately had to increase security and make major security decisions in a few hours. These were implemented overnight.

When the public comes, they see the Market in full swing. Most don't comprehend what it took to build the Market during the two weeks prior to its opening. Working with The Distillery Special Events staff, general contractors had to work as a team to ensure it all ran smoothly. Before any of this could happen, The Distillery Special Events staff had to contract the vendors who would sell their products as well as the variety of service contractors to ensure success.

There were the builders of the huts that would sell goods, food, and beverages. There were electrical contractors required to add electricity to each hut. There were sky-jacks brought in to put up the 40-foot Christmas tree and decorate it. The lighting people put up thousands of lights above the buildings. The vendors set up their wares. The entertainers had to be contracted and scheduled, both on the stage and off. The established restaurants had to ensure they were staffed appropriately and purchase enough food to handle the extra diners. The cobblestone streets had to be checked to ensure no cobblestones were loose. Extra security had to be hired. Portable toilets had to be brought in. Valet parking and parking attendants had to be hired to manage the increased car traffic. Firewood had to be delivered for the outdoor fire pits. Permits had to be obtained for the use of much of the equipment. When the market opened, 80 percent of the work had already been done!

Now it was time for the next ten percent, which occurred during the two-week event. Any on-site crisis had to be dealt with so that the guests didn't know. A snow storm meant the plows had to be ready and the salters had to quickly salt the cobblestones to ensure no one fell and injured themselves. Security had to be on the lookout for anything that could go wrong. Entertainers had to be on time, and outdoor fires had to be watched.

No sooner had it begun it was over. Now, it was time for the last ten percent: teardown and analysis. Again, all contractors had to work together to ensure everything was dismantled and safely taken away. Electrical and sound systems came down first, followed by the center stage. As all this happened, the vendors removed their goods. Security was, as always, there 24 hours a day. Lastly, the huts came down; the wood slats were stored on tractors and taken away. Two days later, if you walked The Distillery, you would never know a two-week Market had just taken place. Why? Because all service contractors worked as a team to design and set up the Market, to ensure safety during the Market, and to tear it down efficiently.

For more information about The Distillery's Toronto Christmas Market, find the website using a search engine.

Key Words and Terms

For definitions, see Glossary.

drayage	exhibitor-appointed contractors (EAC)	request for proposal (RFP)
exclusive services	general services contractor (GSC)	service contractors
exhibitor service manual	material handling	specialty service contractors

Review and Discussion Questions

1. What types of services do specialty contractors provide?

2. What are some of the questions that should be asked in an RFP?

3. Describe the difference between a general (official service contractor) and an exhibitor-appointed contractor.

4. How can the GSC assist the show/event organizer as it prepares for an exhibition/event/conference?

5. You are the event manager of a large conference that includes a trade show component. The trucks are ready to move and bad weather sets in. Winter storms are everywhere on the route. Who do you contact? What alternative plans can you make? What if the trucks can't get there in time to set up?

About the Chapter Contributor

Sandy Biback, CMP Emeritus, CMM, has been involved in the design and implementation of business events/conferences/trade shows for over 30 years. Biback has taught a variety of courses related to meetings and conventions in a post-graduate program at Centennial College in Toronto. She has previously taught online for the University of Nevada, Las Vegas, and George Brown College in Toronto. She is the CEO of Imagination + Meeting Planners, Inc. She was a former member of the Professional Convention Management Association (PCMA) and is a founding member; she was also the Past President of the Canadian Society of Professional Event Planners (CanSPEP). She works on special projects that capture her passion to make the industry a better profession.

Previous Edition Chapter Contributor

Susan L. Schwartz, CEM.

Destination Management Companies can create corporate team building activities.
crazymedia/Shutterstock

CHAPTER 7

Destination Management Companies

Chapter Objectives

- Define a destination management company as well as its structure and services.
- Outline a destination management company's organization.
- Describe the elements involved in the business model of destination management companies.
- Discuss strategies and tools for finding and selecting a destination management company.
- Describe at least eight best practices in destination management companies.

One of the many career opportunities that exist within the MEEC industry is providing local destination management services. These services include being a liaison between the host organization's meeting planner and the suppliers, such as on-site meeting management, hotel services, convention centers and bureaus, airlines, transportation, and catering. Typically, when thinking about careers in the MEEC industry, one may not always consider working on the supplier side of the business. However, services provided at the event destination play a key role in the successful planning and execution of meetings, conventions, and events. This chapter will discuss the business and services provided by destination management companies (DMCs).

Destination Management Company: Definition, Structure, and Services

A **destination management company (DMC)** is a professional services business that possesses extensive local knowledge, expertise, and resources. It specializes in the design and implementation of events, activities, tours, transportation, and program logistics. Depending on the company and the staff specialists in the company, DMCs offer, but are not limited to, the following: creative proposals for special events, guest tours, VIP amenities and transportation, shuttle services, on-site staffing, team-building, golf and sport outings, entertainment, décor and theme development, and on-site registration services and housing services.

Destination management companies may also be known as **ground operators** (a term originally used for DMCs before their services in the industry expanded to what it is today) or **professional congress organizers (PCO)**—a predominantly international term. PCOs are a type of DMC who are especially helpful to those planning international events, and are members of the International Association of Professional Congress Organizers (IAPCO). Destination management companies offer a critical layer of services and are hired by meeting and event professionals to provide local knowledge, experience, and resources for corporate and association gatherings. DMCs work cooperatively with transportation companies, airlines, hotels and resorts, convention centers, and other service suppliers in the delivery and implementation of MEEC activities. Successful MEEC events require comprehensive local knowledge of destination infrastructure, local laws and statutes, and regulations. Meeting and event professionals must work with local professionals who have verified information about supplier availability, capabilities, and capacities, gained through actual project work, to ensure a successful event.

When discussing DMCs and their services, the industry denotes this as the client project, which is typically referred to as a program whether it is a meeting, exhibition, event, or convention. A program includes all activities and services provided by the DMC to the client while visiting a destination over a specified time.

Services Provided by Destination Management Companies

Meeting and event professionals work closely with DMCs to provide recommendations for local destination resources that will best fit and satisfy the goals for a gathering. After these services are determined, a contract is written for the DMC to plan, set up, and deliver those services. Services typically offered by DMCs include:

- Budgeting and resource management
- Creative itineraries
- Creative theme design
- Dining programs
- Entertainers
- Event production
- Event venue selection
- Hotel selection
- Incentive travel
- Meeting support services
- Sightseeing and tour options
- Speakers
- Special event concepts
- Sport events (e.g., golf, tennis, and fishing tournaments)
- Staffing services
- Team-building activities
- Transportation planning and delivery
- VIP services

DMCs may make arrangements for special events within a program, such as this gala complete with entertainment and dancing.
Jim DeLillo/Alamy Stock Photo

DMC services facilitate networking among attendees, celebrating accomplishments, and introducing new ideas and/or products. In today's competitive environment, where the impact and return on investment of meetings and events are expected to be measured, professionals rely on DMCs to provide unique and creative event concepts that will accomplish the specific goals of the event, be consistent with other activities carried out in the client's program, and stay within the client's budget. Full-service DMCs provide both meeting management support services, such as transportation arrangements and on-site staffing; and all aspects of event production, such as staging, sound, décor, and lights. DMCs are often a reliable resource for entertainment solutions, from a small trio for background music at an intimate cocktail party to headline entertainment for large special events. Familiarity and access to local musicians and entertainers is an important criterion when selecting a DMC. In addition, DMCs often suggest and supply décor, such as props, floral designs, and decorations, to enhance event spaces and venues.

Transportation logistics are often a key service provided by DMCs. These services include airport meet-and-greet services, hotel transfers, baggage management, and shuttles. Moving groups of participants—large or small—are an important component of most events, which require precise timing and execution, local expertise, and management responsibility. This is best provided by a professional DMC to ensure attendee comfort, convenience, and safety. In addition, many DMCs will provide customized sightseeing tours and recreational activities, such as golf and tennis tournaments.

Because of the creative element associated with meetings and events, and the variety of each group's needs and expectations, the list of services provided by DMCs is almost limitless. It is important to note that, while one client may require a DMC to manage and execute the entire event, another client may contract a DMC to provide only one or two components of the event.

Destination Management Company versus Destination Marketing Organization

The DMC business process has been compared to, and often confused with, the services provided by a **destination marketing organization (DMO)**, sometimes referred to as a **convention and visitors bureau (CVB)**. Although they are very different organizations, there are some similarities between their services. DMOs optimize the exposure of a specific destination, leading it to develop innovative experiences for visitors and enabling the community to develop a sustainable infrastructure for tourism and travel to that particular location.

Most DMOs are quasi-government, not-for-profit organizations whose purpose is to sell their destination to tourists, business travelers, and convention visitors alike. Often funded by both tax dollars and membership fees, DMOs maintain an unbiased view of their destination's supplier and vendor members. They work with the planner to arrange site visitations, provide marketing materials about the locale, and direct planners to local suppliers of meeting services and venues. See Chapter 3 for more detailed information about DMOs.

Unlike DMOs, DMCs are for-profit businesses who can negotiate and sign supplier contracts on behalf of the meeting client. They too have an expertise of their destination and use that in-depth knowledge to recommend, and eventually book, special event venues, transportation, tour guides, restaurants, and so forth, on behalf of the client.

Today's consumers expect a destination to offer customized product and service offerings that match their needs. The destinations that manage to maximize the satisfaction levels of customers' expectations, and support consumers throughout the buying process, will be the ones to survive and yield maximum benefits. Therefore, DMOs work with the interests of both the community at large and the private companies that provide many of these services.

Business Structure of DMCs

Some prerequisites are essential to the destination management process:

- Staff
- Temporary field staff
- An office
- Technology
- Licenses and insurance
- Community contacts
- Customer contacts
- History
- Destination resources

Staffing is probably the most obvious of the prerequisites. Office staff for sales, logistics, accounting, and administrative duties is all necessary to have. In addition, temporary field staff includes such positions as tour guides, greeters, and on-site supervisors. These people often work on a contract basis for each event as it arises and may be temporarily hired by other DMCs.

A strategically located office is a basic necessity for a DMC. Convenient proximity to major hotels, convention facilities, tourist attractions, and event venues is a must. In today's competitive environment, DMCs must have access to the best possible technology. DMC clients are usually associations and major corporations that are accustomed to technology, and expect to work with DMCs that are also proficient in using electronic communications. Communications equipment, office computer capabilities (including database management), imaging software, and high-speed Internet are all expected to be standard tools in today's DMC. The quick processing of information, and the ability to make on-the-spot changes and produce professional documents and graphics are becoming an industry standard and a necessity for DMCs.

Given the nature of the services provided by DMCs, they must be legally insured for business liability, as well as other standard coverages, such as workers' compensation and automobile insurance. Each destination will have unique laws and licensing requirements for DMC services. Meeting and event professionals must ensure that their chosen business partners are adequately insured and knowledgeable about local ordinances that could affect the successful operation and production of their events.

As with many businesses in the service sector, DMCs compete in a relationship driven industry. Customers and professionals will literally put their reputations and jobs on the line when selecting a DMC. DMC management and staff should have extensive community contacts among hotels, attractions, convention bureaus, airports, law enforcement, and the supplier community, and must articulate their commitment to building and sustaining positive relationships with their clients. It is through the cooperation from these business partnerships, gained through repeated work experiences, that a DMC can properly service the diverse needs of its clients.

Reputation outside of the destination community, that is, in the client community, is very important to the long-term success of a DMC. The most valuable asset a DMC has is its history of success, which is the best verification a professional can rely on when choosing a DMC partner.

Finally, the destination community must have the necessary resources to support the DMC in the execution of a well-run program or event. It must have a competitive service environment, with many suppliers that have good reputations.

The Destination Management Company Organization

Destination management companies come in a variety of sizes and organizational structures. Given the nature of the services that they provide, it is possible to get started in this business with little start-up funding. This section will discuss the range of organizations that operate as DMCs.

Independent Operator

Independent destination management companies are locally owned and operated by small businesses that often got their start as a ground operator. For many years, these DMCs were the backbone of destination management and provided a limited array of targeted services, such as transportation operator, tour organizer, staffing, or special event management. Today, independent DMCs are still a major factor in the industry and many have expanded their services to compete with larger national DMCs. The long-term success of independent DMCs is largely predicated on the ability of the owner to develop lasting relationships and goodwill by exceeding clients' expectations. Although it is relatively easy to start this business, the hours and challenges can be long and arduous.

Multi-Services Operator

Destination management companies that offer multi-services are typically larger organizations rather than independent operators. Over time, these organizations establish large networks of service offerings. These multi-services suppliers must be staffed with well-trained professionals who can put together complex, diverse client programs. Often the larger multi-services operator has staff and offices in multiple destinations and can offer its clients a significant advantage in securing high-quality services at a lower cost than can typically be found with an independent operator. Examples of such organizations include Hosts Global Alliance, which services over 300 destinations, and Allied PRA, which services over 100 domestic destinations and numerous global partners as well.

Destination Management Networks

Because local one-destination DMCs do not enjoy the same economy of scale that national or international DMCs do, networks of DMCs have been formed. An example of this is The DMC Network. This group was formed in order to pool resources from individual one-city DMCs for sales and marketing purposes. Other such DMC groups exist primarily for the sharing of mutual sales and marketing efforts and expenses.

Destination management networks are a collection of independent destination management companies that pay a fee or commission to be affiliated with a national or regionally based organization. Destination management networks provide meeting and event professionals peace of mind when dealing with DMCs in unfamiliar locations. This arrangement allows for smaller, independent DMCs to remain autonomous while gaining significant advantages typically afforded to larger multi-services, multi-destination DMCs.

In some cases, particularly with DMC networks, it makes sense to employ professional representation firms to call on particular market segments. Usually, this representation is contracted for a particular geographic location, such as New York, Chicago, or London. These companies typically call on potential and existing customers in the geographic area on behalf of a DMC network. They will seek to familiarize professionals about the DMC network while uncovering leads for future business. When appropriate, these representation firms will sometimes also serve as a local liaison between the customer and a DMC partner.

Business Model of Destination Management Companies

DMC clients are those who plan meetings, exhibitions, events, conventions, and **incentive travel programs**. When describing the business model of DMCs, the terms customer, client, and professional are used to describe the person, organization, or company for which the DMC is providing services. In some instances, the customer, client, and professional can be three separate entities or be the same. The **customer** is the organization that will be securing and paying for the services provided by the DMC. The client is the representative of the organization who is in a leadership role when making the decision to purchase DMC services. The professional, who represents the customer's organization, is the person (or persons) with whom the DMC works directly to plan and coordinate programs and events.

It is important to note that those who participate in the planning of the services provided by a DMC are almost always staff of the DMC, such as a corporate sales force. It is common for DMCs to service the leisure traveler or tour groups that partner outside of the DMC organization. Increasingly, the value of DMC services is being recognized by large tour operators, and they are often contracted to assist with transportation and/or tours for large groups. A good example of this is a cruise ship that employs a DMC to manage land tours, transportation, and excursions.

A DMC may be contracted directly with an organization whose employees or members will be participating in the program, or it may be contracted with a third party or independent professional meeting professional who is offering their meeting services to the participating organization (customer). (See the flow chart in Figure 7-1.)

Most meeting and event professionals consider the DMC as a local extension of their own office and staff while at the destination. They expect the DMC to be their eyes and ears in the destination, always acting on their behalf, offering unbiased, experience-based

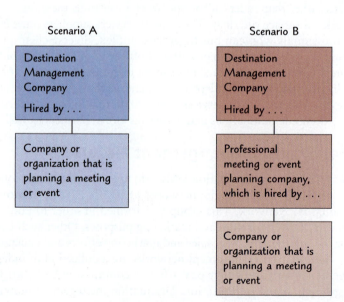

FIGURE 7-1
Sample DMC flow chart.

suggestions on logistics, venues, event concepts, and social program content. Professionals depend on DMCs to help them design event programs that meet their specific needs, which can vary in size, budget, length, and purpose.

Clients

Destination management companies receive business from several categories of customers. Their contracted programs may come from corporate, association, incentive-based, or special event clients.

Corporate Accounts

Given the recent challenges facing the world economy, corporate clients organizing meetings are receiving greater scrutiny. In the past, corporate meetings holding a half-day of meetings while spending the remainder of their day on the golf course would not generate much attention. Today, just the location where the corporate meeting is being held can generate negative publicity. When planning and organizing meetings, DMCs must be sensitive to the constraints and attention that face corporate clients.

In addition, corporate clients are reassessing the value of holding face-to-face meetings. It is very important that DMCs focus on working with their clients to ensure that the meetings and events have a higher level of value than could be achieved by not hosting a face-to-face or virtual event.

The following is a list of sample event programs that DMCs work on with corporate clients:

- National sales meetings
- Training meetings
- Product introductions
- Dealer and/or customer meetings

Association Accounts

Associations are organizations that are created to support an industry, common interest, or activity. Associations can range from local, state, regional, national, and international groups. Most associations exist to provide networking and educational opportunities to their membership. When carrying out these activities, associations will hold a variety of meetings, conventions, and conferences.

In today's competitive environment, potential conference/convention attendees are being more selective as to which meetings they will attend. Attending a meeting out of town is costly in terms of both time and money. One of the factors involved is the return on investment (ROI) that individuals believe they will receive by attending the event. DMCs can provide considerable resources and support to help clients create events that will be offered to their membership with the highest impact. The following is a list of sample event programs that DMCs work on with association clients:

- Industry trade shows (food, construction, aircraft, etc.)
- Professional trade shows and conferences (for architects, doctors, teachers, etc.)
- Fraternal organizations (VFW, Lions, etc.)
- Educational conferences (medical symposia and other professional groups)
- Political conventions

Incentive-Based Organizations

Incentive-based meetings and events are organized to recognize and reward employees who have reached or exceeded company targets. This segment of the meetings and event market continues to experience rapid growth. Today's organizations are recognizing the value of providing rewards and recognition for employees' outstanding performance. These events can typically last between three and six days in length and can range from a modest to extravagant getaway for employees and their partners. DMCs can provide the organizing client a range of services that are customized based on the budget of the organization and the desires of the employee. The following is a list of sample event programs that DMCs work on with incentive-based clients:

- Sales incentives
- Dealer incentives
- Service manager incentives

Special Event Clients

Local corporations, associations, for-profit and not-for-profit organizations may also use the services of a DMC for a singular, stand-alone event such as a gala, fundraiser, anniversary celebration, walk/run challenge, or other celebratory event that needs their expertise of local resources and logistics.

Destination Management Company Operations

Unlike hotels, resorts, convention centers, and restaurants, a DMC does not require an extensive capital investment to start up and operate its business. The DMC office is usually located in office space somewhere near the location where most meetings and events take place. Proximity to major airports can be an advantage, since so many program services involve group arrivals and departures.

Primary responsibilities and job titles for a DMC vary from company to company. Many DMCs are small, stand-alone, single-office companies that are locally owned. Other larger companies may have offices in multiple destinations with local staff fulfilling management responsibilities on all levels. (See Table 7-1 with categories of job responsibilities that follows.)

To be successful, a DMC's job tasks include finding business leads, proposing appropriate services, contracting services, organizing the group's arrival, delivering contracted services, and following up with billing and program reconciliation. These task areas are carried out by contracting with supplier companies, hiring field staff, and assigning program staff. Field staff, who carry out such functions as tour guides, hospitality desk staff, and airport meet and greet staff, are usually temporarily contracted employees who are

TABLE 7-1

Categories of DMC Job Responsibilities with Sample Job Titles

Management and Administration	Operations and Production
General Manager	Director of Operations
Office Manager	Director of Special Events
Accounting Manager	Operations Manager
Executive Assistant	Production Manager
Administrative Assistant	Transportation Manager
Receptionist	Staffing Manager
Research Assistant	
Sales and Marketing	**Field Staff**
Director of Sales	Meet and Greet Staff
Director of Marketing	Tour Guide
Director of Special Events	Transportation Manager
Sales Manager	Event Supervisor
Sales Coordinator	Field Supervisor
Proposal Writer	Equipment Manager
Research Analyst	

hired by a DMC only for the term of the program. It is common for field staff in a destination to work for more than one DMC as the needs arise for their services.

The job titles listed earlier are examples and will vary from company to company. However, sales and promotion, operations and production, and management and administration are the basic responsibilities of all DMCs. As in most companies, the levels of authority and reporting lines vary, and are usually based on the size of the company and the qualifications of its staff. For example, a Director of Special Events title may appear under both the sales and marketing function and the operations and production function. The position can be either or both, depending on the company and the individual executive's area of expertise.

In many cases, DMCs do not own the transportation equipment, props, décor, or other supplies that the DMC packages and sells to its customers. It is common for DMCs to buy or rent from selected suppliers and manage these products and services in the context of the larger event program. As such, the DMC becomes a contractor for the services of a myriad of local supplier companies.

A critical characteristic for the long-term success of DMCs is the ability to objectively recommend and select suppliers for the services contracted. A DMC's value proposition to meeting professionals depends on their ability to select the best provider for the services that meet the client's budget and program specifications. Clients must feel confident that the DMC is earning its money for the management services provided and not from some inflated financial arrangement made with its supplier companies.

The Sales Process

For DMCs to be successful, new business projects must be continually found and secured for the company. Business opportunities may present themselves in a variety of ways. Not all DMCs service all the clients listed earlier in the chapter. Some DMCs have created successful businesses by specializing in associations' convention business, corporate meetings, or international travel groups. Some DMCs may work with individual travelers, while others focus heavily on the domestic incentive market. However, most DMCs operate in multiple markets, which are usually determined by the nature of their destination.

In other words, the infrastructure and appeal of the destination will often dictate which of the previously discussed market segments DMCs will do business with. A destination's infrastructure, such as its convention centers, convention hotels, resorts, and airport facilities, all play into the equation. Other destination assets, such as natural and man-made attractions, play heavily into whether or not corporations will plan important meetings and/or incentive travel rewards in a location. Beaches, forests, weather, recreational facilities, fishing, arts, gambling, and theme parks can all enhance a destination's appeal.

Identifying New Business Opportunities

The first stage of the sales process is to discover new business opportunities and pursue those leads. Almost all new business opportunities involve going where the customers are or where the customers do business, such as attending industry trade shows or conferences. Some examples of these trade shows are the American Society of Association Executives (ASAE) Annual Meeting and Exposition, IMEX America (held in Las Vegas), IMEX Frankfurt, and Holiday Showcase (held in Chicago). Sales executives representing DMCs must carefully research these trade shows to maximize their sales and marketing resources. Knowing in advance which potential customers will attend, and knowing what business opportunities they represent will ensure an increase in the DMC's prospects for creating new client relationships.

DMCs will often get **leads** on new accounts through requests by meeting and event professionals that have gone through a DMO. Once the lead has been passed on by the DMO, the DMC will communicate through direct and electronic communications and presentations. These presentations almost always exhibit the DMC's competence using examples of their past successful programs. Once it has been established that the DMC has the expertise to meet the client's needs, it will respond to the client's request for proposal (RFP).

Some customers, particularly corporate customers, incentive companies, and meeting management companies, will designate a preferred DMC in selected destinations. For DMCs, this is known as a **house account**. Whenever house account planners require services, the chosen DMC can help without going through the often-onerous competitive bidding process. These accounts are very important and require careful maintenance. There is considerable competition for them, and competing DMCs are always active in their attempts to take over these accounts. Periodic visits to these customers and open lines of communication are vital in maintaining these relationships. In addition to continued good service, part of the successful maintenance of these relationships may include membership in the same industry organizations as the professionals. Attending these organizations' conferences and meetings allows DMC representatives to visit and network among existing and potential planner clients.

Sales efforts at the destination level are considered by most DMCs to be an important part of the sales plan. Creating relationships with local industry representatives who conduct business with the same customers and planners is an efficient way for DMCs to identify new business opportunities. For example, networking at local hospitality industry functions, such as the local Hospitality Sales and Management Association International's (HSMAI) monthly meetings or convention bureau mixers, is a common practice among successful DMCs. In addition, staying abreast of industry news, people who work in the industry, and knowing changes in services and staffing within the local industry make for a well-informed DMC.

Collateral materials are essential to a comprehensive sales and marketing plan. Collateral materials include brochures, letterheads, business cards, proposal shells, and fact sheets for the various activities and services offered by the DMC. In addition to these materials, a DMC will often produce a company newsletter to enhance the company's image and recognition in the industry. Increasingly, electronic media is being used.

Request for Proposal

Typically, potential DMC customers will request that two or more DMCs bid on its program, based on a set of specifications in their RFP. Each DMC will then provide detailed, creative proposals for services that will best satisfy the client's specifications. These proposals are almost always developed with no cost with the intention to win the customer's favor, which is a major issue.

Responding to a client's RFP often incurs a considerable cost for the DMC, and requires staff time to formulate a customized proposal; therefore, DMCs must choose wisely when determining what potential business to pursue. Today, the cost for collecting and submitting bids to a client's RFP is controlled by the development of standards for submitting these RFPs electronically. The Events Industry Council (EIC) has been a leader in the development of these standards; and templates for electronic formats can be found and retrieved under the **Accepted Practices Exchange (APEX)** guidelines. The APEX guidelines are a type of best practices (glossary, forms, and procedures) adopted by the industry for a variety of event planning components.

Destination management companies will prepare detailed proposals for services, which are based on the planner's specifications and budget. A meetings and events professional will provide the DMC with information so that the DMCs' proposed itinerary can be designed to best suit the group's purpose, demographics, and expectations. Initial proposals will often include more than one suggested itinerary, providing the client with several options, costs, and details about proposed services.

Once a DMC has secured the sales lead, contacted the customer, and convinced the client to consider the DMC, the DMC will be asked to provide a proposal of services. The following items must be considered and addressed in this proposal stage:

- Project specifications
- Research and development
- Creativity and innovation

- Budgets
- Response time
- Competition

As a DMC begins to determine exactly what to offer a customer, the client's project specifications become a valuable tool. A great deal of detailed information is usually included in these specifications, such as:

- Group size
- Choice of hotel, resort type
- Meeting space allotments
- Dates of service
- Types of services required
- Demographic information about the attendees
- Management's goals for the meeting or event
- Approximate budget
- History regarding past successes and challenges
- Deadlines for completion and proposal submission

Armed with the client's specifications and other information, the DMC will determine what items to offer in the proposal of services that will best fit the client's expectations. The first step is often a series of creative meetings among DMC staff to discuss what might best satisfy the client's specifications. After these meetings, research and development should begin. Availability of suppliers, venues, transportation, and entertainers, plus bids for services like catering, transportation equipment, and venue costs, are all reviewed and incorporated into the proposal. Costs for all items must be identified for accurate budgeting.

Creativity and innovation are usually highly valued in winning proposals. Selected programs will reflect the customer company; therefore, creativity and innovation along with a thorough and well-designed program tends to win. Response time is critical when responding to clients' proposals; however, there is a trade-off as creativity takes time, and a proposal that does not meet the clients' deadline will rarely receive the business.

A final and critical step in the proposal process is pricing. Several factors must be considered when pricing the proposal, such as:

- Total estimated costs for delivering the proposed services
- Staff time and involvement necessary before, during, and after the program
- Amount of DMC resources necessary to operate the program
- Unknown costs, which are factored into the planning stages
- Factors surrounding supplier choice and availability
- Time of the year and local business activity during a particular season
- Costs of taking staff and company capacity off the market for this customer
- Factors regarding competitive bids on the project

Prior to making a final decision on how much effort to dedicate to a given opportunity, a DMC should ask the following types of questions. The answers may show that, ultimately, the best decision is for a DMC to choose not to bid on a client's RFP.

- What is the revenue potential of the business opportunity?
- What is the value of a future relationship with the customer?
- How much proposal work will be involved in the bid?
- How many companies are bidding?
- Which competitors are bidding?

- What success rate does your company have on similar projects?
- What success rate do your competitors have?
- What time of year will the program be operating?
- What are the approximate odds of winning the program?
- How profitable will the program be?

Given the variety among proposal elements offered by competing DMCs, a client may not choose a winning bid based solely on price. The client, in awarding the bid, may consider other important factors, such as:

- Is the proposal feasible?
- What is the perceived value of services offered?
- Will the participants appreciate the suggested program?
- Will the quality be sufficient enough to make the program a success?
- Is the DMC capable of producing the program or event in an acceptable manner?

Site Inspections

While DMCs may be involved in site inspections, they do not usually organize nor sponsor them. This responsibility lies with the DMO at the locale (see Chapter 3, on DMOs, for more information).

Program Development

The execution and civility of business transactions are supported through contractual agreements and are essential in all aspects of the meetings and events industry. Hotels, convention centers, cruise ships, airlines, and DMCs all produce contracts with their clients, which precisely spell out the details of the purchase and the obligation for both parties. Depending on the size and complexity of the program and the services provided by the DMC, contracts can vary in size.

After a program is contracted, a transition begins: moving from the active selling of the program to the operations and production of the program. Now, all suppliers contracted by the DMC are notified that the program is definite and their services are confirmed. The operations staff, which is typically different from the sales staff in larger DMCs, meets with the sales representatives to review the customer's needs, program goals, and any details that will be a factor in the successful delivery of the program.

During this phase of the business process, the participants that are actively engaged can fluctuate, requiring the DMC management to constantly monitor costs and other details. With the active involvement by the client, activities and services may be added or removed from the program during this phase. It is important that the DMC representatives are available, responsive, and note these changes. As a contracted member of the customer's team, the DMC is responsible for the destination management portion of the larger, overall customer event. Therefore, the DMC must be fully cooperative and flexible. The program's project manager, either an operations or events manager, will assume primary responsibility for the entire program or event. During the setup period, each activity and service for the program is reviewed and confirmed in detail. Full-time and part-time professional program managers, supervisors, tour guides, and escorts are scheduled well in advance.

Program Execution

Destination management companies require the coordination of staff and suppliers into one cohesive program of products and services. After finding the opportunity, creating proposals, earning the professional's confidence, contracting the program, and careful preparations, it is up to the operations and production staff to successfully deliver the program. At this point, everything is on the line: The image of the customer's organization, the reputation of the planner, future prospects for the DMC with the planner, the DMC's reputation at the destination, and the opportunity to profit from the contract are all at risk.

The successful execution of the client's program is very important. If the program is for a large association's convention, the members' perception of the organization is at stake. The American Medical Association, Radiological Society of North America, and the National Automobile Dealers Association are examples of associations that employ a DMC. Meeting and event professionals for these associations are orchestrating major events with thousands of participants on an ongoing basis. The participants' perception of the convention can easily be affected by the quality of the shuttle transportation to and from the convention hall, the quality of the networking events, cocktail parties, meal service, and activities like the annual golf tournament and optional sightseeing tours. All of these services are potentially the DMC's responsibility. The events must live up to the participants' expectations. The activities and tours must be entertaining and well run. The participants are the association planner's customers, and membership renewals and future convention attendance will be affected by the quality of the program delivery.

Similar dynamics are in effect with corporate programs. Exhibiting at a trade show gives the exhibiting corporation an opportunity to entertain their customer through special event programs developed by their contracted DMC. Insurance companies reward top sales producers with incentive programs that effectively show the best of their workforce how the company's top executives value their contributions. Computer companies and software companies produce new product introduction events either as stand-alone events or in conjunction with industry conventions. Often, the success of these events has the future of the sponsoring companies at stake.

Through these examples, one can clearly see the tremendous pressure of running a logistically sound and high-quality program. These pressures are riding on the shoulders of the meeting and event professionals and the DMCs. The DMC's operations and production staff have one chance to deliver the program. When mistakes or missteps occur, the event cannot be rescheduled for the next day. If the bus and limousine suppliers do not provide equipment as ordered, the departure time cannot be changed. It is the reliability of execution that is the most important issue in the success of a program; price runs a distant second to reliability. However, all DMCs are not equal, and choosing the best fit for a particular program is essential. A close working relationship that fosters confidence, easy communication, and mutual understanding requires that the planner's DMC contact be readily available. Likewise, the planner must be immediately available to the DMC's operation manager throughout the course of the program.

Transportation Services

Transportation management is often a major part of a DMC's business. It encompasses routing, vehicle use, staff requirements, special venue considerations, equipment staging areas, staff scheduling and briefings, maps, and signage. Transportation scenarios and requirements are usually scattered throughout the program itinerary.

Corporate programs usually begin with airport transfers. Airport transportation services customarily include **meet and greet** services and luggage management. Management of the arrival manifest by the airport transportation manager is a key component of the service. The arrival manifest is a detailed list of each guest's name, arrival flight, and arrival time. The manager develops schedules with the **arrival manifest** as a guide. People change flights, miss flights, fail to accurately supply flight information, and flights can be delayed or canceled. Because of the inaccuracies common to arrival manifests, the transportation manager must not only expect surprises, but also plan for them. Constant communication is necessary between the DMC and the airlines, the transportation equipment suppliers, and the airport meet and greet staff. Equally important is the need to keep open communication with both the hotel(s) to which the participants are being transferred and the meeting professional, who may be receiving information about individual participants' changes in travel plans.

Meeting and greeting guests at the airport and arranging their transportation to the hotel is only one of the many services provided by a DMC.
Imtmphoto/123RF

When airport transfers are run properly, the participants receive a friendly welcome by someone who knows their name, after which they are directed to the proper baggage belt to identify their luggage. Motor coaches, minibuses, vans, sedans, and limousines could all be used. A DMC must proactively manage the changes and challenges of airport transportation. The first impression made on a participant is the arrival transfer, and the last impression is the departure transfer.

Transportation requirements of clients often include shuttle services between event venues and the participating hotel(s). Shuttle supervisors, dispatchers, and directional staff, sometimes referred to as human arrows or way finders, manage this personalized service. Whatever the transportation requirement, the DMC is expected to plan, prepare, and deliver the service in a timely and efficient manner.

DMCs arrange ground transportation. In Thailand this includes transport by elephant.
Hong Hanh Mac Thi/Alamy Stock Photo

Production of Events

Event production is also typically a major part of a DMC's services. Events can be large or small, on a hotel property, or in a remote location. Some examples of events are

- Cocktail receptions and networking events
- Breakfasts, luncheons, and dinners
- Dining events at unique venues
- Gala dinner events
- Extravagant theme parties
- Outdoor and indoor team-building events
- Guest and children's programs

Operational staff must be familiar with all the necessary municipal regulations regarding insurance, fire safety codes, crowd control, and police requirements. When considering all these issues, there is no substitute for experience, and working with a DMC that has a known track record of success is very important.

Whether planning and operating sightseeing tours, a scavenger hunt, a golf tournament, or running a hospitality desk, strong organizational skills, sound preparation, and a sense of commitment and responsibility are essential traits for a professional DMC operations manager. When everything is riding on the performance of the firms, planners will often bond with the managers and become dependent on them to be their on-site consultants in the community.

Meeting and event professionals will often have to deal with on-site questions and requests for VIP arrangements with little advanced notice, and the DMC staff will support them in securing appropriate arrangements. Some examples of last minute requests that DMCs are asked to take care of are

"Where can I send my VP of marketing and her husband for a romantic dinner? She just realized that today's their wedding anniversary!"

"My company president is arriving early in the corporate jet. Can we get a limo to the executive airport in 45 minutes?"

"The boss just decided he wants a rose for all of the ladies at tonight's party."

"Can we get Aretha Franklin to sing 'Happy Birthday' to one of our dealers during her performance at the party tonight?"

A wise person once said, "It is often the little things, the details that separate great events from ordinary ones." Knowing someone's favorite wine, song, or dessert can turn an ordinary event into one that will be remembered forever. These are things that are not included in the contract, but add special touches to an event and are great opportunities for the production staff to demonstrate their passion of service to the client. A production manager who has developed strong relationships with suppliers can often count on their suppliers to be swept up in the process and suggest ideas for program improvement on their own. Suppliers will do this because they want the event to be the best in order to establish an ongoing relationship with the DMC for possible future events. Planners are often pleased to be presented with options. Examples of on-site event upgrades include being offered confetti cannons for the dance floor area, additional accent lighting, or separate martini bars.

Much of an operations or production manager's day is spent confirming and reconfirming services. Constant communication with vendors and suppliers is critical to ensure that final participant counts and timing are accurate. One common task to ensure success of events is the **advancing of a venue**, which is when DMC staff arrives well ahead of a group to make sure that the service staff and the event location are prepared and properly set up. Details, such as the number of seats, room temperature, serving instructions, menu inclusions, and beverage service, are all examples of items that should be verified when advancing a dinner event.

Throughout each event, operations and production managers must carefully monitor the original contracted services and all changes that occur after the original itinerary and contracts. Every addition to the program, such as changes in participant counts, times of service, and additional services, must be documented. Accurate, up-to-the-minute data on the actual services delivered must be kept for billing purposes. To avoid billing disputes, it is also important to identify that an authorized representative for the client has accepted the change or addition. Ideally, these authorizations are in writing and approved in advance by the client.

Wrap-Up and Billing

The final invoice for a program should mirror the contract of services agreed upon prior to the execution of the program. Actual services delivered should be outlined along with the number of participants that each charged item is based on. In most cases, items are billed either on lot costs or on a per-person basis. Lot costs are fixed and independent of the number of participants, such as bus tours, the price of an entertainer, or a décor package for a ballroom. Per-person pricing is based on the actual number of participants, such as food and beverage at a luncheon that is billed at a fixed price per person, plus tax and gratuities.

All additions or deletions to the originally contracted services should appear on the invoice. The grand total for the program should be reflected along with all deposits and payments received prior to the final billing. When possible, final billing details should be reviewed and approved by the planner or representative on-site at the completion of the program, while details about the program's operation, additions, and changes are still fresh in everyone's mind. The more time that elapses between the time the program is completed and receipt of the final invoice, the more likely there will be disputes about program details, such as participant counts, times, and items that were approved to be added to the program.

Finding and Selecting a Destination Management Company

When the time comes for meeting and event professionals to find and select a DMC, there are several steps and guidelines that are helpful in ensuring a successful outcome. When searching for DMC candidates, it is best to begin with contacting industry professionals that are managing and executing meetings and events on a regular basis. One of the best benefits of networking is having contacts that can be called on to provide advice and guidance when searching for suppliers. If the meeting and event professional is lacking suitable connections, contacting industry groups, such as the Professional Convention Management Association (PCMA), Meeting Professionals International (MPI), International Live Events Association (ILEA), and the American Society of Association Executives (ASAE), can be a valuable source. Also, the destination's CVB or DMO will have listings of DMCs that operate in and around its destination.

Association of Destination Management Executives

An important resource in finding a DMC is the **Association of Destination Management Executives International (ADMEI)**. Founded in 1995, ADMEI is committed to the initiative that professional destination management is a critical and necessary component to every successful meeting or event. As a primary goal, ADMEI continuously seeks to identify and promote the value of destination management as a necessary resource for planners of meetings, events, and incentive travel programs. ADMEI's goals also include becoming the definitive source of information, education, and issues-based discussion on destination management for the meetings, events, incentive, and hospitality industries.

Professionals holding positions in the destination marketing field can gain an important professional designation. The designation of *Destination Management Certified Professional (DMCP)* was introduced by ADMEI in January 2000. This professional certification is only available to individuals who have qualified for an extensive examination administered by ADMEI. Applicants are screened through a detailed questionnaire, which chronicles the applicant's experience and industry education. ADMEI has also developed the Destination Management Company Accreditation (ADMC) program designed to promote professional standards and recognize those firms that demonstrate excellence in the practice of destination management, and who adhere to the standards set forth by ADMEI. The ADMC designation assists the meeting planning community by identifying those DMCs that adhere to ADMC standards of practice, ethics, and industry knowledge.

Once a list of potential DMCs has been identified through references or research of the various industry associations, it is time to identify the best of the group. Factors that may be important before soliciting the RFP selection include:

- How long has the company been in business?
- What are the experience levels of the management and staff?
- What are the perceptions of the planner with the personalities of the management team?
- Is the DMC an affiliated member of any meeting and events professional organizations?
- Is the DMC adequately bonded, relative to the size and complexity of the program?
- What is the quality of the references provided by the DMC both in size of previous programs and ranking of the professionals providing the references?

The next step in the process is selecting a DMC that best meets the needs and budgetary guidelines. At this point, meeting and event professionals should formally notify potential DMCs by a RFP. Once the final selection has been made, it is important to begin working with the selected DMC to ensure that they have historical information related to the organization's participants that may impact the execution of the program.

Best Practices in DMCs

The destination management industry's varied representatives are not immune to the need for change. The following is a list of eight areas that DMC operators should take seriously to enhance their leadership and stature in meeting and event management circles and beyond.

1. *Take the Lead in Green Practices.* Be proactive in initiating sustainable practices by implementing leading edge methods for leaving a smaller carbon footprint, educating other parts of the hospitality industry through professional organizational training activities and the development and distribution of training materials. In addition, DMCs should develop new partnerships to share these activities and materials with other businesses in both the private and public sector.

2. *Work Together in Consortiums.* The DMC industry will continue to see a consolidation of service organizations. It will be important for smaller, niche DMCs to bond together in consortiums to ensure that business remains in the local community, and that the overall experience for meeting and event professionals is seamless from planning, execution, and payment.

3. *Identify and Develop New Business from Drive-To Markets.* Given the uncertainty of the economy and the unfriendly skies, businesses will begin to look for more local and regional sites for holding their meetings and events. This should lead DMCs to focus on developing new clients from locations that are closer to their destinations.

4. *Develop Crisis Networks.* Issues surrounding the safety and security of meeting attendees will continue to be a concern for corporations and associations. Successful DMCs will develop, implement, and execute crisis plans and business continuity networks in partnership with other organizations within their communities.

5. *Emphasize Standards of Conduct and Operations.*   DMCs will continue to receive scrutiny about the behavior of staff used to provide client services. It will become increasingly important that DMCs implement high standards of conduct for their employees and operations. Standards and operational policies should be defined, recognized, and understood by every employee, client, and the public in general as part of an established image and reputation.

6. *Relationship Management Strategy.*   Corporations and associations that conduct business and meetings are quickly consolidating their travel, meeting, and event expenses into a more economically efficient model. Local and niche DMCs will need to build strong, lasting relationships with meetings and event professionals to ensure that they are on the list of approved vendors.

7. *Attentive to Competitive Forces.*   Given the ubiquity of the Internet, and its convenience, successful, large DMCs no longer need a continuous presence in a local market. Local, niche DMCs will need to increase the quality of customer contacts and services to meetings and events professionals and their attendees, to remain relevant in a competitive marketplace.

8. *Ethical Business Protocols.*   DMCs rely heavily upon their confidential intellectual property, creative ideas, and research conducted for a specific client program. The industry's (DMCs, planners, as well as suppliers) adherence to the ADMEI Code of Ethics is vital for the continued growth and professionalism of the industry.

Summary

The niche that DMCs provide in the MEEC industry is important for meeting and event professionals. These organizations provide a crucial service because the customer companies and organizations that sponsor meetings and events will always need access to local expertise. The depth of local destination knowledge, contacts, and connections; the community standing; buying power; and hands-on experience with the implementation of programs and events are not readily available to organizations outside of the destination. DMCs have evolved in some interesting ways. Many of the earlier DMCs evolved from the ranks of wholesale tour operators and ground operators. These early DMCs began by specializing in tours and transportation services for visiting travel groups. In the late 1950s, the specialization in association and higher-end corporate programs demanded a wider range of services, including dining programs, expanded activities, and special events.

Today, the competitive landscape of DMCs is filled with multi-destination, national DMC companies that operate networks around the world. However, just as individual one-of-a-kind hotels still prosper along with giant hotel chains, so do unique and specialized one-destination DMCs. The services requested of DMCs by meeting and event professionals are still evolving; and destination management services have been secured as a key component for success in the meetings and events industry.

First known as ground operators, DMCs are still crucial in providing reliable ground transportation and guided tours for their clients.
S_oleg/Shutterstock

Today's network of professionals that work in the destination management segment of the MEEC industry have a wide range of industry associations for support, and trade shows and conventions for marketing their services. Chief among them is ADMEI and its ADMC accreditation and executive certification programs.

The long-term outlook for DMCs is bright. The meeting and event industry that DMCs support is robust, and many existing firms are financially sound and poised to gain market share and increase their brand recognition despite temporary threats and business slowdowns. The industry is full of opportunities for long-term successful career options for new meeting and event professionals.

CASE STUDY

Working with a DMC

Natalie works for a professional association of financial managers in Chicago and has booked her conference of 1,000 participants for the late spring in San Diego. This is the first time the event or Natalie have been to that destination. To familiarize herself with the city she arranged for a site visit where she was escorted around the town by a member of the sales team of the San Diego Tourism Authority, the city's destination marketing organization (DMO). They visited many hotels, attractions, special event venues, and golf courses, and discussed ways in which the authority could be supportive in helping to market the conference to her membership. The DMO also provided her with a directory of member suppliers (tour and transportation companies, golf courses, décor companies, event venues other than hotels, and restaurants). Prior to signing hotel contracts, she worked with the DMO in narrowing the hotel venue down to four properties where she eventually chose two to host the conference.

Now that Natalie had firm dates and a location for her program she began to think about a number of special events and activities her planning committee had recommended. As she thought about it and the additional workload involved, it became clear that she needed a partner in this endeavor. The DMO could only point her in the direction of suppliers. They were not planners and, to be fair to all of their members, they could not negotiate contracts or recommend one supplier over another.

It was then that Natalie turned to a destination management company (DMC). She referred to the DMO's membership directory, asked for recommendations from industry colleagues, and sent a request for proposal (RFP) to her top three DMC choices. Natalie was planning the following:

- A golf tournament where she needed a golf course, transportation, awards, tournament planning, continental breakfast, lunch, and on-site supervision.

- An adventure tour: In previous years they had done desert jeep tours, horseback riding, and swamp tours with airboats. She needed venue recommendations, transportation, a place for lunch, and supervision.

- An opening reception held at one of the hotels, needing theme décor and entertainment.

- A historical cultural tour of the city requiring a planned route, bus transportation, qualified tour guides, and on-site supervision

- Two VIP dinners at high-end restaurants for 35 people each on two different nights. A private room was required. Floral arrangements needed to be ordered, and transportation provided.

- Private transportation for the President, Chairman of the Board, and a keynote speaker to and from the airport.

Once the DMC's proposals arrived, and after a careful review, Natalie chose to interview two of them during a site visit to San Diego. The DMCs met with Natalie, clarified the objectives and the audience for each event and used their expertise of the city to develop a total program for the association. Rather than Natalie having to manage negotiations and contracts for each of these events and the many suppliers, she turned to a DMC as a one-stop shop. She was able to develop a trusted partnership where the DMC became her eyes and ears in San Diego. In essence, she hired an event planner for herself.

1. Did Natalie do a complete job?
2. What would you have done differently?
3. What else would you have done?

Key Words and Terms

For definitions, see the Glossary.

Association of Destination
   Management Executives (ADMEI)
advancing of a venue
Accepted Practices Exchange (APEX)
arrival manifest
convention and visitors bureau (CVB)

customer
destination management company
   (DMC)
destination marketing organization
   (DMO)
ground operators

house account
incentive travel programs
leads
meet and greet
professional congress organizers (PCO)
request for proposal (RFP)

Review and Discussion Questions

1. What is a destination management company?

2. What services are offered by DMCs?

3. Compare and contrast the difference between a DMC and a DMO.

4. Create an organizational chart for a DMC.

5. How do DMCs generate their business leads?

6. What are the resources DMCs provide to a meeting and event professional?

7. Describe the differences between the types of accounts that secure the services of DMCs.

8. What professional organizations support the professionals that work in the destination management industry?

9. List the services provided by ADMEI.

10. Describe the key factors that are considered when meeting and event professionals are selecting a DMC.

About the Chapter Contributor

William R. Host, CMP, is an Associate Professor of hospitality and tourism management, focusing on meeting and event management in the Manfred Steinfeld School of Hospitality & Tourism Management at Roosevelt University in Chicago, Illinois. Prior to his teaching, Bill spent over 30 years in the industry as a meeting professional for not-for-profit organizations before forming HOST Meetings & Events Management.

Bill was installed in the MPI Chicago Area Chapter Hall of Fame in 2006 and was named by the PCMA Education Foundation as their 2010 Education Honoree for Lifetime Achievement.

Previous Edition Chapter Contributors

Brian Miller, Associate Professor at the University of Delaware.

Terry Epton, Executive Vice President, Host Global Alliance.

Weddings are an example of life-cycle special events.
IVASHstudio/Shutterstock

CHAPTER 8

Special Events Management

Chapter Objectives

- Provide an overview of the history, definition, and main components involved in special event planning.
- Outline a number of helpful special event planning tools.
- Discuss the many different considerations that go into special event marketing.

- Clarify the steps in preparing for a special event.
- Discuss the elements of a special event budget.
- Articulate the steps in breaking down a special event.
- Outline current trends and best practices in special event management.

Other components of the meetings, expositions, events, and conventions (MEEC) industry are special events. Unlike most other events in the MEEC industry, they do not occur regularly and may only happen once. Thus, the planner of special events must be very creative as each event is a new product. This makes planning special events both challenging and rewarding.

A Working Definition of a Special Event

A *special event* is an umbrella term that encompasses all functions that bring people together for a unique purpose. Most events require some sort of planning on the part of the organizer. A special event, such as a city festival or fair, can mean working with **community infrastructure**, merchandising, promoting, and, in some cases, dealing with the media. The event can be as small as the local community Kiwanis picnic or as large as the Olympics. Special events are imbedded in MEEC, and at amusement parks, parades, **fairs, festivals, and public events**.

The Events Industry Council (EIC) glossary includes the following definition related to special events:

> *Special Event*   One-time event staged for the purpose of celebration; unique activity.
>
> *Special Events Company*   A company that produces events which include a variety of creative elements including décor, special effects, theatrical acts or other entertainment. They may produce stand-alone events or functions within a larger programme such as a gala dinner during a convention.
> *Source:* www.eventscouncil.org/APEX/glossary.aspx. The APEX glossary is a product of the Events Industry Council, copyright 2016, Used with Permission. www.eventscouncil.org

A special event can bring organizations together for fundraising; establishing a city or community as a local, regional, or national destination; and to stimulate the local economy. The event can also be an opportunity for an association or a corporation to favorably position itself within a community or with the mass consumer. Sponsoring a specific type of event can provide a marketing edge and another avenue for reaching customers. For example, Mercedes-Benz automobiles sponsor numerous PGA golf tournaments, in part because the demographics of the audience match its target clientele. It also does the same thing with the US Open tennis tournament. Coors Light sponsors NASCAR races, Allstate sponsors the Sugar Bowl football game, and Macy's sponsors the Thanksgiving Day parade, and the list goes on and on.

Orchestrating a special event takes more than an idea. It takes planning, understanding your target market, having basic operational knowledge, using effective communication, working with volunteers or volunteer organizations, working within a budget, promoting the event, and even creating the logistics for breaking down an event. Simply stated, the event professional needs to understand the who, what, where, and why of the special event.

History and Background

Festivals and special events have been part of human history since time immemorial. Humankind has celebrated births, weddings, and deaths throughout history and held special gatherings like the Olympics and gladiatorial combat. However, most historians credit the use of the term special event in modern history to a Disney Imagineer named Robert Janni. The problem Disney faced was that the families who frequented the theme park were worn out after a day of adventure and most left by 5 PM each day, even though the park stayed open hours longer. In order to keep attendees at the park, he proposed producing a nightly parade, called the Main Street Electric Parade, with numerous floats decked out with lights. It was a success in keeping people in the park in the evening. When asked by a reporter what he called this parade, he replied, "A special event." The use of special events to attract or maintain crowds is still used to this day.

USING FESTIVALS IN THE OFF-SEASON: "ROCKIN' MOUNTAINS"

The typical image of the Rocky Mountains and Colorado is one of snow-covered peaks in winter dotted with skiers. But what happens when summer rolls around and people cannot ski? What do the ski resorts do, shut down? The answer is a resounding "No!" They put on music festivals using the same facilities occupied by skiers in the winter. The setting is idyllic, with music carrying through the clean air with the awesome backdrop of mountain peaks.

This use of Colorado mountain ski facilities to host off-season musical events started in 1949, when concerts were held in the town of Aspen. At the time, it was called the Goethe Bicentennial celebration. One of the events included the Minneapolis Symphony Orchestra playing in a tent that held 2,000 people. This special event has continued and grown into the Aspen Music Festival and School. Recently the event included more than 800 international musicians performing in over 300 events during the eight-week session. There are four major **venues**. The largest one is a tent that holds more than 2,000 people and is made from the same fabric as the Denver airport terminal.

Another ski resort that has turned to musical events to attract visitors in the off-season is Telluride, Colorado. Nearly every summer weekend, the town hosts a musical event. The biggest special event is the Telluride Bluegrass Festival, which has been held for over 40 years. It runs for four days in June and is capped at 11,000 people per day. Telluride also hosts a Jazz Festival, a Chamber Music Festival, and a Blues and Brews Festival.

In Winter Park, just west of Denver, numerous weekends are occupied with music festivals. Concertgoers sit on the slopes and watch bands perform against the backdrop of the Continental Divide. The Winter Park Music Festival boasts a lineup of old-school music acts like Molly Hatchet and Cheap Trick. In July, they host the Winter Park Jazz festival for two days with artists covering a variety of genres. Also in July, and covering two weekends, is the Winter Park 30 Solshine Music Festival. This event features local artists and is free to audiences.

Breckenridge also hosts a summer concert series that runs from late June until the middle of August. The event features everything from classical to rock music. They finance the event through a unique structure, raising one-fourth of its money through the Bon Appetit Series, which includes more intimate gatherings that range from country music concerts and wildflower hikes to scavenger hunts on Peak 7, tours of South Park, cabaret evenings, and Texas Hold'em tournaments.

It All Begins with a Relationship

What do these special events have in common: a wedding reception, a 5K charity run, the Macy's Thanksgiving Day parade, and a company picnic? All are special events, though they are very different. And, all are planned by someone who must understand the goals, the needs, and the desires of the client they are serving. The event professional has a responsibility to the client to do everything in his/her power to reach these goals, while working within the parameters of the given location, city, or facility.

How does the event professional begin to truly understand the vision of his/her client? And how does the client begin to trust the efforts of the event professional? Special events management begins and evolves by developing a very important relationship between the client and the event professional. The event professional must listen to the clients, hear their words, and see their vision. The event professional should have the capability to make that vision into a reality for the clients.

An event professional and a client must have clear lines of communication between them. And, as they talk and listen to each other, a viable plan can unfold. The event professional must always understand that the success of any event must begin with a relationship. Listen to the client, do what you say you will do, tend to the little things, and keep lines of communication open.

THE PRESIDENTIAL INAUGURATION DAY PARADE

While the tradition of the Inaugural parade dates back to the Inauguration of George Washington, the first organized parade unfolded at the Inauguration of James Madison in 1809. Here, Madison was escorted to the Capitol by a troop of cavalry. After taking his oath of office, Madison then watched the parade of militia. In 1841, William Henry Harrison's Inauguration introduced floats to the parade. In addition, military bands, political groups, and college groups became parade participants.

As history progressed, African Americans joined Abraham Lincoln's Inaugural parade for the first time, increasing even further the number of participating groups in the parade. In 1873, President Grant reordered the events of the Inaugural Day to make the parade *after* the Inaugural Ceremony, rather than *before*. This tradition continues today.

Reviewing stands were built in 1881 for the Inauguration of President James Garfield. To combat the cold and sometimes harsh weather conditions, the grandstands became enclosed. Reviewing stands were also built for visitors.

Women became participants of the parade in 1917, and then, in 1921, President Warren Harding became the first president to ride in an automobile. This set a precedent until 1977, when President Jimmy Carter chose to walk in the parade with his wife and daughter, from the Capitol to the White House. The first televised Inaugural Parade was held in 1949 for President Harry S. Truman.

The largest parade occurred in 1953 at the Inaugural Parade of President Dwight D. Eisenhower. The parade included 73 bands, 69 floats, horses, elephants, military troops, and civilian and military vehicles. The parade lasted for over four-and-a-half hours.

The size and sophistication of the parade has developed tremendously over the last 200 years, and the Inaugural Parade has evolved into a nationally lauded special event. At the 2009 Inauguration Parade, President Barack Obama hosted 15,000 participants, including 2,000 military personnel. Forty-six bands were chosen to participate of the 1,000 that applied. Today, millions of Americans can view the parade, whether via television, Internet access, or in person. This parade has truly become a tradition of celebration for all Americans.

Today, the Armed Forces Inaugural Committee is responsible for the organization of the parade, and the Presidential Inaugural Committee is responsible for selecting all the participants of the parade.

Fireworks make an event even more special.
Elen_studio/Shutterstock

No matter what the profile of the event, each and every special event is special to someone, or to many. It becomes a great challenge to meet (and exceed) the expectations of your client, and this is one of the key roles of the event professional.

One very successful event, which draws more than 100,000 visitors to Central Pennsylvania in the summer, is the Central Pennsylvania Festival of the Arts. This festival, with its nationally recognized Sidewalk Sale and Exhibition; gallery exhibition; and music, dance, and theatrical performances in a variety of traditional and non-traditional venues, brings people to downtown State College and the University Park campus of Penn State to celebrate the arts. The festival was founded in 1967, and was recently ranked first on the list of 100 Best Fine Arts and Design Shows in America by Sunshine Artist magazine.

Examples of Special Events

A film festival can be a dream come true for moviegoers as they seek out famous actors who might be walking right next to them, as they do on the streets of Park City, Utah, during the Sundance Film Festival. Founded in 1981, the festival has grown to become internationally recognized, attracting tens of thousands of visitors each year to this quaint little town to view over 3,000 film submissions.

- Civic Events
  - Centennials
  - Founders' Day
- Mega-Events
  - Olympics
  - America's Cup
  - United Nations Assembly
  - World Expos
- Festivals and Fairs
  - Marketplace of ancient days
  - Community Event
  - Fair = not for profit
  - Festival = for profit
- Expositions
  - Where suppliers meet buyers
  - Education
  - Entertainment
- Sporting Events
  - Super Bowl
  - World Series
  - Masters Golf Tournament
  - FIFA World Cup
- Social life-cycle events
  - Weddings
  - Anniversaries
- Birthdays
- Reunions
- Bar/Bat Mitzvahs
- Meetings and Conventions
  - Political National Convention
  - National Restaurant Association convention in Chicago
  - PCMA annual conference
- Retail Events
  - Long-range promotional event
  - Store opening
- New product launches
  - X-box
  - Apple
- Religious Events
  - Papal Inauguration
  - The Hajj (Mecca)
  - Easter
  - Kwanzaa
- Corporate Events
  - Holiday parties
  - Annual dinner
  - Company picnics
  - Conferences/meetings

FIGURE 8-1
Framework for Special Events.

Special events like this came from a historical tradition that ultimately grew to attract thousands of visitors to some very remote areas. Continuing to attract visitors requires planning and planning tools, such as an understanding of community infrastructure, merchandising and promoting the event, developing sponsorships, and working with the media. This is the art and science of special events management.

A special event is a celebration of something—that is what makes it special. Special events can include those listed in Figure 8-1.

Planning Tools for Special Events

Special events management, like any other form of managing, requires planning tools. The first of these tools is a vision statement of your event. This vision statement should clearly identify the who, what, when, where, and why of the event. As the event begins to unfold, it is important to keep those involved focused on the vision. This can be accomplished by continually monitoring, evaluating, and, where possible, measuring the progress toward the outlined goals of the event (see Chapter 12 on Planning and Producing MEEC Events).

The "who" of planning an event are those people or organizations that would like to host and organize it. In the case of the St. Patrick's Day Parade in Chicago, Illinois, it is the city that hosts and coordinates the marchers, the floats, and the bands. The "what" was a parade demonstrating Irish pride and local tradition. The "where" of the Parade was downtown Chicago, with floats and bands marching down Michigan Avenue. The answer to the big question of "why" is tradition, pride, fun, and tourism. This, in turn, promotes the city and brings revenues to local businesses. When the city decided to serve as the host of this event, it needed to incorporate the tools of special event management.

Some of the management tools that are used in staging events are as follows:

- Flow charts and graphs for scheduling. Look at any program for a meeting/event; there are start and end times, times for coffee breaks, a time for lunch, and a time that the

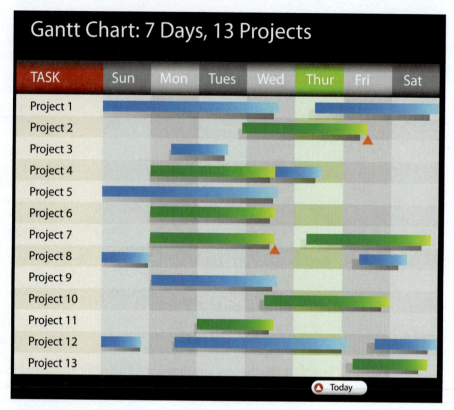

Example of a generic Gannt Chart
John T Takai/ Shutterstock

meeting resumes and ends. The flow chart can be romantic, like a wedding ceremony **agenda**. It can show the order or sequence of floats for a parade, the program for a talent show, or the agenda for a weeklong international conference. A flowchart scheduling an event's activities helps guide attendees and guests, and makes the execution of the event flow smoothly. **Gantt Charts** are often used for many of these tasks.

- Clearly defined set up and breakdown **schedules**. These provide the event manager with an opportunity to determine tasks that may have been overlooked in the initial planning process.

- Policy statements developed to guide in the decision-making process. Policy statements provide a clear understanding of commitments and what is expected to fulfill them. Some of the commitments to be considered are human resources, sponsors, security, ticketing, volunteers, and paid personnel.

Understanding Community Infrastructure

Another key ingredient for planning a successful event is an understanding of the infrastructure of the community where the event is to take place. This infrastructure might include the CEO of the company, politicians, prominent business leaders of the community, civic and community groups, the media, and other community leaders. Without a "buy-in" from city leadership, a community is less inclined to be supportive. The role of business leaders in the community could be to provide sponsorships, donations, staff, or a possible workplace for the coordination of the event. Many times, community groups serve as volunteer workers for the event, and are also an extension of the promotions for it.

Early on, it must be recognized whether a community or a company is truly committed to hosting any type of special event that will call on its support. This support not only includes financial commitment, but also the required physical and emotional commitment it will take to manage an event from start to finish. For a promoter or special events management company to maintain a positive reputation, there needs to be a solid infrastructure in place.

Special Event Marketing Considerations

Merchandising and Promoting the Special Event

Merchandising and promoting a special event is another planning tool for attracting attendance and increasing the overall profitability for an event. Just because a community decides to host a craft fair or street festival does not mean that there will be the attendance necessary to meet vendors' and visitors' needs. Profit for the vendor and a memorable experience for the attendee are two main objectives for a special event. The special event requires all the promotional venues that an event management company or civic group can afford.

Understanding and utilizing the **promotional mix model** is pivotal in order to meet the goals of the event marketing plan. The role of promotion in special events management is the coordination of all the seller's efforts to set up channels of information and persuasion to sell or promote the event. Traditionally, the promotional mix has included four elements: advertising, sales promotion, publicity and/or public relations, and personal selling. However, this author views direct marketing and interactive media as additional elements of the promotional mix. The latter includes social media such as LinkedIn, Facebook, Twitter, and so on. Modern-day event marketers use many means to communicate with their target markets. Each element of the promotional mix is viewed as an integrated marketing communications tool. Each of these elements of the model has a distinctive role in attracting an attendee to the special event. Each takes on a variety of forms, and each has certain advantages.

Promotional Mix

Advertising is defined as any paid form of non-personal communication about the event. The non-personal component means advertising that involves mass media (e.g., TV, radio, magazines, mobile phones, websites, and newspapers). Advertising is the best known and most widely discussed form of promotion because it is the most persuasive, especially if the event (e.g., a home and garden show) is targeted toward mass consumers. It can be used to create brand images or symbolic appeals for the brand, and generate immediate responses from prospective attendees.

There are many elements of the promotional mix for special events. These include:

Direct marketing is a form of advertising that communicates directly with the target customer with the intent of generating a response. It is much more than direct mail or catalogs. It involves a variety of activities, including database management, direct selling, telemarketing, direct-response ads, the Internet, and various broadcast and print media. The Internet has also fueled the growth of direct marketing. One of the advantages of email marketing is the ability to measure response rates.

Engagement marketing, or sometimes called experiential marketing, is a strategy that engages and invites consumers to be a part of a brand experience. This creates a face-to-face opportunity for the event designer. You can also co-brand as a means for increasing response. One of the more successful campaigns was Zappos "Google Cupcake Ambush" where Zappos gave away free pairs of shoes to customers who received a cupcake by trying Google's new photo app.

Interactive or Internet marketing also allows for a back-and-forth flow of information. Users can participate in and modify the form and content of the information they receive in real time. Unlike traditional forms of marketing, such as advertising, which are one-way forms of communication, this type of media allows users to perform a variety of functions. It enables users to receive and alter information and images, make inquiries, respond to questions, and make purchases. Many event attendees will go to a website to garner information about a special event, such as a concert, and purchase their tickets directly online. For a special event, such as the Aspen Music Festival, attendees can go to the festival's official website, view the schedule, learn about the event and the surrounding area, purchase tickets, and request additional information—all forms of direct marketing. In addition to the Internet, other forms of interactive media include jump drives, cloud storage, kiosks, and interactive television.

Sales promotion   is generally defined as those marketing activities that use incentives or discounts to increase sales or attendance. A popular form of sales promotion is the coupon. Many events will use a two-for-one attendance coupon to stimulate attendance on slower days. In addition, merchandise is often offered when purchasing several tickets at once.

Publicity and public relations   is divided into two components. Publicity is the component that is not directly paid for or has an identified sponsor. When an event planner gets the media to cover or run a favorable story on a special event, it affects an attendee's awareness, knowledge, and opinions. Publicity is considered a credible form of promotion, but it is not always under the control of the organization or host of the event. In the case of South by Southwest (SXSW), prior to the event, the organizers send out press releases highlighting the performers or acts that are participating in the event. During the event, reporters and camera crews cover the action on a daily basis. If those reporting the event have a positive experience, it will favorably affect the public's perception of the event. Unfortunately, the reverse is also true; the event professionals have little control.

Social Media   has exploded as a preferred strategy for promotional initiatives. Social Media reaches the masses with minimal expense and relative ease of effort. This is also known as viral marketing. While there are many vehicles of social media, some of the more commonly used mediums include Facebook, blogging, LinkedIn, Pinterest, Google+, and Twitter. Each of these mediums allows a message to be sent simultaneously to many people, projecting a controlled and positive message to the reader. In addition, the message that is sent is delivered immediately to the reader. (For more information, see Chapter 11, Technology.)

There are a variety of special events that take place to promote a destination or an occasion. One example is the SXSW event held in March each year in Austin, Texas. This nine-day event is the premier gathering of music, film, and interactive professionals.

The purpose of public relations is to systematically plan and distribute information to attempt to control or manage the image and/or publicity of an event by building beneficial relationships with stakeholders and consumers. It has a broader objective than publicity because its purpose is to establish a positive image of the special event. Public relations and publicity are favored by festival and event directors because they reach the audience they are attempting to attract. Public relations can be the reason for hosting the special event altogether. Tobacco companies have used special events like a NASCAR race or tennis tournament to create a more positive image with consumers.

Personal selling is the final element of the promotional mix model, and it is a form of person-to-person communication in which a seller attempts to assist and/or persuade prospective event attendees. Typically, group tour sales are one of the best prospects for personal selling of a special event. There are several touring companies that purchase large groups of tickets for special events. Unlike advertising, personal selling involves direct contact between the buyer and seller of the event, usually through face-to-face sales. Personal selling is by far the most expensive form of promotional activity when considered in terms of the number of consumers reached. Some examples of events that group tours attend may include: the Indianapolis 500, the Kentucky Derby, or the Jazz

Fest in New Orleans. Group tour organizers will meet face-to-face with event professionals or talk via the telephone to purchase tickets for an event.

BRANDING A DESTINATION

South by Southwest

South by Southwest (SXSW) is a group of festivals and conferences that take place every spring in Austin, Texas, and covers music, film, and interactive technologies. It began small in 1987 but has grown every year since its inception. Currently, it is the largest music festival of its kind in the world, boasting over 2,200 bands on 113 stages. The film festival is focused on attracting new directors, while the interactive portion is focused on emerging technology. SXSW has launched a number of new products during the event, but two of the more notable are Twitter and Foursquare. John Mayer launched his career by performing at SXSW. The film festival has launched numerous films over the years including The Hurt Locker, which went on to win the Academy Award for Best Picture in 2010.

While the focus of the event has been to promote the three industries, it has also become a primary source of bringing tourism to Austin. It continues to be the single most profitable event for the City of Austin's hospitality industry. In 2016, the event created the following impact to the local economy:

- 87,971 registrations
- 14,415 individual hotel registrations totaling over 59,000 room nights
- 140,000 conference and festival participants
- A direct economic impact of $220.1 million (directly related to the local economy)
- An indirect impact of $57.6 million (increases in sales, income, and jobs associated with companies that benefit from SXSW expenditures)
- Induced impacts of $47.6 million (spending by individuals as a result of increased earnings as a result of the conference)
- Total economic impact $325 million

Sponsorships for Special Events

Sponsorships help to ensure profitable success for an event. They are an innovative way for event organizers to help underwrite and defray costs. Sponsorships should be considered more than just a charitable endeavor for a company—they can be a strong marketing tool.

Event sponsors provide funds or in-kind contributions, and receive consideration in the form of logo usage and identification with the event. Recent trends of sponsorships show rapid growth. Sponsorship can take many forms. A large corporation, for instance, may have the means to provide financial sponsorship for an event. Mid-size and smaller organizations, however, may need to be more creative in their sponsorship methods. A smaller organization may, for example, provide product, rather than a financial contribution. Therefore, you may not see their banner hanging at the event, but you will have their product in your hand.

Many types of special events require sponsorship to be successful. Sporting events have long been the leader in securing sponsorships for teams and athletes. However, their market share has dropped, because companies have begun to distribute sponsorship dollars to other events, such as city festivals and the arts. This shift in sponsorships from sports events to that of festivals and the arts over the past decade has emerged because companies are cognizant that a sponsorship can be an effective tool for overall company marketing plans. Sponsors are beginning to recognize that festivals are now as attractive as sports at generating a return on investment (ROI).

THE GREAT GARLIC COOK-OFF

Gilroy, California

The Annual Gilroy Garlic Festival is held in the Garlic Capital of the World, Gilroy, California, at Christmas Hill Park during the last full weekend of July.

This festival's origin lies in the pride of one man, Rudy Melone. Melone felt that Gilroy should celebrate its superior production of the "stinking rose," otherwise known as garlic. He then began what has been referred to as the preeminent food festival in America.

In December of each year, the Gilroy Garlic Festival begins its request for original garlic recipes. Citizens of Canada and the United States are asked to participate. Recipes are then submitted by amateur chefs, and eight are chosen to participate in the festival cook-off. Winners are awarded monetary prizes for their well-done work.

Another tradition practiced by the Gilroy Garlic Festival is the nomination of a "Miss Gilroy Garlic Festival Queen." Contestants are judged on a personal interview, talent, a garlic speech, and evening gown competition. The queen represents Gilroy at various festivities before and during the festival.

Over the last thirty-five years, the Gilroy Garlic Festival has attracted over four million attendees and raised over ten million for local nonprofit organizations. Over 4,000 volunteers are recruited to work the event and participate in activities like picking up trash, parking cars, and serving lemonade. The Gilroy Garlic Festival is not only known for its garlic pride and knowledge, but also for its ability to bring the community of Gilroy together. Its website states, "Where else can one feast on food laced with over two tons of fresh garlic, enjoy three stages of musical entertainment, shop in arts and crafts, view the great garlic cook-off and other celebrity cooking demonstrations, spend time in the children's area, visit interactive displays set up by many of our sponsors, soak up some glorious sunshine, and mingle with a fun bunch of garlic-loving people?"

There are five compelling reasons why company sponsorships are an important option to consider:

1. Economic changes (both upturns and downturns)
2. Ability to target market segments
3. Ability to measure results
4. Fragmentation of the media
5. Growth of diverse population segments

Changes in the economic climate of the country affect the goals, spending, and expectations of sponsoring organizations. In times of economic health, companies (both large and small) may be willing and able to more freely spend their promotional dollars on sponsorship. In economic downturns, however, organizations are likely to feel the necessity to account for the return they are receiving on their promotional spending. In other words, the sponsorship is seen as an investment, and the organization would like to know if, in fact, they are receiving a return on their investment. In either economic climate, sponsorships promote intangible benefits of company visibility and overall goodwill.

When looking for sponsorships for a special event, organizers must determine if the event fits the company. Event professionals must always examine the company's goal, and be sure to research the competition. Special event organizers should aid the sponsors with promotional ideas that will help them meet their goals. Promoters of an event need to ensure that sponsors get their money's worth. Remember that sponsors have internal and external audiences to whom they are appealing.

Cross-promotional opportunities allow the sponsor to achieve the greatest visibility possible by capitalizing on more than one promotional opportunity within one event. For example, if PepsiCo sponsored an event, then that company would likely gain notable visibility through banners, logos, and so on. However, to further capitalize on this sponsorship, PepsiCo might further request that only Pepsi products be sold at the event. They are gaining visibility through the product that is being served at the event, and they may likely be earning revenue on the product that they are serving. This sponsorship would, therefore, serve as a triple benefit to the corporation. The internal audience of a corporation is its employees, and they must also be sold on the sponsorship of the event. A company needs to provide opportunities for employee involvement. If the special event is a charitable marathon, employees may be asked to actually participate in the marathon or raise funds for the charitable cause. Those employees who participate may be featured in promotional material or press releases.

NEW YORK CITY MARATHON

Sponsorship

The New York City Marathon boasts over 50,000 runners with more than two million spectators, and is one of the largest live sporting events in the world, being broadcast to over 330 million viewers in more than 154 territories. Television coverage includes a live five-hour telecast on ABC Channel 7 in New York, a two-hour national telecast on ESPN, and various international live and highlight shows.

New York Road Runners and the New York City Marathon are fortunate to have the support and commitment of sponsors and strategic partners. Their continued support makes the New York City Marathon a world-class event year after year.

Sponsors

Title Sponsor:

    Tata Consultancy Services (TCS)

Additional Sponsors

Airbnb

United Airlines

New Balance

fitbit

The Rudin Family

Foot Locker

Poland Spring

PowerBar

Gatorade

Hospital for Special Surgery

Tiffany & Co.

UPS

Selling to the external audience of the corporation (the consumer) is done in a variety of ways. First, the company might feature its logo on the event's products. The company can promote its affiliation with the special event by providing its logo for outdoor banners and specialty advertising items, such as T-shirts, caps, or sunglasses. The types of specialty products are limitless, and are excellent venues for advertising. The sponsoring company may wish to appoint an employee spokesperson to handle radio or television interviews.

Working with the Media for an Event

Generating media coverage for a special event is one of the most effective methods for attracting attendance. Ideally, an event organizer wants to garner free television, radio, and print coverage. To attract the media, a promoter must understand what makes for good coverage and what does not.

When a camera crew is sent to film an event by TV station assignment editors, they will look for a story that can be easily illustrated with visuals captured by a camera. They also look for a vignette that can entertain viewers in thirty seconds or less. If an event organizer wants television or radio stations to cover the event, he or she needs to call it to their attention with a press release or press conference. There are no guarantees that the station or the newspaper will air the footage or print the story; however, the chances are better if a camera crew shoots footage or a reporter does an interview. Remember, special events provide ideal fodder for the evening news. This can be an interview with a celebrity who will be attending the event or an advance look at an art exhibit.

Event organizers try to present the unusual to the media. In 2007, Kentucky Fried Chicken decided to unveil a redesign of the company logo for the first time in over ten years. The logo revision included bolder colors and changing the founder Col. Harland Sanders from his customary white suit and black bow tie into a red apron against a matching red background. To unveil the logo redesign, the company decided to create an 87,000-square-foot version that could be seen from space. The logo for this event was created out of 65,000 one-foot tiles that were set up in the Las Vegas desert. The new logo was then filmed by the Google satellite and uploaded to YouTube and Google Maps, resulting in over 600,000 views.

KFC logo created in the Las Vegas desert.
NASA Image Collection/Alamy Stock Photo

This also resulted in the story being carried on national news broadcasts, and resulted in a multitude of media coverage over the next several weeks. Promoters of special events have long recognized what TV and radio coverage can do for an event.

Here are some helpful hints for attracting television and radio coverage:

- Early in the day is considered the best time to attract cameras and reporters. Remember, a crew must come out, film, get back to the studio, edit the film, and have the segment ready for the 5 or 6 PM newscast that night.

- The best day of the week to attract news crews is Friday. This is because it is usually a quiet news day. Saturday and Sunday have even fewer distractions, but most stations do not have enough news crews working the weekend who can cover an event.

- Giving advance notice for a special event is very helpful to assignment editors. Usually about three days notice, with an explanation of the event via a press release and telephone follow-up, is very helpful in securing media coverage. If an interview is involved, a seven-day notice is a good time allotment for coverage.

Understanding the Target Market for Your Special Event

Bringing special events to a community has not changed much over the years; however, consumers have changed. They are much more selective and sophisticated about the events they will attend. Since the cost of attending events has risen, consumers are much more discerning about how they spend their entertainment dollars. This creates a demand for quality for any special event.

Understanding your target market is one of the most important components for the overall success of the event. It is critical for the event marketer and event professional to know the participant audience. Age, gender, religion, ethnicity—all must be understood. Depending on the type of event, the event professional must understand participant's restrictions (e.g., religious, or dietary) and participant's needs. The event must be based on the overall needs and desires of the target market.

The most valuable outcome a special event can generate for a community is positive word of mouth. To create this positive awareness, an organizer recognizes that the event cannot appeal to all markets. A promoter will determine the target market for the community's event.

Target marketing is defined as clearly identifying who wants to attend a certain type of event. For example, a Justin Bieber concert has been determined to appeal to a young female audience between the ages of twelve and sixteen. To stage a profitable concert, promoters will direct their advertising dollars to that particular targeted audience. Subsequently, all promotional items will also be geared toward that age group.

A VERY SPECIAL WEDDING

A couple from Texas wanted to be sure that their wedding was special, so they decided to have it in New Orleans. They were enamored with the charm of the city: moss-draped oak trees, antebellum homes, and horse-drawn carriages. They decided to invite 100 people and contacted a local destination management company (DMC) to make the arrangements. Their specification was that the DMC arrange a rehearsal dinner for 12 people and a reception for 100. Such costs as transportation to New Orleans, hotel accommodations, and the church were not part of the bid. Their stated budget for this wedding reception and dinner was $300,000. That's right, over a quarter of a million dollars, or $3,000 per guest! When the event professional heard this, her reaction was twofold: (1) how could she possibly put together this event and spend that much money, and (2) if that was their proposed budget, she would try to upsell them.

The rehearsal dinner was held in a private dining room at the famous Arnaud's restaurant in the French Quarter. The real money was spent on the reception. They rented the art deco Saenger Theater for the evening, but there was a problem. Like most theaters, the floor sloped toward the stage. So, they removed all the seats and built a new floor that was level, not sloped. The interior of the theater was so beautiful that it needed little decoration. The New Orleans Police Department was contracted to close the street between the church and theater to cars so that the period ambiance would not be disturbed for the couple and their guests while being transported in their horse-drawn carriages. When the couple and their guests entered for the evening, they were greeted by models in period costume and served mint juleps while a gospel group sang. A blues band followed, and the night was topped off by not one, but two, sets by Jennifer Lopez who owns a home in New Orleans. The affair was catered by Emeril Lagasse and only included heavy hors d'oeuvres, not even a sit-down dinner. The ultimate cost for this event was almost $350,000 and the couple was delighted.

The planner was Nanci Easterling of Food Art, Inc.

Most communities know that a special event will have a positive economic impact on the community and the region. This has created competition to attract events. A city will commonly use inducements to lure a special event to the community. These inducements may include free entertainment space, security, parking, and even a key to the city for the celebrity providing the entertainment. Citywide is a commonly used term for these large events or conventions that impact the entire city. Citywides are key to urban economics. When a large event or convention is hosted in a particular city, the economic effects are positive. Hotel rooms may completely sell out across the city, eateries are busy, and retail and cultural attractions may flourish due to the citywide.

A successful event has two vital components. One is that the community is supportive of bringing the event to the city, and the other is that the event meets the consumers' needs. For example, every year on Labor Day weekend, New Orleans is host to a special event called Southern Decadence. This three-day event, attended by over 150,000 LGBT people, generates over $150 million for the city.

Preparing for the Special Event

Basic operations for staging an event need to be established and include the following.

1. Secure a venue.
2. Obtain **permits:**
   a. Parade permits
   b. Liquor permits
   c. Sanitation permits
   d. Sales permits or licenses
   e. Fire safety permits

3. Involve **government agencies** where necessary (e.g., if using city recreation facilities, work with the department of parks and recreation).

4. Involve the health department if there will be food and beverage at the event.

5. Meet all relevant parties in person so that any misconceptions are cleared up early.

6. Secure all vendors and suppliers for the event.

7. Recognize the complexities of dealing with the public sector. Sometimes public agencies have a difficult time making decisions.

8. Recognize the logistics that a community must contend with for certain types of special events, such as street closures for a marathon.

9. Set up a security plan, which may include the security supplied by the venue and professional law enforcement. (Pay attention as to which security organization takes precedence.)

10. Secure liability insurance (the most vulnerable areas are those liabilities attached to liquor and liquor laws).

11. Determine ticket prices if the special event involves ticketing.

12. Determine ticket sale distribution if the special event involves ticketing.

The type of special event being held will determine the degree of preparedness needed. The larger the event, the more involved the checklist. Preparedness should produce a profitable and well-managed event.

Software and Tools for Special Events

Event planners are faced with a wide variety of tasks to complete for each event and there is a plethora of tools available to assist with these tasks. While there are too many to include here, it is important to identify the types of tools you need. Are you looking for project management help or something for attendee engagement?

One of the most common management tools is Google Drive. Planners can use the features for managing documents, folders, and spreadsheets, and it is also a great tool for collaboration. While this is one option, there are a number of tools to consider. If you are looking for an overall event management software, Whova makes software that handles everything from registration, on-site check-in, attendee polling, and name badge creation, and it also has an event app.

If you typically use an Excel spreadsheet for managing tasks, you might want to consider Smartsheet. This is a tool that also allows live collaboration and communication. The program has a very easy to use dashboard, although there is a short learning curve for new users.

Basecamp is another good management software. Although not as new as some of the others it is still a very solid performer in the project management space.

If you and your event team have mastered project management but lack good communication you might want to consider a program like Slack. This tool allows users to share and discuss ideas from anywhere, and is a great way to keep your team informed.

Food and beverage events require some separate tools to manage these types of events. Caterease is one of the industry leaders in this space. Ticketing is another area that planners are commonly looking for help. TicketSpice is one of the most powerful ticketing solutions available.

Floor plan design programs are also an important tool to the special event planner. AllSeated makes a program that allows the user to design floor plans, manage guest lists, and create visual seating charts.

Finally, audience engagement is the latest area that event planners are attempting to influence. EventMobi is one of the leaders in this market. They have a customizable app, built-in audience response tracking, and gamification, registration, and reporting tools. While we have only touched on a small portion of the range of products available to the planner, it is clear that help is available for any task you might have when producing a special event.

GETTING A PERMIT

San Diego, California's event permitting process is fairly typical for most moderate-sized cities. The city publishes a guide to indicate to the event organizers what permits are necessary for their event. The city's website has a planning guide and access to all the forms that might be required for any event.

Events or organized activities for 75 or more people that involve street closures, or include event components, such as the use of alcohol, on-site cooking, food sales, or large-scale temporary structures, requiring the coordination of many city departments or other agencies, are typically reviewed through the Citywide Special Event Permit Process. Examples include festivals, parades, runs/walks, farmer's markets, and other planned group activities.

For an application to be considered complete, applicants must submit the following required minimum information—in sufficient enough detail for the material to be understood and assessed—in the sections of the Citywide Special Event Permit Application that follow:

Host Organization Section (Complete)

Event Summary Section (Complete)

Event Infrastructure Section (All aspects that relate to the specific event)

Operational Plan Section (All aspects that relate to the specific event)

Site Plan/Route Map Section (Complete)

Community Outreach Section (Complete)

Insurance Section (Complete including all required certificates of insurance and endorsements)

Signature Section (Complete)

Any required documentation relevant to the permit application processes and requirements set forth in the Special Events Planning Guide and Citywide Special Event Permit Application (Complete)

Applicants are responsible for obtaining all permits, authorizations, and/or exemptions required by other agencies with jurisdiction for any element of the event (e.g., Alcohol Beverage Control Permits, Health Permits, California Coast Guard, California Coastal Commission approval, etc.).

https://www.sandiego.gov/sites/default/files/legacy/specialevents/pdf/planningguide.pdf

The Special Event Budget

For any event to be considered a success, it must also be considered profitable. Profitability requires understanding the concepts of budgeting and financing an event. (See Chapter 13: Planning MEEC Gatherings for more information.) The basic items that make up the costs for a special event include the categories that follow.

Rental Costs

Depending on the type of event, renting a facility, such as a convention center or ground space to put up a tent, requires payment of a daily rental charge. Convention centers usually sell the space based on a certain dollar amount per square footage used. Most facilities charge for space even on the move-in and move-out days. Multiday events can usually negotiate a discount.

There are, of course, variations to the rental cost of an event space. If, for example, an association is holding a conference in a hotel, the event space may be free of charge or offered at a reduced rate if a certain number of hotel rooms are booked by the participating group. Furthermore, if the group requires food and beverage, often the rental space is provided at a reduced rate or complimentary with the establishment of a **food and beverage minimum**.

Security Costs

Most convention centers, rental halls, and hotels provide limited security. This could mean that a guard is stationed at the front and rear entrances of the venue. Depending on the type of event, such as a rock concert performed by a band that has raucous fans, more security may be required. European Soccer (Football) matches require even more security. Actual costs will depend on the city and the amount of security needed.

Production Costs

These are the costs associated with staging an event. The costs vary depending on the type of special event. For example, if the special event is a large home and garden show, there are costs associated with the set up of the trade show booths. As with many home and garden shows, exhibitors bring in elaborate garden landscapes that are very time consuming and labor intensive to set up and breakdown. Labor costs for decorators need to be calculated to estimate the production costs based on the type and size of the trade show booth. There are also electrical and water fees needed for a home and garden show, and these costs must be included in the production costs. Other production costs include signage or banners for each booth, and pipe and drape fees.

Labor Costs

The city where the special event is being held will affect the labor costs involved in the set up and breakdown of the event. Some cities are unionized, and this can add higher costs to an event because of the higher wages. Holding an event in very strict union cities means that the organizer of the event must leave more of the handling to the union crew. In some cities, the union allows the exhibitor to wheel his or her own cart with brochures and merchandise. In other cities, exhibitors cannot carry anything other than their own briefcases.

When selecting a city for an event, the role of unions has been an important influence. Most special event organizers will pass the higher costs on to the exhibitor or will increase ticket prices.

Marketing Costs

The costs associated with attracting attendees can make up a large portion of the budget. Here, the event organizer examines the best means of reaching the target market. Trying to reach a mass audience may mean running a series of television commercials, which can be very expensive. Most event organizers use a combination of promotions to attract the attendee. There will be elements of advertising, direct marketing, publicity, public relations, sales promotion, interactive or Internet marketing, and personal selling. All of these need to be budgeted.

Talent Costs

Virtually all special events use some type of talent or performers. They may include keynote speakers, bands or orchestras, sports teams, vocalists, animals, and so on. While the organizer may have grandiose thoughts about the quality of the talent used, price must be considered and matched to the special event budget—a high school class reunion probably cannot afford to have Jennifer Lopez or Taylor Swift perform.

Before an event, it is essential that an event professional do a projection of all costs and revenue. These projections are essential to whether a community will host another event. Repeat events are much easier to promote, especially when the organizers have made a profit. Before and during the event, it is critical that billing updates are completed and presented to the client on a regular (sometimes daily) basis. Any discrepancies or new costs should be handled at the point they occur. There should be no cost surprises at the end of an event.

Breakdown of the Special Event

Special events have another thing in common: They all come to an end! Taking down or **breaking down** the event usually involves many steps. Once the attendees have gone, there are a variety of closing tasks that an organizer must complete.

First, the parking staff should expedite the flow of traffic away from the event. In some cases, community police can assist in traffic control.

A debriefing of staff should take place to determine what did or did not happen at the event. There may be issues pending that will need documentation. It is always best to have written reports to refer to for next year's event. Consider having the following sources add information to the report:

- *Participants:* Interview some of the participants from the event. A customer's perception and expectation is an invaluable insight.
- *Media and the Press:* Ask why it was or was not a press-worthy gathering.
- *Staff and Management:* Get a variety of staff and other management involved in the event to give feedback.
- *Vendors:* They also have a very unique perspective on how the event could be improved. Exhibitors and vendors *must* complete a survey. Because of their great perspective, exhibitors can provide some outstanding and constructive feedback for planning the next event.

The following should also be included in a final report on the event:

- Finalize the income and expense statement. Did the event break even, make a profit, or experience a loss?
- Finalize all contracts from the event. Fortunately, almost everything involved with putting together the event will have written documentation. Compare final billing with actual agreements for any discrepancies.
- Send the media a final press release on the overall success of the event. Interviews with the press could be arranged. This could be especially newsworthy if the event generated significant revenues for the community.
- Provide a written thank you for those volunteers who were involved with the event in any way. A celebration of some sort with the volunteers may be in order, especially if the event was financially and socially successful.

Once the elements of breakdown have taken place, the organizers can examine the important lessons of staging the event. What would they do or not do next year?

Trends and Best Practices in Special Events

Less is the new more. Clients are seeking the simple with a "flare."

- Clients want to appear to be responsible in their spending. Excessive overspending is no longer the desirable trend.
- "Stylish minimalism" refers to the idea that clients still want style, flare, and innovation in the overall event but choose to uphold a conservative budgetary perception.
- Quality is paramount, but at a cost that the client sees as a value.
- Frivolous events are seen as wasteful; events should have a purpose.
- Many events are now targeted toward service or charitable causes. This provides purpose to an event. Events may be targeted toward medical concerns (e.g., cancer research, heart disease, autism awareness, etc.) or toward relief on a national or international level (Haiti Relief, Hurricane Irma Relief, etc.).
- Clients are looking for an entire package—an experience. The event planner is truly planning an experience, often referred to as experience management. Some event planners believe that a good event should captivate the audience and offer change every half hour.
- Going environmentally green: event professionals are urged to consider green solutions. Earthy, environmentally friendly efforts are becoming the expectation. Interestingly, because of the perceived lack of sophistication, eco-friendly efforts are more likely to be

incorporated into an event, rather than a primary means of service. For example, recycled coffee cups may be offered at a coffee station, along with china cups and saucers.

- Technology is key in promotional efforts. More Internet promotions are desired, as event managers are able to quantify the number of hits that they receive on their promotional initiative.

- Technology will also impact the meeting space. Google Glass has the opportunity to create a more personal, staged, and shared attendee experience.

- Gamification—adding games to the meeting/event mix—can create a healthy competition and measurable ROI for your events.

- Every client has his/her own unique set of needs and wants. Every client wants the undivided attention of the event professional; his/her needs must be recognized throughout the entire planning and execution of the event.

- Quality, cost, and relationships are three components that must be in balance for every special event.

- Face-to-face events are here to stay.

Summary

Creating a memorable event requires that an organizer meet and exceed an attendee's expectations. Recognizing that the special event could be for a meeting or convention, a parade, a festival, a fair, or an exhibit requires understanding the objectives of the event. Having the planning tools in place is the keystone for success in managing the gathering. Special events management works with and understands the community infrastructures to help support the event.

It can be costly if an event professional does not decide which part of the promotional mix model for an event will be used in advance. The promotional mix model includes advertising, direct marketing, interactive or Internet marketing, sales promotion, publicity, public relations, and personal selling. Helping to defray costs by seeking sponsorships for a special event is another way to successfully market an event, and it is also an important marketing tool for corporation sponsors. Generating and working with the local and/or national media is the most effective way for attracting attendance. An organizer also needs to understand what makes for good media coverage, and whether it is for print or broadcast. The target market for a special event must always be considered in the objectives, promotions, and continuation of an event.

The basic operations and/or logistics for the event follow planning and promoting. A checklist of the items that need to be handled or considered is a must for any event professional. Event professionals should also create checklists that will help develop the overall special event budget. This budget requires regular reviews of the statement of revenues and expenditures. The breakdown is the final step and includes another checklist for the closure of the event. Always remember your volunteers—without them, the event would not take place!

CASE STUDY

Bad Timing at the Banquet

Rob Clifford is the director of food and beverage at the Homey Hotel in New York, New York, which has a ten-room, 6,000 square foot banquet/meeting facility.

Sue Chase is an event planner in New York City who has been planning a very important employee recognition/awards dinner banquet for a large, local company in the city. She has arranged to have the dinner at the Homey Hotel. The dinner will be for 450 people, served buffet style with three separate buffets, and the total for the event has come to approximately $10,000.

The schedule for the evening is supposed to go as follows:

5:30 PM—Arrival of Guests/Cash Bar Opens

6:00 PM—Welcome speech given by the president of the company

(Guests mingle after welcome speech, before dinner)

7:00 PM—Dinner (Buffet is to be opened)

8:30 PM—Awards are given

10:00 PM—Adjourn

Rob has spoken to Sue about the schedule for the night, and she has told him that they still plan on eating, and want the food ready at 7 PM.

During the welcome speech, the president of the company welcomed his employees, recognized the board of directors, and briefly talked about how the night will go. Unexpectedly at the end of his speech, around 6:15 PM, he gives the board of directors the go-ahead to begin helping themselves to the buffet. The board of directors followed by three other groups of VIP guests sitting at reserved tables got up and proceeded to the buffet lines. The Homey Hotel hadn't planned to put their cold food out on the buffets until 6:35 PM, followed by their hot food around 6:45 PM. The Homey banquet staff immediately began bringing out food, but it took almost 15 minutes to get all the food ready on all three buffets. All food was brought out while the board of directors and the VIP guests were standing in line, waiting.

Although Rob and the rest of the Homey staff acted quickly to this unexpected change, the president of the company was furious that the board of directors, his VIP guests, along with himself had to wait in line while food was put out and into chaffers. Because of how unhappy he was about the food, the president of the company is refusing to pay the full amount of money that he owes to Sue, and Sue is demanding a discount from the Homey Hotel food and beverage department. The Homey feels that they did their job by speaking to the event planner prior to the beginning of the event to confirm the time that the food should be out, and that it is not their fault that the president invited guests to the buffets 45 minutes prior to the scheduled time.

Do you feel that the Rob should honor the request and discount their event? Why or why not?

Produced by *George G. Fenich* from East Carolina University.

Key Words and Terms

For definitions, see the Glossary.

agenda	food and beverage minimum	promotional mix model
breaking down	Gantt Chart	schedules
community infrastructure	government agencies	venues
fairs, festivals, and public events	permits	

Review and Discussion Questions

1. Discuss the types of events that a city might host.
2. What does the vision statement of an event provide for an organizer?
3. Discuss the importance of the event professionals' client relationship in event planning.
4. Discuss the types of planning tools that aid in successful event management.
5. What are the distinctive roles of the promotional mix model?
6. What are the benefits for sponsorships at a special event?
7. What are some tips for working with broadcast media?
8. What are some basic operations for staging an event?
9. Discuss costs associated with the event budget.
10. Outline the elements of breakdown for a special event.
11. Consider special event opportunities for your community. How would you offer advice as an event professional to encourage attendance?

About the Chapter Contributor

David Smiley received his Master of Science degree in Hospitality & Tourism Management from the University of Central Florida and holds a Bachelor of Science degree from Pennsylvania State University in Recreation and Park Management. After serving 22 years in the industry, including 10 years with Rosen Hotels & Resorts, he is now a lecturer in the School of Public Health at Indiana University Bloomington. He also serves as the advisor to the school's student chapter of the Student Event Planning Association (SEPA), and is the advisor to the Professional Tourism and Event Management Club.

Previous Edition Chapter Contributors

Joy Dickerson, Widener University.
Cynthia Vannucci, Metropolitan State College in Denver.

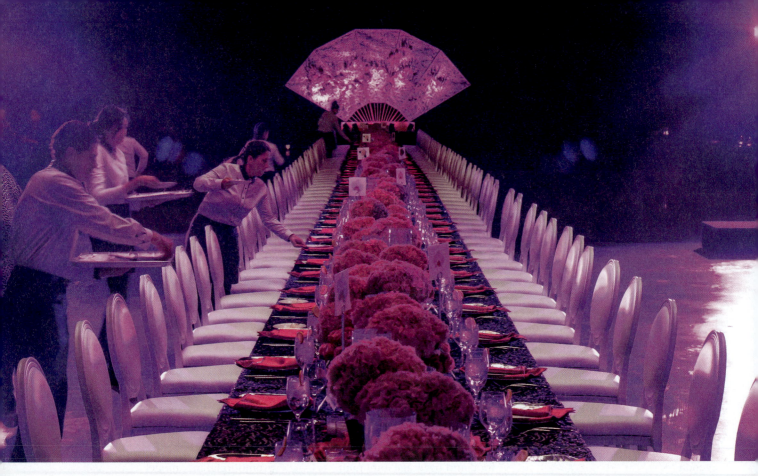

Banquets are a major component of food and beverage in MEEC.
Jenna Dosch Photography

CHAPTER 9

Food and Beverage

Chapter Objectives

- Clarify the different types and requirements of catered events.
- Discuss the specific requirements and considerations related to beverage events.
- Outline items to consider when choosing, planning, and arranging rooms for an event.
- Outline important service requirements to consider when planning a food or beverage event.
- Name current trends and best practices in food and beverage practices for events.

Food and beverage is an area that many event professionals shy away from by outsourcing planning and negotiation to third-party planners. It is often a mystery to many event professionals as to what is negotiable, how caterers price their services, and where caterers will make concessions.

The Events Industry Council (EIC) Glossary provides the following definition:

Caterer (1) a food service vendor, often used to describe a vendor who specializes in banquets and theme parties. (2) An exclusive food and beverage contractor within a facility.

The quality of the food and beverage functions can make a major impact on the overall impressions of a meeting/event. The first thing to consider when planning a catered event is to answer the question, "What is the purpose?" Is it merely to satisfy hunger, or is it for a break to reenergize, for socializing and networking, to present an award, to honor dignitaries, or to keep an audience entertained for the speaker?

While many simply see food as fuel, for others it is an important component of an overall experience. From planning menus to negotiating prices, catering is one area not to leave to chance. It is one of the major expenses of a meeting/event and an area where Murphy's Law prevails. Furthermore, the importance of cuisine must be emphasized. The choices and preparation of food have changed dramatically over the past few years—whether to go organic, ethnic, or vegetarian, for example. It is posited that food revenue is increasing steadily due to the increased choices of cuisine. However, beverage revenue may be in decline because sponsors of events do not want to assume liability for alcohol consumption.

Questions to ask when planning for food and beverage:

1. Who will I work with planning the event?
2. Who will be on-site during the event?
3. When can I expect your written proposal?
4. What is your policy regarding deposits and cancellations?
5. When is the final payment due?
6. Are there other charges for set up, delivery, overtime, and so on?
7. Do you take credit cards? PayPal? Online payment?
8. When must I give you my final guarantee?
9. What percentage is overset above the guarantee?
10. What is the sales tax, and what are your gratuity and/or service charge policies?
11. What are the chef's best menu items?
12. What are your portion sizes?
13. Will wine be poured by the staff or placed on the tables?
14. How many staff will be working at the event?
15. What are your substitution policies for vegetarian plates and special meals?
16. Could you pass wine or champagne as guests arrive?
17. How many bartenders will be used during the cocktail hour?
18. Do you provide table numbers?
19. What size tables do you have?
20. What are the options for linen, chair covers, china, stemware, flatware, and charger plates?
21. What decorations do you provide for tables, buffets, and food stations?
22. Are you Americans with Disabilities Act (ADA) compliant?
23. Can you provide a podium, mike, and overhead projector?
24. What are your green initiatives?

Catered Events

Catered events generally have one host and one bill, and most attendees eat the same meal. (Exceptions would be if an attendee arranged vegetarian, low-fat, or other special meals.) A mandatory gratuity or service charge is added to the check, which can typically range from 18 to 24 percent of the total bill, and taxes can add another 5 to 9 percent. The distribution of this gratuity or service charge varies widely among venues and companies. A gratuity differs from a tip, as a tip is voluntary and is given at the discretion of the client for service over and above expectations. A gratuity is generally 100 percent distributed to team members. A service charge includes a percentage distributed to team members (which may include servers, bartenders, and sometimes the management team), and a percentage that is retained by the property. The lesson here is, when in doubt, ask. In many countries and cultures, service charges and tips do not exist.

Catered events can be held in just about any location. **Off-premise catering** requires transportation of food—either prepared or to be prepared on-site—to a location such as a tented area, museum, park, or attraction. Sometimes food is prepared in a kitchen and is transported fully cooked to the event site. At other times food is partially prepared in a kitchen and is finished at the site, or everything can be prepared from scratch at the site. Mobile kitchens can be set up just about anywhere, using generators and/or propane and butane as fuel to heat cooking equipment. Off-premise caterers generally must rent equipment, including tables, chairs, chafing dishes, plates, flatware, and glassware.

On-Premise Catering

On-premise catering is defined as being held in a facility that has its own permanent kitchens and function rooms, such as a hotel, restaurant, or convention center. This allows the facility to keep permanent furniture, such as banquet style tables and chairs in their inventory. Event professionals are almost always required to use the catering department of the venue at the site of the meeting. In a citywide convention, one hotel is usually named the host hotel and holds most of the food functions, although some events often move attendees to a variety of venues. However, many meetings/events have at least one off-premise event, often the opening reception, closing gala, or themed event. Attendees want to experience some of the flavor of the destination, and they often get cabin fever if they never leave the hotel. Events can be held at an aquarium, museum, winery, or historic mansion. For example, in St. Louis, many events are held at Busch stadium, home of the world champion Cardinals baseball team. In San Diego, some large conventions actually take over the entire Gas Lamp District for an evening.

Most meals are catered on-premise during a meeting. Serving attendees all at once prevents strain on restaurant outlets, keeps attendees from leaving the property, and ensures that everyone will be back on time for the following sessions.

Conference centers offer a complete meeting package, which includes meals. Breakfast, lunch, and dinner are generally available in a cafeteria-type set up at any time the group decides to break. This keeps the group from having to break just because it is noon if they are in the middle of a productive session. If more than one group is in the facility, they will each be assigned different areas of the dining room. Refreshments are usually available at any time as well, allowing breaks at appropriate times. Conference centers can also provide banquets and receptions on request.

Convention centers and stadiums usually have concession stands open. More and more, exhibitions are holding their own opening reception or providing lunch on the show floor to attract attendees into the exhibits. Most convention centers are public entities, and the food service is contracted out to companies like Aramark or Sodexo. These contract food service companies often have exclusive contracts, and other vendors or caterers are not allowed to work in the facility.

The venues mentioned earlier generally also have full-service restaurants on the property. If the group will use the restaurant, check the capacity and hours relative to the needs of the group. For example, the association ICHRIE held one of its annual conventions at a major hotel in Palm Springs, California, during late July. They attracted about 700 attendees and were virtually the only people in the 1,500-room hotel. ICHRIE felt that the five freestanding restaurants would be more than adequate to meet the dining needs of the group (dining off-site was not a practical option). This would normally be true. However, since it was low season for the hotel, they closed all but two of the restaurants, with the result that ICHRIE convention attendees were faced with waits of over two hours to be seated for dinner.

Event professionals also need to stay abreast of current food trends. They do so by reading trade journals, such as *Meeting News, Successful Meetings, Convene,* or *Meetings and Conventions.* Many of the event and food trade publications, such as *Event Solutions, Special Events, Event Manager Blog, Bizbash, Catersource,* and *Smart Meetings* are wonderful resources as well and can be accessed online.

Off-Premise Catering

In Orlando, it is much easier logistically to transport a 20-person board of directors' dinner to a local restaurant than to transport 1,000 plus attendees to Disney World. As an event professional, you may be responsible for simultaneously coordinating both on-premise and off-premise catering events. In this case, a shuttle bus system should be set up to transport attendees back and forth, which can be expensive.

Many excellent restaurants have banquet rooms, and bigger restaurants have banquet sales managers. Arnaud's in New Orleans has a six-person sales staff, so banquets are big business. In Las Vegas, a trend has been for celebrity chefs to create their own signature restaurants within the hotel, separate from the hotel's own food service operations. These restaurants, such as Spago in the Forum Shops at Caesars Palace or Delmonico's at The Venetian, also have their own banquet sales staff. Websites, such as OpenTable, make it easy to research what local restaurants have to offer.

For an off-premise event, the first step for an event professional would be to create an RFP and send it to event managers or caterers in the area. The RFP would include basic information, such as the objective of the event, information on the company, workable dates, number of attendees, and approximate budget, as well as any special requests, such as the need for a waiter-parade area. Many catering companies have online RFPs. Once the event professional has had the opportunity to review the proposals and interview, if possible, a site inspection would follow. During the site inspection, the event professional should look at the ambiance of the space, the level of cleanliness and maintenance, and other amenities that may be required, such as parking and restrooms.

In many cases, off-premise events will be outsourced through a destination management company (DMC). DMCs are familiar with the location and have relationships established with unique venues in the area. For example, in Las Vegas the Liberace Mansion is available for parties. In New Orleans, Mardi Gras World, where the parade floats are made, is an outstanding setting for a party. Just about every destination has some distinctive spaces for parties: Southfork in Dallas, the Rock and Roll Hall of Fame in Cleveland, the Getty Museum in Los Angeles, and so on.

DMCs also know the best caterers, decorators, shuttle companies, entertainment, and any other supplier of products or services you may require. While DMCs charge for their services, they often can get quantity discounts because of the volume they purchase throughout the year. And if there is a problem with the product or service, the DMC can usually resolve it faster because of the amount of future business that would be jeopardized.

Two of the challenges with off-premise events are transportation and weather. Shuttle buses are an additional expense for the event. Weather can spoil the best-laid plans, so contingency measures must be arranged. Back-up shelter should be available, whether it is a tent or an inside function room. For example, outdoor luaus in Hawaii are frequently moved inside at the last minute because of the frequent tropical storms that pop up there.

During the initial site inspection, obtain a copy of the facility's banquet menus and policies. Do they offer the type of menu items that would be appropriate for your group? Ask if they are prepared to handle custom menus if you decide not to use their standard offerings. When planning custom menus, always check the skill level of the culinary team in the kitchen and the availability of special products that may be required.

Other important considerations include the demographics of the group. Menu choices would be different for the American Truck Drivers Association as compared to the International Association of Retired Persons. You need to consider gender, age, ethnic background, profession, and so on.

Style of Service

There are many ways to serve a meal, from self-service to VIP white-glove service (see Table 9-1). While there is some disagreement on a few of the following definitions, the

TABLE 9-1

Types of Functions

Continental breakfast	Typically includes an assortment of breads, pastries, juice, and coffee, although it can be upgraded with an addition of sliced fruit, yogurt, and/or cold cereals. Most are self-service with limited seating, unless an additional fee for seated continental service is assessed. Continental breakfast is excellent for the budget, speed, and efficiency.
Full, served breakfast	The entrees are plated in the kitchen and would normally include some type of egg, like Eggs Benedict; a meat, like bacon or sausage; a potato item, like hash browns; fruit; and coffee. When deciding on breakfast service, planners need to consult their history and guarantee accordingly as attendance is invariably lower since not everyone indulges in breakfast and many will use the time to visit the gym or to catch up on work.
Breakfast buffet	Includes a wide assortment of foods including fruits and fruit juices, egg dishes, meats, potatoes, and breads. Buffets are good as the times are longer, allowing for latecomers to be accommodated. In certain situations, buffets are cheaper than a full, served breakfast.
Refreshment breaks	These are often beverages only, but may include snacks, such as cookies, bagels, or fruit. Remember that such breaks are to refresh and energize. The food and beverage selection should reflect this objective. Such break buffets are put out longer so the food items selected should be able to accommodate the length and not dry out. Refreshment breaks are often themed.
Brunch	This is a late-morning meal and includes both breakfast and lunch items. A brunch can be a buffet or a plated, served meal.
Buffet lunch	This can be a cold or hot buffet with a variety of salads, vegetables, meats, and so on. A deli buffet may include a make-your-own sandwich area.
Box lunch	Normally only available for carrying away from the hotel to an off-premise location. They can be eaten on a bus if there is a long ride to a destination (such as a ride from San Francisco to the Napa Valley for a day of activities) or eaten at the destination (such as a picnic area to hear the Boston Pops Orchestra). Box lunches can also be provided to attendees at a trade show.
Full, served lunch	This is a plated lunch, usually a three-course hot meal, and often includes a salad, a main course, and a dessert. A one-course cold meal is sometimes provided, such as a Grilled Chicken Caesar Salad.
Receptions	These are networking events with limited seating, which allow for conversation and interaction during the event. Food is usually placed on stations around the room and may also include butler style service. Beverage service is always offered at these events. Light receptions may only include dry snacks with beverages, and often precede a dinner. Heavy receptions would include hot and cold appetizers, perhaps an action station, and are often planned to replace a dinner.
Dinner buffet	This would include a variety of salads, vegetables, entrees, desserts, and beverages. Often, meats are carved and served by attendants.
Full, served dinner	This could be a three- to five-course meal, including an appetizer, soup, salad, main course, and a dessert. Food is pre-plated in the kitchen and served to each guest seated at round tables in the dining room. This style of service is often referred to as American Style Service.
Off-site event	This is any event held away from the host hotel. It could be a reception at a famous landmark, such as the Queen Mary at Long Beach, or a picnic at a local beach or park.
Theme party	This is a gala event with flair. It can be a reception, buffet, or served meal. Themes can run the gamut. An example would be an international theme, where different stations are set up with food from Italy, China, Japan, Mexico, Germany, and so on.

following are based on the EIC glossary. The White House protocol is also being followed in this book. The White House publishes the *Green Book*, which explains how everything is to be done for presidential protocol. However, because of confusion in the area, it is important to be sure that the event professional and the catering representative agree on what the service styles mean for the event. (Unfortunately, the *Green Book* is not available to the public, as it also includes information on presidential security, among others.) The style of service will often influence the types and varieties of foods offered. The common service styles that can be used include the following.

Buffet

Food is attractively arranged on tables. Guests serve themselves and then take their plates to a table to sit and eat. Beverages are usually served at the tables. Buffets are generally

Dessert buffet table.
Jenna Dosch Photography

more expensive than plated served meals because there is no portion control, and surpluses must be built in to assure adequate supplies of each food item. However, staffing costs are lowered by eight to ten percent or more. Be sure to allow adequate space around the table for lines to form, and to allow efficient replenishment by the service staff. Consider the flow, and do not make guests backtrack to get an item. For example, place the salad dressings after the salad so that guests do not have to step back on the next guest to dress their salad. Provide 1 buffet line per 100 guests, with 120 being the point to break into 2 lines.

Attended Buffet/Cafeteria
Guests are served by chefs or attendants. This is more elegant and provides better portion control.

Combination Buffet
Inexpensive items, such as salads, are presented buffet style, where guests help themselves. Expensive items, such as meats, are served by an attendant for portion control.

Action Stations
Sometimes referred to as performance stations or exhibition cooking. **Action stations** are similar to an attended buffet, except food is freshly prepared as guests wait and watch. Because action stations have more flair and interaction, and are more distinctive, they are part entertainment. Some common action stations include foods such as pastas; quesadillas; fajitas; sushi/sashimi; oyster shucking; lettuce wraps; paninis; French fry; mashed potatoes; comfort foods; soups; espresso; pizzas; s'mores, chocolate dipped fruit; grilled meats or shrimp; omelets; crepes; flaming desserts such as baked Alaska, crepes suzette, or bananas foster; Caesar salad; Belgian waffles; and carved meats.

Reception
Light foods are served buffet style or are passed on trays by servers (**butler service**). Guests usually stand and serve themselves and do not usually sit down to eat. Receptions are often referred to as "Walk and Talks." Small plates should always be included for these events, since some cost control can be managed by selecting the appropriate service pieces. Some receptions serve only finger food (food eaten with the fingers), while others offer fork food (food that requires a fork to eat).

Family Style/English Service

Guests are seated, and large serving platters and bowls of food are placed on the dining table by the servers. Guests pass the food around the table. A host often will carve the meat. This is an expensive style of service. Surpluses must be built into the price to account for potentially high food cost and additional service equipment.

Plated/American Style Service

Guests are seated and served food that has been pre-portioned and plated in the kitchen. Food is served from the left of the guest. The meat or entree is placed directly in front of the guest at the six o'clock position. Beverages are served from the right of the guest. When the guest has finished, both plates and glassware are removed from the right. **American Service** is the most functional, most common, most economical, most controllable, and most efficient type of service. This type of service usually has a server/guest ratio of 1 to 20 or 1 to 30, depending on the level of the facility.

Preset

Some foods are already on the table when guests arrive. The most common items to preset are water, butter, bread, appetizers, and/or salad. At luncheons, where time is of the essence, the dessert is often preset as well. These are all cold items that hold up well.

Butler Service

At receptions, *butler service* refers to having hors d'oeuvres passed on trays, where the guests help themselves.

Russian Service

(1) Banquet Russian: The food is fully prepared in the kitchen. All courses are served either from platters or an Escoffier dish. Tureens are used for soup, and special bowls for salad. The server places the proper plate in front of the guest, who is seated. After the plates are placed, the server returns with a tray of food and, moving counterclockwise around the table, serves the food from the guest's left with the right hand. With this style of service, the server controls the amount served to each guest. (2) Restaurant Russian: Guests are seated. Foods are cooked tableside on a *réchaud* (portable cooking stove) that is on a *gueridon* (tableside cart with wheels). Servers place the food on platters (usually silver), and then guests serve themselves. Service is *from the left*.

Sliders are a food item that can be served at a reception.
Ievgeniia Pidgorna/Alamy Stock Photo

Chef preparing food on a *réchaud.*
Vacancylizm/Shutterstock

White glove service.
Evgeny Litvinov/Shutterstock

Banquet French

Guests are seated. Platters of food are assembled in the kitchen. Servers take the platters to the tables and serve from the left, placing the food on the guest's plate using two large silver forks or one fork and one spoon. Servers must be highly trained for this type of service. The use of the forks and spoons together in one hand is a skill that must be practiced. Many hotels are now permitting the use of silver salad tongs.

Cart French

commonly used for banquets, except for small VIP functions, this style is used in fine restaurants. Guests are seated, and foods are prepared tableside using a réchaud on a gueridon. Cold foods, such as salads, are prepared on the gueridon, sans réchaud. Servers plate the finished foods directly on the guest plate, which is then placed in front of the guest *from the right*. Bread, butter, and salad are served from the left, while beverages are served from the right. All are removed from the right.

Hand Service or Captain

Guests are seated. There is one server for every two guests. Servers wear white gloves. Foods are pre-plated. Each server carries two plates from the kitchen and stands behind the two guests assigned to him or her. At a signal from the room captain, all servings are set in front of all guests at the same time, synchronized. This procedure can be used for all courses, just the main course, or just the dessert. This is a very elegant and impressive style of service used mainly for VIP events because there is significant additional labor required.

A La Carte

Guests are given a choice of two to three entrees, with a minimum of two predetermined courses served before the entrée choice.

Waiter Parade

An elegant touch where white-gloved servers march into the room and parade around the perimeter carrying food on trays, often to dramatic music and lighting. This is especially effective with a Flaming Baked Alaska Dessert Parade. The room lighting is dimmed, and a row of flaming trays carried by the waiters slowly encircles the room. When the entire room is encircled, the music stops and service starts. (Flaming dishes should never be brought close to a guest. After the parade, the dessert is brought to a side area, where it is sliced and served.)

Mixing Service Styles

The event professional can change service styles within the meal. The whole meal does not have to conform to one type of service. For example, the appetizer can be preset, with the salads Frenched (dressing added after salads are placed on table), the main course served American with a dessert buffet.

Menus

In times past, menus rarely changed. Today, change is necessary to keep pace with the changing tastes of the public. Most food trade journals run features on "What's Hot and What's Not." Table 9-2 lists some items that are generally always hot, while Table 9-3 lists consumption guidelines.

TABLE 9-2

Hot Menu Items

Seasonal food	The use of locally grown produce, in season, was first popularized some years ago by Chef Alice Waters. These foods are served when they are at the peak of flavor, enhancing the quality of the event.
Ethnic foods	The unique cuisine of many areas of the world has come into the United States with the influx of peoples from other cultures. The American palate has grown beyond the ethnic foods of the past, such as Italian, Chinese, and Mexican, to include the foods of many Asian countries, the Middle East, and South America.
High-quality ingredients	People may pinch pennies at the grocery store, but when they eat out at a banquet, they want the best. No longer satisfied with frozen, sweetened strawberries, they want fresh Driscoll strawberries on their shortcake. They want giant Idaho baked potatoes and prime Angus beef.
Fresh ingredients	Frozen, canned, and dried foods, once seen as the newest, greatest technology, have worn out their novelty. The loss of these food's flavors during preservation has made fresh food highly prized. Fresh ingredients also mean local sourcing, with many establishments naming the specific farms that products are sourced from.
New and unusual ingredients	With improvements in production, technology, and transportation, new foodstuffs have appeared in marketplaces that were previously unknown to most Americans. These include artisanal breads and cheeses, heirloom tomatoes, lemon grass, Yukon Gold potatoes, purple potatoes, and blood oranges.
Safe foods	Organic foods and foods free from pollution and pesticides.
Highly creative presentations	Plate presentations are increasingly important. We eat with our eyes before anything hits our taste buds. Contemporary presentations should focus on the primary menu components, and garnishes should be minimal (based on the time food might be on display or stored in a hot box).
Excellent service	Food served promptly (while still hot) with friendly, courteous services are important considerations in the enjoyment of a meal.
Sustainable	For consumers, sustainability means food sources that promote good health, help protect the environment, are fair to workers, and does not harm animal populations.

TABLE 9-3

Food Consumption Guidelines

Type of Reception	Type of Eaters	Number of Hors D 'Oeuvres per Person
2 hours or less (dinner following)	Light	3–4 pieces
	Moderate	5–7 pieces
	Heavy	8+ pieces
2 hours or less (no dinner)	Light	6–8 pieces
	Moderate	10–12 pieces
	Heavy	12+ pieces
2–3 hours (no dinner)	Light	8–10 pieces
	Moderate	10–12 pieces
	Heavy	16+ pieces

Food Consumption Guidelines

The most important information in deciding how much food to order is the history of the group: Who are they? Why are they there? A pretty good determination can be made based on previous years. If this is a new group, or the history is not available, then consider the demographics of the attendees.

Some General Guidelines

Guests generally eat more during the first hour of a reception and may eat an average of seven hors d'oeuvres per person during this hour. These general guidelines will vary based on the demographics of the group.

The amount of food consumed may also depend on how many square feet of space is available for guests to move around in (smaller equals less consumption).

In general, menu offerings tend to lend themselves towards assembly-line production and service. Certain delicate items cannot be produced and served in quantity without sacrificing culinary quality. For example, lobster, soufflé, rare roast beef, medium-rare tuna, rare duck breast, or salmon steak are difficult to prepare and serve satisfactorily to more than a handful of guests at a time. One technology that has grown in popularity that has ameliorated concern for this is *sous vide*. *Sous vide* cooking, which means "under vacuum," involves vacuum sealing foods in plastic, then cooking at a precise temperature in a water bath. This yields a product with a consistent result and taste since the food cooks in its own natural juices. There is also ease of cooking as no attention is needed while cooking, and, very importantly, their is reduction of waste since nothing is dried out.

Menu Restrictions

Banquet servers should know the ingredients and preparation method of every item on the menu. Many attendees have allergies or are restricted from eating certain items like sugar, salt, nuts, or gluten, due to health concerns. Others do not eat certain foods due to their religious restrictions, and others are vegetarians who do not eat meat. The question of allergies and food restrictions should be posed as early as possible. For conventions, attendees are asked to provide information on food restrictions on the convention registration form.

Guests with special diets will influence the types of foods served. Some people cannot tolerate monosodium glutamate or MSG (allergic reactions); onions and garlic (digestive problems); certain spices or peanuts (allergic reactions); sugar (diabetes); salt (high blood pressure, heart problems); fat (weight problems, high cholesterol); wheat, rye, or barley (celiac disease); or milk products (allergic reactions, lactose intolerance), and those with hypoglycemia have to eat something every few hours.

Vegetarians often make up approximately 10 to 15 percent of a group. There are three basic types of vegetarians:

- Type one: Vegetarians who will not eat red meat, but will eat chicken and fish.
- Type two: Lacto-ovo vegetarians who will not eat anything that has to be killed, but will eat animal by-products (cheese, eggs, milk, and so on).
- Type three: Vegans who will not eat anything from any animal source, including animal by-products such as honey, butter, and dairy.

When in doubt, assume attendees who identify themselves as vegetarian are vegans. To simply serve a vegan a plate of vegetables with butter and/or cheese would not be appropriate.

Other dietary restrictions include people who are lactose intolerant, which means they have difficulty digesting anything containing milk or milk products. Today, people have imposed dietary restrictions upon themselves in an effort to eat in a healthier fashion, including those on low carbohydrate diets, high fiber diets, and so on. An acute allergic reaction to a food may manifest itself as swelling of the eyelids, face, lips, tongue, larynx, or trachea. Other reactions can include difficulty breathing, hives, nausea, vomiting, diarrhea, stomach cramps, or abdominal pain. Anaphylactic shock is a severe whole-body reaction that can result in death. The eight most common food allergies are diary, egg, peanut, tree nut, seafood, soy, wheat, and carmine.

Religious restrictions may also impact food and diet. For example, people who maintain a Kosher diet will not eat anything that does not follow Kosher guidelines, will not mix dairy products with meat products, and will keep separate china and separate kitchens for dairy and for meat. Kosher food must follow stringent rules and pass the approval of a *mashgiach* who does not have to be a rabbi, but must be recognized in the community as a person authorized to give certification for *kashruth*. Kosher food conforms to strict Judaic laws regarding the type of food that may be eaten as well as the kinds of food that can be combined during a meal. In addition to the kinds of animals considered kosher, the laws state that animals must be killed in a specific manner. In kosher service, with the exception of glass and silverware that can undergo a curing period, meat products must not be served on any plate that has ever had dairy products on it. Pork, shellfish, rabbit, and hindquarter cuts of beef and lamb are examples of foods that are not allowed for various reasons.

It is a good idea to have attendees fill out a form indicating if they have menu restrictions. This information can then be communicated to the catering manager, who will ensure that the proper number and type of alternative menu items are available. At meetings of the National Association of Catering Executives, attendees are provided with complete menus of every event, along with a form where they can indicate which meals they need to have changed.

Contracts

Normally, formal catering contracts are required. Sometimes they may be forgone in place of a signed **banquet event order (BEO)** or a signed letter of agreement. A BEO, sometimes referred to as a function sheet, is a venue's internal communication system between departments. It is also the building block upon which accounting and record keeping systems are constructed. A resume is a summary of function room usage for a particular convention or meeting. The resume usually includes all BEOs. The resume focuses on major highlights while deferring to the pertinent BEOs for specific details. A catering contract, or letter of agreement, usually contains a combination of standard, boilerplate language, plus language specifically tailored to the event.

Food and Beverage Attrition

Most event professionals do not like **attrition** clauses, although they benefit both event professionals and venues, because they set down legal obligations for both sides and establish liability limits. When a contract is signed, both parties want the food and beverage guarantee to be met. But caterers want to be certain and up-front, while event professionals want to wait until the last minute to give the final guarantee. If the guarantee is too high, the event professional might have to pay for it in the form of attrition.

Attrition hits the event professional in the pocketbook if the **guarantee** is not met. The event professional agrees in the contract to buy a specific number of meals or to spend a specific amount of money on group food and beverage; the caterer's obligation is to provide the service and the food. If the guarantee is not met, the event professional must pay the difference between the guarantee and the actual amount or an agreed-on percentage of the actual amount (see Chapter 10 on legal issues for more information on attrition).

Beverage Events

Reasons for a Beverage Event

Beverage events are popular and include refreshment breaks and receptions. Beverage breaks not only provide liquid repasts and possibly a snack, but also allow the attendee to get up, stretch, visit the restroom, call the office, and possibly move into another room for the next break-out session.

Receptions are slightly different because most include alcoholic beverages and probably more variety and quantity of food options. Reasons for receptions include:

Socializing: To provide a relaxed atmosphere that encourages interaction among guests.

Networking: To provide an opportunity to discuss business and develop new contacts.

Planners typically plan and purchase for only three main types of beverage functions: cocktail reception, hospitality suite, and poured wine service. A key consideration in finalizing a beverage menu is based on the demographics and history of the group.

Categories of Liquor

The categories of alcoholic beverages offered to a customer for a catered event are liquor (distilled spirits), wine, and beer. The caterer typically offers tiers of these options, representing different price and quality levels: Well, Call, and Premium brands. The event professional will choose the tier most appropriate for their guests and the event budget.

Well Brands: These are sometimes called house liquors. It is less expensive liquor, such as Kentucky Gentleman Bourbon. Well brands are served when someone does not call for a specific brand.

Call Brands: These are priced in the midrange and are generally asked for by name, such as Jim Beam Bourbon or Beefeater's Gin.

Premium Brands: These are high-quality, expensive liquors, such as Crown Royal, Chivas Regal, or Tanqueray Gin.

Spirits

All premium brands are available in 750-ml and 1-liter bottles. One 750-ml bottle equals 20 (eleven 4-ounce) servings; a 1-liter bottle equals 27 (eleven 4-ounce) servings (see Table 9-4). Consumption will average three drinks per person during a normal reception period.

Wine/Champagne

All premium brands are available in 750-ml bottles and many are in 1.5 liters (magnums). There are other sizes as well, such as:

Split (187-ml)
Half bottle (375-ml)
Bottle (750-ml) = five 5-ounce servings
Magnum (1.5-liter bottle) = ten 5-ounce servings
Double magnum (3-liter)
Jeroboam (3-liter for sparkling, 4.5-liter for still)
Imperial (6-liter)
Methuselah (6-liter)
Nebuchadnezzar (15-liter)

Consumption will average three glasses per person during a normal reception period, assuming that 50 percent of the people will order wine; you should order thirty 750-ml bottles for every 100 guests.

TABLE 9-4

Number of Drinks per Bottle

		1 Ounce	$1\frac{1}{4}$ Ounce	$1\frac{1}{2}$ Ounce
1-Liter	33.8 ounces	33	27	22
750-ml	25.3 ounces	25	20	16

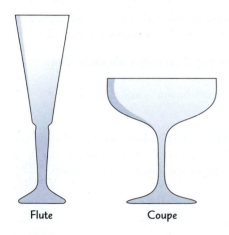

Flute   Coupe

FIGURE 9-1
Flute and coupe.
Pearson Education, Inc.

Champagne should be served in a flute glass instead of the classic coupe because there is less surface exposed to the air, so the bubbles do not escape as fast, causing the champagne to go flat (see Figure 9-1).

Beer

The caterer should always offer a variety of domestic and imported choices, as well as a contemporary list of craft beers from small, independent, and traditional brewers (Dogfish Head 60 Minute IPA, Bell's Two Hearted Ale).

How Beverages Are Sold

By the Bottle

This method is common for open bars and poured wine at meal functions. The event professional pays for all of the liquor bottles that are opened. A physical inventory is taken at the beginning and end of the function to determine liquor usage. Most venues charge for each opened bottle, even if only one drink was poured from it. This method saves money but is inconvenient to monitor and calculate. The event professional will not know the final cost until the event is over. Usually, the group history will give some indication of how much consumption to expect. Open bottles may not be removed from the property. Unopened bottles may not be removed unless the venue has an off-sale liquor license. You can, however, have them delivered to a hospitality suite or to the room of a VIP to use during the meeting. This method is less and less common, with the exception of wine.

By the Drink

This is also called a consumption bar. The host is charged for each individual beverage consumed during the event. Normally, the price per drink is high enough to cover all relevant expenses (limes, stirrers, napkins, and so on). Individual drink prices are set to yield a standard beverage cost percentage set by the hotel. This is the amount of profit the hotel expects to make from the sale of the liquor. Cost percentages range from 12 to 18 percent for spirits and usually around 25 percent for wine. The event professional will not know the final cost until the event is over.

Per Person

This method can be more expensive for the event professional, but involves less work and aggravation. The event professional chooses a plan, such as premium liquors for one hour, and then tells the caterer how many people are coming ($25 per person × 500 guests = $12,500). Costs are known ahead of time—no surprises. Tickets are collected from attendees at the door, and the guarantee is monitored. The key to selecting this, or any other method, is to know your group. Know their drinking capacity and pattern by, ideally, reviewing their past history.

Charge Per Hour

This is similar to per person. This method often includes a sliding scale with a higher cost for the first hour. This is because guests usually eat and drink more during the first hour, and then level off. You must provide a firm guarantee before negotiating a per-hour charge. Or, you can combine *per person, per hour*: $25 per person for the first hour, and $20 per person for the second hour, so hosting 100 guests for a two-hour reception would cost $4,500 ($25 × 100 = $2,500 (+) $20 × 100 = $2,000 (=) $4,500). No consideration is given for those who arrive late or leave early; the fee is $45 per person, regardless.

Open Bar

This is also called a host bar. Guests do not pay for their drinks; a host or sponsor pays for them. Guests usually drink as much as they want, of what they want. Liquor consumption is higher because someone else is paying. The sponsor can be the meeting itself, an exhibitor, a similar organization, and so on. For example, at the Super Show, which features sporting goods, Nike may sponsor a bar.

Cash Bar

This is also called a no-host bar. Guests buy their own drinks, usually purchasing tickets from a cashier to exchange with a bartender for a drink. At small functions, the bartender may collect and serve, eliminating the cost of a cashier. Cashiers are usually charged as extra labor. Cashiers provide better control, and speed up service. Bartenders do not have to handle dirty money and then handle glassware.

Combination Bar

A host purchases tickets and gives each attendee a certain number (usually two). If the guest wants a third drink, he or she must purchase it him or herself. Or, the host can pay for the first hour, and the bar reverts to a cash bar for the second hour. This method provides free drinks to guests, but retains control over costs and potential liability for providing unlimited drinks.

Limited Consumption Bar

This is pricing by the drink, and a cash register is used. The host establishes a dollar amount. When the cash register reaches that amount, the bar is closed. The host may decide to reopen as a cash bar.

CALCULATE TOTAL COST TO DETERMINE THE BEST OPTION

If the hotel charges $80 for a bottle of bourbon that yields twenty-seven 14-ounce drinks, each drink costs the client $2.96. If guests are expected to drink two drinks per hour for a one-hour reception for 1,000 people, purchasing by the bottle would cost $6,000.

If purchased by the drink, at $4.00 per drink, the same group would cost $8,000.

If purchased at $10 per person, it would cost $10,000.

So, you can see, the hotel makes more money selling per person. Selling by the bottle is becoming less and less common.

Labor Charges

Extra charges are usually levied for bartenders and/or bar backs, cocktail servers, cashiers, security, and corkage. These items are negotiable, depending on the value of the business. For example, if a bar sells over $500 in liquor, the bartender charge may be waived.

A **bar back** is the bartender's helper at the bar—restocking liquor, keeping fresh ice, cleaning glasses, and so on—so that the bartender will not have to do it him or herself during service.

Corkage is the fee added to liquor brought into the venue but not purchased from the venue. The venue charges this fee to cover the cost of labor, use of the glasses (which must be delivered to the room, washed, and placed back in storage), mixers, olives, lemon peels, and so forth. Corkage is not available at all properties and depends on venue policy.

Considerations for the number of bartenders include the number of bars scheduled, types of drinks, number of attendees, hours of operation, amount of bar back work, and applicable union or company human resources policies. The standard ratio is one bartender for every 100 attendees. If guests all arrive at the same time, a ratio of 75 (or down to even 50) is appropriate. At large events with over 1,000 attendees, a ratio of 100 is appropriate. To alleviate pressure on bartenders, ask for a few servers to pass glasses of champagne, still wines, bottled waters, or juices. This will also add an extra touch of elegance to the event. Unless the event is very small, at least one bar back is needed. Considerations for the number of bar backs include the number of bars scheduled; capacity of each bar set up; distance between the bars and the kitchen; ease of retrieving stock; hours of operations; number of attendees; variety of liquor stock, glasses, and garnishes; and, lastly, the applicable union or company human resources policies.

Hospitality Suites

Hospitality suites are places for attendees to gather outside of the meeting events. They are normally open late in the evening, after 10:00 PM, but occasionally around the clock. Three types of hospitality suites are

Morning: Continental breakfast
Afternoon: Snacks and sodas
Evening: Liquor and snacks

Some suites offer a full bar, and some only offer beer and wine. Some have lots of food, others have only dry snacks. Some offer desserts and specialty coffees. Consider ordering more food if the attendees have had an open evening.

Hospitality suites are usually held in a client's suite on a sleeping room floor, are usually handled by room service, and usually sold by catering. Sometimes they are held in a public function room and are both sold and serviced by catering.

Hospitality suites can be hosted by the sponsoring organization, a chapter of the organization, an exhibitor, a non-exhibiting corporation, an allied association, or a person running for an office in the organization.

Watch for underground hospitality suites where unofficial parties pop up. In these types of hospitality suites, you only gain legal liability and lose revenue. The court case resulting from the Tailhook Scandal, in which a female was groped in a hallway at a military meeting at the Las Vegas Hilton, set a precedent that a hotel can no longer claim that it does not know what is going on within the property.

Another factor to keep in mind is that liquor laws vary from state to state, county to county, and country to country. You should always check the laws in the specific location where your event is being held.

EXAMPLES

In Las Vegas and New Orleans, liquor can be sold 24/7 and carried plus consumed in public places.

In California, liquor cannot be sold between 2 AM and 6 AM.

In Atlanta, liquor may not be served until noon on Sundays.

In some states, liquor may not be sold at all on Sundays.

There are generally four types of illegal liquor sales, wherever you are located:

- Sales to minors
- Sales to intoxicated persons
- Sales outside legal hours
- Sales with an improper liquor license

There are on-sale licenses, off-sale licenses, and beer and wine licenses. Licenses also stay with the property. For example, if your hotel has a liquor license, it is not valid in the public park across the street. The caterer would need to obtain a special temporary permit.

Event professionals who wish to bring their own liquor into an establishment must check local laws and be prepared to pay the establishment a per-bottle corkage fee.

Rooms

Room Set Ups

The way the room is set up is critically important to the success of any event. The room set up can affect the flow of service, the amount of food and beverage consumed, and even the mood of the guests. The ambiance can make or break a meal function—be it a continental breakfast or a formal dinner. (See Figure 9-2)

Room set up includes tables, chairs, decor, and other equipment, such as portable bars, stages, and audiovisual equipment. It is essential that the event professional com-

Grand Hall

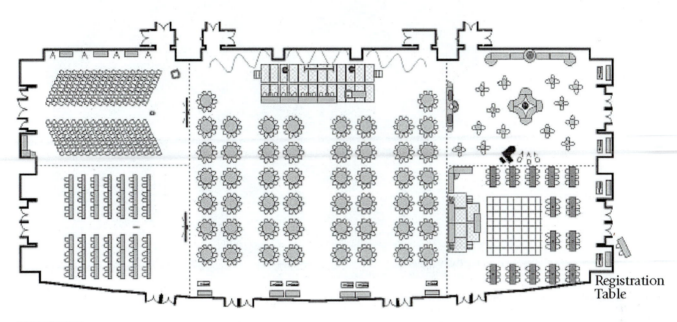

FIGURE 9-2
Sample room layout.
Pearson Education, Inc.

municate *exactly* how they want the room to be set to the banquet set up manager. This is accomplished on the banquet event order (BEO) form and by using room layout software. These types of programs allow the placement of tables, chairs, and other equipment into a meeting room plan. Room software demos may be viewed on a number of websites, including Social Tables, Meeting Matrix, All Seated, and Room Viewer.

Aisle Space

Aisles allow people to move easily around the room without squeezing through chairs and disturbing seated guests. They also provide a buffer between the seating areas and the food and beverage areas. Aisles between tables and around food and beverage stations should be a bare minimum of 36-inches wide (three feet), but it would be preferable to have 48 inches. Also, leave a three-foot minimum aisle around the perimeter of the room. Cross aisles should be six-feet wide. Check with the local fire marshal for local rules and regulations as these vary from location to location.

Tables

Allow ten square feet per person at rectangular banquet tables. Allow 12.5 square feet per person at rounds. This assumes the facility is using standard 20- by 20-inch chairs.

Remember to deduct space taken up for furniture before calculating the number of people. Include large sofas found in many hospitality suites, buffet tables, portable bars, plants, decor and props, check-in tables, and so forth. Also, allow three square feet per person for dance floors. And always remember to check local fire codes.

Tablescapes

The tabletop is the stage—it sets expectations and should reflect the theme of the event. Once seated, the focus is mainly on the table, so it is imperative that it not be overlooked.

The centerpiece should not block sight lines for people sitting across the table from each other. Centerpieces should be low or high with a Lucite or slender pole in the middle portion.

The *cover* is the place setting and includes placement of flatware, china, and glassware.

Napery is the term to include all table linens, including tablecloths, overlays, napkins, and table skirting.

Other décor may include ribbons, greenery, or other items relating to the theme of the meal.

A "wow" tablescape presentation.
Sophie McAulay/Alamy Stock Photo

EXAMPLES INCLUDE

- Trailing flower garlands or ribbons between place settings
- Different colored napkins at each cover
- Creative napkin folds at each cover
- Creative centerpieces

Major props for **tablescapes** can be rented from prop houses, service contractors, or party stores, or can be provided by the venue, hotel, or club. Other props are small, decorative pieces that can be found in many places, such as:

Auto supply stores
Toy or crafts stores
Garden centers
Ethnic food stores or import shops
Travel agencies (destination posters)
Sports clubs or stores
Medical supply stores
Military surplus stores

Room Rental Charges

Can they be waived? It varies depending on the venue. If the event also requires the use of sleeping rooms, it is easier to negotiate the room rental charge from the hotel. When undertaking catering events at hotels that are handled by the catering department rather than the sales department, because there are no room nights involved, an event professional rarely encounters a rental fee for the space. Rather, there will be a minimum revenue requirement based on the amount of space needed for the event. The group may have to spend $50,000 in food and beverage to secure a ballroom for an event, which frequently means that guests eat *very* well. However, in event venues, otherwise known as off-premise venues, it depends on how the venue has set up its charge/profit schedule. Most off-site venues charge a rental fee. Some charge a rental fee, some an admission fee per guest, and a few charge both and then add on catering, rentals, and service costs. The types of charges are almost always dependent on the size or projected profitability of the event. Everything is negotiable. At several venues, it may be possible to negotiate removing the rental charge when bringing a large or highly profitable event to the property; it varies depending on the venue.

Service Requirements

Labor is a major cost for catering. Most properties use a staffing guide to formalize policies in an effort to contain labor costs.

One bartender per every 100 guests is standard. If guests will arrive all at once, or you do not want long lines, you could have a bartender for every 50 or 75 guests, but there may be an additional labor charge. See Table 9-5. If a dinner involves a wine pairing for each course, or has three or more wines, a dedicated wine service team is commonly added.

Service is critical. Many excellent meals are ruined by poor service. Meal service levels can run from one server per eight guests to one server per forty guests. Most staffing guides allow for a ratio of 1 to 32, but most event professionals want 1 to 20 or 1 to 16 with either poured wine or French Service.

Savvy event professionals negotiate for the following:

General

Rounds of ten to one server for every two tables, busser for every six tables

Rounds of eight to one server for every five tables, busser for every eight tables

With Poured Wine or French Service

Round of ten to two servers for every three tables

Round of eight to one server for every two tables

Buffets 1/30 to 40

One server per 30 to 40 guests

One runner per 100 to 125 guests

TABLE 9-5
Space Requirements

Space Requirements for Tables			
Rounds	60-inches round =	5-feet diameter =	Round of 8
	72-inches round =	6-feet diameter =	Round of 10
	66-inch round =	Compromise size	Seats 8–10
Rectangle	6-feet long	30-inches wide	Banquet 6
	8-feet long	30-inches wide	Banquet 8
Schoolroom or classroom	6- or 8-feet long	18- or 24-inches wide	
Half-moon table	Half of a roundtable		
Serpentine	$\frac{1}{4}$ hollowed-out	round table	
Space Requirements for Receptions			
Minimum (tight)	$5\frac{1}{2}$–7 square feet per person		
Comfortably crowded	$7\frac{1}{2}$ square feet per person		
Ample room	10+ square feet per person		

French or Russian Service

Rounds of eight or ten

One server per table

One busser per three tables

Supervision

One room captain, with one section captain for every 250 guests (25 rounds of 10).

Set Over Guarantee

The set over guarantee is negotiable, depending on the property. It is the percentage of guests that the hotel will prepare for beyond the guarantee, in case additional, unexpected people show up. The following are **set over guarantees** at a major Las Vegas property.

Average overset is 3 percent, but you must look at the numbers, not just the percentages. less than 100 guests = the guarantee is the set.
100 to 1,000 guests = 3 percent overset with a maximum of 50.
Over 1,000 guests = 3 percent overset.

Cocktail Servers

Cocktail servers can only carry from 12 to 16 drinks per trip. Counting the time to take the order, the time to wait for the drinks at the service bar, and the time it takes to find the guest and deliver the drink, it takes at least 15 minutes per trip to the bar. This only makes it possible to serve from 48 to 64 drinks per hour. Cocktail servers are usually only used at small or VIP functions.

Service Timing

Fifteen minutes before you want to start serving, dim the lights, ring chimes, start music, open doors, and so on to get the guests to start moving to their tables.

The salad course should take from fifteen to twenty minutes, depending on dressing or style of service. The main course should take from 30 to 40 minutes from serving to plate removal. Dessert should take from 20 to 30 minutes.

A typical luncheon: one hour and fifteen minutes
A typical dinner: two hours

Trends and Best Practices

- Global and sustained efforts to embrace and integrate green products and practices.
- Use of clean/slick/simple presentations and efficient service.
- Focus on big/bold flavor profiles.
- Use fresh, locally/regionally sourced, sustainable foods and products from outstanding specialty producers (Cowgirl Creamery and Niman Ranch).
- Include a signature portfolio of house made items (potato chips, jams, yogurt, jerky, olives, and spice rubs).
- Make strategic use of well-known branded products (Boars Head, Starbucks, Evian, and Pellegrino).
- Consider tapas style small plates as reception choices.
- The food truck, which is popular now even in Paris! This is an interesting addition to receptions as a themed station.
- Provide craft beer options and bolder options for varietal wines.
- Invest in improved display and action station equipment (hinged chafing dishes, small convection burners, steamers, deep-fryers, self-draining cold beverage containers, stainless steel buffet table tops, rolling/folding buffet tables, display racks, and lighted back-bar units).

Food Trends

- *Classic Dishes Are New Again:* Fads are on hold. People are looking for sophisticated interpretations of familiar food.
- *Chicken Is Back in Style:* There is a movement toward anti-luxury, so chicken is preferred over beef for a closing dinner. Variations in chicken preparation are far more common than in the past, ranging from pan roasted, braised, sofrito, confit, to ballotine.
- *Small Surprises:* Even if budgets for meals are reduced, a "wow" item can be included to build some buzz.
- *Breakfast Can Be Tweaked:* Some venues are allowing multiple groups to share the same breakfast buffet, thus saving cost. Another trend is to consolidate breakfast and lunch into brunch, thereby making it one meal instead of two, which results in cost savings.
- *Easier Prep:* Event professionals will choose foods that don't require extra labor such as making special sauces or preparing individual servings.
- *Meal Mingling:* More meals are focusing on networking opportunities in lieu of a large, long, sit-down meal. Lunches are going toward a more grab-and-go style or to small, tapas style items. Dinners are often replaced by receptions.
- *Organic Décor:* Using cotton tablecloths instead of linen, low-cost candlescapes instead of laurels. Compostable plates and utensils are now more common.
- *Locally Grown:* The green movement has created more interest in products that are locally grown. The story of where food came from is being included on printed menus.
- *Waste Reduction:* There is continued focus on reducing the waste produced by meetings, conventions, and events.
- *Small Plate:* As clients become more health conscious, and with the advent of small plate cuisine, such as tapas and dim sum, small plates are gaining popularity allowing clients to taste more with every meal. This also goes with some events that forgo a formal dinner format, replacing it with an extended cocktail hour with heavy hors d'oeuvres.

Summary

Food and beverage is an integral part of most meetings and events. Astute planning can save a tremendous amount of money. Knowing what is negotiable and how to negotiate is critical. Food and beverage events create memories and provide a necessary service beyond being a refueling stop. While most attendees do not specify food and beverage events as a reason for attending a meeting, when asked later about a meeting, they will often rave (or complain) about these events. Catered events often set the tone of the meeting and create great memories that can result in future business, not only from the event professional, but also from every guest in attendance.

CASE STUDY

Catering Safety and Sanitation

Food and beverage production and service must be carried out in a safe and wholesome manner. Anyone handling foods must be trained to practice safety and sanitation procedures to ensure that guests do not fall victim to accidents and food-borne illnesses. All commercial foodservice operations must adhere to the sanitation standards set forth by their local health districts. Certifications exist that prove adherence to safety and sanitation standards. These include sanitation guidelines developed by the National Restaurant Association Educational Foundation, such as ServSafe and the Hazard Analysis and Critical Control Points certification (HACCP). Food contact equipment should be certified by the National Sanitation Foundation (NSF). Equipment should meet the guidelines of Underwriters Laboratories (UL) and the American Gas Association (AGA). The Department of Labor, as well as the state worker's compensation agency, all have relevant standards that require adherence.

1. Have you earned any of these certifications?
2. If not, will you?
3. What other food or beverage certifications can you identify?

Key Words and Terms

For definitions, see the Glossary.

action station	butler service	on-premise catering
American Service	catered events	off-premise catering
attrition	caterer	room set up
banquet event order (BEO)	corkage	set over guarantees
bar backs	guarantee	tablescapes

Review and Discussion Questions

1. What is the first step for an event professional when planning for an off-premise event? List five types of functions and give a brief description of each.

2. Describe how Family Style/English Service and Plated/American Style service differ.

3. What is the most important information to consider when deciding how much food to order for a group?

4. What is the average number of hors d'oeuvres a guest will eat during the first hour of an event?

5. What are the three categories of liquor?

6. What is the function of a hospitality suite, and what are the three types?

7. What are the important aspects of an event that are affected by how the room is set up?

8. When catering an event at a hotel, and no room nights are involved, which department handles the booking of the event?

9. Why is it imperative that the tabletop not be overlooked?

About the Chapter Contributors

Donnell Bayot, PhD, CHE, CPCE, CFBE is the Director of Academic Affairs for the International School of Hospitality (TISOH) in Las Vegas, Nevada. Donnell is President-Elect for the 3,500 member National Association for Catering and Events (NACE). Donnell is a 2014 Pacesetter Award winner from the Convention Industry Council (now the Event Industry Council) and his PhD dissertation was on the development of a competency model for catering and event professionals.

Gary L. McCreary, CPCE CMP CSEP is the Vice President of Catering and Convention Operations at The Venetian/The Palazzo Resort Hotel & Casinos in Las Vegas, Nevada. Gary is Immediate Past President of the Foundation of NACE (National Association for Catering and Events). Gary is a graduate of the University of North Texas where he earned a degree in Hotel and Restaurant Administration.

Previous Edition Chapter Contributors

Perry Lynch joined the faculty of the Rosen College of Hospitality Management at the University of Central Florida in 2006, after a 23-year career in catering and convention service with Marriott Hotels.

Patti J. Shock is the academic consultant for The International School of Hospitality and emeritus professor and chair in the Harrah College of Hotel Administration at the University of Nevada–Las Vegas. Patti has authored six textbooks on catering, and received over 30 industry and academic awards, culminating in her induction into the Hall of Leaders of the Convention Industry Council (now Event Industry Council).

Contracts are a critical legal factor in MEEC.
Maksym Dykha/Shutterstock

CHAPTER 10

Legal Issues in the MEEC Industry

Chapter Objectives

- Cover the most important elements of negotiation in MEEC.
- Note the specifics to consider when dealing with contracts in this industry.
- Discuss the importance of crisis preparedness and management.
- Clarify the points and impact of the Americans with Disabilities Act as it pertains to MEEC.

- Articulate the legal importance of intellectual property as it has to do with this industry.
- Outline potential labor issues to consider in the industry.
- Discuss important ethical concerns to consider in MEEC.
- Outline current trends and best practices regarding legal issues in MEEC.

Whether we like it or not, we live in a very litigious society. Thus, legal issues are becoming increasingly important, especially in the MEEC industry. There are legal aspects or issues in almost everything we do as meeting planners and organizers. Contracts are a part of virtually every event, and have become increasingly complex.

183

One reason that contracts can be so long and complex is that the parties to the contract try to eliminate as much ambiguity as possible. Ideally, contracts will be as clear as possible for the average person. We enter into negotiations regardless of whether we are the buyer (meeting organizers) or suppliers (hotels, DMCs, caterers, etc.). We must be concerned about risks, such as force majeure (emergencies, crises, or disasters), people getting injured, and failures to perform. We also must be concerned with national, state, and local laws that impact how we put on an event, who we employ, and the entertainment we use. In this chapter, we delve into many of these issues and provide some insight into legal issues. Remember that this chapter does not take the place of consulting with an attorney who is knowledgeable about MEEC and licensed to practice in your jurisdiction. Furthermore, legal and ethical issues vary by country. This chapter uses a US framework, but has broad applicability around the globe.

Negotiation

Negotiation is the process by which a meeting planner and a hotel representative (or other supplier) reach an agreement on the terms and conditions that will govern their relationship before, during, and after a meeting, convention, exposition, or event.

Negotiation Strategies

While many believe that the goal of a negotiation is to create a win–win situation, some say there can be no win–win because, generally, one or both parties must compromise on some things. The real winner may be the party who is better prepared entering the negotiation and has the best bargaining leverage. In this regard, hotel representatives generally have an advantage over planners, since the hotels usually know more about the planner's organization than the planner knows about the lodging industry or the specific hotel under consideration.

There are almost as many approaches to negotiating strategy as there are negotiators. The following are some tips on negotiating:

- *Do your homework.*   Develop a game plan of the outcomes sought, and prioritize your wants and needs. Learn as much about the other side's position as you can.
- *Keep your eyes on the prize.*   Do not forget the outcome being sought.
- *Leave something on the table.*   It may provide an opportunity to come back later and renew the negotiations.
- *Do not be the first one to make an offer.*   Letting the other person make the first move sets the outside parameters for the negotiation.
- *When there is a roadblock, find a more creative path.*   Thinking outside the box often leads to a solution.
- *Timing is everything.*   Remember that time always works against the person who does not have it and that 90 percent of negotiation usually occurs in the last ten percent of the time allocated.
- *Listen, listen, listen . . . and do not get emotional.*   Letting emotions rule a negotiation will cause one to lose sight of what result is important.

When negotiating meeting contracts—or any contracts—it is wise to keep some general rules in mind. The following general rules will help with the negotiation of a meeting contract:

- *Go into the negotiations with a plan.*   A skilled negotiator knows his or her bottom line, that is, what is really needed, what is just wanted, and what can be given up to reach a compromise.
- *Always go into a contract negotiation with an alternative location or service provider in mind.*   Bargaining leverage is better if the other party knows you can go somewhere else with your business.

- *Be thorough.* Put everything negotiated in the contract. Develop your own contract if necessary.

- *Do not assume anything.* Meeting industry personnel change frequently, and oral agreements or assumptions can be easily forgotten or misunderstood. Put it in writing.

- *Beware of language that sounds acceptable but is not specific.* For example, what does a "tentative first option" mean? Words like reasonable, anticipated, and projected should be avoided, since they mean different things to different people.

- *Do not accept something just because it is preprinted on the contract or the proposal is given to you by the other party.* Everything is negotiable. (See Case 1: SXSW Entertainment Contract).

- *Read the small print.* For example, the boilerplate language about indemnification of parties in the event of negligence can make a major difference in the resolution of liability after an accident or injury.

- *Look for mutuality in the contract's provisions.* For example, do not sign a contract in which the hold harmless clause only protects one of the parties. Such provisions should be applicable to both parties. And never give one party the unilateral right to do anything, such as change the location of meeting rooms without consent of the meeting organizer.

CASE 1. SXSW ENTERTAINMENT CONTRACT

In 2017, in the wake of a change in federal government that brought with it declarations of sweeping changes in immigration policy among other things, SXSW, an annual music, media, and film festival, came under fire because of a controversial clause in its contract with musicians who wanted to play at the festival. The clause read in part:

> *Foreign Artists entering the country through the Visa Waiver Program (VWP), B visa or any non-work visa may not perform at any public or unofficial shows, DAY OR NIGHT, in Austin from March 10–19, 2017. Accepting and performing at unofficial events (including unofficial events aside from SXSW Music dates during their visit to the United States)* **may result in immediate deportation, revoked passport and denied entry by US Customs Border Patrol at US ports of entry."** *(emphasis added)*

(Strauss & Yoo, 2017)

One entertainer declined to participate in the event because of this language that he (and others) perceived as threatening to non-US artists, despite the fact that the language had been in previous year's contracts, but had gone unnoticed.

SXSW, in crisis management mode after the debate over this language went public, reiterated their support of foreign artists and their stance on government issues. They claimed to have put this in the contracts as a reminder of the responsibility of the artists traveling to the United States, and to protect SXSW in the event of "egregious acts" by foreign acts. Although it was too late at the time of the public backlash to go back and change all of the existing contracts, SXSW indicated that it would consider whether to modify the contract language in the future. Everything truly is negotiable.

Strauss, M., & Yoo, N. (2017, March 2). SXSW under fire over artist deportation contract clause. Pitchfork. Retrieved from http://pitchformk.com/news/72013-sxsw-under-fire-over-artist-deportation-contract-clause/

Negotiating Hotel Contracts

In addition to the general rules that are applicable to all contract negotiations, there are some special rules about hotel contracts that should also be kept in mind.

- *Understand revenue streams.* Remember that a meeting contract provides a package of funds to a hotel. Think in terms of overall financial benefit to the hotel (i.e., its total income from room rates, food and beverage, and so on), and allocate this to the organization's benefit.

- *Finalize details.* Never sign a contract in which major items, like room rates, are left to future negotiation. Future rates can always be set as a percentage of the then-current rack, or maximum increase over the then-current group rates. This applies to rooms, catered food and beverage, audiovisual, and other expense items.

- *Specify special room rates*—such as for staff and speakers—and indicate any upgrades for them. Indicate whether these are included in the complimentary room formula, and specify what that formula is.

- *Specify when function space will be finalized.* While it is preferable to have specific meeting and function rooms designated in the contract, a secondary negotiation position is that they should be assigned at least 12 months prior to the meeting/event, depending on the time of the first promotional mailing. Do not permit a change in assigned meeting rooms without approval of the meeting organizer, but be prepared to agree to alternate space, or to pay for the original space if the group numbers decrease significantly.

- *Get changes in writing.* Do not agree to any changes that are not spelled out either in the contract or in a later addendum. If an addendum is used, make sure that it references the underlying agreement and supersedes the language in it; and if it is signed at the time of the agreement, make sure that the agreement references the addendum. Be sure that all documents are signed by individuals who are authorized to bind the parties.

Naming Names

One of the most frequently overlooked yet most important parts of a hotel contract includes the names of the contracting parties. While the meeting's organizer is listed (an independent planner should always sign as an agent for the organizer or have an authorized representative of the organizer sign), the name of the hotel is, in almost all cases, simply listed as the name on the hotel marquee, like "Sheraton Boston."

But the hotel's name is merely a trade name—that is, the name under which the property's owner or management company does business. In today's hotel environment, it may be a franchise of a national chain operated by a company that the planner has never heard of. For example, one of the country's largest hotel management companies is Interstate Hotels & Resorts, Inc. Included in the more than 300 hotels that it manages are properties operating under the following chain names: Marriott, Holiday Inn, Hilton, Sheraton, and Radisson. Thus, if a contract with one of Interstate's properties simply states that it is with the "Gaithersburg (MD) Marriott," the planner might never know that the actual contracting party is Interstate Hotels & Resorts.

Every meeting contract should contain the following provision, usually as the introductory paragraph.

> "This Agreement dated _____ is between (official legal name of entity), a (name of state) (corporation) (partnership) doing business as (name of hotel) and having its principal place of business at (address of contracting party, not hotel) and (name of meeting organizer), a (name of state) (corporation) (partnership) having its principal place of business at (address of meeting organizer)."

Sleeping rooms generate the major share of hotel revenue, so this is often the biggest concern to hotels.

Catered food and beverage is also important but only if it is the right kind of food and beverage function, since not all functions are equal in value. For example, a seated dinner for 100 people is worth more to a hotel—in revenue and profit—than a coffee break or continental breakfast for the same number of people.

The type of entity organizing the meeting. Hotels know from experience that certain types of meeting attendees are likely to spend more at hotel food outlets (restaurants, room service, etc.) than other types of attendees who may venture outside the property for meals at more expensive restaurants. From experience, a hotel is also able to estimate the number of attendees who will not show up or who will check out early. Early departures and no-shows deprive the hotel of expected revenue.

If a meeting planner is going to successfully negotiate with a hotel, the planner should:

- Understand the relative strengths and weaknesses of the meeting as a piece of business that the hotel may be interested in: "how much is the piece of business worth?"
- Understand how a hotel evaluates meeting business.

- Understand the competitive marketplace in which the hotel operates—for instance, its strengths, weaknesses, and occupancy patterns.

- Position the meeting in its best light, using detailed information and history of prior meetings to support this approach. The hotel may base its evaluation of a meeting, especially one it has never hosted before, on its perception of the industry or profession represented by the meeting organizer. Thus, the meeting organizer can counter any negative impressions, or play up positive ones, by providing the hotel with as much information as possible on the organizer's **meeting history**. Especially helpful is information pertaining to previous meeting room blocks and subsequent room utilization, total spending on sleeping rooms, food and beverage, equipment rental, and ancillary services like recreational activities or in-room movies.

- Many hoteliers, particularly those who have been in the industry for many years, sum up meeting negotiations with this simple maxim: "**Dates, rates, and space**—*You Can Only Have Two.*" (See Table 10-1) By this maxim, for example, the planner can get the dates and meeting space he or she wants for a meeting, but may have to give a little on the rate. Much more than space, room rates, and meeting dates are negotiable. Consider contract issues, such as earning complimentary rooms for a certain number of reserved rooms, cutoff dates, rates after cutoff, attrition and cancellation clauses, meeting or exhibit space rental, comp suites, staff rates, limo service, audiovisual rates, VIP amenities, parking fees, and food and beverage provisions. In short, *everything* about a hotel (supplier) contract is negotiable. Likewise, in any other vendor or supplier contract, there are many negotiable items.

- Determine where the meeting organizer can be flexible. A negotiation often requires both parties to make concessions to reach an equitable, acceptable agreement. For example, if a planner understands that the meeting's space-to-rooms ratio is greater than customary, the planner can help his or her position by altering the program format, eliminating 24-hour holds on meeting or function space, which allows the hotel to sell the space in unused hours. The planner who refuses to be flexible is not likely to get the best deal. Changing arrival and departure dates to more closely fit the hotel's occupancy pattern can also lead to a successful negotiation. Moving the meeting forward or backward one or more weeks can also result in savings, especially if the preferred time coincides with a period of high sleeping room demand.

To understand how a hotel approaches a meeting negotiation, the planner must first know about the hotel. Some of the necessary information is obvious:

- The hotel's location—is it near an airport, downtown, or close to a convention center?
- The hotel's type—is it a resort with a golf course, tennis court, and other amenities; a convention hotel with a great deal of meeting space; or a small venue with limited meeting facilities?

However, some of the information that is important to know is not so obvious, and may in fact change depending on the time of the year. For example, it is important to know the mix between the hotel's transient business (that derived from individual business

TABLE 10-1

Rates, Dates, and Space . . . You Can Only Have Two

The Cocoa Society wants to meet in Portland, Oregon, ideally the week after Memorial Day. They would like to keep their rates under $200 a night. They need 20,000 sq. ft. of meeting space. In a negotiation, they may get options like the following.

Rates	Dates	Space
$199/night Run of House	June 1–4	12,000 sq. ft. at a rental of $2,500/day total
$199/night Run of House	May 15–19	20,000 sq. ft. complimentary
$289/night Run of House	June 1–4	20,000 sq. ft. complimentary

guests or tourists) and groups. Within the group sector, it is valuable to know how much business is derived from corporate, government, and association sources. It is also important to know what the hotel regards as high season, when room demand is highest; and low season, when demand is at its annual low. This information is important because it helps the planner understand the hotel's position in the negotiation process, and it may provide some helpful hints in structuring a planner's proposal to meet the hotel's needs.

Seasonal fluctuations may be driven by outside factors, such as events in the city where the hotel is located. For example, an informed planner will know that it is difficult to book rooms in New Orleans during Mardi Gras or during that city's annual Jazz Fest (in late April and early May) because hotels can sell their rooms to individual tourists at higher rates than to groups. Many hotels in Palm Springs, California, are heavily booked during spring break; therefore, favorable meeting rates may be difficult to obtain then.

The arrival and departure patterns of the majority of a hotel's guests are also important for a planner to know. For example, a hotel in Las Vegas is generally difficult to book for weekend meetings, because the city attracts large numbers of individual visitors who come to spend the weekend. A hotel that caters to many individual business guests may have greater availability on Friday and Saturday nights, when business travelers are not there. A national survey indicates that, for typical hotels, occupancy is lowest on Sunday evenings and highest on Wednesdays.

While hotels generate revenue from a variety of sources—and have recently become more sophisticated at analyzing these profit centers—the primary source of hotel income is sleeping room revenue; one industry research report estimates that, overall, more than 67 percent of all hotel revenue is generated from sleeping rooms.

Hotels set their sleeping room rates—at least the published or so-called **rack rates**—in several ways. First, the hotel wants to achieve a total return on its investment. However, since nearly 50 percent of all rooms in all hotels are sold at less than rack rate, hotels vary their actual rates depending on a number of supply and demand factors, including time of year (which is a function of demand).

Most hotels have adopted the concept of **yield management**, also called revenue management, which was pioneered by the airline industry. In this approach, hotels can vary their rates almost daily, depending on the actual and anticipated demand for rooms at a particular time. The yield management concept may have some negative impacts on meeting planners. For example, a planner who books a meeting fifteen to eighteen months in advance may find that, as the meeting nears, total hotel room utilization is lower than

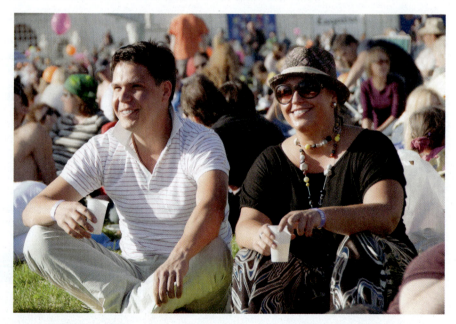

Jazz Fest draws upward of 100,000 attendees per day to New Orleans in late April.
Anton Gvozdikov/Shutterstock

the hotel anticipated. Therefore, the hotel, hoping to generate additional revenue, will promote special pricing, which may turn out to be less than what was offered to the meeting organizer. A contractual provision prohibiting this practice, which many hotels will not agree to, or at least giving the meeting organizer credit toward its room block for rooms booked at these lower prices can help take the sting out of yield management practices.

Contracts

In far too many instances, **contracts** for meetings, conventions, and trade shows, and the ancillary services provided in connection with these events, contain self-serving statements, lack specificity, and fail to reflect the total negotiation between the parties. This is understandable since neither meeting planners nor hotel sales representatives generally receive training in the law governing these agreements.

By definition, a contract is an agreement between two parties that details the intention of the parties to do (or not do) specific things. For example, at its most basic, a meetings contract says the meeting's organizer agrees to use a certain number of rooms and services and the hotel agrees to provide the rooms and services outlined.

A contract need not be called a contract but can be referred to as an agreement, a letter of agreement, a memorandum of understanding, and sometimes a letter of intent or proposal. The title of the document or understanding is not important—its contents are. For example, if a document called a proposal sets forth details of a meeting and contains the legal elements of a contract, it becomes a binding contract when signed by both parties. So, don't let the name at the top of the document mislead you.

The essential elements of a contract are

- An **offer** by one party.
- Acceptance of the offer as presented by another party. This is typically done by signing the contract.
- **Consideration** (i.e., the price negotiated and paid for the agreement). Although consideration is usually expressed in monetary terms, it need not be, for example, mutual promises are often treated as consideration in a valid contract.

Offers can be terminated prior to acceptance in one of several ways:

- At the expiration of a specified time (e.g., "This offer is only good for 24 hours." After 24 hours, the other party cannot accept it because it expired.).
- At the expiration of a reasonable time period.
- On specific revocation by the offeror. In this case, however, the revocation must be communicated to the offeree to be effective.

A rejection of the offer by the offeree, or a proposal of a counteroffer terminates the original offer, but a request for additional information about the offer is not construed as a rejection of the offer. For example, if an individual responds to an offer by saying, "I accept, with the following addition," this is not really an acceptance, but a proposal of a counteroffer, which the original offeror must then consider and either accept or reject.

Often, a meeting contract proposal from a hotel will contain a specified termination period for the offer. These offers are usually couched in the phrase, "tentative first option" or in a similar wording. Because the meeting organizer pays or promises nothing for this option, it is, in reality, nothing more than a contract offer, which must be specifically accepted by the meeting planner. There is no legal obligation on the part of the hotel to keep the option or offer open for the time period stated.

In a meeting context, the hotel, venue, or vendor is usually the offeror, that is, the written agreement is generally proposed, after some preliminary negotiation, by them to the planner. The meeting organizer becomes the offeree, but a counteroffer is often made.

For an offer to be accepted, the acceptance must be unequivocal and in the same terms as the offer. Any deviation from the offer's terms is not acceptance; it is a counteroffer, which must then be accepted by the original offeror for a valid contract to exist.

Acceptance must be communicated to the offeror using the same means as the offeror used. In other words, if the offer is made in writing, the acceptance must be in writing. Mere silence on the part of the offeree is never construed as acceptance, and an offeror cannot impose an agreement on the other party by stating that the contract will be assumed if no response is given by a specified date.

As indicated, consideration is the price negotiated and paid for the agreement. While consideration generally involves money paid for the other party's promise to perform certain functions—for example, money paid to a hotel for the provision of sleeping rooms, meeting space, and food and beverage functions—it could also be an exchange of mutual promises, as in a barter situation.

Consideration must be what the law regards as sufficient, not from a monetary standpoint, but from the standpoint of whether the act or return promises results in either a benefit to the promisor or a detriment to the promisee. The fairness of the agreed exchange is legally irrelevant. Thus, the law is not concerned about whether one party overpaid for what he or she received. One need not make an affirmative promise or payment of money; for instance, forbearance, not doing something that someone is legally entitled to do, can also be a consideration in a contract.

It is important that both promises are legally enforceable to constitute valid *consideration*. For example, a promise to commit an illegal act is not *consideration* because the law will not require one to commit that act.

Statute of Frauds

Although a contract does not have to be in writing to be enforceable, every law student learns that it is better to have a written document since there can be less chance for a misunderstanding about the terms of the agreement. However, under what is called the "Statute of Frauds," some contracts must be in writing to be enforceable. This statute was first passed in England in 1677, and in one form or another has become a part of the law of virtually every state in the United States. The exception is Louisiana, where law is based on French Napoleonic code.

Among the agreements that must be in writing are contracts for the sale or lease of real estate, and contracts that are not to be performed within one year of agreement. The latter includes contracts for meetings and other events that are to be held more than one year in the future. The former could also include a meeting contract, since the agreement might be construed as an organizer's lease of hotel space. The law requires these contracts to be in writing because they are viewed as more important documents than ordinary agreements. However, as indicated, planners are strongly encouraged to put all contracts in writing to avoid the possibility of misunderstandings.

A valid written contract must contain the identity of the parties, an identification or recitation of the subject matter and terms of agreement, and a statement of consideration. Often, where the consideration may not be obvious, a contract will state that it is entered into for "good and valuable consideration, the receipt and sufficiency of which are acknowledged by the parties."

When a contract is in writing, it is generally subject to the so-called parol evidence or the four-corners rule of interpretation. Thus, where the written contract is intended to be the complete and final expression of the rights and duties of the parties, evidence of prior oral or written negotiations or agreements, or contemporaneous oral agreements cannot be considered by a court charged with interpreting the contract. Many contracts contain what is often called an entire agreement clause, which specifies that the written document contains the entire agreement between the parties and supersedes all previous oral or written negotiations or agreements.

Parol Evidence

Parol evidence (or evidence of oral agreement) can be used in limited instances, especially where the plain meaning of words in the written document may be in doubt. A court will generally construe a contract most strongly against the party that prepared the written document; and if there is a conflict between printed and handwritten words or phrases, the latter will prevail.

Many contracts, especially meeting contracts, contain addenda prepared at the same time as, or sometimes subsequent to, the signing of the contract. In cases where the terms of an addendum differ from those of the contract, the addendum generally prevails; although, it is a good idea when using an addendum to specifically provide that, in the event of differences, the addendum will prevail.

Key Hotel Group Meeting Contract Clauses

Planning and executing a meeting may involve the negotiation of several contracts. Obviously, the major—and perhaps most important—agreement is the one with the hotel and/or trade show facility. However, there can also be agreements covering a myriad of ancillary services, such as temporary employees, security, audiovisual equipment, destination management (e.g., tours and local transportation), entertainment, outside food and beverage, exhibitor services or decorating, and housing bureaus. Moreover, agreements may be negotiated with official transportation providers like travel agencies, airlines, and rental car companies.

Attrition, cancellation, and termination provisions in a hotel are frequently confusing. If not carefully drafted, they can lead to many problems (and much expense) if a meeting organizer does not fill the room block or wishes to change his or her mind for some reason. For more information on these and other hotel group meeting contract clauses, see the Events Industry Council's Accepted Practices Exchange (APEX) Contracts Accepted Practices (www.conventionindustry.org/Files/APEX/APEX_Contracts.pdf).

Attrition

Attrition clauses (sometimes also referred to as *performance* or *slippage clauses*) provide for the payment of damages to the hotel when a meeting organizer fails to fully utilize the room block specified in the contract. Most hotels regard the contracted room block as a commitment by the meeting organizer to fill the number of room nights specified. However, in at least one case, a court determined that the room block did not represent a commitment by the meeting organizer; that decision was predicated, in part, on contract language that indicated that room reservations would be made by individuals and not by the meeting organizer.

A well-written attrition provision should provide the organizing entity with the ability to reduce the room block by a specified amount (e.g., 10 to 20 percent) up to a specified time prior to the meeting (e.g., 6 to 12 months) without incurring damages. Thereafter, damages should only accrue if the organizer fails to occupy a specified percentage (e.g., 85 to 90 percent) of its adjusted (not the original) room block. Occupancy should be measured on a cumulative room night basis, not on a night-by-night basis.

Because hotels sometimes offer rates to the general public as part of special promotional packages that are lower than those available to the meeting attendees, it is important that the meeting room **pickup** be measured by all attendance, regardless of the rate paid. This may involve some extra work on the part of the hotel and the meeting organizer, but the result could save the organization money, especially if the meeting attendance is not as expected. For example, the meeting contract could include language like the following.

> **EXAMPLE**
>
> Group shall receive credit for all rooms used by attendees, regardless of the rate paid or the method of booking. Hotel shall cooperate with Group in identifying these attendees and shall charge no fee for assisting Group.

Using this language, an organization would submit its meeting registration list to the hotel and ask that the hotel match the list against those guests who are in-house at the time. An alternate approach, which many hotels reject, is to have the hotel give the group its in-house guest list and have the group do the matching.

A contract between The Cocoa Society and Fountain Hotel initially included the following attrition clause (it is not favorable to the Group).

Clause 1. This Agreement is therefore based on Group's use of 200 total room nights. Group agrees that if Group uses less than the room block established in this agreement, Hotel will be harmed. Hotel will allow Group 10 percent room block shrinkage without any liquidated damage payment. For shrinkage over and above this allowance, the Hotel will require payment from Group for each unused room night at the confirmed group average rate plus applicable tax for your committed room block. This payment will not be in effect with respect to any unused room nights within your committed block for any night during your stay in which all of the available rooms in the Hotel are sold.

After modification by The Cocoa Society, the clause read as follows.

Clause 2. This Agreement is therefore based on Group's use of 200 total room nights. Group agrees that if Group uses less than the room block established in this agreement, Hotel will <u>may</u> be harmed. Hotel will allow Group 10 percent room block shrinkage without any liquidated damage payment. For shrinkage over and above this allowance, the Hotel will require payment from Group for each unused room night at 75 percent (profit margin) of the confirmed group Run of House rate plus applicable tax for your committed room block. Group will receive credit against attrition damages for all room nights Hotel is able to resell. The parties understand the Hotel will resell Group rooms only after the rest of its inventory has been sold.

To see how significant a few changes to an attrition clause can be in terms of financial damages, compare the calculations with Clause 1 and Clause 2. Examples assume that the Group picked up 150 room nights.

Clause 1

$200 - 150$ room nights $= 50$ room nights unsold

Shrinkage $(200 \times 10\%) = 20$ room nights shrinkage

50 room nights unsold $- 20$ room nights shrinkage $= 30$ room nights for attrition damages

30 room nights $\times$ \$235/night $=$ US\$7,050 attrition damages

Clause 2

$200 - 150$ room nights $= 50$ room nights unsold

Shrinkage $(200 \times 20\%) = 40$ room nights shrinkage

50 room nights unsold $- 40$ room nights shrinkage $= 10$ room nights for attrition damages

10 room nights $\times$ (\$200/night $\times$ 75% profit margin) $=$ US\$1,500 attrition damages

FIGURE 10-1
Calculating Attrition Damages

Damages triggered by the failure to meet a room block commitment should be specified in dollars, not measured by a percentage of some vague figure, such as "anticipated room revenue." The latter may provide the hotel with an opportunity to include estimated spending on such things as telephone calls, in-room movies, and the like. The specified damages should be based on the hotel's lost profit, not its lost revenue. With sleeping rooms, for example, the average industry's profit margin is 75 to 80 percent, so the per-room attrition fee should not exceed 80 percent of the group's single room rate. The industry standard for food and beverage profit is 25 to 30 percent. In any event, damages for failure to meet a room block commitment should never be payable if the hotel is able to resell the rooms; the contract should impose a specific requirement on the hotel to try and resell the rooms and, if possible, require the hotel to resell the rooms in the organization's room block first. (See Figure 10-1).

Attrition clauses often appear in the portion of a contract that discusses meeting room rental fees, with the contract providing that meeting room rental fees will be imposed, typically on a sliding scale basis, if the room block is not filled. If the clause appears in conjunction with a meeting room rental, it should not also appear somewhere else, resulting in a double charge, and language should be inserted making it clear that the meeting room rental fee is the only charge to be imposed if the room block is not completely utilized.

Cancellation

This is the provision that provides for damages should the meeting be canceled for reasons other than those specified in the termination provision. Often, this provision in a hotel-provided agreement is one-sided. It provides damages to the hotel in the event the meeting organizer cancels. A properly drafted agreement should provide for damages in the event either party (including the hotel) cancels without a valid reason. However, as indicated previously, some contract drafters believe that damages should not be specified in the event of a hotel cancellation, because it only provides the hotel with an amount that it can use to buy out of an agreement. An alternative approach is to specify what the group's damages will include if the hotel cancels. This is called an actual damages clause (as contrasted with liquidated damages, mentioned later). This includes listing things like: increases in food and beverage costs or rooms at a substitute hotel, additional marketing materials, site inspection trips to find a new hotel for the meeting, and so on. Although it seems like bad business for a hotel to cancel a meeting, it does happen. (See Case 2).

The meeting organizer should not have the right to cancel solely to book the meeting in another hotel or another city, or for the hotel to book another, more lucrative meeting in place of the one contracted for.

The damages triggered by a cancellation by the group are sometimes stated on a sliding scale basis, with greater damages being paid the closer to the meeting date the cancellation occurs. Damages should be expressed as liquidated damages or a cancellation fee, not as a penalty, since the law generally does not recognize penalty provisions in contracts. As with damages in an attrition clause, damages should be expressed in dollar amounts, not room revenue (so that sales tax can be avoided), and should only be payable if the hotel cannot resell the space.

CASE 2.   SYLVANIA VERSUS BOCA RATON RESORT & CLUB

Osram Sylvania, Inc. signed a contract with the Boca Raton Resort & Club for a national sales meeting to take place in October 2007. Sylvania had a long history with the hotel, having held 17 meetings at the hotel since 1984. So imagine Sylvania's surprise when the hotel cancelled in 2007 the contract that had been negotiated and signed in 2004! Because the contract was signed during a recession period for the United States, the rates Sylvania was able to negotiate in 2004 may have been more favorable than the market rates in 2007. This is why negotiating contract clauses are so important—you

may think the hotel will never cancel (it is unusual), but it does happen. Sylvania never got to meet at the Boca Raton Resort & Club in 2007, but through a settlement, they did return in 2008.

Bassett, M. (2007, August 1). The seller's market strikes again. *MeetingsNet.* Retrieved from www.meetingsnet.com/checklists/sellers-market-strikes-again
MeetingsNet. (2007, September 21). OSI settles meeting flap. *Corporate Meetings & Incentives.* Retrieved from www.meetingsnet.com/corporate-meetings/osi-settles-meeting-flap

---

Termination

Sometimes called a **force majeure** or an **Act of God** clause, this provision permits either party to terminate the contract without damages if fulfillment of the obligations imposed in the agreement is rendered impossible by occurrences outside of the control of either party. This usually includes such things as labor strikes, severe weather, and transportation difficulties. Typical language says that performance will be excused due to circumstances beyond the control of the parties that makes it illegal or impossible to hold or host the meeting. Sometimes the provision also uses the term impracticable, which means while it may not be absolutely impossible, it is functionally impossible.

A meeting organizer should be able to terminate the contract without payment of damages, if the hotel ownership, management, or brand affiliation changes; if the meeting size outgrows the hotel; if the hotel's quality rating (e.g., as measured by the American Automobile Association) changes; or for reasons that make it inappropriate or impractical to hold the meeting there. The latter language should be broad enough to cover objectionable policies or laws, where a group decides not to hold a meeting in a particular location because of action taken by government. For example, the organizer of a major shooting sports trade show—SHOT—canceled the event after the sponsoring city sued the gun manufacturers who were the show's major exhibitors.

Because of the differences in contracts supplied by hotels, and because it is often so easy for planners, even experienced ones, to overlook key elements of a contract, many meeting organizers are developing their own standard contract. While many meeting organizers may be unsure of the costs involved in having a competent attorney prepare this type of document, such costs are minimal when compared with the time (and there-fore expense) involved in reviewing each and every contract proposed by a hotel, whether the review is conducted by counsel, or by a meeting planner or other staff member.

An organizer's development of its own contract will ensure that its needs are met, and will minimize the chances of subsequent legal problems caused by a misunderstanding of the terms of the agreement.

Dispute Resolution

No matter how carefully a contract is written, disputes may occur either because the parties might disagree as to their individual rights and obligations, or because one of the parties may perform less than was promised. These controversies seldom involve prece-dent-setting legal issues; rather, they concern an evaluation of facts and the interpretation of contract terms. When these differences arise, parties often prefer to settle them pri-vately and informally in the kind of businesslike way that encourages continued business relationships.

Sometimes, however, such resolution is not possible. This leaves the aggrieved party with three options: forget the possibility of reaching a solution and walk away from the problem, go to court and sue, or resolve the dispute through other means.

Going to court can be an expensive and time-consuming proposition, with crowded court dockets delaying a decision for several months, or, in some cases, several years. Attorney fees can mount up quickly, especially if extensive pretrial proceedings are involved. Depending on the court's location, one of the parties may have to expend addi-tional fees for travel expenses. Since court cases are matters of public record, potentially adverse publicity may result.

For this reason, arbitration is gaining favor as a means of settling disputes. Arbitration is one form of alternative dispute resolution. In arbitration, one or more arbiters are cho-sen to hear each party's side of the dispute and decide about the outcome. Under rules administered by the American Arbitration Association, arbitration is designed for quick, practical, and inexpensive settlements. It is, at the same time, an orderly proceeding, gov-erned by rules of procedure and standards of conduct prescribed by law. Either party can utilize lawyers, but there is a minimum of pretrial procedures. If arbitration is chosen as the dispute mechanism procedure in the contract, the parties also generally agree that the results are binding; that is, they cannot be appealed to a court of law. The contract should also specify the location of the arbitration. Arbitration is not generally a matter of public record, so all the proceedings can remain private.

If the parties choose arbitration as a means of settling disputes, the choice should be made before disagreements arise, and language governing the arbitration option should be included in the meeting contract. If arbitration is not selected, the contract should spell out which state's law (e.g., where the meeting took place or where the meeting organizer is located) will be utilized to resolve a court dispute.

Under the American system of justice, each party to a court suit or arbitration pro-ceeding is required to bear the costs of its own attorneys unless the agreement provides that the winning party is entitled to have the loser pay its attorneys' fees and costs.

Finally, a well-drafted contract should specify the damages to be awarded in the event of a breach by either party. Such an approach takes the decision out of the hands of a judge or an arbitrator, and leaves the dispute resolver only to determine whether a breach of the agreement occurred. Damages are typically stated as liquidated damages; that is, damages that the parties agree in advance will be the result of a breach. Courts will generally not honor a contract provision that imposes a penalty on the one breaching the agreement, so this term should be avoided. For example, a conference was held in a Las Vegas hotel, but the meeting organizer failed to pay the $57,000 master bill presented by the hotel for the meeting expenses. After multiple unsuccessful efforts to get the meeting organizer to pay the bill, the hotel decided to bill the individual attendees for a pro rata share of the master bill. After many upset attendees and much negative media, the hotel reversed its position and went back to pursuing the meeting organizer for the payment.

Crisis Preparedness and Management

What Is Risk? What Is Crisis Preparedness?

All meetings involve an element of **risk**. *Risk* is the possibility of suffering loss or harm. *Risk management* is the process of assessing, analyzing, and mitigating the risk, or the possibility of an adverse event. Realized risks (those that actually happen) are classified based on their scope and impact and may be an emergency, crisis, or disaster. Or a realized risk may just be one of the many little things that goes wrong in the process of planning and managing events—a routine business incident.

Imagine that an exhibition is to be held outdoors and during set up, torrential rains come, making it impossible to complete the set up or to hold the exhibition. Inclement weather is an example of a risk. It could create a business incident (the exhibition is delayed in opening), an emergency (lightning struck a would-be exhibitor), or a crisis (the lightning caught the exhibitor materials on fire and now there is a fire raging out of control). Now imagine that the wise exhibition planner has rented tents under which the exhibits can be placed so that the show can go on. That's part of crisis preparedness.

Crisis Management

Once the meeting professional has assessed and analyzed risks, they will have determined which crises have (1) the highest probability of occurring or (2) the greatest impact if they do occur. This is when crisis preparedness and management kicks in. Crisis management can be broken down into four stages:

1. Mitigation
2. Preparedness
3. Response
4. Recovery

The earlier outdoor exhibition example can be used to illustrate the steps of emergecy management.

Mitigation

Conducting a risk assessment and analysis will also help the planner determine which mitigation measures should be implemented. Examples of some common mitigation measures include:

- Contracts—signed prior to the meeting or event, contracts mitigate risk by narrowing or shifting liability to the responsible party, or specifying exactly what the monetary damage fees (e.g., attrition or cancellation) might be for underperformance of the contract.
- Insurance—the mitigation effect of insurance is that it shifts some of the liability for financial loss to the insurance company. In exchange for paying a premium, the meeting/event organizer knows that the insurance company will pay a claim for loss or damage if it falls within the boundaries of the insurance policy.
- Security—hiring security guards to provide physical security and/or monitor a property is a way of mitigating the risk of injury or loss.

In our rain example, in the *mitigation* stage, the planner would try to determine what he or she could do to mitigate the risk—that is, decrease the probability that rain would occur (and quickly realize it's hard to control the weather). The planner would also mitigate the crisis—decrease the consequences if it did rain. Realizing that the latter was more manageable, the planner would have had a tent rental company on standby (or rented them just in case, if the budget allowed), contracted with a backup indoor venue, and purchased event cancellation insurance in case the exhibition was rained out.

Preparedness

In the preparedness stage, the planner institutes activities like training of staff, emergency drills, and preparing documentation like a crisis plan and an incident report form. This is the stage at which people involved with the meeting—meeting organizer staff, facility staff, and vendor staff—are assigned roles for monitoring emergency indicators and gathering information that will be needed if a crisis does occur, like a list of contact information for staff and attendees.

In our rain example, the *preparedness* stage would include assigning someone to carefully monitor the weather reports on the days leading up to the exhibition.

Response

Should a crisis adversely affect a meeting or event despite the best planning, the meeting/event professional needs to have an emergency response team ready to respond. Depending on the nature of the crisis, the response may be as simple as sending an announcement to participants about a change in the program. Or, it may be as complex as having to help coordinate a crisis evacuation and provide first aid to the injured. A simple response will be up to the planner's risk team. A complex response will likely require emergency professionals: firefighters to put out a fire, police to regain control of a crowd, and emergency medical professionals to administer first aid. The response must fit the crisis.

The tricky thing about response is figuring out both *when* to respond and *how*. If two days prior to the event dates, the weather forecast is calling for 60 percent chance of rain on the exhibition date, should the planner implement the rain plan? Does that mean getting the tents or just alerting exhibitors to a possible change in plans? If the planner waits until the morning of the exhibition, does that give him or her enough time to implement the rain plan? The answers to these questions really depend on the size and scope of the event as well as the nature of the plan.

Recovery

Recovery also depends on the nature of the crisis. If the rain in our ongoing example is so bad that the outdoor exhibition has to be cancelled, recovery would include insurance paying claims for the losses suffered by the exhibition organizer, as well as the actions by the organizer to overcome any bad press.

A crisis is likely to result in loss or harm and can cause damage to property, people, or to more intangible aspects—like the organizer or planner's reputation. In the case of the outdoor exhibition, recovery might just include refunding the exhibitor's or attendee's fees who didn't attend, or filing a claim with the insurance company. In the case of a full-blown disaster or crisis, however, the recovery stage can be much more serious and take a much longer time.

How do you plan for natural risks like fires and tornadoes?
Concept use/Shutterstock

Muratart/Shutterstock

Americans with Disabilities Act

The US **Americans with Disabilities Act (ADA)** of 1990 makes it illegal to discriminate against or fail to provide a "reasonable accommodation" for persons with disabilities. The ADA places responsibility on the owners and operators of places of public accommodation (hotels, restaurants, convention centers, retail stores, zoos, parks, etc.) to make reasonable accommodations for equal enjoyment by persons with disabilities.

A **disability** is "a physical or mental impairment that substantially limits a major life activity of an individual."

A **major life activity** under the original ADA includes performing manual tasks, walking, seeing, hearing, speaking, breathing, learning, and working. The ADA Amendment Act of 2008 modified this somewhat, as mentioned later.

The ADA may include people with mobility, hearing, or vision limitations as well as those with "invisible disabilities" such as multiple sclerosis, epilepsy, or other conditions that may not be immediately visible.

Under Title III of the ADA, places of public accommodation (including hotels, restaurants, convention centers, retail stores, etc.) must provide a reasonable accommodation for persons with disabilities unless doing so creates an undue hardship. The ADA Technical Assistance Manual and case law help outline what constitutes undue hardship. Just because an accommodation (such as sign language interpreters or printing large print materials) may be expensive does not necessarily mean it is an undue hardship.

The following is the stated purpose of the ADA:

1. to provide a clear and comprehensive national mandate for the elimination of discrimination against individuals with disabilities;
2. to provide clear, strong, consistent, enforceable standards addressing discrimination against individuals with disabilities;
3. to ensure that the federal government plays a central role in enforcing the standards on behalf of individuals with disabilities; and
4. to invoke the sweep of congressional authority, including the power to enforce the Fourteenth Amendment and to regulate commerce, to address the major areas of discrimination faced day-to-day by people with disabilities.

For more information on the Americans with Disabilities Act, see the US government's ADA website, www.ada.gov.

The ADA Amendment Act of 2008 became effective January 1, 2009. It was passed because the US Justice Department realized that people were using the ADA more to exclude people (your disability isn't specifically listed, so you get no accommodation) rather than to include people (you fit the criteria of a person with a disability, so we will provide this accommodation for you). As a result, the definition of a person with a disability under the ADA as Amended (ADAAA) includes a non-exhaustive list of major life activities and major bodily functions. The ADAAA rules require the law to be construed broadly and inclusively instead of narrowly as it was under the original ADA. This means some issues like food allergies and dietary restrictions, which have, in the past, been deemed not to fall under the ADA, may be covered in the future. (See Case 3.)

CASE 3.   US DEPARTMENT OF JUSTICE VERSUS LESLEY UNIVERSITY (2013)

When Lesley University required students to purchase a meal plan, but then wouldn't provide accommodations for those with serious food allergies, the US Department of Justice got involved and, using the language of the ADAAA, negotiated a settlement with Lesley University that required them to provide reasonable accommodations for students with food allergies. An Iowa Court of Appeals case, Knudsen versus Tiger Tots Community Child Care Center (2013) was decided shortly after the Lesley University case. Knudsen said the ADAAA should be applied. These cases should be taken as a sign that the law is turning. Planners should expect to see more cases using this new ADAAA rationale and, thus, elevate the liability risk for issues arising from food allergies to a higher level.

Title III of the ADA covers public accommodations, which applies to meeting planners and organizers, as well as facilities and vendors. Meeting organizers must (1) determine the extent to which attendees have disabilities and (2) make reasonable efforts to accommodate the special needs of those attendees at no cost to the attendee. As a result, we now see sections on registration forms asking if the attendee has any special needs. An example is the attendee who is hearing impaired. The planner would have to provide a sign language interpreter, large print materials, or other accommodation that would allow the person with a disability to fully participate in the meeting to the extent possible. Readers may have seen these interpreters in class or during important speeches. For those with vision impairment, the planner may have to provide documents with extra-large type or produced in Braille. Failure to accommodate attendees with disabilities can result in legal action and fines. Furthermore, the accommodations requirement is not limited to attendees; it applies to employees as well.

The planner must be aware of the ramifications of the ADA, and be sure that all the facilities used meet the standards. The planner must also be sure that their activities and programs meet the guidelines set forth in the act. Be aware, however, that this act only applies to events and meetings in the United States. Canada, for example, does not have the equivalent of the ADA, and many of its facilities do not meet the standards put forth in the act. Accessibility and accommodation of those with disabilities varies significantly from county to county.

Intellectual Property

There are three main areas of intellectual property: patents, trademarks, and copyrights.

Patents

Patents are property rights for inventions. Patents allow the inventor of a device or process to protect their invention for a period of time. There are three types of patents:

Utility patents, for new and useful processes, machines, articles of manufacture, composition of matter, or any new and useful improvement thereof;
Design patents, for new, original, and ornamental design for an article of manufacture; and
Plant patents, for the invention or discovery of a distinct and new variety of plant.

Patents are not widely discussed in the meetings industry, although there was once a claim made by a company that they had invented the online registration process. This company sent demands for money to associations who were using online registration for their meetings. ASAE & the Center for Association Leadership got involved and the issue ultimately went away.

Trademarks

A trademark (or service mark) is a word, name, symbol, or device that is used with goods (or services) to indicate the source of the goods and to distinguish them from the goods of others. For example, Campbell's Soup puts their name on their cans so consumers know it is their soup. By eating different brands of soup, consumers count on a trademark to tell them what to expect. Likewise, Ritz-Carlton® puts their name on their hotels so you know where you are staying and what to expect. For more information, see the US Patent & Trademark Office (www.uspto.gov).

Copyrights

Copyright is a form of protection provided to the authors of "original works of authorship," including literary, dramatic, musical, artistic, and certain other intellectual works, both published and unpublished. In the meetings industry, copyright covers event proposals, music played at events, photographs, videos, and more. Copyright protection attaches at the time the work is fixed in a durable medium. A singer may riff and come up with an original song to sing, but until the song lyrics are written down or the music is recorded, it is not copyrightable. For more general information on copyrights, see the US government's copyright website www.copyright.gov.

Music Copyright

Many meetings and trade shows feature events at which music is played, either by live musicians or using prerecorded CDs. Music may be provided as a background (such as at a cocktail reception) or as a primary focus of attention (such as at a dinner dance or concert). At trade shows, individual exhibitors, as well as the organizing entity, can provide music.

Regardless of how music is provided, it is important to remember that under the federal copyright act, the music is being performed, and according to many court decisions, the entity organizing the event is considered to be controlling the performance, even if that control means only hiring an orchestra without telling them what to play. The only recognized exemption to the performance rule is for music played over a single receiver (radio or TV) of a type usually found in the home.

The **American Society of Composers, Authors, and Publishers** (**ASCAP**) and **Broadcast Music, Inc.** (**BMI**) are membership organizations that represent individuals who hold the copyright to approximately 95 percent of the music written in the United States. ASCAP and BMI exist to obtain license fees from those who perform copyrighted music, including radio stations, retail stores, hotels, and organizations that organize meetings, conventions, and trade shows. A 1979 decision of the US Supreme Court conferred on ASCAP and BMI a special, limited exemption from normal antitrust law principles. This decision has enabled them to develop blanket-licensing agreements for the various industries that utilize live or recorded music.

Following negotiations with major meeting industry organizations (such as the International Association of Exhibits and Events and the American Society of Association Executives) in the late 1980s, both ASCAP and BMI developed special licensing agreements and fee structures for meetings, conventions, trade shows, and expositions. These special agreements were designed to replace earlier agreements under which hotels paid licensing fees for meetings held by others on the property. Although the negotiated agreements technically expired at the end of 1994, ASCAP and BMI have extended them on a year-to-year basis, with slight increases in licensing fees. Under court decrees, ASCAP and BMI are forbidden to grant special deals to individual meetings, so the agreements, which must be signed, are the same for all meetings and cannot be altered to meet the needs of a particular meeting. Failure to sign these agreements—agreements with *both* organizations must be signed—could subject a meeting or trade show organizer to costly and embarrassing litigation for copyright infringement.

Under copyright law, an organization cannot meet its obligation by requiring the musicians performing the music, or the booking agency or hotel that provided the musicians, to obtain ASCAP and BMI licenses. The entity organizing the event must obtain the requisite licenses.

CASE 4. TRADEMARK INFRINGEMENT AT AN EXHIBITION

Jibbitz, Inc., the official maker of snap-on accessories for Crocs (shoes), attended the World Shoe Association trade show as an exhibitor. At the trade show, the Jibbitz exhibit staff noticed another exhibitor promoting the sale of snap-on accessories for Crocs. Because Jibbitz, Inc. (as a wholly owned subsidiary of Crocs, Inc.) was the only official maker of these accessories, it filed a copyright and trademark infringement lawsuit against the other exhibitor. Jibbitz, Inc. was awarded $56 million in damages. www.law360.com/articles/56002/crocs-awarded-56m-in-suit-over-shoe-charms

Speaker/Entertainment Copyright

An organization organizing a meeting will often want to make audio or video recordings of certain speakers or programs, either for the purpose of selling copies to meeting attendees to those who could not attend, or for archival purposes.

Speakers or program participants have a common law copyright interest in their presentations, and the law prohibits the organizing organization from selling audio or video copies of the presentation without obtaining the written permission of the presenter. Many professional speakers who also market books or recordings of their presentations frequently refuse to provide consent to be recorded by the meeting organizer.

Permission can be obtained by having each speaker whose session is to be recorded sign a copyright waiver, a simple document acknowledging that the speaker's session is going to be recorded and giving the organizing entity permission to sell the recordings of the speaker's presentation. If the recording is to be done by a commercial audiovisual company, a sample waiver form can usually be obtained from that company, or the sample form following this summary can be used.

Labor Issues

Preparation for on-site work at meetings and trade shows often involves long hours and the use of individuals on a temporary or part-time basis to provide administrative or other support. It is therefore important for organizations to understand how federal employment law requirements impact these situations.

The Federal Fair Labor Standards Act (FLSA) in the United States, adopted in 1938, is more commonly known as the law that prescribes a minimum wage for a large segment of the working population. Another major provision of the FLSA, and one that is frequently misunderstood, requires that all workers subject to the law's minimum wage coverage *must* receive overtime pay at the rate of 1½ times their regular rate of pay *unless* they are specifically exempted by the statute.

There are many common misconceptions that employers have about the FLSA's overtime provisions, including the following, all of which are not true:

- Only hourly employees (and not those paid on a regular salary basis) are eligible for overtime.
- Overtime pay can be avoided by giving employees compensatory time off instead.
- Overtime need only be paid to those who receive advance approval to work more than forty hours in a week.

Over the years, the Department of Labor regulations and court decisions have made it clear that overtime pay cannot be avoided by a promise to provide compensatory time off in another workweek, even if the employee agrees to the procedure. According to the US Department of Labor, the only way so-called *comp time* is legal is if it is given in the same week that the extra hours are worked or in another week of the same pay period, and if the extra time off is sufficient to offset the amount of overtime worked (i.e., at the time-and-one-half rate).

The use of comp time is probably the most common violation of FLSA overtime pay requirements, and it occurs frequently. This is because many employees, particularly those who are paid by salary, would rather have an extra day off from work at a convenient time to deal with medical appointments, holiday shopping, or simply an attitude adjustment. Compensatory time is also frequently, but not legally, provided when a nonexempt employee works long hours in connection with a meeting or convention, and is then given extra time off in some later pay period to make up for the extra work.

Overtime cannot be limited to situations where extra work is approved in advance. The law is also clear that premium pay must be paid whenever the employee works in excess of 40 hours per week—or is on call for extra work—even when the extra effort has not specifically been approved in advance. Thus, if a nonexempt employee works a few extra hours in the days prior to a meeting to complete all assignments for that meeting, the employee must be paid overtime.

Overtime pay is not limited to lower salaried employees or those paid on an hourly basis. The FLSA requires *all* employees to receive overtime unless they fall under one of the law's specific exemptions. The most generally available exemptions are the so-called white-collar-exemptions for professional, executive, and administrative employees.

To determine whether an employee falls within one of these exemptions, one should review the FLSA and applicable regulations and interpretations carefully. What is explained here is simply a summary. It is also most important to remember that the exemptions only apply to those whose actual work activity falls within the definitions; job titles are meaningless in determining whether an employee is exempt.

Under modifications made to the FLSA in 2014, to qualify for white-collar-exemption, an employee generally must:

1. be salaried, meaning that they are paid a predetermined and fixed salary that is not subject to reduction because of variations in the quality or quantity of work performed (the "salary basis test");

2. be paid more than a specified weekly salary level, which is $913 per week (the equivalent of $47,476 annually for a full-year worker) under this final rule (the "salary level test"); and

3. primarily perform executive, administrative, or professional duties, as defined in the department's regulations (the "duties test").

It is important for all employers to know which of their employees are exempt from overtime pay requirements and which are not. This is especially significant when employees are asked to work long hours at meetings or conventions, particularly those held out of town, or those who pitch in and help complete a large project. When in doubt about overtime, an organization should review job descriptions with a competent human resources professional or experienced counsel.

Ethics in MEEC

The preceding part of this chapter deals with legal issues, and the event professional can look to legislation or legal advisors for assistance in dealing with them. There are many other issues, actions, or activities in MEEC that may be legal but may raise questions of ethics. Ethics guide our personal and professional lives. Furthermore, the issue of ethics has come to center stage with the unethical practices of businesses like Enron, Tyco, Martha Stewart, and others. Ethics is addressed on today's evening news and on the front page of newspapers. The MEEC industry, by its very nature, offers a multitude of opportunities for unethical behavior or practices.

How someone responds to an issue regarding ethics is personally and culturally based. What is ethical behavior in one community or society may be considered unethical in another. Loyalty to personal friends versus an employer is another ethical consideration faced in the MEEC industry. Ethical issues and personal conduct are an important aspect of any industry, including MEEC. The topic cannot possibly be covered in a few paragraphs. Thus, readers are encouraged to seek additional sources of information on this topic.

Supplier Relations

Some planners feel suppliers are out to make a buck and will do anything they can to get the contract for an event. Some believe that suppliers and vendors will promise anything, but may not deliver on their promises. While promising more than can be delivered, or embellishing their abilities may be legal, it may not be ethical. On the other hand, many suppliers and vendors feel that meeting/event professionals tend toward overstatement, for example, in estimating the number of rooms they will use in a hotel and the amount their group will spend on food and beverage. This too is an ethical question. The solution to these issues is to put everything in writing, preferably in a contract.

Even with a contract, the buyer (planner or organizer) and the seller (vendor or supplier) should be as open, forthright, and honest as possible in dealing with each other. A relationship not built on trust is a fragile relationship, at best. Furthermore, given the increasing importance of relationship marketing, honest and ethical behavior can lead to future business.

Still another ethical issue deals with the ownership and use of intellectual material. Destination management companies (DMCs) in particular often complain that meeting planners submit requests for proposals (RFPs) to many suppliers and the DMCs spend quite a bit of time, energy, and money to develop creative ideas and programs to secure the planners business. However, there are many cases in which a planner will take the ideas developed by one DMC and have another implement them, or the planner may then do this on his or her own. Is this legal? Yes. Is it ethical? No.

Still another issue for suppliers relates to the offering of gifts. Should an event professional accept gifts and privileges from a supplier or vendor? If amenities are accepted, is there some obligation on the part of the planner to repay the supplier by steering business in the vendor's direction? When does one cross the line from ethical to unethical behavior? Is it proper to accept a Christmas gift, but not proper to accept football tickets when offered? Event professionals working for the US government are prohibited from accepting any gift with a value of $50 or more.

Another ethical question regards so-called familiarization or "fam" trips. Fam trips bring potential clients on an all-expenses-paid trip to a destination with the hope that they will bring their business to the community. But what if a planner or organizer is invited on a fam trip to a destination, but has no intention of ever holding a MEEC gathering in that location? Should the planner accept the trip? If accepted, is there some implicit expectation that the planner *will* bring business to the locale? Although it is perfectly legal to accept a trip with no intention of bringing business to the locale, is it ethical?

The planner or organizer of a large MEEC gathering has significant clout and power based on the economic and social impact of the gathering. He or she may ask for special consideration or favors based on this power. It may be ethical to exert this influence on behalf of the group, such as when negotiating room rates, catering rates, and complimentary services. However, is it ethical for the planner or organizer to request personal favors that only benefit him or herself? Is it ethical for the planner to accept personal favors from a supplier or community?

Examples of ethical issues and questions abound in the MEEC industry. An individual must adhere to a personal code of ethics, and many industry associations have developed their own code of ethics to which members must adhere. Colleges and universities have recognized the need to address ethics by implementing courses on the subject. The discussion of ethics in this chapter is meant to make readers aware that ethics is an important aspect of the study of the MEEC industry, but it is not meant as a comprehensive treatise.

Trends and Best Practices Regarding Legal Issues in MEEC

- Legal issues and precedents continue to vary by geographic region, and even within the same country. As the meetings industry gets progressively more global, the laws of other countries become more important as well.

- Laws that are seemingly unrelated to the meetings industry will nonetheless affect the meetings industry.

- The protection of intellectual property becomes a greater challenge as technology makes it easier to take photos (including by drone), make copies, or "snip" a protected piece of writing.

- Who has the upper hand in negotiation—the organizer or the vendor—will depend upon the economy. In a good economy where demand is strong, the supplier has the upper hand; in a weak economy, it is the organizer or buyer.

- The line between ethics and law will continue to be gray, but more organizations will formalize ethics policies to avoid public relations nightmares, especially via social media.

Summary

Legal issues are an increasingly important factor in the MEEC industry. This chapter is meant to provide insights into some of these issues, such as negotiation, contracts, labor, and intellectual property. There are other issues that were not discussed, and entire books are devoted to them. Readers are reminded to seek legal counsel whenever appropriate.

Now that you have completed this chapter you should be competent in the following Meeting and Business Event Competency Standards.

MBECS—Skill Measure Value of Meeting or Business Event

Sub skills	Skills (standards)
A 3.04	Evaluate effectiveness of risk management plan

MBECS—Skill 6: Manage Risk Management Plan

Sub skills	Skills (standards)
C 6.01	Identify risks
C 6.02	Analyze risks
C 6.03	Develop management and implementation plan
C 6.04	Develop and implement emergency response plan
C 6.05	Arrange security

MBECS—Skill 17: Engage Speakers and Performers

Sub skills	Skills (standards)
H 17.04	Secure contracts and communicate expectations

MBECS—Skill 32: Professionalism

Sub skills	Skills (standards)
K 32.03	Demonstrate ethical behavior

CASE STUDY

Alcohol and Event Liability

Sydney, a recent college graduate, has just been hired by D&T Events in a mid-sized city. D&T houses five event planners as well as a large wait staff. The company will supply staff to serve food and alcohol, however, D&T does not actually provide the food and alcohol. Their main purpose is to plan, down to the last detail, everything that an event needs to have in order to be a success.

After going through training and working as an assistant to Madison, one of D&T's top event planners, Sydney was set to work her first big event. The event was the wedding reception of Ms. Ashley Jones to Mr. Caleb Chamberlain, a very prominent businessman well known throughout the Raleigh area. Caleb was notorious for having lavish parties and bringing in a lot of revenue for both Madison and D&T.

Set up for the wedding reception went off without a hitch and Sydney felt a new-found confidence in her position as an event planner's assistant. However, about thirty minutes into the reception Madison got a phone call and had to leave immediately due to a family emergency. Before Madison left she instructed Sydney to make sure she did everything the Groom asked and not to do anything that might upset him. Sydney had also been made aware before the event of Caleb's background and how important his business was to the company. Caleb's wishes were always granted and so she passed on the information to the bartender and wait staff to make sure they were also aware of the situation.

Sydney made it most of the way through the reception alone without a problem and thought she was home free until she heard a guest being loud and boisterous. She made her way through the crowd to see who was responsible for the disturbance only to find that the rowdy guest was none other than the best man. Sydney took notice of the fact that not only was the best man slurring his words, stumbling, and attempting to start fights with other guests, but he also had two drinks in his hands. Sydney quickly went to the bartender, a D&T employee, and asked how much the best man had been served. The bartender informed her that when she tried to cut off the best man, Mr. Chamberlain came over and made it very clear that he paid a lot of money for this reception and his best man was to have whatever he wanted. Therefore, the bartender, under direct orders from Sydney, granted Caleb's wishes and continued to serve the best man.

Being that Sydney was fresh out of college, she remembered the Hospitality Law class that she took and the chapter about alcohol. She knew that she could be held financially liable if the best man were to injure himself or someone else after he was served too much alcohol at her event by her staff. Sydney knew the best course of action to take was to cut the best man off and ask him to leave, but she also knew how important Mr. Chamberlain's business was and how much she could hurt her company if she upset him.

1. Do you think Sydney should risk her job and Caleb's business by continuing to serve his best man or should she do what is legal and deal with the repercussions from Madison and D&T?

2. What would you do if you were put in Sydney's situation?

Produced by George G. Fenich from East Carolina University

Key Words and Terms

For definitions, see the Glossary.

Act of God	contracts	offer
Americans with Disabilities Act (ADA)	copyright	parol evidence
	dates, rates, and space	pickup
American Society of Composers, Authors, and Publishers (ASCAP)	disability	rack rates
	force majeure	risk
attrition	major life activity	yield management
Broadcast Music, Inc. (BMI)	meeting history	
consideration	negotiation	

Review and Discussion Questions

1. Discuss the negotiation process. What are the important points for each party to be aware of?

2. What are the three elements of a legal contract?

3. What are the most important clauses in hotel group sales contracts? Why?

4. Discuss negotiating contracts.

5. Discuss attrition and strategies for dealing with it.

6. What is the difference between cancellation and termination with regard to events?

7. Discuss the different types of crises a planner may face and how to deal with them.

8. What is the ADA, and how does it impact events and gatherings?

9. What are the three types of intellectual property, and why should a planner or organizer be aware of them?

10. What are some of the labor issues unique to MEEC?

About the Chapter Contributor

Tyra W. Hilliard, PhD, JD, CMP has devoted her career to justice and safety in the hospitality and meetings industry.

Twenty-five years of professional experience combined with extensive education and research allows Tyra to provide a well-informed but practical approach to crisis preparedness and legal issues. Her experience in the hospitality and meetings industry includes stints as a meeting planner, convention and visitors' bureau sales representative, catering manager, association executive, attorney, and professor.

She has published several research-based articles on crisis preparedness and the meeting planner. She is widely quoted on legal and crisis management issues in academic and industry publications.

She has been invited to share her irreverent approach to law, crisis management, and risk management with groups worldwide. She also teaches college courses in business, hospitality, and event management, including courses in hospitality and event law, and crisis management for hospitality and events.

She is one of a very few people to have a PhD in Hospitality, be a practicing attorney, and be a certified meeting professional (CMP).

Contact Information:

Tyra W. Hilliard, Ph.D., JD, CMP, Assistant Professor
College of Coastal Georgia
One College Drive
Brunswick, GA 31520
Phone: (912)279-4568
thilliard@ccga.edu
http://www.tyrahilliard.com

Previous Edition Chapter Contributor

James M. Goldberg is a principal in the Washington, DC, law firm of Goldberg & Associates, PLLC.

Virtual Reality Technology.
LJSphotography/Alamy Stock Photo

CHAPTER 11

Technology and the MEEC Professional

Chapter Objectives

- Outline the impact of virtual site selection and research on the MEEC professional's event planning.
- Cover the evolution of marketing and communications for the MEEC professional in our digital world.
- Discuss the importance and continuing changes in online registration.
- Cover the rise and importance of social media in planning and executing an event.
- Define some of the most important desktop tools for the MEEC professional.

- Discuss the importance of understanding on-site tech infrastructure.
- Clarify tech tools and processes that improve attendee interaction and communication.
- Outline some of the most effective post-conference technology applications.
- Articulate the ways the industry is using virtual and augmented reality to better prepare for events.
- Discuss the ways in which webinars and hybrid meetings can assist when face-to-face events are not possible.

Technology in meetings, expositions, events, and conventions (MEEC) has changed dramatically over the past decade and continues to do so. The dominance of mobile over desktop/laptop devices changes how content is delivered and consumed. Social media has become the primary source of information (and Facebook may have finally exceeded Google as the dominant Web service). Mobile apps have replaced printed programs for conferences, yet may also be becoming an old school approach as well. And the dawning of the age of mixed reality and artificial intelligence have given us a glimpse of what meetings of the future may look like.

However, the fear remains for many planners that the virtual tools available will eradicate the need for live meetings. Most experts agree that this will not happen, as we are still a species of social animals who craves face-to-face communication. But more and more, the savvy planner will need to create a blended experience for their attendees. Organizations that don't adapt to technology will quickly become legacy institutions.

What does this mean for today's MEEC professional? It's straight forward, actually: Professionals that don't embrace the new tools, especially while they try to engage their younger constituents, will struggle to succeed. A basic understanding of technology is as important a skill set for today's planner as their knowledge of site selection, food and beverage, and room set ups.

The changing nature of technology also makes us look at organizing this information better. Rather than grouping tech into pre-event, on-site, and post-event silos, many of the tools play across these categories. Therefore, the information in this chapter will be more tool-specific rather than timing-based.

More than ever, today's planner needs to understand all the technology tools available, if for no other reason than to be able to correctly decide which ones are the best for their group.

From mature to breaking technologies, this section will provide the information required for you to be knowledgeable about what technology is impacting our industry, and how it will help you be more successful.

Virtual Site Selection and Research

Back in the day (albeit many, many thousands of days ago), planners would have huge encyclopedic books that listed critical information about facilities for meeting professionals. The Internet changed all that in the 1990s, and, as hotels and convention and visitor bureaus (CVBs) saw the value in replacing their traditional marketing with Web-based tools, the planner's research palette expanded exponentially. This process is still changing, as the incoming wave of mixed reality tools (which will be discussed later in this chapter) will ultimately bring the planner to the site without ever leaving their office.

Virtual Tours

Industry stats have estimated that over one half of all meetings are booked without a formal site inspection—a number, which continues to grow. While there is no substitute for visiting a hotel, the Web's visual capabilities have allowed planners to at least get a sense of a facility if time or budgetary restrictions prevent their inspection.

The concept of a virtual site inspection has morphed over the years from its meager beginnings of using only pictures of meeting rooms to videos and 360-degree panoramic tours of meeting spaces and sleeping rooms. Ongoing development of virtual reality for virtual walkthroughs will change the game even further.

However, most hotels and facilities haven't gone in this direction yet. What are the reasons?

Although there are many reasons for this, a key reason is a combination of an industry that struggles with embracing new technology and integrating it into their processes, and not wanting to spend money on technology that is still in its formative stages.

Ten years ago, a virtual world named Second Life had the techy part of our industry buzzing about the future of site selection and other services. Starwood Hotels' brand, Aloft, was developed a decade ago, and used Second Life to showcase design ideas to their potential customers. However, Second Life was way ahead of its time (and the processing power of computers needed to run it), and never took off. With the virtual reality and augmented reality devices that are available now and with new devices on the horizon, it wouldn't be surprising if we soon saw some progressive properties embracing these tools.

Online RFPs

As the Web developed in the mid to late 1990s, one of the first tools available, both through convention and visitors bureau websites, as well as hotel and third-party planning sites, allowed the planner to create an efficient online request for proposal (RFP, which is the tool many planners use to distribute information to hotels about potential meetings). While the model has been adapted from a fee-based RFP to a free approach, the idea remains the same: Allow the planner to input their specs easily, and allow the Web to be the conduit for distributing the information to potential cities and hotels.

Without standardization, each RFP has its own nuance, which costs the planner time when completing each one of the required RFPs. Planner's still need to determine which vehicle (CVB-based, hotel-based, or third-party based) is best to distribute their meeting specs. This lack of standardization has plagued, and will continue to plague, our industry.

Some planners eschew the RFP forms, and just use email and the Internet to save time in their process. This allows an office-based spec sheet to be distributed via email technology. This is saving significant time in helping planners distribute their meeting requirements.

Meeting Industry Portals and Information Resources

While less elegant, but still enormously useful, industry information portals continue to thrive. While search engines are incredibly useful for general research, our industry portals have a great deal of information available to the savvy Web user who can find resources and tools with just a few clicks.

Any discussion of information portals for the hospitality industry begins with the website of Corbin Ball (www.corbinball.com). Linking onto his favorite's page from his home page presents the viewer with nearly 3,000 industry-related websites, which are organized categorically. Corbin updates the site frequently, and has plenty of additional information of value for the meeting professional.

Liz King's techsytalk (http://techsytalk.com) is a great tech resource and portal for planners, as well as a host to one of the industry's top annual tech conferences. Combining a newsletter, blog, podcast, and industry news, her site is not to miss.

While perhaps not a true portal, another not-to-miss site is the Event Manager blog (www.eventmanagerblog.com/). Filled with great articles and meeting planner resources, Julius Solaris has created this page as another critical tech resource for our industry.

Naturally, convention and visitors bureau pages are rich with information for the planner to plan their meeting. Replacing the more archaic printed city meeting planning guides, all information is now available through their websites, which are accessible via drop down menus.

If you're looking for a non-traditional destination, the Unique Venues (www.uniquevenues.com/) site is your friend. College campuses, cruise ships, and business offices are all part of this rich resource for planners. A great blog and traditional magazine enhance the information provided by them.

Through Google Groups (http://groups.google.com), the Meeting Industry Forum continues to be a leading destination for planners and suppliers to exchange ideas and best practices. Many of its users love that no sales or marketing is allowed in this space.

Marketing and Communications

As more and more new events are created, the amount of work needed to market your brand and conference has become more important than ever. Clearly, the best marketing tool you have is the completion of a successful conference that meets and exceeds the needs of its audience. But getting people to an event is becoming more and more of a challenge.

Most planners and suppliers would agree that the decision process of their customers occurs increasingly later in the selling cycle. People don't confirm attendance months ahead of time anymore. This makes marketing a critical part of the successful planner's toolbox, with technology being the primary (sometimes sole) distribution medium for these efforts.

It is clear that a critical, if not overwhelming, part of the marketing process today occurs through social media channels. These components will be covered in the next section of this chapter, which is dedicated to social media.

Websites and Strategic Communications

There was a time when one-way communications was common: Information was sent from the event organizers to (potential) attendees. In the past few years, as websites and social networks have become synonymous with real-time communication, event communication has become a two-way model.

Websites are still an important part of the communication conversation. Not only do they need to integrate a two-way communication model, but they must also serve the purpose of efficiently providing critical information to conference goers. The best online event models have a navigable, easy to find website that is easy to make purchases from, as well as a successful social media strategy.

Event Websites

Although overshadowed by the social media revolution, one-way tools are still important. Today, the event website is what the conference marketing brochure was a generation ago. It is a place to provide information, create interest, and hopefully get people to register for the conference.

The best websites integrate a two-way strategy, using elements such as blogs/comments, or a live social stream with clear links to all essential social channels. However, having a site that allows people to find out everything they need to know about an event is of critical importance. The core rules of a successful conference website include

- Clear, easy to find information
- A focus on the five W's (who, what, where, when, and why)
- The ability to make and process a sale (in our industry, this would include the payment process on the registration form)

A frequent issue with event organizers is not getting information on the website early enough. While there is no definitive time frame, if you're running an annual event, information about next year's meeting should be ready to go live the day this year's meeting concludes. This is just common sense, if people are pleased with the conference, why shouldn't you allow them to register for next year when their memories are still vivid from the past event? Yet, many planners don't establish their website as early as they should. Perhaps this is part of the same problem as the sales/purchase cycle becoming shorter.

Mobile Websites

Unfortunately, many planners (and suppliers) focus all their efforts on their website as if the desktop/laptop platform is the only game in town. However, by mid-2015, mobile usage surpassed traditional computer usage. This means that a well-designed website could be considered of secondary importance to a well-designed mobile site. In fact, many people would make the argument that a mobile website and effective use of social media is all that a planner needs these days.

The phrase, responsive Web design, has been used to identify a website that optimizes itself for whichever platform (desktop, tablet, or phone) is being used to access the site. While this makes sure that the content is clear on all platforms, it doesn't embrace the fact that mobile and desktop users often have different needs when they're searching for content.

The critical question that planners need to ask themselves, or discuss with their Web designers, is what content is most important for the mobile user. It should always include easy access to registration and other critical event information, and do so without allowing slower-loading videos and resources to hog up the channel. The planner can't assume that the user is on a device using exceptional bandwidth (they may be using their cellular signal). The planner needs to be sure that the content gets to their potential customer efficiently. The six-second rule is a good tool for planners to use. If the page doesn't load on a mobile device in six seconds or less, you may want to reconsider what is being sent to the mobile device, and trim accordingly.

E-blasts

Twenty-five years ago, a planner could (and would) send out as many direct mail pieces as they could. They would do so as frequently as their budget would allow, since they knew that the more information that landed on the desk of the buyer, the greater the likelihood that they might attend the event. Fifteen years ago, the same planners would have taken advantage of email as the primary marketing tool. And, if they used it correctly, they could reap great benefits from a well-orchestrated e-blast strategy.

However, as we stated earlier, the rules have changed. We are so inundated with spam email (some experts have estimated that the percentage of spam we receive is as high as 85 percent of our daily email) that multiple, unsolicited emails are having the inverse effect: People are tuning out all communications with that sender.

Instead of just blasting the audience with email after email, the planner may be wise to heed a different set of marketing rules to best promote their conference to their audience.

Opt In

Just because you have obtained an email address, it is not an open invitation to commence spamming. The Federal Trade Commission's CAN-SPAM act of 2009 (www.ftc.gov/tips-advice/business-center/guidance/can-spam-act-compliance-guide-business) forces all businesses, including the events business, to comply with proper rules about email marketing. In fact, the technology-savvy (and proper) approach would be to establish a dialogue, and confirm that the recipient wants to be included in future mailings.

Don't Overdo It

Once you've received the OK to email, don't begin a barrage of mindless communications. The result of too many emails from a single person or organization is the tuning out of all of them. We get hit with far too many messages daily, so we're looking for ways to reduce the number on which we need to focus. It is better to spend time on creating useful messages, sent occasionally, rather than mindless reminders sent repetitively.

What's in It for Me (Technology-Version)

Think about What's in It for Me—WIIFM—from the perspective of your customer: Why would they want to read your emails? If all you are doing is sending information about the conference, it will look just like a continuous hard sell. Since this is a marketing medium (as well as one that can finalize the sale), use the technology to create a dialogue of important information for your customer. Give them educational information. Inform them of useful tools to help them become better at their job. Oh yes, you can also tell them about your conference's benefits, but that information is better received in an environment of trust than in one of constant sales.

Keep It Simple

Don't write a novel in every email. Over the past generation, we have become accustomed to sound bites; planners must understand that people don't have time to read lengthy emails (you can always give access to more information, but allow them the choice to venture down that path). Keep your messages easy to read and as short as possible. Videos attract more attention than photos, which, in turn, attract more attention than plain text. And, if you're providing any links, make sure they work.

Room Design Software

How the planner shares information with the facility is another level at which technology can provide efficient communication, as it ensures that the planner's wants are interpreted correctly by the facility. Conference resumes create a very effective flow chart of what must happen, and at what time.

Certain aspects of your event, themed parties, banquets, or just unique set ups, are not as efficiently communicated by the written word. In these cases, planners use computer aided design (CAD) room design software to enhance communications.

Our industry has many versions of this type of software. They tend to be simple to use, but can range in price. Two of the top providers of this are Social Tables (www .socialtables.com/) and AllSeated (www.allseated.com/). Some work better for meetings; while others focus on special events. Social Tables is a premium model, while AllSeated is free for planners to use. They both have 3D room tour capabilities.

Selling the Show Floor

Another way technology is enhancing event communications and marketing is by assisting the trade show manager in selling the show floor. Traditional exhibit sales were focused on a document called the *exhibit prospectus*, along with a generic layout of the show floor.

By posting the show floor diagram on the Web, and using its interactivity, the trade show manager can now offer potential buyers a better look at where they might want their booth. Advantages of this include updated layouts (as the show floor diagram is frequently modified when exhibitors buy space), as well as helping the buyer locate a floor space that either is near, or far away, from their competitors (depending on their approach). The use of colors to represent booths can help differentiate between which ones are available, and the ones where premium costs apply.

Almost every trade show now uses some kind of virtual enhancement with the trade show floor selling process. These sites also include a downloadable version of the exhibit prospectus, as well as other information of use for the exhibitor.

Online Registration

A few years ago, when event technology was discussed, the topic of online registration would dominate the conversation. One of the first critical benefits of Web technology to our industry, the ability to register for an event online, truly enhanced marketing and communication for event organizers.

Currently, online registration is a relatively mature technology. However, it is interesting to note that some meetings still do not use online registration. Many meetings, especially internal meetings where attendance is mandatory, do not wish to incur the expense of establishing a professional online registration presence, preferring to use more traditional, or even email, approaches to handling meeting registration.

With this said, there are still several issues that confront planners when establishing an online registration process. The largest one for many planners is the integration of data. Even in the best of circumstances, not all of the attendees will use an online service; the planner's challenge is to make sure that, when he or she integrates the data, there are no inaccuracies or duplication of records. Ensuring that an online service can properly export into whichever tool you are using to maintain the remaining records (such as Excel) is a critical question to ask when considering companies to use.

Another issue that is raised by organizations using online services is about added, unexpected expenses. One area of concern is in the creation of additional reports. The planner has two approaches to offset this issue. One approach is to know all the reports that he or she might require, and negotiating it into the package when purchasing the service. The other, more tech-savvy, approach is to learn how to use the report-writing feature. Many online registration services use the product *Crystal Reports* to generate reports for the client.

There are too many online resources that can perform the online registration service to list. Researching these using an industry portal, such as Corbin Ball (www.corbinball .com) and his industry favorites, will give the user a plethora of options from which to choose.

Social Media

Has **social media** overtaken websites as the critical go-to information tool for events; This issue is still in debate but if nothing else, the combination of a well-designed website (both mobile and desktop optimized) and the use of multiple social media channels enhance the marketing and communication efforts of the planner. Can a planner even imagine holding an event without, at the very least, a Facebook page (and possibly an event-specific page) being part of their communication strategy?

Primary Social Channels

The past decade has seen the ascension and dominance of social channels and e-services. Social networks have always been at the root of this industry's success. A conference gathering about a specific topic, such as the Annual Widget Convention, is nothing more than a large social network of professionals gathering to learn and share from one another.

The only difference is now the social network is online as well as face-to-face. The applications created over the past decade have enabled real-time communication in this area. Facebook, Instagram, Twitter, YouTube, and LinkedIn are currently the dominant general social media channels used by planners.

Facebook's event pages, viral marketing, and social interaction abilities make it a great platform for communication (and marketing) about a meeting/event. A good Facebook event page helps create buzz for an event, especially when supported by an active community (as always, the planner needs to understand their own group to see what works best). The most visual of the big three social media networks, and the one with the largest community, Facebook is an essential part of the marketing strategy for all groups.

Social Media.
Odua Images/Shutterstock

Instagram, which is owned by Facebook, is the ultimate visual tool, as photos and videos are its sole domain. While incredibly popular, it's surprising that in 2017 many planners still don't use Instagram as a tool to promote and enhance their event. Its hashtag-centric approach also works very well for use at conferences and events.

Twitter has tried to keep pace with Facebook, but, while it has a very engaged audience, user numbers are far below Facebook. Twitter's true benefit is in its ability to curate content from its stream by its users. Whether using hashtags or lists, these features can turn the noise of social media into nuance. Twitter walls, especially for larger conferences and events, are becoming more standard. These tools allow the posts, which use the conference hashtag, to be aggregated and exclusively shown.

YouTube, owned by Google, is the number one video channel available. Any savvy planner will create a YouTube channel that contains the various videos they want to use to promote and highlight their event. YouTube, like Facebook, supports 360-degree video, which will be discussed in the section on mixed reality.

LinkedIn is considered more of a business network than a social network. However, it is also more of an individual networking tool. While they have groups (which are a great tool), there is no place to promote an event directly. The Senior Planners Industry Network (SPIN) is one of the many vibrant meeting communities on LinkedIn.

By no means are these services the only social networks available for the planner. Customizable networks (some free, some premium) are in favor with many groups. The benefits of a customized network are just what they seem to be: to be able to design the event's layout and content to meet its specific needs. One such service is Pathable (www.pathable.com), which helps create dialogue and networking between attendees before, during, and after an event, especially when integrated within the event app.

Live Streaming

In February 2015, right before the SXSW (South by Southwest) conference, an annual pilgrimage for tech aficionados, the live streaming video app *Meerkat* was released. It was an immediate sensation at SXSW, as it became the app of the conference (no small feat). However, right after the conference, Twitter, which Meerkat used to distribute the videos, cut off Meerkat's use of their social graph, and purchased a competing fledgling product, *Periscope*.

This scenario was the beginning of the battle of live streaming. For the events industry, live streaming brings up a mixed bag of responses. Those in favor of it highlight how easily it can extend the meeting to those who cannot attend, while those against it harp on the fact that people can easily broadcast content for which they do not have the rights or permissions.

No matter which side of the live streaming debate you're on, it has become a frequently used tool within social media channels. Both Facebook and YouTube have made it simple to broadcast live and post to their services. There's no disputing that the value of video on social media channels far exceeds any other type of post, so the conversation about live streaming in meetings has only begun.

Blogging

The **blog**, or Web log, is an online diary that is posted to the Web. Now considered an old school social channel, blogs are still an effective way to impart information to your customers and followers. Blogging inherently is a two-way medium, as most blogs allow for people to respond and further the discussion on the posted blog.

The use of a blog for the marketing of a conference is simple. You can easily create a dialogue between organizers and their audience. Since blogs have a built-in comment functionality, it is a two-way communication tool that can greatly help organizers get a pulse of what is on the minds of their attendees. Savvy planners have used bloggers outside of their organization to help them share content to those not in attendance. In some cases, organizations provide event bloggers complimentary registration, and provide them first row seating to do their posts.

While blogs are a very easy point of entry into social media, and a great way to enhance your Web presence, it is surprising how few planners and suppliers maintain and update blogs on a regular basis. To some extent, the explosion of Facebook and Twitter are to blame. Still, planners would be wise to create and update a blog to help enhance their event communications. As mentioned earlier, Julius Solaris' Event Manager's blog (www.eventmanagerblog.com/) is a great example of a successful industry blog.

Podcasting

Like blogging, podcasts are very much an old school tool in the realm of social media. While podcasts are very much in vogue for listening to a variety of educational and entertainment shows, their use within the meeting industry is nominal.

Consider the event planners' boss blog. Well written and informative, it provides a great tool for communication with your colleagues—as long as they are at their computer. But how about that long morning and evening commute? Many organizations have taken their blogs, and other information, and enabled the user to listen to it on their mp3 player by creating **podcasting** content.

The event podcast is essentially an extension of what planners have been doing for many years. A generation ago, planners would record sessions, and then distribute (sell) the audiotapes to those who couldn't attend. Podcasts can do this by digitizing the recording. However, as our attention spans have gotten shorter (and with the proliferation of free available podcasts online), the event podcast may find itself to be more of a marketing tool than a revenue stream. Still, it provides a great way to extend the event to those who couldn't attend.

Hashtags

No conversation about social media is complete without a discussion on the importance of hashtags. Essentially a keyword or phrase that helps target social posts to an interested audience, hashtags drive two social services, Twitter and Instagram.

In the world of Twitter, the hashtag establishes and feeds a threaded conversation that everyone can view and join in. Some events establish a single hashtag for their event, sending out information before and during the event through Twitter, while providing attendees an opportunity to also be apart of the dialogue. With larger, more tech-savvy groups, some events have multiple hashtags, allowing for more focused dialogues to occur.

While hashtags in Twitter are part of a successful post, it can be said that in Instagram, it's all (and only) about the hashtags. There is no limit on the number of hashtags usable in an Instagram post (Twitter's limit is based not only on the 140-character cap, but also on making the post easily readable). Many top-notch Instagram users believe 15 to 20 or more hashtags on a post is the way to maximize their reach.

Hashtags in both services (they can be used in Facebook, but they don't have the value there) allow for the content curation necessary for open channels to streamline content to those who are interested. In our industry, hashtags aren't only the domain of conferences, but they are also a great way to curate and receive content about our industry. *#eventprofs* is one of the top respected meeting industry tags in use. The hashtag search tool, Hashtagify.me (http://hashtagify.me/), allows users to see which hashtags are used alongside ones they already know about—a great way to find out more relevant hashtags about your industry.

Social Selling

The marriage of event marketing and social media channels isn't complete without mentioning the use of advertising within social media channels (and, of course, Google as well). Paid social media is an often underutilized tool for getting past the noise of social media channels to deliver content onto the screens of potential attendees.

Targeted ads (prevalent on Facebook), often referred to as *re-targeting*, allow organizations to identify target demographics (e.g., 35 to 44 year olds in New York and Connecticut who are interested in Widgets) and serve ads onto these users' Facebook pages. Since Facebook heavily curates the content that people see (no, you don't see the posts from everyone you're following), they have forced businesses to consider ads, or the option of paid boosted posts, to hopefully ensure that your message is seen by those you want to see it.

Outside of Facebook, most other social channels accept paid placement. *Promoted Tweets* is a tool on Twitter allowing the event organizer to increase the amount of people who see their posts. Like Facebook, it comes with targeting tools. Both Instagram and LinkedIn also have ad functionality within their channels.

For all social channels, the cost of ads tends to be much less expensive than more traditional advertising. Following the successful Google model, these reasonably priced tools can certainly help the tech savvy planner to promote their conference without depleting their marketing budget.

Event Apps

Is the printed program guide dead? It depends, as always, on whom you ask. The proliferation of event-specific apps has allowed planners to drive all event content directly to attendees' mobile devices. Clearly a more ecologically sustainable approach to content distribution at events, event apps have become an industry standard.

Although it is ultimately the planner's decision about what content is provided within the event app, there are some consistent elements that frequently enhance the attendee's experience. These include sections for the program, maps, local information, social media, gamification, among a variety of others.

By making these social posts part of the app, the event app can help drive online discussions about the event, enhancing event marketing and awareness.

Some of the top industry providers of event apps include:

- Quick Mobile (www.quickmobile.com/)
- EventMobi (www.eventmobi.com/)
- Double Dutch (doubledutch.me/)
- Trip Builder (www.tripbuildermedia.com/)

With the increased indexing of content located on mobile devices by Google, event organizations need to consider the value of an organization-level app, as well as event apps, to stay relevant digitally.

Desktop Tools

While there are dozens of industry specific software packages on the market, the clear leader in our industry is still the basic Microsoft Office Suite with Word, Excel, Access, and PowerPoint, the meeting professional has the tools on his/her desktop to manage all the components of any event.

For some planners, these tools are too feature rich and outdated in some ways. Online collaborative office-based tools, such as Google Drive (https://drive.google.com), provide more than enough functionality with better collaboration tools for documents. Google Drive's hidden gem, Google Forms, allows planners to create surveys, evaluations, and questionnaires through their service at no cost.

However, this general package does not fill every need. Many planners, especially in organizations with non-centralized meeting departments, need tools that allow information to be shared across the organization. The industry has many tools that foster better centralization of information.

At the core of this need to centralize information is the ability for organizations to get a handle on the amount of purchasing leverage they have. The individual planning a small meeting within a large organization is at a disadvantage in terms of negotiation, unless they can combine their hotel room, contracting with others within the organization. This is where third-party software tools can have a significant advantage over the Microsoft or Google options. While more expensive, they frequently provide exceptional cross-organizational value by allowing organizations to bundle their purchasing needs.

APEX

The Events Industry Council (formerly known as the Convention Industry Council), the organization that manages the Certified Meeting Professional (CMP) examination, has been at the forefront of establishing the Accepted Practices Exchange (APEX) for our industry. The essential concept of APEX is to make the industry more efficient by creating a set of standards that all parties within the industry can accept. A great link to learn more about APEX is found on the Convention Industry website (www.eventscouncil.org/).

As it relates to technology, APEX has created white papers and information on event bandwidth and RFPs, among many other tools.

Virtual Trade Shows

A few years ago, **virtual trade shows** were all the rage as the next big thing. At its most fundamental, a virtual trade show can be an online trade show floor plan with hypertext links to the sites of the exhibitors for the attendees to visit. Virtual trade shows proclaimed that they could also be a virtual experience in itself, with the attendee virtually walking through the event and clicking on information (or in some cases, actually chatting with sales reps). However, while companies are still creating these virtual experiences, they have lost the interest of most groups. Still, it could make a return.

On-Site Event Tech Infrastructure

The meeting professional understands the importance of negotiations with hotels. From rates, dates, and space, to every other aspect of the event, the planner, armed with knowledge and information about their event and the destination, can have a productive interaction with a hotel to create a win–win event.

However, many planners, fearful about, or unaware of, technology, leave out any discussion of the technology during this part of the planning process. This can be a very expensive omission. The technology-savvy planner, however, understands enough about event-supporting technology that they know what they need to plan for (even negotiate) during the initial stages of planning.

Planners need to think about issues of bandwidth, and how they will use the Internet and other technologies to support their goals. Additionally, the technology-savvy planner will think about how their attendees will want to use technology to enhance their meeting experience. While an event professional may not be able to implement all of these technologies, they can identify which ones are most critical (and useful) to successfully implement everyone's goals, thereby allowing the technology to play a spectacular supporting role in the success of the conference.

Bandwidth

Bandwidth is the amount of information that can be transmitted at the same time. The more bandwidth that is available, the more emails, hits to a social networking site, and so on can occur simultaneously. Bandwidth can be a very expensive proposition for planners, especially when they're holding their meetings at convention centers instead of hotels.

Determining how much bandwidth is needed is a difficult task. Here is where the planner may need help, and it can come from their own IT specialists; but only if they understand and plan for their on-site needs. The following is a partial list of planner tasks that uses bandwidth at events:

- Registration networking (for the planner)
- Internet cafes (including email access)
- HQ office and press room bandwidth for office communications
- Speaker Internet access for presentations
- Attendee bandwidth for interactive elements
- Live streaming for sessions and events
- Social channel content distribution

Determining how much bandwidth is needed before the contract is signed will enable you to ensure that the facility can meet your needs, and allow you to negotiate costs to a more reasonable level. The technology provider, PSAV, has developed a *bandwidth calculator* to help event professionals determine their needs.

TECHNOLOGY IS GREAT: WHEN IT WORKS

A MEEC industry conference included a session that was meant to be on the cutting edge of technology. Attendees sitting at tables were each provided with a tablet while others were invited to use their smart devices. All were provided log on information. The concept was to have content streamed to each attendee. Two-way communication was incorporated where attendees could send texts to the presenters and participate in audience polling. The session began well. However, as more and more attendees logged on, communication slowed and, eventually, the entire session crashed. This was due to insufficient bandwidth. Technology is great . . . when it works.

Wired versus Wireless

Most attendees will want to access their email wherever they go in the hotel. With the proliferation of 4G/4G LTE mobile phones (such as the iPhone, Samsung phones, and Google Pixel), the attendee can typically get it on their mobile device. But it is at the meeting space below ground (lacking a strong signal), or even at an international destination, where the attendee might not be able to use their devices.

A facility that allows for the attendees' computer to pick up a wireless signal, whether it is in their guest room or in a public space, is still an important service to provide. Some guest rooms can also provide wired access, but today, wireless is the standard, even with its tendency to drop out (always at the most inopportune moment). Even in guest rooms, the strength of the bandwidth coming from the wireless signal is not always sufficient to allow the guest to adequately check email, let alone browse the Web.

The wireless standard is an engineering specification named 80211. This spec, adopted in the late 1990s, defines how a wireless interface between clients and access points is constructed. However, there are many flavors of 80211. Each one provides a different amount of potential bandwidth to the user. Talk to your IT department about the limitation of 80211, 80211ac, and the latest 80211n standards.

If you ask speakers requiring high-speed Internet access what kind of connection they want for the success of their presentation, they will respond by stating that they prefer hardwired Internet access (an Ethernet cable attached to their computer, as opposed to a wireless connection). As the MEEC industry progresses to create a more seamless broadband experience, wireless may (and should) become the standard. However, a good planner will at least have a hardwired backup in case the wireless signal is not an adequate solution. Planners should also make sure that the bandwidth streaming to the speaker is dedicated for their device(s), and not part of the shared bandwidth that the attendees are using. Otherwise, a busy online audience can negatively impact the needs of the speaker.

Digital Recording and Streaming Media

The general session is a critical part of any annual meeting or conference. The marketing success of many conferences depends on the quality (and name recognition) of the keynote speakers, who establish the tone of a conference.

However, there are many people who cannot attend who would like to watch/hear the talk, either in real time or from an archive. The organization can extend their keynotes (as well as other meeting components) to those who cannot attend by streaming it over the Internet (frequently referred to as webcasting), or creating podcasting content to share or sell.

If you have never done this at a meeting, be aware that significant extra coordination and support is required, especially with video content. You'll need to have cameras (and video/audio engineers) in the session to ensure the recorded material is of good quality. You'll need a company to digitize the video into a format that can be electronically distributed. You will need to determine whether the event should be streamed live (always a riskier proposition) or archived. And will people have free access to it, or will the organization charge a fee for people to virtually attend?

Or, of course, you can have a single person with a phone, running one of the previously mentioned live streaming apps, stand up and provide real-time content at no cost (though clearly not at the same quality). The choice is yours.

While learning about the technical side of events, the MEEC professional must also understand a great deal about their audience, and what they might want to view online. Age and demographics certainly play a role in whether an entire session should be digitized, or if a highlights approach is best for the MEEC professional's group. The adage "know your group" applies to all aspects of event planning, even the technological side.

Drones

For outdoor events, one of the latest technologies is the use of drones to provide aerial photography of the event. A drone is an unmanned aircraft that can be maneuvered by remote control. Used for years by the military for aerial reconnaissance, drones have now fallen into mainstream use. While they are heavily regulated by the Federal Aviation Administration (don't think of flying it indoors, even in a high-ceilinged convention center), many tech savvy photographers are offering drones and drone photographs as part of their package of services.

Attendee Interaction and Communications

Many people think paper badges are "old school." Technology has moved the name badge from a simple identification tool to one that can interact with a variety of planner tech tools, and may ultimately being able to interact with other badges.

Beacons

If you've ever walked into an Apple store and seen small round devices, no more than a few inches in circumference, around the store, you've seen beacon technology at work. A beacon is a Bluetooth-based tool that broadcasts small bits of information directly to a Bluetooth-enabled device, such as your smart phone. The content that is broadcast is typically location specific, and typically targeted for a specific user.

Within meetings and events, beacon technology can interface with phones, or even Smart Badges (badges that have tiny beacon receivers within them). This allows event organizers to pass along content, recognize attendance for continuing education (CE) credits, promote sponsors, and so on. There are a variety of ways it can be used.

Two-way beacon technology is the next wave of this kind of technology. Typically, they are on a wearable tool, such as on a lanyard around an attendee's neck. Two-way beacon technology avoids using the attendee's phone (many of whom keep Bluetooth off for a variety of smart reasons), and sends and receives data directly to and from the wearable device. This opens up a wide-range of possibilities for wearable social media integration and communications between wearable devices. If you really wanted to think long-term, these tools may be integrated with augmented reality to provide floating information above an attendee's head, which could facilitate networking.

NFC and RFID

The following two acronyms, NFC and RFID, are at the core of many of the interactive technologies available on-site at conferences. **Near field communications (NFC)**, which is a short range, high-frequency wireless technology, allowing for information exchange between certain devices. RFID stands for radio frequency identification, and are the tags (readers) used to access these signals. Most people already familiar with RFID tags, as anyone living in a city with tolls from bridges or tunnels can obtain RFID tags (known by a variety of names, including EZPass, SmartPass, etc.) to quickly pay these fees. They also can be used to inventory products in a company's warehouse, enabling it to better track its products.

RFIDs and NFCs are finding a use in our industry as well, mainly for **interactive nametags**.

Lead Retrieval Systems

For many years, trade shows and exhibits have used **lead retrieval** systems to help capture customer information. The process begins with the meeting organizer asking questions during the registration process that will help identify important information for the exhibitor. These questions often include the attendees' purchasing responsibility, and the nature of the products and services in which they may have interest.

The information is coded into a badge, though it needn't be an RFID. From the 1990s through today, many groups still use a simple bar code on the badge (or even a credit card-based system) that contains this information.

When the attendee enters the trade show floor, and interacts with an exhibitor, the exhibit staff member can ask to swipe the badge with their lead retrieval device (typically, these are rented to the exhibitor for the duration of the show by a vendor who is supporting the meeting). Once swiped, this information now resides in their handheld lead retrieval device. At day's end, the exhibitor can download this information to their spreadsheet or database, and have customized thank you notes emailed to the attendee before their work for the day is complete (not to mention excellent information about their prospective clients).

Name badge with imbedded RFID Technology.
ZUMA Press Inc/Alamy Stock Photo

The planner's job in this process is to identify and select a system or service that can support the lead retrieval process. Since exhibitors require this level of information to determine whether exhibiting at a function will potentially help their business, lead retrieval systems are primarily used for trade shows. However, these systems have also been used to help facilitate attendee surveying using automated kiosks around the event.

Also available to the planner is what is known as a reverse lead retrieval system. Instead of the exhibitor scanning the planner's badge, the planner uses a handheld device to scan information positioned in the booth of the exhibitor. When utilized, it is frequently for much larger shows.

Audience Response Systems and Speaker Interaction

If you've ever watched certain audience participation game shows, you've seen the host poll the audience to determine their opinion about a question. The audience is outfitted with small keypads that allow them to answer questions quickly, and have their data tallied immediately. This is the essence of the **audience response system (ARS)**.

Historically, ARS systems have been expensive propositions for the planner to implement, but new technologies have made it a more affordable and necessary part of many meetings in today's two-way communication lifestyle. One such service is Poll Everywhere (www.polleverywhere.com), which uses SMS (texting), in addition to Web and Twitter voting, to interface with a real-time, Web-based poll. The audience members respond, and the data is instantaneously updated and posted for all to see.

Over the past five years, one of the game changers in our industry for audience interaction has been the Crowd Mics app (http://crowdmics.com/). The speaker and the attendees have the app installed on their devices. The speaker can generate live polls through the device; though it's primary (and undeniably coolest) use is turning everyone's smartphone into a microphone to ask questions at an event.

Twitter has also been frequently used to help facilitate interactivity during a session, whether it's for the purpose of providing an audience chat discussion, or used as a way to send messages and questions directly to a speaker. SMS (through texting of questions to a session moderator) is another way that these technologies have created a better real-time connection between a speaker and his/her audience.

This technology allows the meeting organizer and speaker to gain instant information (demographic or otherwise) about attendees, and can be used to customize content and the direction of educational sessions.

Post-conference Technology Applications

Technology has clearly served a great purpose in the marketing and running of meetings. It also continues to be a useful tool once the meeting is completed. From the post-conference evaluation process, to the digital highlights (which can be weaved into the marketing for the next conference), there is more to review regarding technology applications in our industry.

Evaluations and Surveys

Many organizers have moved the meeting evaluation process from a paper-based process on-site (it can be digitized as well), to a post-conference, online approach. While there is much debate over whether post-conference evaluations provide the most accurate information, as well as whether the post-event approach offers the best quantity of completed evaluations, its mainstream usage cannot be ignored.

Regardless of ones' position, it is a system in use by many planners. In fact, Web-based tools, such as Survey Monkey (www.surveymonkey.com/), are becoming increasingly popular for this process. Web-based services not only distribute the evaluations, but also tally them and provide the planner with an easy to read analysis of the questions they posed to the attendees. In fact, many integrated online solutions for meeting professionals include event survey functionality.

Earlier in this chapter we discussed the Google Drive tool known as Google Forms. As a free alternative, this tool can also become the de facto survey distribution tool at no cost to the planner. This service also automatically builds the back-end database of the survey, so all the responses go directly into a spreadsheet that can be analyzed by the planner.

This process should not be limited to conference evaluations. Any meeting professional who is involved in the programming process understands that learning about the needs of their audience is one of the best tools to identify program elements that create greater value for the attendee. The online survey, independent of the conference evaluation, can be of significant support to that process.

Marketing the Media

The essence of post-conference technology is to extend the event past its traditional time borders. A conference is no longer bound to a Monday to Thursday time frame. It can begin with attendee networking months prior to the opening session by using tools, such as the pre-event networking tools previously discussed. After the conference, the planner can provide content to those who didn't attend (or even those who wish to view it again).

As the planner makes arrangements to record and stream activities at their conference, he or she must consider how this information will be delivered. Issues of cost and delivery are a significant part of the conversation. Will the planner charge for virtual attendance? Will they provide complimentary video clips of the event on their website (either to enhance purchasing or help the marketing of future events)?

As for the delivery of digital content, especially in a live environment, the event professional needs to make certain that they have the servers and technology (including bandwidth) available so that whoever wishes to log on and view the event can do so without the signal degrading or breaking up.

The planner's best marketing tool is the success of their previous event. The digitization and distribution of this content is, therefore, an absolutely critical tool for not only generating revenue from this year's event, but also continuing to attract attendees in future years.

Virtual and Augmented Reality

The newest game changing technology in meetings and events falls in the category of mixed reality. In this category, two tools are just finding their way into the MEEC industry: **virtual reality** and **augmented reality**. To say that these are potentially game-changing tools for our industry is an understatement. However, as a new technology that probably hasn't found its "sea legs" yet, its current usage is limited with early tech adopters finding ways to integrate it successfully.

Virtual Reality

Virtual Reality (VR) is an immersive experience, with the user wearing goggles to see content in 360 degrees. The user doesn't see anything other than what is projected inside the wearable device. VR devices fit into three categories: phone-based, computer-based, and stand-alone. Phone-based devices (Samsung Gear and Google Daydream) are used by accessing content by placing a smartphone (brand specific, of course) inside the goggles. Computer-based (Oculus Rift, HTC Vive) are more powerful tools, as the goggles are attached to a powerful PC. The latest category is the stand alone, which, right now, has no actual devices. However, Google has announced *WorldSense*, which will cut the cables and phones out of the VR equation.

For the MEEC industry, VR has many uses—for example, at special events, attendees can try on goggles and experience content (such as multimedia, photos, videos, even games). In fact, integration of VR into event gamification is going to greatly enhance the user's experience. Many hotels and CVBs are already using virtual reality to promote destinations at trade shows and on sales calls. Why talk about your property when the planner can experience it as if they were there? VR is a great marketing vehicle for planners to promote their upcoming meetings as well. And don't forget that 360-degree content isn't limited to goggles, both Facebook and YouTube support 360-degree content on their pages.

THE VIRTUAL TRADE SHOW BOOTH MODEL

RetailNext was looking for a way to stand out on the crowded floor at Retail's Big Show, hosted by the National Retail Federation at the Jacob K. Javits Convention Center. The company decided to try a new tactic to entice attendees to stop at its booth: a life-size, lifelike virtual presenter from Prsonas.

The company positioned the virtual presenter in a high-traffic spot in its booth. While in idle mode, the unit would look around and wave to attract attention from passersby. As attendees got near, motion sensors triggered it to speak a welcome message that invited them to select an option from an attached touch screen, such as watching a video about RetailNext or submitting contact information. As attendees stepped away from the unit, it would say good-bye and thank them for visiting the booth, and RetailNext staff members were nearby to answer any questions.

This was one of the first virtual presenters created with Prsonas's new computer-generated system, which creates a lifelike image entirely through computer animation rather than shooting video of a real actor. Live talent is used for the voice recordings, because it is warmer and more engaging than a computer-generated voice. Clients provide the scripting for the presenter's messages, which can be recorded in multiple languages, and they also customize its appearance, choosing hairstyle and color, eye color, and clothing.

The virtual presenter can be configured to swipe attendee badges for lead capture, or process credit cards for exhibitors that are selling products in their booths. The system captures data such as how many people interacted with the presenter, the duration of the interactions, and which topics on the touch screen were most popular.

Augmented Reality

Many experts expect that augmented reality will be the more useful tool moving forward. Augmented reality is the ability to see content that isn't visible to the naked eye. By looking through a device (phone or tablet), or through a wearable (headset or glasses), the user will see and interact with content that is visible only to them, often dropped into the real world. We can't talk about AR without mentioning the breakout AR tool—Pokémon Go. Many people thought it was the craziest, silliest app ever. But before you completely dismiss it, digest these numbers: It has more than 100 million downloads, and they earned $10 million dollars in daily revenue from both app stores (data from Engadget, September 2016).

Think of augmented reality as QR codes on steroids. Point your device and content comes to life. The difference is, instead of a bar code, the object that can be scanned is, well, anything.

In 2009, a company named Layar created the first augmented reality browser, allowing users to use their mobile devices (supported with built-in GPS and camera) to display real time information on top of live images. A few progressive hotel companies have added an augmented element to their traditional magazine advertisements, providing users with second screen content. A simpler use for planners to the traditional session signage at meetings is to have an augmented video accessible. When the attendee hovers their phone over the sign, they can watch a short video clip of the session or speaker in action.

Google Glass in use.
PA Images/Alamy Stock Photo

Artificial Intelligence and Big Data

As a society, we create as much data in two days as we did from the beginning of time through 2003. Think about that for a second. The volume of videos, pictures, posts, and comments we make on an ongoing basis has helped coin the phrase **big data**. Of course, big data is meaningless unless we can find a way to interpret this information and make it useful to our organization. Massive computing capabilities, once the domain of massively sized computer systems, can now chunk-out and analyze this information, as long as the users can ask the right questions and interpret it without bias.

The hotel industry has clearly seen the power of this. Being able to use digital tools to learn more about their customers provides them with the ability to deliver what their customers want in a timely manner. The more data they get (and properly interpret), the more useful the information. Therefore, hotels (as should planners) love people using their property app with location and Bluetooth services turned on. Every point of data becomes a piece of a puzzle that's getting easier to complete.

However, on the planner side, there are still only a few groups (mainly those with larger trade shows and conferences) who have begun to understand the power of this data. Yet, the same is true for planners as it is for hoteliers: The more you know about your customers, the better you should be able to serve them.

Artificial Intelligence

Even though we may not be aware of it, we are using **artificial intelligence (AI)** tools regularly. Ever have Netflix tell you that people who like a certain movie also watched these films? That's an everyday example of AI in use. When coupled with the big data we just discussed, today's AI can use recursive-learning techniques to better understand the data, and learn from how it connects with people.

A clear use of AI in meetings is integrating with another new tool, chatbots, to create automated responses to user questions from websites and event apps. By definition, a **chatbot** is a computer program that is trained to have conversations with humans, using natural language.

For many planners, one of the most time-consuming activities leading up to the event is in answering the steady stream of questions from the attendees. "When does registration begin?"; "Who's delivering the Tuesday keynote?"; and "At which hotel is the convention located?" are all examples of queries that a chatbot, using AI, could (and are) answering.

AI tools are able to summarize phone conversations into to do lists (http://claire.ai/), transcribe minutes at events (https://swiftscribe.ai/), or even act as your personal assistant (https://x.ai/). These available AI tools have a variety of applications and many more are being developed. In fact, Facebook Messenger uses a host of chatbots from various applications to respond to questions. It makes you ask the question, "Is this really a human being, or is it a chatbot?"

Webinars and Hybrid Meetings

Even though face-to-face interactions are still what most people want (both for their networking and education), online tools, such as webinars and hybrid meetings, provide immense value to support those times when you just can't be there.

Webinars

The creation of a successful webinar is very different than a live event. All day live online events are rarely successful. (Who's going to sit at their desk all day to actively view a meeting?) Short burst training (sometimes as short as 15 to 20 minutes) can be as, if not more, effective than more standard session durations of 60 to 90 minutes. The speaker, who is getting no visual or audio cues from the audience, must be able to keep their audience engaged. Q&A tends to be relegated to a specified time frame following the session.

There are many webinar providers that a planner can use. One such service is ReadyTalk (www.readytalk.com). The planner should make certain that the service they use is priced properly for their needs. Additional questions include how the service handles audio (through the computer or the phone), the maximum capacity of the virtual event, does the service provide interactive tools such as chat and polling, and how easy is it for the event organizers and speaker to switch the view from the platform being used to their desktop, for showcasing their applications and browser.

A more expensive, yet far more interactive approach comes from Cisco, whose *TelePresence* videoconferencing provides face-to-face communications between attendees. With HD and top-quality audio, events or meetings held using this service seems to tear down the walls between real and virtual events.

Hybrid Meetings

If done well, a **hybrid meeting** successfully extends the reach of live events to those who cannot attend. As the name indicates, a hybrid meeting combines a live event with a remote component. Successful hybrid events do not just show remote attendees a video of what's happening at the event. They are designed to deliver unique and enriching experiences for both live and remote audiences. Paying attention to the needs of both audiences is a delicate balance that is required for the creation and delivery of these types of sessions.

There are a host of examples of types of hybrid meetings. From town halls to technical trainings, if you can satisfy both your live and remote audiences, you have the potential of a successful event. These events aren't inexpensive, as it requires AV and content delivery tools to engage with both the remote audience in real time as well as the live audience's experience.

Summary

Do you think that technology has changed rapidly up to now? We haven't seen the rate of change that we should continue to experience moving forward. Short term, the adoption of VR and AR into event management, marketing, and experiences; and a better understanding of AI and chatbots will continue to make significant inroads in our industry. Long-term, well who really knows what's around the tech corner? It's clear that the successful event/meeting planner of today needs to know and integrate technology the same way they understand logistics, and food and beverage. And yet, we haven't even discussed the day where our event food will be produced by tech tools. But that's in the distant future . . . maybe.

CASE STUDY

Using Technology to Attract Millennials

The American Society of Widgets (ASW) is a nonprofit, 501C3 association of members who are in the industry of making, selling, and distributing widgets. The association has been around for 50 plus years and, in recent years, has struggled to stay relevant to a younger group of potential members. With conference attendance plummeting by 50 percent in the past decade, a new, younger executive director was hired to reverse the trend. By understanding the importance of integrating new technologies into the marketing, delivery, and experience of the conference, she could connect with the younger potential members, make the conference meaningful to them, and improve the association's conference attendance and bottom line.

Moral of the story: *Change, while never a comfortable thing to do, is essential to move your mission and your impact forward.* For many people, the use of technology is the biggest driver of change.

1. What technology could the executive director use in her conference marketing efforts?
2. Which social media channels are the ones she would find most success with, and why?
3. How could the organization integrate cutting edge technologies, such as virtual and augmented reality, into the marketing and experience of the event?
4. What common meeting tools and techniques could be used by the association to aggregate big data about the attendees and ensure that future conferences met and exceeded their needs?
5. What are the biggest technological challenges the executive director must overcome to create a more technology-friendly conference?

Key Words and Terms

For definitions, see the Glossary.

artificial intelligence (AI)	chatbot	podcasting
audience response system (ARS)	hybrid meetings	social media
augmented reality	interactive nametags	virtual reality
big data	lead retrieval	virtual trade shows
blog	Near field communications (NFC)	

About the Chapter Contributors

James Spellos is the president of a company called Meeting U located in New York City. The website is meeting-u.com. He is a consultant and frequent speaker on technology issues in the MEEC industry.

Kathryn Hashimoto, PhD is an emeritus member of the faculty in the School of Hospitality Leadership at East Carolina University.

Previous Edition Chapter Contributors

Dennis Rudd, EdD, Robert Morris College Emeritus
Kathleen Taylor Brown, Robert Morris College.

Sustainability is a critical element of the MEEC industry.
Rawpixel.com/Shutterstock

CHAPTER 12

Sustainable Meetings and Events

Chapter Objectives

- Cover the difference between green and sustainable meetings.
- Discuss the reasons to go green with meetings and events.
- Outline important sustainable meeting standards and guidelines.
- Specify steps in creating a process for sustainable practices.

- Outline opportunities to evaluate sustainable efforts.
- Discuss the practice of greenwashing in events and meetings.
- Articulate current trends and best practices in creating sustainable meetings and events.

ROOFTOP GARDEN

Vegetables can grow in the most unexpected places, including the roof of the McCormick Place Convention Center, West Building, in Chcago. Architects planned a green roof to mitigate the environmental impact of the building, and went a step further by creating a lovely terrace event space with skyline views.

The food service provider at the McCormick Place convention center in Chicago is SAVOR. They have collaborated with the Chicago Botanic Garden to plant what is thought to be the Midwest's largest farm-to-fork rooftop garden. This garden is part of a continuing commitment to promote local sustainable agriculture. The partnership is also meant to train city residents for careers in urban agriculture. Further the garden aids in reducing the thermal footprint of the convention center and helps reduce the building's heat island effect. The harvest of herbs and vegetables is used in the creation of menu items like homemade pesto and herb rub.

The rooftop garden provides the food service provider with fresh produce for catering and restaurant operations at the convention center including "Windy City Harvest" menu items served in the 23rd Street Cafe & Market. The 2.5-acre soil based rooftop garden is thought to be the largest in the Midwest. It produced garden products and a seasonal harvest that yield 8,000 lbs. of farm-fresh goods. The products include beans, beets, lettuce, carrots, kale, herbs and peppers that are used in the kitchens. The rooftop garden also houses 2,000 Red Wiggler worms that create 200 lbs. of compost annually. It is also the home to 20,000 honey bees in three hives that produce 50 lbs. of honey a year. Additionally, the views of the Chicago skyline are spectacular. While the garden mainly yields produce during warm weather, the staff planned to extend the growing season by planting cool weather crops like kale, spinach and collard greens for McCormick Place restaurants. Hops have been planted in the garden and are used to produce McCormick Place Every Day Ale. It is the country's first branded ale brewed for a convention center using locally-sourced ingredients.

The garden was conceptualized and planted by employees from the Chicago Botanic Garden's Windy City Harvest (WCH) urban agriculture program.

SAVOR…Chicago provides a limited number of tours of the rooftop garden to local organizations and industry groups.

Provided by Connie Chambers, Savor . . . Chicago.
Jbryson/Getty Images

The author has heard Kermit the Frog say, "It's not easy being green." But what does green mean in terms of the MEEC industry? **Green meetings** are defined in a variety of ways, but the term green has become commonly used to describe a meeting's environmental practices. In other words, how green a meeting is, is usually determined by policies, such as recycling, using energy efficient lighting, or serving pitchers of water as opposed to bottled water. The emphasis on protecting the environment is often a key indicator for green meetings.

The industry started referring to green meetings roughly within the past eight to ten years, when the idea of being green was becoming a popular concept in the lodging arena. This green meeting movement is now evolving, however, to include not just minimizing environmental impact, but to also include efforts that impact the people-side of meetings and events, as well as profits. In other words, taking good care of not only the employees working the meetings and events and the event's attendees, but also those who are impacted in the community where an event may occur—all the while also making a profit—is just as important as taking care of the environment. This triple threat is often referred to as the triple bottom line, or sustainability.

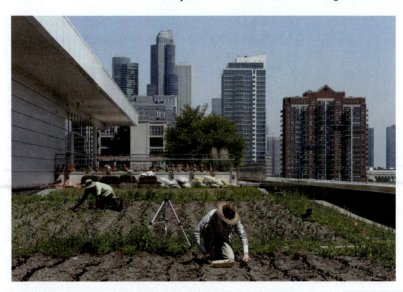

The roof top garden at McCormick Place in Chicago.
Antonio Perez/Chicago Tribune/Getty Images

Green Meetings versus Sustainable Meetings

While sometimes used interchangeably, the terms green meetings and sustainable meetings have different meanings.

Green meetings have been created and executed to curb harmful effects on the environment (e.g., minimize waste and the use of bottled water), while taking the current state of the environment into consideration, it is not usually associated with the overall impact on future generations, or the triple bottom line.

Sustainable meetings are a more encompassing term that includes implementing and executing a plan to save resources while also improving the performance of a meeting or event. This term suggests that the impact that a meeting has on the environment, society, and the economy has been taken into consideration. According to the United Nations Environment Programme's (UNEP) *Green Meeting Guide*, a green or sustainable meeting or event is one that is designed, organized, and implemented in a way that minimizes environmental impacts and leaves a positive legacy for the host community. The Events Industry Council Sustainability Initiative takes the view that the demand sustainability places on our society and industry requires everyone to be part of the solution. By working together, they believe we can all create sustainability and sustainable development in the framework of the events and meetings that occur in our communities. In addition, they emphasize that meeting professionals should source materials that are both environmentally *and* socially responsible.

The widely recognized Brundtland Report, created after the 1983 World Commission on Environment and Development, defines **sustainability**, as "development, which meets the needs of the present without compromising the ability of future generations to meet their own needs." This definition is one of the most often cited, and focuses on three aspects of sustainable development—economic development, social development, and environmental protection. These three aspects, or pillars as many people refer to them, are also called the three P's of sustainability—profit, planet, and people—and are interconnected to each other; none can exist without the others.

TIDBIT

Earth Hour—Coordinated primarily by the World Wildlife Fund, Earth Hour began in Australia in 2007 to help curb the effects of global warming, and conserve energy by encouraging people to turn off their lights for one hour, 8:30 PM to 9:30 PM, toward the end of March. In 2017, 187 countries across 17 continents participated in the event, with 3,000 landmarks switching off their lights.

The movement toward sustainable meetings within the MEEC industry is impacting all areas of meeting planning. As more planners strive to minimize their events' environmental impacts, suppliers are also working to make their products and services more Earth-friendly. Meeting professionals are actively learning the ins and outs of executing sustainable meetings; and meeting suppliers are jumping on board accordingly. When meeting professionals begin planning more sustainable meetings, the ripple effect has an impact on all parties involved.

Why Go Green

The Triple Bottom Line

Perhaps answering the question, "why go green?" includes more than a single bottom line could report. Some experts consider the triple bottom line as a more accurate measure of a company's accomplishments, and a better answer to the question. Considering the triple bottom line of people (social impact), planet (environmental impact), and profit (economic impact) expands the concept of success to include environmental and social accomplishments in addition to the financial accomplishments of an organization. Research suggests that many forward-thinking organizations, associations, and companies are applying the triple bottom line concept as they measure success and answer to stakeholders.

Profit (Economic Impact)

Economic sustainability refers to an organization's, or in this case a meeting's, ability to efficiently and responsibly use resources to ensure all financial obligations are met over time. In the MEEC industry, this is important for both the meeting planner as well as the company or organization holding/requesting the meeting. This makes good business sense, and companies that choose to do so are reporting higher gross profit margins, higher return on sales, higher return on assets, and a stronger cash flow than their less sustainable competitors. Examples of economic sustainability include return on investment (ROI), fair trade, local economy, growth, and business performance. Once a company has made the commitment to become more sustainable within its own organization, it is easier to apply the same principles to their meetings and events.

Taking small steps to become sustainable can make an enormous difference in a company's bottom line. For example, one large event eliminated the use of bottled water and saved $1.5 million at an event attended by 40,000 people over a five-day period. Reusing name badge holders saved another group more than $1,500 in just one year. In addition to the monetary savings to these groups, the amount of waste deposited into a landfill was also reduced dramatically. Oracle's sustainability efforts during their annual OpenWorld event saved the company $1.7 million combined over the past five years. Among their many green efforts, they saved $420,000 by reevaluating their signage policies. Signage is now made from lighter, reusable materials and is sourced from local companies.

Planet (Environmental Impact)

Many efforts that are related to the economic impacts and savings of sustainability are directly related to the environmental efforts associated with those cost savings—thus highlighting the interconnectedness of the triple bottom line (See Figure 12-1 for examples). It is difficult to have one without the other. Perhaps the easiest piece of the triple bottom line to grasp is the focus on environmental sustainability. In fact, it is how most in the industry would describe or define sustainability; participating in and encouraging actions that help our meetings and events reduce the negative impact they may have on the environment. MEEC industry professionals can address environmental issues and impacts of their meetings in many ways. For example, they can reduce the amount of printed materials, such as program guides, maps of a venue, or exhibition materials they use for a meeting. This, by the way, will also save on cost! Many groups have eliminated the practice of automatically printing conference and meeting programs for each attendee. Instead, they take advantage of technology to encourage attendees to use apps via their mobile devices. Event apps have become very user friendly and have evolved over the years to include daily schedules, speaker

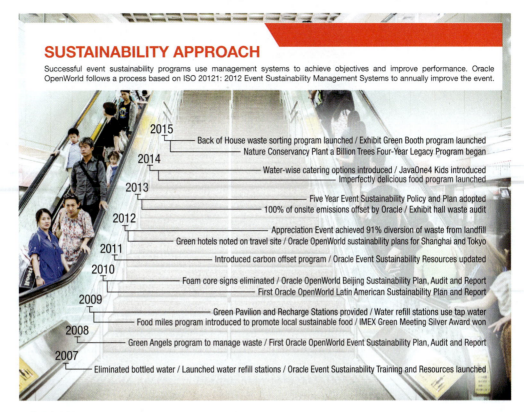

SUSTAINABILITY APPROACH

Successful event sustainability programs use management systems to achieve objectives and improve performance. Oracle OpenWorld follows a process based on ISO 20121: 2012 Event Sustainability Management Systems to annually improve the event.

2015 — Back of House waste sorting program launched / Exhibit Green Booth program launched
— Nature Conservancy Plant a Billion Trees Four-Year Legacy Program began
2014 — Water-wise catering options introduced / JavaOne4 Kids introduced
— Imperfectly delicious food program launched
2013 — Five Year Event Sustainability Policy and Plan adopted
— 100% of onsite emissions offset by Oracle / Exhibit hall waste audit
2012 — Appreciation Event achieved 91% diversion of waste from landfill
— Green hotels noted on travel site / Oracle OpenWorld sustainability plans for Shanghai and Tokyo
2011 — Introduced carbon offset program / Oracle Event Sustainability Resources updated
2010 — Foam core signs eliminated / Oracle OpenWorld Beijing Sustainability Plan, Audit and Report
— First Oracle OpenWorld Latin American Sustainability Plan and Report
2009 — Green Pavilion and Recharge Stations provided / Water refill stations use tap water
— Food miles program introduced to promote local sustainable food / IMEX Green Meeting Silver Award won
2008 — Green Angels program to manage waste / First Oracle OpenWorld Event Sustainability Plan, Audit and Report
2007 — Eliminated bottled water / Launched water refill stations / Oracle Event Sustainability Training and Resources launched

FIGURE 12-1

Oracle's sustainability efforts over the years. Oracle OpenWorld 2015 Event Sustainability Report. *Wayne0216/Shutterstock*

and exhibitor information, social media tools, and calendars with options for personal customization. All this information would typically be presented in a paper program guide.

Carbon Offsets   Large trade shows or conventions also incorporate the option for attendees to purchase carbon offsets as a way to diminish their environmental impact. It is inevitable that attendees need to use some form of transportation (e.g., airplane, car, or train) in order to attend a meeting, which produces emissions that are not good for the environment. In fact, transportation is the largest contributor to an event's environmental footprint, which accounts for 90 percent of the emissions produced by an event with travelers around the world. A **carbon offset** is meant to reduce the carbon dioxide or greenhouse gases produced when we travel—it compensates for the emission, and is meant to balance or cancel them out. Officially, a carbon offset "reduces or offsets carbon emissions through the funding of activities and projects that improve the environment." If, for example, someone flies from Phoenix to New York round-trip for a meeting or event, the trip will produce approximately 806 pounds of carbon per person, assuming the flight is full. The impact will be greater with an emptier plane. The purchase of a carbon offset helps to minimize that impact by funding projects that help reduce carbon and other greenhouse gas emissions. Some projects include planting trees, and investing in renewable energy sources such as windmills, or alternative fuels. This is an option that meeting professionals are now offering their attendees who can choose to voluntarily purchase these carbon offsets. The costs for such programs vary.

People (Social Impact)

In addition to the plant and profit factors of sustainability, it also encompasses people. People are those who attend meetings and events, those who work them, those who organize them, and those in the communities within which they are held. This is

FIGURE 12-2

Example of an event app used for conferences. *DWD-Media/Alamy Stock Photo* realized by equitably meeting the needs of all people affected by the planning or activation of an event. The question that meeting planners must ask themselves is how their events impact both their own employees and the people attending them, as well as those in the local communities where the events are being held. Is that impact a positive one?

To provide a framework for this idea of work with and for people, many companies have adopted the concept of **corporate social responsibility (CSR)**. The concept has been around since the 1950s and has been referred to as a number of different things (e.g., corporate responsibility, corporate accountability, corporate ethics, corporate citizenship, corporate sustainability, and responsible business). According to the World Business Council for Sustainable Development, corporate social responsibility is, the continuing commitment by business to behave ethically and contribute to economic development while improving the quality of life of the work force and their families as well as the local community and society at large. This is right in line with the people-side of sustainability. Another appropriate definition is from *Simply CSR*, which states that CSR is "a long-term approach to business that addresses the needs of communities, people, and their employers. CSR provides frameworks for a successful enterprise that is harmonious with its surroundings. It is an opportunity to generate honest, authentic good-news stories that a business and its community can be proud of. The center of CSR is the people and doing the right thing for people, and all stakeholders in this case, in the MEEC industry."

How does this translate to action in the MEEC industry specifically? Internally, employees who work in organizations that support sustainable efforts could be healthier due to working in an office that is naturally lighted or better ventilated for energy savings. They may be encouraged to take the stairs or ride their bike to work, obviously contributing to their personal health. In addition to obvious health reasons, employees like to be a part of something that is good overall. According to a recent survey, 92 percent of Americans are interested in an increased use of solar power. If you are working for a company that is using solar power, you are likely to feel that you are participating in making a positive contribution. Encouraging employees to become participants in sustainable efforts often means encouraging them to live a healthier and more active lifestyle. This leads to happier and more productive individuals in the workforce. And just as importantly for the entrepreneur or manager, it also has terrific potential for contributing to the bottom line of the company. Examples of such programs might include paid time off to volunteer at a local charity, or one-for-one matching donations to a charity of an employee's choice.

Externally, meeting and event attendees are also positively impacted by sustainable efforts, and enthusiastically participate in reduce, reuse, and recycle programs. They are often interested in also participating in those activities that get them out into communities, or at the very least, help to raise funds for local charities. The trend is to not provide attendees with the same-old meeting experience, but, instead, familiarize them with the local city that they are visiting, and how their impact of being there affects that city and its residents.

These types of activities can take many formats. Some organizations encourage attendees to become actively involved in a project while attending an event, while others may simply ask for donations, or make donations on behalf of the entire organization. Some examples include the following.

Oracle—In partnership with Goodwill's GoodSource program, which provides jobs for those with barriers to employment, Oracle provides jobs at its annual OpenWorld conference. Goodwill GoodSource employees put together 9,800 conference kits—70 percent of all kits given out to attendees. This is a good example of giving back to your community by providing jobs.

Clean the World—Recycles soap and partially used toiletries. Attendees can take a few minutes out of their day to put toiletries into bags to create small toiletry kits that are then given to local homeless or other shelters in need.

Tee It Up for the Troops—This is an organized golf tournament at the annual Club Managers Association of America World Conference, with all proceeds donated to this charitable organization. The golf tournament sells out every year.

Food Runners—Anyone holding a meeting or event in San Francisco can donate left-over food to Food Runners, who then distribute it to feeding programs throughout the city. They typically deliver 15 tons of food per week, which would have other-wise been thrown away.

MOSCONE CENTER

RELEASE DATE: June 29, 2016
CONTACT: NAINA AYYA
PHONE: 415.974.4017
EMAIL:*nayya@moscone.com*

San Francisco's Moscone Center Named 2016 Recipient of CRRA's Award for Outstanding Practices in Venue and Event Resource Recovery

Convention center wins large venue award
from nation's largest and oldest nonprofit recycling organization

California Resource Recovery Association (CRRA), one of the nation's oldest and largest nonprofit recycling organizations, has named San Francisco's Moscone Center as the 2016 recipient of their annual award for Outstanding Practices in Venue/Event Resource Recovery Award.

"We are very proud to accept this award," said Bob Sauter, Acting General Manager, "and we are committed to our sustainability programs here at Moscone Center."

The award will be presented to the Moscone Center at an Awards Ceremony at the CRRA Annual Conference and Tradeshow on Tuesday, August 9 starting at 5:45 PM in the California Ballroom at the Doubletree Hotel in Sacramento, Calif.

The annual award goes to a large event or venue located in California which serves over 2,000 people per day, which has demonstrated excellence in implementing waste reduction, recycling and organics programs, innovative source reduction programs, recovering over 90 percent of event discards, and other programs that demonstrate best practices in event or venue resource management.

Moscone Center is San Francisco's premier convention facility. In FY 2014-15, Moscone Center held 129 events, hosted 1.1 million registered attendees and exhibitors. For over a decade the facility has pioneered large venue sustainability programs. In 2012, Moscone Center attained APEX/ASTM Environmentally Sustainable Event Standards Level 1 as a Sustainable Venue for Environmentally Sustainable Meetings, Events, Trade Shows, and Conferences. In 2012, Moscone North and South attained LEED Gold EB: O+M certification.

California's policy goal is to achieve 75 percent diversion by the year 2020; San Francisco's goal is to attain zero waste that same year. At the close of the FY2014-15, Moscone Center had diverted 2.4 million pounds of materials through donation, recycling and composting. Also for FY2014-15, the facility attained a diversion rate of 56 percent. Facility caterer, SAVOR San Francisco, donated over 117,000 pounds of food product to those in need, equivalent to more than 90,000 meals. Weekly donations continue to be picked up from SAVOR kitchens by SF City IMPACT and other local nonprofits locally feeding those in need.

San Francisco's Climate Action Plan calls for 50 percent of all trips to be made outside of personal vehicles. Approximately 70 percent of SMG's employees, at the Moscone Center, regularly commute using alternative transportation. Moscone Center incentivized the utilization of public transit by offering a commuter check program which has helped employees to save money on transit expenses.

Capital expansion is already underway for Moscone North and South. Slated for completion in 2018, the $500 million expansion will add more than 170,000 gross square feet of flexible meeting space. Minutes away from 22,000 of the city's 33,000-plus hotel rooms, world-class shopping and dining, Moscone Center will remain fully operational during the expansion.

CRRA is California's state-wide recycling association. It is the oldest and one of the largest nonprofit recycling organizations in the United States. A 501(c)(3) organization, CRRA is dedicated to achieving environmental sustainability in and beyond California through Zero Waste strategies including product stewardship, waste prevention, reuse, recycling and composting. CRRA advances local, regional and state-wide waste reduction efforts which result in critical environmental and climate protection outcomes. CRRA members represent all aspects of California's reduce-reuse-recycle-compost economy. Members work for cities and counties, as well as hauling companies, material processors, non-profit organizations, state agencies, and in allied professions. For more information, visit www.crra.com or contact John H. Dane, Executive Director, john@crra.com.

Owned and operated by the City and County of San Francisco, Moscone Center is privately managed by SMG. Moscone Center's website at www.moscone.com contains more information about the facility.

Fighting Hunger—Every year at the annual Foster Farms Bowl football game, the team players and coaches participate in a day of community service by serving food to those in need. In addition, every ticket sold is a meal ticket for hungry families.

Other Benefits of Sustainability

In an industry as hectic as the meetings and events industry, where every detail is important, it is easy to understand why planners, suppliers, vendors, and facility managers want to streamline wherever possible. So why should industry professionals take on the extra challenge of becoming more sustainable? Because doing the right thing, is the right thing to do.

Enhanced Brand Image

Planning or executing a sustainable event is good business. This is especially important for those large corporate and association events that occur around the world. If attendees are aware of the good that event organizers are doing for both the planet and the people for these large events, it will improve their image and repeat attendance. It will also make attendees feel good about attending, especially if they know they can do so and still minimize their impact on the environment and help local communities.

Differentiation

A challenge for some in the MEEC industry is keeping their meeting and events interesting and pertinent to attendees—some of whom attend the same events every year. Sustainability offers a point of differentiation from one year to the next, and, thus, can give attendees something new to look forward to.

Cost Savings

Reducing waste, conserving energy, sourcing local food, or eliminating the use of bottled water lead to cost savings.

Raise Awareness

The MEEC industry has a tremendous opportunity to educate attendees every time they incorporate a sustainable practice into a meeting or event. Attendees of events hail from around the world, and they may not be familiar with such practices, and the benefits they can bring to all stakeholders of a meeting. This may encourage people to make decisions to minimize their own footprint on the environment, and take those practices back to their own businesses or personal lives.

Social Benefits

If planned and implemented carefully, the meeting can benefit the local region by providing jobs, benefiting regional suppliers, promoting better working conditions, and acting as a catalyst for encouraging environmental best practices across the region (UNEP, *Green Meeting Guide*).

Sustainable Meeting Standards and Guidelines

The MEEC industry is moving quickly toward the very real possibility of sustainable meetings becoming the norm of the future. Evidence that corroborates this theory lies in the number of guidelines and certifications that are currently available. These types of standards help identify, unify, and contain these efforts.

Green Meeting Standards

The US Environmental Protection Agency (EPA) and the Events Industry Council Sustainability Initiative have developed nine standards for sustainable meetings and events. These were developed in a collaborative effort between APEX (the Events Industry Council's Accepted Practices Exchange) and ASTM (An ANSI certified international

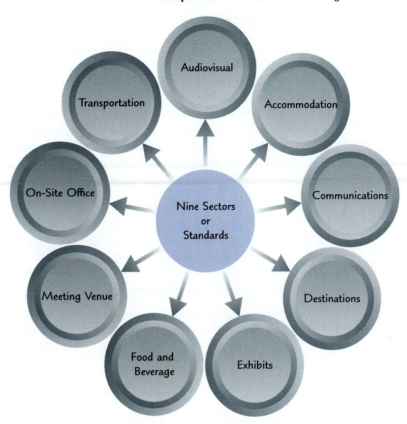

FIGURE 12-3
Standards.

standard development organization) and are the first standards of this kind in the MEEC industry. The standards are referred to as the *APEX/ASTM Environmentally Sustainable Event Standards*. The standards cover nine individual sectors of the MEEC industry, as noted in Figure 12-3, which follows.

Each of the previous standards is broken down into eight subcategories as follows. These include the environmental and social areas to be included in each of the previous nine overall standards. They are

1. Staff management and environmental policy
2. Communication
3. Waste management
4. Energy
5. Air quality
6. Water
7. Procurement
8. Community partners

The ASTM/APEX Green Meeting and Event Standards are designed

- to be measurable,
- in a tiered system to allow for different levels of interaction,
- for both the planners as well as the suppliers, and
- to complement other recognized standards in the MEEC industry such as the ISO 20121(see the following).

For detailed information on these standards, see the Events Council website.

ISO 20121

ISO 20121 is an international management system designed to help MEEC organizations improve the sustainability of their events as they relate to products, services, and related activities. It is the international version of a British standard established in 2007, and was specifically created to coincide with the 2012 London Olympics. ISO 20121 is designed to address all areas of the MEEC industry. Successful implementation of the standard will allow corresponding organizations to seek certification through an independent accrediting body. Although ISO 20121 and ASTM/APEX represent two different approaches to defining a sustainable events standard, they are designed to work independently or in collaboration with one another.

GES ACHIEVES ENVIRONMENTAL SUSTAINABILITY CERTIFICATION

Global Experience Specialists (GES) became the first general service contractor to be certified to an international sustainability standard for the meetings and event industry. GES exceeded Level One and achieved Level Two certification to the APEX/ASTM Environmentally Sustainable Event Standards pertaining to the Evaluation and Selection of Exhibits for Environmentally Sustainable Meetings, Events, Trade Shows, and Conferences.

GES has a long and ongoing commitment to sustainable practices. Its operations in the United Kingdom are ISO 20121 certified, a complex and challenging international standard accreditation that takes a management systems approach to running more sustainable events (GMIC, 2015).

In addition to ASTM/APEX and ISO 20121, there is a plethora of eco-friendly third-party certifications recognized within the MEEC industry. The following is a list of the various certifications or awards that apply primarily to suppliers in the MEEC industry.

A. Accommodations/Venues
- Green Key Global's Green Key Eco-Rating Program
- Audubon Green Lodging Program
- Green Globe 21
- Ecotel Certification
- International Tourism Partnership
- Leadership in Energy and Environmental Design (LEED)
- Energy Star Qualified Buildings

The Hotel Association of Canada's (HAC) Green Key Eco-Rating Program
- Leadership in Energy and Environmental Design (LEED)
- ISO 20121
- Green Globe 21
- Ecotel Certification

B. Catering/Food and Beverage
- Marine Stewardship Council (MSC)
- Fair Trade Certified
- USDA Certified Organic
- Green Restaurant Association
- Green Seal

C. Décor/Trade Show Rentals
- The Sierra Eco Label (prominent in Canada for flowers)
- VeriFlora
- The Flower Label Program (FLP)
- Rainforest Alliance Certification

FREEMAN

IN TUNE WITH SUSTAINABILITY

National Association of Music Merchants

The NAMM Show 2015

LOCATION: Anaheim, CA

AUDIENCE: Music Retailers, Educators, Distributors, Corporate Buyers, Artists

SOLUTIONS: Green Event Plan, Environmental Performance Report, Waste Diversion

CHALLENGES & OBJECTIVES

For more than 30 years, the National Association of Music Merchants (NAMM) and Freeman have collaborated on The NAMM Show, the annual event that attracts more than 99,000 attendees and 1,620 exhibitors. During that time, the event has evolved to meet the diverse needs of the music merchant community.

In recent years, the community has become increasingly interested in ways to reduce the event's environmental impact. In 2013, NAMM approached Freeman to look for ways that The NAMM Show could reduce waste, increase recycling, and reuse event materials to divert waste to local landfill.

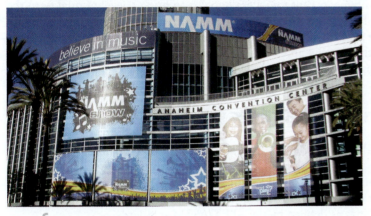

"The Freeman Green Event Plan allows us to tap into their staff expertise and experience from other events. It is a solid foundation to build event sustainability goals now and in the future."

- Cindy Sample
NAMM Director of Trade Show Operations

SOLUTIONS

Working across several departments, Freeman created a Green Event Plan to outline the sustainability efforts that would take place before, during, and after the show. The plan, which can be adapted to any size event in any industry, is now the standard for all Freeman clients who are interested in improving their sustainability efforts by implementing the "5Rs:" Rethink, Reduce, Reuse, Recycle, Repurpose. The Freeman Green Event Plan template included an Environmental Purchasing Policy (e.g., preference for products containing post-consumer recycled content); a "pack in, pack out" policy for exhibitors, encouraging exhibitors to ship only the promotional materials needed and to send remainders back to their offices (instead of disposing of them on the show floor); and an online exhibitor kit, which reduced the amount of paper used and the amount of energy needed to deliver the kits.

To measure the outcomes of the plan, Freeman provided NAMM with a post-show Environmental Performance Report that included data to measure the sustainability of the event and to provide benchmarks for future events. Categories tracked included fuel used to transport Freeman and show management freight; propane usage by forklifts and boom lifts; use and reuse of carpet, graphics, and other materials (e.g., table-top vinyl, Visqueen); and Freeman staff air travel.

"The Loft Restaurant and Lounge" is a popular networking area on the show floor that features comfortable seating areas, newsstands, charging stations, and food and beverages. In designing the area, Freeman utilized several sustainability and waste diversion best practices, including thinking through the life cycle of the materials used and potential reuse or disposal plans.

SUCCESS

Since its inception, the Freeman Green Event Plan template has guided NAMM and Freeman to find innovative ways to produce an environmentally friendly event that still meets the needs of The NAMM Show's attendees and exhibitors.

Innovation highlights include:
- Interior signage is printed on Freeman Honeycomb, a direct-print high-quality corrugated cardboard that is 100% recyclable.

- Carpet in The Loft is made of 50% recycled content and is returned to inventory for future use before eventually being recycled.
- Aluminum extrusions for media racks and charging stations contain 85% recycled content and are returned to inventory for future use before eventually being recycled.
- Mesh banners used on the exterior of the event venue are undated and can be used multiple times.

D. Printing/Promotional/Gifts
- Forest Stewardship Council (FSC)
- The Programme for the Endorsement of Forest Certification Schemes (PEFC)
- The Sustainable Forestry Initiative Program (SFI)
- American Tree Farm System (ATFS)
- Waterless Printing Association
- Rainforest Alliance
- Green Seal

While not all the meeting industry certifications are noted here, the list of these certifications continues to change. New certifications are added, some are blended together, and some have simply outlived their usefulness and have been replaced by a more meaningful certification. From a meeting professional's perspective, it is important to gain a thorough understanding of what is required for each certification that is claimed. Planners must do their homework and verify that the certification in question is of value. They all have individualized requirements, but the overall goal is to bring a level of quality to the ever-evolving practice of incorporating environmentally friendly applications. Due diligence on the part of the meeting professional will ensure that there is no misrepresentation to the attendees of the meeting and will also help guarantee that the sustainable goals for the meeting will be met.

Creating a Process for Sustainable Practices

According to recent studies, more than half of all meeting professionals are considering environmental practices as they plan their conferences. No longer is it possible to limit considerations to sleeping rooms. At all major events held by Meeting Professionals International (MPI), for example, the board of directors purposefully considers the nine areas of sustainable meetings as defined by the APEX/ASTM standards.

Planning, managing, and evaluating a sustainable meeting used to be thought of as difficult and expensive, when in reality, it may be as simple as paying attention to the decisions that are made regarding company policies. Here are some simple steps professionals can follow to make their next meeting more sustainable, as suggested by the Events Industry Council Sustainability Initiative.

Step 1: Create a Plan

Create a plan (management system approach) for identifying your event's sustainability objectives. This plan should include how you will achieve your objectives and what are the key performance indicators to track the success of your plan. Identify specific activities, (such as a certain percentage of waste diversion, percentage of local or organic meals, etc.) metrics for tracking, and outcomes you want to achieve for each objective identified and who is responsible for the end results.

Step 2: Engage Internal Stakeholders in Supporting Your Plan

Establish or create a sustainable meeting policy for your team/department/meeting. Ideally, this policy will reflect the internal values of your company/organization to ensure that it is supported by your event efforts.

Step 3: Engage Vendors in Supporting Your Plan

Make the "ask" of your current vendors at cost savings or cost neutral pricing. Include language in your request for proposal (RFP) process and contracts that includes vendors reporting back to you with the data you need to track your performance. (The first year can be your benchmark year to evaluate and grow in future years).

Step 4: Track Your Performance

Just as we monitor our event budgets, we need to monitor and track the performance of our sustainability action plans. Post-event, ensure accurate reports so you can build on them for future years and use them in your site selection process.

Step 5: Communicate the Results, Celebrate the Success

While continuous improvement is always our goal as sustainability professionals; be sure to pause, breathe, and share the success of your action plan with attendees, vendors, media, and the industry. The more you can quantify your results in human scale terms (amount of money saved, number of trees, amount of CO_2 kept out of the atmosphere), the more engaged you and your stakeholders will be for your plan the following year.

Step 6: Be Innovative and Have Fun!

This step may not technically be on the environmental management action plan; however, it is important for us as meeting professionals to enjoy what we are doing. Our goal is to create rewarding experiences for our attendees. So, if it is aligned with your organization, be creative and include a yoga break, human powered energy stations, or networking events that have a purpose in a local community. Remember to allow for some outdoor or nonscheduled activity time. Your attendees will appreciate your efforts to take care of their sustainable needs.

Used with permission - Events Industry Council. All rights reserved. www.eventscou ncil.org.

Best Planet Practices

Now that best sustainable practices have been established, the following are some specific actions that meeting professionals can take to incorporate best planet practices into their meetings.

Use Technology

Take advantage of technology to reduce the need for paper. With easy-to-use apps or registration companies, there is virtually no need to produce printed materials. To cut down on travel costs, utilize podcasting, webinars, and video streaming. In doing so, event professionals may find an increase in attendance because they are making it easier for more people to attend.

This salad is served on a plate that is totally compostable.
George G. Fenich

Choose a Local Destination

Ninety percent of an event's carbon footprint comes from air travel. Whenever possible, event professionals should choose a destination close to where participants live to reduce the distance that must be traveled to attend. If air travel is necessary, event professionals should choose a venue or hotel that is close to the airport or is within walking distance of off-site events. Research public transportation options in the host city.

Reduce, Reuse, and Recycle

Proper recycling bins should be added to the event supplies list, and the staff should be trained in the proper ways to recycle. Venues should be asked to provide visible and accessible recycling services for paper, metal, plastic, and glass. Banquet managers should be asked about composting options or giveaway programs, as well as the option to use real china for meals. If this is not possible, choose disposable plates made from renewable resources that will biodegrade in a landfill. Collect name badge holders and lanyards for use the next year.

Volume Up

Encourage food and beverage providers to serve sugar, creamer, and other condiments in bulk dispensers rather than individual packets. Find hotels that use dispensers for shampoo and lotions rather than small bottles. Request to have water stations, as opposed to bottled water. Give attendees a water bottle for their personal use throughout the meeting. The latter provides a sponsorship opportunity.

Eat Local

Speak with the banquet manager about using local fruits and vegetables that are in season. Include more vegetarian meals, as they require less carbon energy to prepare. Obtain an accurate headcount prior to finalizing the food to order so that food waste can be minimized.

Decorate with Nature

Use local flowers and plants to decorate your tables and leave them in pots so that you can use them as gifts or prizes. This ensures that they are not wasted once the meeting is over. Some cities have local charities that will collect flowers at the end of an event and donate them to churches, or assisted living facilities around their city.

Decorating with nature.
George G. Fenich

Use Paper Wisely

If print materials are necessary, use chlorine-free, recycled paper, and vegetable-based inks. Print on both sides of the paper and only print materials for a participant if requested. Use print-on-demand stations rather than printing copies for each attendee.

Save Energy

Look for venues and hotels that practice energy efficiency, and have policies in place for doing so. Coordinate with the venue to ensure that lights, audiovisual equipment, and air-conditioning in meeting spaces will be turned off when not in use. Remind attendees to conserve energy in the guest rooms by turning off lights when they leave, and not leaving electronics plugged in and powered on unnecessarily.

Inform Everyone

Tell participants, speakers, suppliers, vendors, and the media about your sustainability efforts and your expectations from them as event partners. Communication is the key to encouraging and securing active participation from all involved parties. For example, in the speaker contract, green expectations should be made very clear so that speakers do not arrive with printed handouts when electronic versions of the handouts are expected.

Sources

Companies will recycle items, such as meeting banners, into useful and creative things like messenger bags, wallets, tote bags, and laptop sleeves.

Evaluation of Sustainable Efforts

If you can measure it, you can manage it. This is a common mantra in many sectors of the business world. It applies equally well to sustainable meetings and sustainable efforts. It is important for meeting professionals and companies to set clear goals in the beginning so that it is possible to measure the success or failure of an event. Fortunately, because of the growing interest in conducting green meetings, a few tools have been created to help in the measurement/evaluation process.

MeetGreen Calculator 2.0

Measuring the impact of sustainable efforts can be challenging. To address this challenge, *MeetGreen* has developed a calculator that is a comprehensive tool used for benchmarking sustainable aspects of an event, regardless of size. The tool allows event professionals to "capture valuable information throughout the event planning process to make it easy to see . . . accomplishments and where improvements can be made. The tool assesses event management practices and measurable outcomes in 14 key categories to audit the environmental impact of conference activities. The calculator integrates aspects of the ISO 20121 and APEX/ASTM Environmentally Sustainable Meeting Standards."

Sustainable Meeting Planner

Another option is the online tool provided by the Sustainable Meeting Planner program. "The SMPP system (Sustainable Meeting Planning Program) is a set of policies and detailed procedures to follow sustainability standards while planning events. It is used to educate, plan, score, improve, audit, report and list" an event's sustainability rating. Many industry associations have partnered with SMPP to provide discounts and support to the program. The metrics are measured against the aforementioned ISO 20121 standards.

Greenwashing

Today, as consumers become more and more aware of environmentally sound practices, companies are responding by incorporating these green efforts into their business standards. As these companies compete for consumers, many become too eager to tout their green campaigns, achievement, or standards. As awareness grows, it is becoming more difficult for even the consumer to distinguish between those companies that are actually implementing green practices and those who are **greenwashing**.

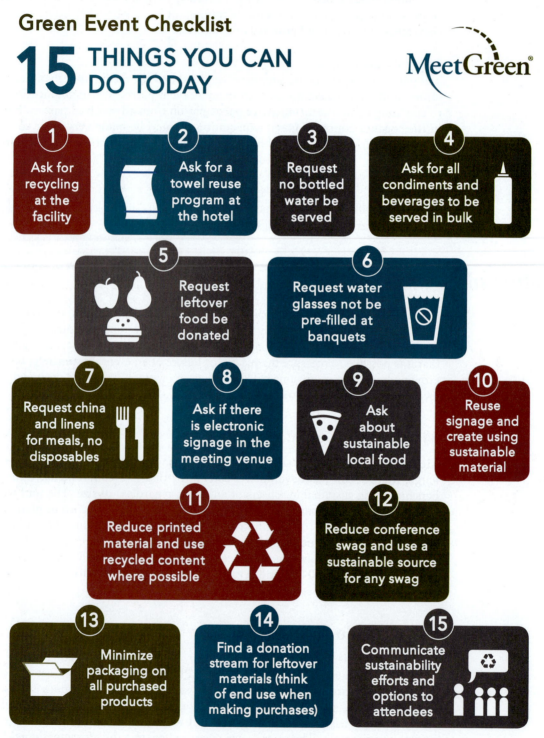

Green Event Checklist

15 THINGS YOU CAN DO TODAY

MeetGreen®

1. Ask for recycling at the facility
2. Ask for a towel reuse program at the hotel
3. Request no bottled water be served
4. Ask for all condiments and beverages to be served in bulk
5. Request leftover food be donated
6. Request water glasses not be pre-filled at banquets
7. Request china and linens for meals, no disposables
8. Ask if there is electronic signage in the meeting venue
9. Ask about sustainable local food
10. Reuse signage and create using sustainable material
11. Reduce printed material and use recycled content where possible
12. Reduce conference swag and use a sustainable source for any swag
13. Minimize packaging on all purchased products
14. Find a donation stream for leftover materials (think of end use when making purchases)
15. Communicate sustainability efforts and options to attendees

FIGURE 12-4
Green Event Checklist.

The term greenwashing refers to any misrepresentation by a company that leads the consumer to believe that its policies and products are environmentally responsible, when its claims are false, misleading, or cannot be verified. Greenwashing is also used to identify the practice of companies spending more money on the campaign to notify customers of their environmentally friendly efforts, than the efforts themselves.

The actual practice of greenwashing began in the mid-1960s when companies were eager to be seen as part of the environmental movement that was taking shape. As these practices continued to evolve, they eventually became known as greenwashing, a term that was first used in an essay written by environmentalist Jay Westerveld in 1968. His essay reviewed the practice of placing a card on the pillow in each hotel room explaining that the hotel encourages reuse of guest towels for environmental responsibility. Upon closer examination of this practice, Westerveld surmised that, in most cases, the hotel's main reason for the practice was to increase profits. To combat this issue in the MEEC industry, meeting professionals must be aware, knowledgeable, and not afraid to ask questions. As this area of the industry continues to evolve, it is the responsibility of all event professionals to stay on top of current trends, regulations, and questions regarding this topic. Meeting professionals must take responsibility for understanding what is being said and ensuring that the terms being used are credible and make sense. Just because something is natural or organic, for example, does not mean that it is healthy. Understanding the criteria for certifications and labels is also important.

A back-of-the-house tour should be part of the due-diligence process of the meeting professional and can be very helpful in validating (or not validating) the green claims being stated by any given company. If a claim was made by the participating venue, for example, that recycling opportunities were readily available, and will be made available for all attendees, evidence of this should be apparent during the back-of-the-house tour. The event professional should be able to observe where the recycled material is stored and the process that takes place once it is removed from the event space. If the venue has made claims that local produce is used for all meals, evidence of this could be apparent during this tour as well. Lastly, planners must practice being green within their departments and companies so that they can be an advocate and lead by example. While there are numerous checklists available that can be used to assist meeting professionals with planning a green meeting, the checklist included in Figure 12-4 is a good place to start. Once a planner is aware of the obstacles greenwashing can present, it is easier to identify those areas of concern and proceed in a positive manner with the planning of a green meeting.

The following three examples provide insights regarding sustainable efforts in practice.

GRAND CAROLINA RESORT AND SPA

The resort was chosen to host 1,000 delegates over six days. While it was not particularly green at the outset, management responded to the client's greening requirements by altering standard operating procedures and implementing capital improvements, such as installing solar panels. Delegates joined in the effort by reducing their own consumption while on-site.

For the duration of the event, data was collected each day on utility usage and waste generation, and reported the following morning at general sessions. Total consumption was compared with the average of a similar convention held the previous year. The results were impressive: Total electricity consumption had been reduced by 21 percent, water use by 48 percent, and solid waste by 34 percent. The greening measures were estimated to save the resort over one million dollars per year.

As the need for measurable outcomes continues to grow and companies look for ROI on green strategies, the ability to measure sustainability factors will become increasingly important. Look for new and more sophisticated tools that track carbon, energy, and water footprints, and overall conference achievements. Newer tools will work hand-in-hand with established tools such as paper savings calculators and the MeetGreen Calculator.

OREGON CONVENTION CENTER REPLACES LIGHTING FIXTURES WITH ENERGY EFFICIENT TECHNOLOGY

The Oregon Convention Center recently replaced all lighting fixtures in the building's Oregon Ballroom, Portland Ballroom, and its entire loading dock area. Incandescent and fluorescent fixtures were all changed to a modern, energy efficient LED lighting technology.

The annual energy savings is estimated to be 1,144,076 kWh, with an annual cost savings of approximately $76,000, meaning the replacement project will pay for itself in less than three years.

In the Oregon Ballroom:

- The convention center substituted 400-watt quartz can lighting fixtures for 40-watt LED fixtures.
- Two 32-watt fluorescent lamps were replaced with a single 18-watt lamp.
- 15-watt incandescent bulbs were replaced with 3-watt LED bulbs.

In the Portland Ballroom:

- The convention center substituted 400-watt quartz can lighting fixtures with 40-watt LED fixtures.
- Two 32-watt fluorescent lamps were replaced with a single 18-watt lamp.
- 40-watt fluorescent lamps were replaced with 22-watt LED's in the ballroom chandeliers.

On the loading dock:

- The convention center replaced two 32-watt lamps for two 11-watt lamps in each fixture.

These lighting replacement projects could not have been completed without the support of the Energy Trust of Oregon, which will reimburse nearly a third of the cost upon project completion.

The "Energy Trust of Oregon has been an important and valuable partner with OCC for nearly a decade," said Josh Lipscomb, OCC Facilities Manager. "Over this time, they've supported our energy saving projects with over $800,000 in cash incentives."

"While the cost and energy savings are impressive, the new LED fixtures also provide more flexibility and significantly better lighting levels in all the areas, allowing us to set the perfect mood for any type of event," added Scott Cruickshank, OCC Executive Director.

The Oregon Convention Center is owned by Metro and managed by the Metro Exposition and Recreation Commission. OCC is a LEED Platinum certified facility hosting groups from around the world and bringing millions of dollars into the Portland and Oregon economy.

BEST PRACTICES IN MEETINGS, EXHIBITIONS, EVENTS AND CONVENTIONS-SANDS EOC 360° MEETINGS PROGRAM

Introduction

The Las Vegas Sands Corporation is achieving high praise in Green Meetings standards throughout the world. The Sands Expo and Congress Center facility at the Venetian and The Palazzo Las Vegas was the first venue in the world to achieve ASTM International's Advanced "Level Two" certification for green meetings venues in September 19, 2013. In April 2014, the Venetian Macao became the first in Macao and one of two integrated resorts in Asia alongside its sister property in Singapore to receive the ISO 20121 Event Sustainability Management System certification.

As a first step, the Las Vegas Sands Corporation has begun their commitment for Green Meetings by constructing their buildings to have high performance facilities. This requires controlling building expenses and maintenance. Energy Reduction Management reports keep track of energy consumption which include occupancy sensors that adjust temperatures and turn off lights when people are not present. Low e-glass and insulated water pipes and heaters are part of the construction. Energy efficient lighting is used throughout all the buildings to aid in reaching green meeting goals. Water reduction management systems are used along with water-efficient landscaping and the use of water efficient plumbing fixtures. These systems allow Sands properties to minimize their sustainable energy use. These controls allow breakdowns for costs and energy use for any additional events that may be on the property. As a result, they can keep track of each of the events individually and create reports that allow event organizers the opportunity to assess the goals each step of the way to make sure they are on track.

Best Practices

The Sands ECO 360° Meetings Program, was launched in 2011. This created a holistic approach to identify and create choices and options in conjunction with its clients. The goal is to minimize the environmental impact of operations through the implementation of sustainable practices. To begin planning an event, a Green Meeting Concierge team introduces event planners to the array of standard sustainable practices, green meeting options, and community programs. Meeting planners can assess their energy and water options goals to minimize usage. In addition, standard sustainable practices like resource conservation, air quality pollution prevention, recycling, and purchasing procedures are assessed. In this way, the planners can see the impact of their event on the environment.

Planners are asked to set 3 major goals like improve waste diversion rates or communicate sustainability or increase sustainable food for the events. Goals are developed for energy conservation in audio & visual, material conservation, waste manage, sustainable procurement, and sustainable food.

In addition, the Green Meeting Concierge can also suggest options that go beyond the standard goals. Clients are invited to join local sustainable efforts to give back to the community. Things like donating leftover materials from daily operations of the event and allocating time and resources to local environmental events or encouraging staff to participate in green community projects are some of the options available. Another option is to organize a Corporate Social Responsibility (CSR) event for attendees to work with the community. Once the goals have been selected by the clients, the Green Meeting team develops a customized program to implement those goals for the meeting/event.

Therefore, planners can assure stakeholders that this venue has a comprehensive sustainability program. Once the meeting is over, an Event Sustainability Report is produced documenting the sustainability highlights that have been accomplished. The Sands ECO 360° The report summarizes the event's carbon footprint by calculating the energy consumption, water usage, carbon emissions, and recycling rate. These event impact statements can be used as a benchmark for future events.

Produced by Kathryn Hashimoto from East Carolina University

Trends and Best Practices

The following are some of the best practices in MEEC sustainability.

- Increasing numbers of planners will have sustainable meeting policies that will extend to suppliers.
- Sustainable meeting practices will continue to be incorporated into increasing numbers of events.
- Increasing numbers of groups will have policies associating all three factors of sustainability—people, profit, and planet—with their meetings and events.
- Many national governments, or large corporations, are likely to demand that the meetings and events they organize and sponsor incorporate sustainable elements.
- There will be increasing accountability, and requirements for planners to prove their meetings and events are sustainable.
- There will continue to be an increased focus on cost versus benefits of sustainability. Being able to document and calculate the true cost of sustainability versus the true benefits will be crucial.
- Some sustainable activities that are now voluntary will become legal requirements.
- Educational training and workshop programs for providers of sustainable events will become more abundant.

Summary

This chapter summarizes the most recent developments in the MEEC industry as related to sustainability. Sustainability is not a fad; it is a fact of life in the twenty-first century. The challenge is how to incorporate sustainability into meetings and events, and show how these efforts impact the bottom line, the environment, and the people, while also providing attendees with a good experience.

Now that you have completed this chapter you should be competent in the following Meeting and Business Event Competency Standards:

MBECS—Skill 2: Develop Sustainability Plan for Meeting or Event

Sub skills	Skills (standards)
A2.012	Implement sustainability management plan
A2.02	Demonstrate environmental responsibility

Key Words and Terms

For definitions, see the Glossary.

carbon offset
corporate social responsibility (CSR)

green meetings
greenwashing

sustainability
sustainable meetings

CASE STUDY

The New Manager Takes the Hotel in a Green Direction

Nick Saltmarsh is the new general manager at a very nice boutique hotel in Charleston, South Carolina, called the Harbour-View Inn. With the recent push to go green in South Carolina, Nick was aware that, as a new general manager coming in, he would have to get the ball rolling on this going green issue and really push the subject. When Nick first started managing the HarbourView Inn there was next to nothing being done in the way of going green. When Nick chose to hold a staff meeting he informed the employees that this was going to have to be a team effort and everyone would have to be on board to make the necessary changes to be certified as a green property.

During the staff meeting Nick held a discussion and everyone brainstormed what their departments could do to put a stop to waste. The housekeeping, front desk, and restaurant were the main culprits for significant waste. The front desk needed to stop the ridiculously excessive waste of paper, and start shredding and recycling it. The restaurant had always thrown containers, cardboard boxes, and packaging straight into the trashcan, and they were now going to recycle all of that. The housekeeping staff was going to attempt to reuse untouched items, and the front desk agents made recycling cards for each room that explained that if guests hung their towels up it would be a sign that they do not need new towels to preserve water. They also posted something similar for the bedding.

As far as the meeting rooms go, everything mentioned previous played a part on the meeting space, because the restaurant caters the meetings and the housekeepers clean the rooms. The paper wall hangings ended up being transferred into dry erase boards so that less paper would be wasted and the lights were changed to LED lights to conserve energy. Most of the guests that hold meetings at their property would be staying in the hotel too so this created going green awareness.

Nick realized that at first the Harbourview Inn may take a hit financially, but in the long run the property will gain the respect of its clients and save money on energy preservation. The HarbourView Inn just received their certification from the South Carolina Green Hospitality Alliance, which put them one step ahead of most properties with meetings competition in Charleston.

The HarbourView Inn has been implementing the greening of their property for about a year now, but they still have a long way to go. There is so much that can be done to help the environment, and, yet, in our industry it is very hard not to waste, because it is the nature of the business.

1. What do you think the HarbourView Inn's next step should be in their quest to continue to go green?
2. What else could they do to be more sustainable?

Produced by George G. Fenich from East Carolina University

Review and Discussion Questions

1. Discuss the economic advantages of a meeting going green.
2. How does a meeting manager evaluate green efforts?
3. Explain the difference between the terms green meetings and sustainable meetings, and give examples for each that supports your answer.
4. Describe how an event planner can ensure that a venue is not greenwashing.
5. What is corporate social responsibility (CSR)? What role does CSR play in the MEEC industry?
6. What is the triple bottom line, as applied to the MEEC industry?
7. Define sustainability.
8. Describe best practices for incorporating sustainability into your meeting or event.

Internet Sites for Reference

Events Industry Council—www.eventscouncil.org/
Events Industry Council Sustainability Initiative—www
    .gmicglobal.org/
ISO 20121—www.iso20121.org/
MeetGreen—www.sustainablemeetingplanner.com/

Sustainable Meeting Planning Program—www.susta
    inablemeetingplanner.com/
Terrapass—www.terrapass.com/

About the Chapter Contributor

Michelle Millar, PhD is an Associate Professor and Department Chair at the University of San Francisco's School of Management, in the Department of Hospitality Management. Dr. Millar teaches meeting and event management, corporate event management, introduction to the hospitality industry, and sustainable business. She is a certified hospitality educator who earned her master's degree at Temple University, and her PhD from the University of Nevada, Las Vegas.

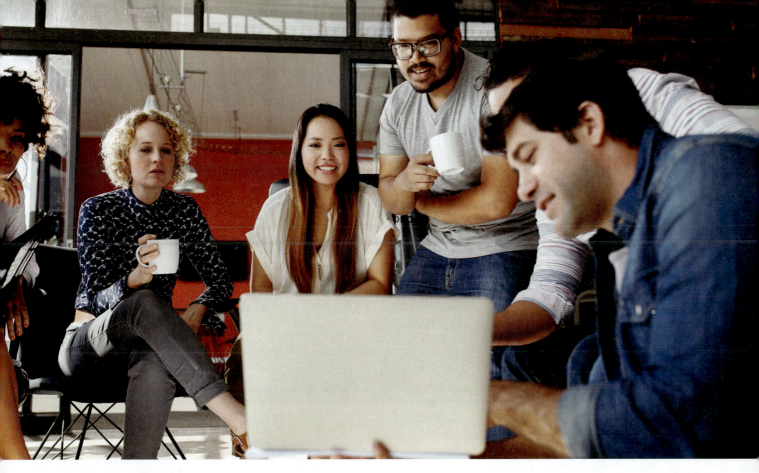

Groups of people plan MEEC events.
Ammentorp Photography/Alamy Stock Photo

CHAPTER 13

Planning MEEC Gatherings

Chapter Objectives

- Discuss the importance and process of setting goals and objectives when planning MEEC gatherings.
- List the considerations to keep in mind during the site selection planning process.
- Articulate the areas of concern when program planning for an event.

- Outline the many logistical considerations to keep in mind when planning a MEEC gathering.
- Discuss the main considerations in direct and indirect marketing and promotion that a MEEC professional must consider when planning a gathering.

A meeting/event professional or organizer may be familiar with all the elements of the MEEC industry. However, it takes good planning, organizing, directing, and control to put these diverse elements together and make it work. To accomplish this, the organizer needs to understand the group, its wants, and its needs: Who are they? Why are they here? Then objectives can be set that will guide the program delivery to meet these wants and needs while staying within budget constraints. It should be noted that

It takes good marketing to get people to attend a MEEC event.
George G. Fenich

this chapter is on planning MEEC events; the following chapter will focus on producing events. There are two new textbooks available that go into more detail. They are meant to be read in sequence: The first is *Planning and Management of Meetings, Expositions, Events and Conventions*, while the second is *Production and Logistics in Meetings, Expositions, Events and Conventions*. Both are by the author of this text, George G. Fenich, PhD. The reader is reminded that the process and steps of planning are the same for any event, whether business or leisure oriented.

Setting Goals and Objectives

Determining the Meeting and Event Goal(s)

The first thing a meeting/event professional needs to ask is (1) Who is the group? and (2) What is the objective of this event? These simple questions are the basis of much of the planning process.

A meeting goal defines the purpose of the MEEC gathering and provides a clear direction for the organization. It simply answers why the organization exists, and why the event is happening.

An *objective* is defined as something strived for or to be accomplished. All meetings and events should begin with clear, concise, and measurable objectives. Objectives are the basis for virtually all components of the planning process, whether it is for corporate meetings, association meetings, special events, exhibitions (formerly referred to as trade shows), or virtual meetings held via the Internet. The objective of the meeting will impact site selection, food and beverage (F&B) requirements, transportation issues, communication channels, and especially program content.

Most people attend meetings for three reasons: education, networking, and to conduct business. Some people participate in association **annual meetings** for their networking and educational offerings. Others may attend primarily to develop business relationships and to generate leads or make sales. If the meeting/event professional does not design the program content and scheduling to accommodate these objectives, then the attendees may become dissatisfied.

Another key point is that program planning, especially for association meetings, begins months or years before the actual event. The average meeting attendee does not understand how much effort goes into planning even simple events, let alone something as complex as an association's annual meeting and trade show/exhibition. As with much of the hospitality industry, the real work goes on behind the scenes, and unless something goes wrong, the attendees are blissfully unaware of the planning process and the coordination and cooperation necessary to produce an event.

Good meeting objectives should focus on the attendees. What will make the attendees want to attend the meeting? What will be their return on investment (ROI)? What makes the event more desirable than that of a competitor? The following are some of the key meeting planning components that are directly affected by the meeting objectives.

Needs Analysis

As part of setting objectives for a meeting, a needs analysis must be undertaken. A **needs analysis** is a method of determining the expectations for a particular meeting. A needs analysis can be as simple as asking senior management what they want to accomplish at a meeting and then designing the event around those expectations. It should be remembered that the needs of corporate and association meeting attendees are very different (see Chapter 2). The first step is to know the attendees by asking the question, "Who are they?" A meeting/event professional must collect demographic information of both past and prospective attendees. This is much easier for an annual event, such as an association meeting or corporate management meeting. The meeting/event professional keeps a detailed **group history** of who attended the meeting, their likes and dislikes, and all pertinent information that can be used to improve future meetings. Questions to consider include the following:

- What is the age and gender of past attendees?
- What is their level of expertise—beginner, intermediate, or advanced?
- What is their position within the organization's hierarchy—new employee, junior management, or senior management?
- What hotel amenities are preferred—indoor pools, spas, tennis courts, exercise rooms, wireless Internet access?
- Are there specific dietary restrictions for attendees (e.g., Kosher, Muslim, vegetarian, diabetic, gluten-free, food allergies, or other medical dietary needs)?
- Who is paying the expenses? Most people are more cost-conscious if they are paying out of their own pocket rather than on a company expense account.
- Will meeting attendees bring guests or children to the event?
- Are networking opportunities important?
- How far are attendees willing to travel to attend the meeting?
- Will international guests who require interpreters attend?
- Are special accommodations needed for people with disabilities?
- What are the educational outcomes expected at the meeting?

Some of this information can be answered by questions on the event registration form. Other information can be obtained through association membership or company records. Most meeting/event professionals do some type of evaluation after an event to provide feedback that can be used to improve the next meeting. This is covered later in this chapter. An excellent resource is to go to the Event Council's website and download their RFP workbook from their APEX (Accepted Practices Exchange) tab. By completing this important step, the planner can often immediately rule out certain venues, thus streamlining the site selection and planning process.

Developing *SMART* Objectives

Once the meeting/event professional has determined the needs of the attendees and the sponsoring organization, objectives must be written in a clear and concise format so that all parties involved in the planning process understand and are focused on common goals.

A common method of writing effective meeting objectives is to use the **SMART** approach. Each letter of the SMART approach reminds the meeting/event professional of critical components of a well-written objective.

Specific: Only one major concept is covered per objective. For example, instead of stating, "I want my event to be more successful" state, "I want my event to generate more revenue than last year."

Measurable: Must be able to quantify or measure that objectives have or have not been achieved. For example, instead of stating, "I want my event to generate more revenue" state, "I want my event to generate 100 percent more revenue than last year."

Achievable: Is it possible to accomplish the objective? So, instead of stating, "I want my event to generate 100 percent more revenue than last year" state, "I want my event to generate 30 percent more revenue than last year.

Relevant: Is the objective important to the overall goals of the organization? For example, instead of stating, "I want my event to generate 30 percent more revenue by selling souvenirs" state, "I want my event to generate 30 percent more revenue from ticket sales."

Time-constrained: The objective should include when the objective must be completed or be time-bound. So, instead of stating, "I want my event to generate 30 percent more revenue" state, "I want my event to generate 30 percent more revenue from ticket sales in the next six months."

It is also good to begin meeting objectives with an action verb (e.g., achieve, promote, understand, or design) and include cost factors if applicable. Additionally, be sure to include by the name of the person or department responsible for achieving the objectives.

Examples of Meeting Objectives

- The Meetings Department of the International Association of Real Estate Agents will generate attendance of 7,500 people at the 2018 annual meeting to be held in Orlando, Florida, USA.
- The Education Committee of the National Association for Catering Executives (NACE) will create a NACE professional certification program by the 2018 annual meeting.
- The Brett & Co, Pharmaceutical Corporation will hold a two-day conference, October 2 and 3 in Chicago, Illinois, for the 12 regional sales managers to launch five new product introductions for 2018. Total meeting costs are not to exceed $15,000.
- Jill Miller will complete the graphic design for the convention program by May 3, 2018.

Designing well-written meeting objectives is a very important activity for the meeting/event professional. Objectives serve as signals to keep the planning process focused and on track. At the end of the meeting, the meeting/event professional can communicate to management what objectives were achieved or exceeded, or what was not achieved and why. If objectives are met, it helps demonstrate the ROI that the meeting/event professional provides to the organization. If objectives are not met, then management can focus on new ways to achieve the outcome for the next meeting.

Site Selection

The site selection process can begin after meeting objectives have been developed. The meeting goals and objectives will guide the meeting/event professional in deciding the physical location for the event, type of facility to use, transportation options, and many other meeting components. Depending on the type of meeting, site selection may take place days, weeks, months, or years before the actual event. For major conventions, a city is usually selected three to ten years in advance. Some large associations, such as the American Library Association, have determined meeting sites (cities) decades into the future. However, small corporate meetings usually have a much shorter lead time of a few weeks or months.

The association meeting professional is usually not the final decision maker when it comes to which city will be selected to host a convention. Typically, determining the actual site selection is a group decision made by a volunteer committee, with much input from the board of directors and the association staff. The meeting professional will review numerous reference materials, talk with other meeting/event professionals, and may make recommendations, but usually does not personally make the final decision. The corporate meeting/event professional may have more influence over site selection, especially for smaller meetings. But for larger corporate meetings, the CEO or chairman of the board may make the decision. Sometimes, locations are chosen because of the availability of amanities like golf, shopping, or a spa, not because the meeting facilities are outstanding. It differs with each organization.

Large travel expos, such as IMEX in Frankfurt, Germany; or IMEX America held in Las Vegas, Nevada, are also great opportunities for meeting/event professionals to gather information about possible locations for their meetings and events. They employ a hosted buyer strategy where the exhibitors pay for the travel expenses of the meeting/event professionals (buyers) in return for guaranteed appointments (see Chapter 5, Exhibitions and Trade Shows, for more information on IMEX and the hosted buyer concept).

Other factors to consider in site selection are the rotation of locations and the location of the majority of the attendees. In the United States, the meeting/event professional may want to rotate their conventions and hold a major convention in the East (Boston) one year, the South (New Orleans) the next, the West (San Francisco) the third year, and the Midwest (Chicago) the fourth year. This allows attendees to enjoy a wide variety of meeting locations, and attendees who live on one side of the country are not always traveling many hours, and through several time zones, to attend the meeting. But if most of the attendees live on the East Coast, it may be preferable to hold the meeting in a city conveniently located there. However, some conventions, such as the National Association of Broadcasters, MAGIC Marketplace, International Builder's Show, or the Consumer

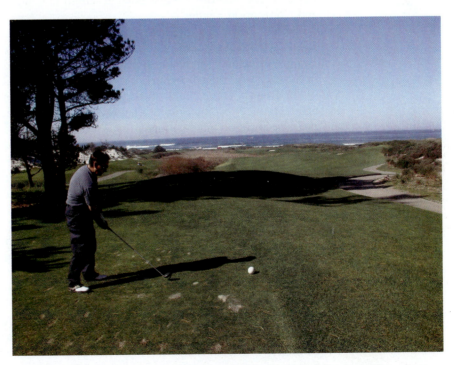

The Links at Spanish Bay, part of the famous Pebble Beach Golf Resort, is often chosen as a site for small meetings and incentive trips.
George G. Fenich

Electronics Show, are so large that they are extremely limited to their choice of cities due to the amount of sleeping rooms, meeting, and exhibition space required.

Cost is another consideration. In addition to the costs incurred by the meeting/event professional for meeting space and other essentials, the cost to the attendee should be considered. Some cities, mostly first-tier cities, are notoriously expensive for people to visit (the average daily rate [ADR] in New York City is over $250 per night plus tax). It all depends on what is important to the attendees—cost or location. Another option is to hold a meeting in a first-tier city at a first-class property in the off-season or during slow periods, such as around major holidays. Most hotels discount prices when business is slow. As witnessed by the global economic downturn that began in 2008, most hotels had to reduce their rates to attract a shrinking volume of MEEC gatherings. As economies and the willingness to spend money on travel continue to improve, rates for many services have and will continue to rise.

The mode of travel is another factor in site selection. How will the attendees get to the location, by air, road, or rail? In recent years, most major airline carriers have been struggling to survive, resulting in a number of mergers and acquisitions in the industry. Many people are still cautious about flying due to terrorism threats, the ordeal of getting through security at airports, packed airplanes, additional baggage fees, food charges, government imposed travel restrictions, and a host of other challenges that make air travel distasteful. The availability of flights (**air lift**) can also be an important consideration in site selection. Those cities with the greatest number of flights include Chicago, Atlanta, Dallas, and New York. There are some cities that are convention destinations (have a convention center) but have no air lift, including Anchorage, Alaska; Huntington, West Virginia; Davenport, Iowa; and Wheeling, West Virginia.

The type of hotel or meeting facility is another major consideration. There are a variety of choices, including metropolitan hotels, suburban hotels, airport hotels, resort hotels, and casino hotels. In addition, there are facilities especially designed to hold meetings called conference centers. The International Association of Conference Centers is an association in which the member facilities must meet a list of over thirty criteria to be considered an approved conference center. Visit their website for more information. Other options are full-service convention centers, cruise ships, and university campuses. These facilities are discussed at length in Chapter 4, Meeting, Exposition, Event and Convention Venues.

Meeting space requirements are also critical in the site selection process. How many meeting or banquet rooms will be needed? How much space will staff offices, registration, and pre-function areas require? Floor plans with room dimensions are readily available in the facilities' sales brochures or on their websites. Good diagrams will also provide ceiling heights, seating capacities, entrances and exits, and location of columns and other obstructions. Most major hotel chain websites will provide direct links to their hotels and their specification information.

Once the meeting objectives are clearly defined and the basic location and logistics are drafted, the meeting professional creates a request for proposal (RFP). The RFP is a written description of all the major needs for the meeting. The Events Industry Council (EIC), a federation of over thirty MEEC industry associations, has created a standardized format that may be used. It is copyright free.

After the completion of the RFP, it is disseminated to hotel properties and convention facilities that may be interested in submitting a bid for that meeting. Typically, the meeting/event professional can submit the RFP via the Internet directly to preferred hotels and the Destination Marketing Organization (DMO) or Convention and Visitor Bureaus (CVBs) of desirable cities for distribution to all properties, or can submit it to the DI website. Planners can also opt to send their RFP to national hotel chains, such as Marriott or Hyatt, directly. The RFP also serves to allow hotels to examine the potential economic impact of the meeting and decide whether or not to create a bid for it. DI offers members an economic impact calculator. If the group has limited resources and can only afford an $89 room rate, then major luxury hotels may not be interested in the business. However, smaller properties or hotels in second-tier cities may be very interested in hosting the event. If a meeting facility decides to submit a proposal, then the sales department will review the meeting specifications and create a response.

Familiarization or **fam trips** are another method of promoting a destination or particular facility to a meeting/event professional. Fam trips are a no- or low-cost trip for the meeting/event professional to personally review sites for their suitability for a meeting or event. These trips may be arranged by the local DMO or CVB, or by the hotel directly. During the fam trip, the hotel or convention facility tries to impress the meeting/event professional by showcasing its property, amenities, services, and overall quality. Throughout the visit, the meeting/event professional should visit all F&B outlets, visit recreational areas, see a variety of sleeping rooms, check all meeting space, monitor the efficiency of the front desk and other personnel, note the cleanliness and overall appearance of the facility, and, if possible, meet with key hotel personnel. A seasoned meeting/event professional always has a long list of questions to ask. A lot goes into the selection of a hotel.

Once the meeting/event professional has reviewed the RFPs and conducted any necessary site visits, then the negotiations between the meeting/event professional and the sales department at a facility can begin. This process can be quite complex, and careful records of all communications, concessions, and financial expectations should be well documented.

Event Budgeting

Budgetary issues are usually the next major consideration when planning a meeting or event. How much will it cost to produce the event? Who will pay? How much will attendees be charged for registration, if anything? What types of F&B events are planned, and what will be served? Will meals be provided free or at an additional cost to the attendee? What additional revenue streams are available to produce and promote the meeting? Are sponsorships possible? If the event is being held for the first time, the meeting/event professional will have to do a lot of estimation of expenses and potential revenues. An event that has been held before benefits by having some historical data to compare to and project costs from. The basis for a meeting budget can be developed by establishing financial goals, identifying expenses, and identifying revenue sources.

Establish Financial Goals

Financial goals are important and should be easily measurable. They may be set by the meeting/event professional, association management, or by corporate mandate. Basically, financial goals determine the monetary expectations of the event. Not every meeting or event is planned for profit. For example, an awards ceremony held by a company to honor top achievers represents a cost to the company. Similarly, a corporate sales meeting may not have a profit motive. The ultimate goal of the meeting may be to determine how to increase business, and, therefore, profit, but the meeting itself is not a profit generator; it is an expense for the company. On the other hand, most association meetings rely heavily on conventions to produce operating revenue for the association (see Chapter 2 for more details). For most associations, the annual meeting (and often the accompanying trade show) is the second highest revenue producer after membership dues. The financial goal for an annual meeting may be based on increases or decreases in membership, general economic trends, political climate, competing events, location of the event, and many other influences. For any event, there are three possible financial goals:

- *Break-even:* Revenue collected from all activities cover the expenses. No profit is expected.
- *Make profit:* Revenues collected exceed expenses.
- *Deficit:* Expenses exceed revenues.

Identify Expenses and Revenue Sources

It is suggested that expenses be categorized by their different functions:

- *Fixed costs:* are expenses incurred regardless of the number of attendees, such as meeting room rentals or audiovisual equipment.

- *Variable costs:* are those expenses that can vary based on the number of attendees (e.g., F&B).
- *Indirect costs:* should be listed as overhead or administrative line items in a program budget. These are expenses of the organization not directly related to the meeting, such as staff salaries, overhead, or equipment repair.

Expenses will vary according to the overall objectives of the meeting and will be impacted by location, season, type of facility, services selected, and other factors. For example, a gallon of Starbucks coffee in San Francisco at a luxury hotel may cost $90 or more. A gallon of coffee at a moderate-priced hotel in Oklahoma City may only cost $25 or less.

There are many ways to fund meetings and events. Corporations include meeting costs in their operating budgets. The corporate meeting/event professional must work within the constraints of what is budgeted. Associations usually have to be a bit more creative in finding capital to plan and implement an event. Associations must justify the cost of the meeting with the expected ROI of the attendee. It can be quite expensive to attend some association meetings. Consider a hypothetical example of one person attending an association annual meeting: transportation ($500), accommodations for three nights ($700), F&B ($300), registration fee ($500), and miscellaneous ($200), for a total of $2,200. Depending on the city and association, this amount could easily double. It is a complex process to create an exceptional and affordable event. If the registration fee is too high, people will not attend. If it is too low, the organization may not achieve revenue expectations. But there are more possible sources of funding available other than registration fees. These include the following:

- Corporate or association funding
- Private funding from individuals
- Exhibitor fees (if incorporating a trade show/exhibition)
- Sponsorships
- Selling logo merchandise
- Advertising fees, such as banners or ads in the convention program
- Local, state, or national government assistance
- Selling banner ads or links on the official website or on social media platforms
- Renting membership contact lists for marketing purposes
- Establishing official partnerships with other companies to promote their products for a fee or percentage of their revenues
- Contributions in cash or in-kind (services or products)

Estimating expenses and revenues can be accomplished by first calculating a break-even analysis—in other words, how much revenue must be collected to cover expenses.

Program Planning

Once the basic objectives of the meeting have been identified, the site selected, and the budget set, the meeting program can be developed in detail. Some major concerns involved in this process are as follows. Is the programming to be designed in a way that facilitates communication between departments within a corporation? Is the programming geared toward training new employees in the use of a particular computer system? Is the programming geared to educate the members of a professional association and lead toward a certification? To address these concerns, the meeting/event professional must consider several factors, including the following:

- Program type
- Content, including track and level
- Session scheduling

- Speaker arrangements
- Refreshment breaks and meal functions
- Ancillary events
- Evaluation procedures

Putting together a good meeting program requires the meeting professional to select appropriate program types, understand what content is appropriate and interesting to attendees, and schedule the different formats into a master agenda.

Program Types

Each type of program or session is designed for a specific purpose, which may range from providing information to all attendees, discussion of current events in small groups, hands-on training, and panel discussions. The following are typical descriptions of the major program types and formats.

A **general session** or **plenary session** is primarily used as a platform to communicate with all conference attendees at one time in one location. Typically, the general session is what kicks off the meeting and includes welcoming remarks from management or association leadership; outlines the purpose or objectives of the meeting; introduces prominent officials; and recognizes major sponsors or others who helped plan the event, ceremonial duties, and other important matters of general interest. General sessions can last between 1 and 1.5 hours. Often, an important industry leader or a recognizable personality will give a **keynote address** that helps set the tone for the rest of the meeting. For a corporate meeting, this may be the CEO or the chairman of the board. An association may elect to hire a professional speaker in a particular subject area, such as business forecasting, political analysis, leadership and change, technology, or a topic that would be motivational to the audience. Many meeting/event professionals use highly recognizable political, sports, and entertainment personalities. At a recent association convention, the famous basketball player Magic Johnson was the keynote speaker. Other associations have hired former presidents as keynote speakers. These individuals are hired not because of their personal knowledge of the association and the various professions it represents but as a hook to attract people to come to the meeting. As a note, it is not uncommon to spend $75,000 to $100,000 or more (plus travel expenses) to hire a well-known sports or entertainment figure to speak at a general session. General sessions may also be held at the end of a convention to provide closure and summarize what was accomplished during the meeting, or as a venue for presenting awards and recognizing sponsors. Attendance at closing general sessions is typically smaller than with opening sessions as people make travel plans to return home early.

A concurrent session is a professional development or career enhancement session presented by a credentialed speaker who provides education on a specific topic in a conference-style format. Alternately, several speakers may form a panel to provide viewpoints on the topic at hand. Group discussions at individual tables may also be incorporated. Concurrent sessions typically serve groups of 150 plus attendees, and several sessions may be offered simultaneously at a specific time. They typically last between 1 and 1.5 hours.

Workshops or **break-outs** are more intimate sessions that offer a more interactive learning experience in smaller groups. Participants may learn about the latest trends, challenges, and technologies of a specific field. These sessions are often presented by experienced members or peers of the association and may involve lectures, role-playing, simulation, problem solving, or group work. Workshop sessions usually serve groups of 150 or fewer attendees. These are the mainstay of any convention, and dozens or even hundreds of workshops may be offered throughout the course of the event, depending on the size of the meeting. A large association, such as the American Library Association, has more than 1,000 workshop sessions at its annual convention. Workshops typically last from fifty minutes to an hour.

Roundtables and discussion groups are small, interactive sessions designed to cover specific topics of interest. Basically, eight to twelve attendees convene around a large round table, and a facilitator guides discussion about the topic at hand. Typically, several roundtable discussions will take place in one location, such as a large meeting room or ballroom. Attendees are free to join or leave a particular discussion group as desired. Roundtables can also be useful for continued and more intimate conversation with workshop speakers. The role of the facilitator is to keep the discussion on track and not allow any one attendee to monopolize the conversation. Roundtable discussion groups may also employ a subject matter expert to inform and moderate the group.

Poster sessions are another more intimate presentation method often used with academic or medical conferences. Rather than utilizing a variety of meeting rooms to accommodate speakers, panels or display boards are provided for presenters to display charts, photographs, a synopsis of their research, and so on for viewing. The presenter is scheduled to be at his or her display board at an appointed time so that interested attendees may visit informally and discuss the presentation.

Program Content

The average attendee will only be able to sit through three to six sessions on any given day. It is critical that the attendee be as well-informed as possible about what each session will offer and the appropriateness of the session to his or her objectives for attending the meeting. For association meetings, programming objectives are developed months in advance and used extensively in marketing the convention to potential attendees. Program content is not a one-size-fits-all proposition. The content must be specifically designed to match the needs of the audience. A presentation on "Basic Accounting 101" might be good for a junior manager, but totally inappropriate for the chief financial officer. A good way to communicate to attendees how to select which programs to attend is to create tracks and levels. A **track** refers to separating programming into specific genres, such as computer skills, professional development, marketing, personal growth, legal issues, certification courses, or financial issues. A variety of workshops can be developed that concentrate on these specific areas. **Levels** refer to the skill level the program is designed for, whether it is beginning, intermediate, or advanced. Thus, the speaker who is assigned a session can develop content specifically tailored for a particular audience. Attendees can also determine if a session meets their level of expertise.

The following is an example of a typical description of a session.

SESSION DESCRIPTION

Workshop 14: Effective Marketing through Social Media and Email Marketing
Frank Wise, PhD
3:30 PM to 4:45 PM (1530–1645)
Room 314

With over 132 billion email messages sent daily and billions of users on thousands of social media platforms, how can your company develop an effective marketing strategy to capitalize on these technologies? What are the most effective options to do so?
Attend this session to:

- Discover the top ten steps in developing effective electronic media marketing messages.
- Discuss a variety of delivery platforms.
- Enhance your own effectiveness with social media.

Track: Marketing
Level: Intermediate

Session Scheduling

The meeting/event professional must orchestrate every minute of every day to ensure that the meeting runs smoothly and punctually. Each day's agenda should be an exciting variety of activities that will stimulate attendees and make them want to attend the next meeting. One of the biggest mistakes meeting/event professionals make is double-booking events over the same time period. If a meeting/event professional schedules workshops from

8:00 AM to 1:00 PM and the tee time for the celebrity golf match is at 12:30 PM, then he or she stands to lose any of the attendees who want to attend the golfing event. Trade shows/exhibitions are another challenge. If workshops are scheduled at the same time that the trade show floor is open, attendees must choose between the two options. If attendees choose to attend the education sessions, the exhibitors will not get the traffic they expect. Conversely, if attendees go to the trade show rather than attend sessions, there may be empty meeting rooms and frustrated speakers.

Another major issue is allowing enough time for people to do what comes naturally. Do not expect to move 5,000 people from a general session into breakout sessions on the other side of the convention center in ten minutes. Plan thoughtfully. Allow sufficient time for people to use the restroom, check their email, text messages, or voicemail, say "hello" to an old friend, and comfortably walk to their next workshop. If these delays are not planned for in advance, then there may be attendees disrupting workshop sessions by coming in late, or worse, by skipping sessions.

The following is a description of the schedule for an association meeting.

EXAMPLE OF AN ASSOCIATION MEETING SCHEDULE

While no two conventions are the same, the following timeline provides a good idea of a typical meeting's flow.

Day One

8:00 AM: Staff office and pressroom area set up

Exhibition set up begins
Pre-convention meeting with facility staff
Registration set up

Day Two

8:00 AM: Association board meeting

Registration opens
Staff office opens
Exhibition set up continues
Set up for pre-convention workshops

1:00–4:00 PM: Pre-convention workshops (with break)

Various committee meetings
Program planning committee finalizes duties for meetings

5:00 PM: Private reception for board members and VIPs
7:00–9:30 PM: Opening reception

Day Three

6:30 AM: Staff meeting
8:00 AM: Registration opens

Coffee service begins

9:00 AM: General session
10:30 AM: Break
10:45 AM: Concurrent workshops
12:00–1:30 PM: Lunch
1:30–5:00 PM: Exhibition opens
5:00 PM: Registration closes

(Continued)

Day Four

6:30 AM: Staff meeting

8:00 AM: Registration opens

  Coffee service begins

9:00 AM–4:00 PM: Exhibition opens

12:00–1:30 PM: Lunch provided on show floor

1:30–2:30 PM: Workshops

2:45–3:45 PM: Workshops

4:00–5:00 PM: Workshops

  Teardown of trade show begins

5:00 PM: Registration closes

7:00 PM: Cocktail reception

8:00–10:00 PM: Banquet and awards ceremony

Day Five

7:00 AM: Staff meeting

8:00 AM: Registration opens

  Trade show teardown continues

9:00–10:30 AM: Closing session

  Pack up staff office

  Pressroom closed

10:45 AM–12:00 PM: Program planning committee meets

12:00 PM: Registration closed

3:00 PM Post-Conference Meetings

Logistical Considerations

Registration

To attend most conventions or exhibitions, some type of registration is typically required. Even weddings require an RSVP. Registration is the process of gathering all pertinent information and fees necessary for an individual to attend the meeting. It is much more than merely collecting money. Registration data are a valuable asset to any association or organization that is sponsoring an event. Registration begins several weeks or even months prior to the event, and usually lasts right up to the final day. Discounts are often provided to attendees who register in advance. They are offered an **early bird rate** incentive to pay fees early. The association can then use that money to pay deposits or bills coming due. By registering early, the meeting/event professional can determine if registration numbers are at anticipated levels. If not, it can increase marketing or negotiate with the hotel or meeting facilities about lowering expectations and financial commitments that may have been promised.

  Data collected on the registration form may include name, title, occupation, address, email, phone, fax, membership category, desired workshop sessions, social functions, optional events, method of payment, special medical or dietary needs, and a liability waiver. A recent addition has been to ask attendees where they are staying while at the convention and their length of stay, so that the impact of the meeting can be determined. Some organizations inquire about the size of the company, number of employees, or financial responsibility of the attendee (such as does he or she make or recommend purchase decisions). This registration data can be used before, during, and after the meeting.

Prior to the meeting, the data can be given or sold to exhibitors or advertisers so that they can promote their company, products, and services before the actual event. It may also be used to market to potential attendees who have not committed to attending. Advertising "we have 7,500 qualified buyers attending this year's convention" may entice more companies to register or exhibit. Preregistration data can also help the meeting/event professional monitor interest in special events or particular workshops that may be popular. If a particular workshop is getting a lot of interest, then the meeting/event professional can move it to a larger room or increase seating.

During the meeting, registration data can be used as a promotional tool for the press to gain media attention for the organization, sponsors, and exhibitors. It can also help the local DMO in justifying the costs of marketing and soliciting groups to come to their city. Hard facts, such as using 3,000 rooms and 200,000 square feet of meeting space, are music to the ears of hospitality companies. For the attendees, technology now allows them to automatically access, via smartphone or computer, who is at a particular meeting and save the list for future use.

After the meeting, registration data can be used to update association membership records, solicit new members, or be sold to interested parties. Most importantly, it can be used to help the meeting/event professional with logistics and to promote the next meeting. By examining registration data over time, it gives the organization a better view of who is attending its meeting and if there are any apparent trends, such as changes in gender, age, education, or the title of attendees.

Registration Fees

There may be several different pricing structures for a single meeting. For association meetings, members typically receive a discount on the cost of registration. This helps encourage people to become members of the association. But not all members will pay the same price. For example, in 2018, the Professional Convention Management Association (PCMA) charged professional members (meeting/event professionals), $1,095; suppliers (hotel sales people, CVBs), $1,295; university faculty, $525; and student members, $275. These were the early bird preregistration prices available until about six weeks prior to the convention. After the **cutoff date** for preregistration, all prices increased by $50 to $100. Additional fees of $200 were added if the registrant did not stay in the **room block** at a host hotel. All attendees, regardless of how much they paid, received the same opportunities for education and networking, and were invited to the scheduled meals, breaks, and receptions. However, additional activities, such as golf, tours, or special entertainment functions, incurred a separate cost.

For some events like the Exhibitor Show, an annual trade show for people in the exhibition industry, registration fees are priced based on what the attendee wants to attend. Entrance to the trade show is free, but education sessions may cost $295 or more per workshop. Additional events, such as dinners and receptions, may be purchased separately. All-inclusive registrations at the Exhibitor Show are also an option with full registration and attendance to all education programs, costing well over $1,500.

Associations usually offer substantial registration discounts to their members. The non-member rate to attend may well exceed the difference between the cost of membership and the member rate, making it desirable to join the association. This is a clever way for associations to increase their membership base and provides an opportunity to promote other products and services to new members. Registration fees are often waived for members of the press, speakers, and local dignitaries. Complimentary registrations must be monitored closely because there may be costs involved if the meeting has F&B, or if other events are available.

Preregistration

Preregistration is the process of registering attendees weeks or months in advance of an event. This benefits the meeting/event professional in several ways. It provides information about who will be attending a meeting or event. It can help the meeting/event professional determine room capacities for educational sessions, and can help the session speaker to estimate the number of people who may attend a session. Typically, advanced payment is also required to preregister. By receiving payment weeks or months ahead of the event, the meeting/event professional can use that money to pay bills or make necessary deposits for services. The early bird discount is a major incentive to preregister. Logistically, as people are arriving for the event, preregistration can reduce congestion in the registration area, as well as reduce long lines and waiting time. A quick check-in to collect a name badge and other meeting materials, and to confirm the person's arrival is all that is necessary.

Whether it is paper-based or electronic, the prospective attendee must complete a registration form; the more simple and easy it is to complete, the better.

Housing

Not all meetings require housing arrangements. But if housing is needed, there are basically four methods of handling housing for attendees.

1. Attendees arrange for their own room. Lists of hotels may be provided, but the meeting sponsor makes no prior arrangements regarding price negotiations or availability.
2. A group rate is negotiated by the meeting/event professional at one or more properties, and attendees respond directly to the reservations department of their choice.
3. The meeting sponsor handles all housing, and attendees book rooms through them. The sponsor then provides the hotel with a rooming list of confirmed guests.
4. A third-party **housing bureau** (outsourced company) handles all arrangements either for a fee or is paid by the DMO.

Having attendees make their own hotel reservations is the easiest method. It totally removes the responsibility from the meeting/event professional and the contract liability from the meeting organization. However, the hotel facility is going to base its pricing to host the event on the total revenues it anticipates from the group. Sleeping rooms represent the largest amount of potential revenue for the hotel. If rooms are not blocked (set aside for the group), it is most likely that a premium will be charged to the organization for renting meeting space and other services (e.g., F&B, AV, etc.). The room block is a key negotiation tool for the meeting/event professional.

The last three options require that the meeting/event professional establish a rate for the attendees. The room rate will reflect prior negotiations with the hotel sales department in which the total value of the meeting to the facility is considered. A certain number of rooms will be reserved, called a block, and rooms are subtracted from this inventory as attendees request them. This can be a gamble for the meeting/event professional. As with F&B events, the meeting/event professional must estimate how many people will be attending. If the meeting/event professional blocks 100 rooms and only 75 rooms are used by the group, he or she may be held responsible for part, or all, of the cost of those unused rooms. The difference between rooms blocked and rooms picked up (actually used) is called attrition (for more information on attrition, see Chapter 10, Legal Issues in the MEEC Industry).

A serious challenge to meeting/event professionals these days is attendees booking rooms outside the block. That is, the attendee opts to bypass the hotels for which the meeting/event professional negotiated special pricing and find other accommodations or even less expensive accommodations within the host hotels. If the host hotel charges $199 per day and a smaller and less luxurious hotel down the street is charging $99, a certain percentage of the attendees will book the alternative property for the lower price. Sometimes, by calling the hotel directly or by using a discount hotel broker on the Internet, attendees can get better prices in the same hotel for less than what the meeting/event professional negotiated. If large numbers of attendees do this, then the meeting/event professional is going to get stuck paying for a lot of unused rooms. One method of reducing this potentially expensive problem is to establish review dates in the hotel contract, whereby the meeting/event professional can reduce (or increase) the **room block** by a certain percentage at a certain time. The closer to the actual meeting dates, the less likely the hotel will allow a reduction in room block. The hotel must have time to try and sell any unused rooms and recoup any losses. A hotel room is a perishable commodity; if it is not sold each day, the potential revenue is lost forever.

Having attendees call or reserve rooms online directly with the hotel is a good option. The attendees should benefit by the negotiated room rate, and the hotel handles the reservation processing directly. The meeting/event professional will need minimal involvement. For larger meetings, where multiple properties are used, it is advisable to provide a range of hotel prices to accommodate the budgets of all the attendees.

> ### REGISTRATION AND HOUSING COMPANIES
>
> Several companies have evolved that specialize in handling both conference registration and housing. Examples include companies such as ConferenceDirect and Experient.
>
> Outsourcing the housing process to a third-party vendor or DMO is most prevalent with medium and large meetings. Some groups, such as the National Association of Broadcasters or the Consumer Electronics Show, are so large that they require most of the hotel rooms in the host city. Housing for a so-called *citywide* meeting is best left to professionals who have the most current technology and are well equipped to handle thousands of housing requests. The housing bureau may charge a fee per transaction. This cost may be paid by the sponsoring organization, or, in some cases, the local DMO will absorb some or all of the cost. Indeed, many DMOs, and even hotels, operate their own housing bureaus as a service to meeting/event professionals.

Handling attendee reservations in-house is possible, but is easiest with small groups. If the event is a small, high-profile event, the meeting/event professional can have attendees reserve rooms with the organization, and a **rooming list** will be created to give to the hotel. The rooming list should include type of room, ADA requests, smoking or nonsmoking, arrival and departure dates, names of additional guests in the room, and special requests. Handling reservations in-house can be quite time-consuming and may require additional staffing. Alternatively, a housing bureau can be of great assistance.

Refreshment Breaks and Meal Functions

As with scheduling workshops, it is important to provide time for attendees to eat and relax throughout the day. F&B functions should be thoughtfully planned, as they are important, yet expensive. However, it may be more productive to feed attendees than have them wandering around a convention center or leaving the property to find something to eat. Refreshment breaks provide the opportunity to catch up with old friends, make new business contacts, network, and grab a quick bite or reenergize with a cup of coffee or tea. Breaks and meals are excellent sponsorship opportunities and companies gain attendee recognition.

Speaker Arrangements

For large conventions, it is almost impossible for the meeting/event professional to independently arrange for all the different sessions and speakers. The meeting department often works together with the education department to develop the educational content of the meeting. In addition, a program committee comprised of industry leaders and those with special interests in education will volunteer to assist the meeting/event professional. These volunteers will work diligently to arrange what topics are appropriate for sessions, and who the likely speakers might be. It is the job of the committee to be the gatekeeper of educational content. Subcommittees may be created to focus on finding a general session speaker, or on developing workshops, concurrent sessions, student member events, and so on.

Most associations cannot afford to pay all of the speakers at a large convention, and use volunteer speakers instead. A moderate-sized convention of 2,500 people may have 100 or more sessions offered at a three-day event. Remuneration for speakers may range from providing no assistance at all to paying a speaker fee and all expenses, such as the case with a paid general session speaker.

Benefits of Using Volunteer Speakers

- Reduces expenses (the person may already have budgeted to attend the meeting, so no housing or transportation costs are required)
- He/she is knowledgeable about important industry topics

- Popular industry leaders may increase attendance at sessions
- Builds relationships between speaker and event sponsor

Challenges of Using Volunteer Speakers

- May not adequately prepare for presentation
- May not be a good presenter, even if knowledgeable about the topic
- May have a personal agenda; uses session to promote self or company

A more expensive, but often more reliable, source for speakers is to contact a *professional speaker* from a speaker bureau. A **speaker bureau** is a professional talent broker who can help find the perfect speaker to match your event objectives and your budget. Typically, a speaker bureau has a stable of qualified professionals who can talk on whatever topic you desire. Fees and other amenities range from the affordable to the outrageous. If you are a small midwestern association of county clerks, you are not going to be able to afford a world-famous athlete as your keynote speaker at your annual meeting. However, you might be able to afford a gold medal Olympian from the 1990s who can talk about teamwork and determination for a bargain price of $4,000.

Providing high-priced, popular, paid speakers will most likely increase attendance at your meeting. The smart way to provide such talent is to have the costs of the speaker sponsored by a key exhibitor or leader in the industry. The general session is a high-profile event, and it may be cost-effective for a company to fund the keynote speaker to promote itself to a maximum number of attendees. For example, a $30,000 speaker for a group of 5,000 attendees is only $6 per attendee. That may be less expensive than designing and distributing a traditional mailing!

Sports stars are often used as keynote speakers in an effort to draw more attendees to a convention.
dotshock/Shutterstock

Another source for speakers is local dignitaries, industry leaders, and university professors. As they are local, you will not incur transportation and lodging costs. In addition, their services are often free or very affordable. The local DMO or university can assist you in finding people who are willing to assist you. A small gift or honorarium is customary to thank these individuals for their time and effort.

Speaker guidelines should be developed to inform the speakers (paid and nonpaid) of the logistics required to speak at an event as well as to clearly define the expectations of the organization. Speaker guidelines vary from one group to the next, but most should include the following:

- Background information about the association
- Date and location of meeting
- Special events or activities the speaker may attend
- Date, time, and location of speaker's room for presentation
- Presentation topic and duration
- Demographics and estimated number of attendees for the session
- **Room set** and audiovisual equipment requests and availability
- Request for short biography
- Names of other speakers, if applicable
- Remuneration policy
- Dress code
- Location of **speaker ready room**, where he or she can practice or relax prior to speaking
- Instructions for preparing abstracts or submitting final papers (typically for academic conferences)

- Instructions for having handouts available
- Transportation and lodging information
- Maps and diagrams of hotel or facility
- Deadlines for all materials that must be returned
- Hints for speaking to the group (e.g., attendees are very informal, attendees like time for questions and answers at the end of session)

It is not uncommon to include a variety of contractual agreements that must be signed by the speaker. A presenter contract is a written agreement between the presenter and the sponsor to provide a presentation on a specific topic at a specific time. A contract should be used regardless of whether the speaker will be paid or not. The contract will verify, in writing, expenses that will be covered, the relationship between the two parties, promotional material needed to advertise the session, deadlines for audiovisual and handout materials, disclosure statements pertaining to any potential conflict of interest, selling or promoting products or services, penalties for failure to perform the presentation, and allowable conditions for termination of the contract.

If the session will be recorded in any digital format and made available on a website or online video platform, the speaker must be informed and must sign a *recording, internet authorization and/or waiver.* Some speakers do not want their presentation materials to be accessed on the Internet, because they may be easily copied and used by others. Selling digital recordings of programs is an additional revenue stream for associations. Since attendees are limited in the number of sessions they can attend each day, by purchasing recordings of missed sessions, they can have the information from the sessions they missed. Additional information on the use of speakers, entertainers, and performers can be found in Chapter 10.

Audiovisual Equipment

Most hotels and meeting facilities do not allow meeting/event professionals to provide their own audiovisual equipment, such as LCD projectors, television monitors, and DVD players. The rental and servicing of this equipment is a significant revenue stream for facilities. Audiovisual equipment is extremely expensive to rent. In many instances, it costs as much to rent the equipment as it does to buy it. A 40-inch television, which may be purchased at a discount store for $350, may cost the meeting/event professional that amount in rental fees *each day*!

Thus, controlling audiovisual costs is very important. The event professional may wish to inform speakers that only an LCD projector and laptop computer are available. Thus, the speaker can craft his or her presentation to the media available. Another good idea is to provide speakers with a template to use in preparing overheads and handouts. You can request that all slides and handouts be developed with a certain font, such as Arial or Times New Roman, and dictate the text and background colors that should be used. Also provide a crisp logo for the organization or event. This will provide some uniformity to the look of your meeting.

To reduce expenses and conserve resources, most groups have opted to put all handouts on an app, flash drive or stored in the Cloud and make it available for free or for a nominal charge. Likewise, some groups post all the handouts on their company website rather than distribute it at the meeting. Others will provide print on demand stations for those attendees who desire a hard copy. If handouts will be used, remember to request a master copy well in advance of the meeting.

Marketing and Promotion

Plan an event and people will come, right? Not necessarily. The costliest mistake in event management is not having an audience. No amount of lavish decoration, fine food, effective room design, engaging speakers, energetic entertainment, flawless audiovisual, or elaborate staging will compensate for an event that few attend. Despite all efforts to coordinate and manage a well-run event, if the intended audience does not attend or if the attendance numbers are too low, the event will not be deemed a success. It is impossible to underestimate the importance of event marketing and event communications.

Some events and meetings have minimal marketing or promotional requirements. For example, a corporate sales meeting, where employee attendance is mandatory, might only require an email notification. Social events, such as a wedding, birthday party, or an anniversary do not typically require extensive marketing. Events that depend on audience revenues, and events that exist to create awareness require more extensive marketing in order to guarantee an audience.

In some organizations event marketing efforts might be handled by an entire team of event professionals. They might also hire contractors who specialize in marketing, public relations, and promotional campaigns. In contrast, there are some organizations where an event professional has the sole responsibility for all event marketing efforts. In either case, it makes sense for the event professional to be involved in the marketing and public relations (PR) efforts to assure that the event objectives are clearly represented and that there is a consistency in the meeting or event look, design, and theme concepts.

(adapted from *Planning and Management of MEEC* by *George G. Fenich*)

Identifying Target Markets

Two pivotal elements to planning a successful marketing strategy are to identify the target audience and to use the right marketing promotions to reach them. Determining who the ideal event or conference audience will be should be part of an analysis that is done in the initial program planning stages. Knowing whom the desired audience is will help the event professional determine what type of marketing to implement.

By understanding a little bit about the consumer behavior of their target market, the event professional can identify the best way to reach them. Examining what motivates people to attend some events and avoid others is part of the analysis that helps in understanding their response or buying behaviors. In the initial planning stages of the event process, the event professional should outline who the event **stakeholders** are. A stakeholder is one who has stake in an enterprise. Typical event stakeholders are the producing organization of the event, the decision-makers, the sponsors, the exhibitors *(if the event has exhibitors)*, the organization membership *(if the event is for an association or other membership organization)*, the beneficiaries *(if the event is to promote a cause or is a benefit event)*, the participants *(such as the speakers, presenters, volunteers, and performers)* and, most importantly, the attendees or audience who will attend the event.

Types of Marketing for Events

Direct Marketing

Direct marketing is marketing by means of direct communication with consumers. When referring to events, the term, consumers, refers to your potential event attendees. Some of the more common forms of direct marketing for events include the following.

Email   Email marketing has become the more predominant technique for the direct marketing of events. The cost effectiveness and ability to reach a wide audience makes email marketing very appealing. There are several good software programs that can help an event professional with bulk email distribution.

When sending invitations using personal email accounts, the event professional needs to consider the recipients' concern about receiving spam emails and getting computer viruses. They will also want to make sure the email reaches the recipient.

Telephone   The telephone remains one of the best ways to connect with people on a one-to-one basis. Sometimes that personal touch is necessary to encourage people to attend an event. Some event organizers organize a *telephone tree*, which involves having several volunteers divide up a phone list to make direct phone calls to lists of contact names. Some event professionals use third-party telemarketing companies or internal sales reps (ISR's) to help make phone calls.

For a telephone calling campaign to be successful, event professionals create a phone script for those who will call the target audience. A phone script helps callers use compelling language that will resonate with the potential guests. This phone script also functions as a sales pitch to help those making phone calls to remember all of the critical details such as the date, location, time, and how to get tickets.

Advertising   An advertisement is a public notice. In most cases, advertising refers to paid forms of commercial advertisements (also called ads). The most common forms of commercial advertising are print media ads, such as newspapers and magazines; broadcast media ads, such as television and radio commercials; and online media ads, such as on websites, search engines, social networking sites, and Web video commercials. Commercial advertising may also take many other forms from billboards, to mobile telephone screens, bus stop benches, aerial banners and balloons, humans wearing signs (called human billboards), bus and subway train signs, and much more.

Because advertising can be expensive, event professionals want to target their advertising dollars to the people most likely to attend the event. Ads can be placed in relevant trade magazines, journals, or publications in order to provide exposure, not only for the event, but also for the organization. For example, if an event were to be targeted to an audience of event professionals, a few professional trade journals where the event might be advertised could be *Convene, Successful Meetings,* or *Meetings and Conventions Magazine.* If the event had a target audience of bankers, the event might be advertised in the American Bankers' Association publication, *ABA Banking Journal.*

Some media outlets will offer trade-out advertising in exchange for a service that the event organization can provide. For example, an event manager for a large exhibition might trade exhibit space to a publishing company in exchange for an advertisement in their publication. A radio or television station might be willing to become an event sponsor for marketing exposure at the event in exchange for free advertisements on their radio or television station.

Many community events use posters or flyers (also called circulars, handbills, or leaflets) as a form of advertisement. Distributed and posted in public places where the target audience might assemble, this is often a lower-cost option to more expensive forms of commercial advertising.

Mail   Before the Internet, direct mail was the preferred marketing technique for promoting attendance at conferences and events. This included sending materials directly to an individual through the postal service. It was a costly and time-consuming method of marketing, but it is still effective and commonly used for smaller meetings and events. Many organizations still use the postal service mailing for save the date postcards, letters, and meeting reminders. Invitations to VIPs, especially in a corporate setting, are best done in hard copy.

Indirect Marketing

Also known as word-of-mouth marketing, indirect marketing is promotion using non-traditional and innovative means. Whereas direct marketing is marketing directly to the target audience; indirect marketing involves indirect communication about the event to create marketing buzz about an event. Buzz is the humming sound that flying bees make, marketing buzz expresses the idea of people passing along the word from one person to another about a brand, product, or in the case of event marketing, an event.

Social Media   Social media refers to all types of internet communications. Interactive discussions on online news sites, blogging, online discussion communities, micro blogging, mobile technologies for communication, and social networking sites are all forms of social media. In prior decades, marketing for events meant one person calling their friends and telling them about something they were planning to attend. These days, word-of-mouth marketing tends to also involve social media.

The World Wide Web has become an effective way to connect to people. The event professional might create a Facebook page, a Twitter feed, a LinkedIn discussion board, or any other social media platform to notify others, encouraging them to pass the word along to their friends. Social media marketing has become such a phenomena that many companies hire staff to manage social media platforms, and to monitor social media dialog about the companies' products or services.

Event professionals might also encourage further word-of-mouth marketing buzz and online social interaction by offering special discounts tickets to their event. Advertising pay for two and the third person is free, or buy one, get one free (known by the acronym BOGO) are common strategies to encourage people to invite their friends to an event.

Summary

Planning a meeting or event is a long process that often requires input from many people or committees. Setting event goals and clearly defined objectives is the first essential step in creating effective program content and managing logistics. The objectives will impact site or city selection, type of facility used, and the services required. The meeting/event professional must also understand the motivations of the attendees: Why should they attend? Is attendance voluntary or mandated by management? Planning a corporate event, compared to an association event, can be a very different process. Education has replaced recreation as the driving force for most meetings.

Once the objectives are clear, a needs analysis should be conducted to further guide the meeting/event professional in selecting an appropriate meeting space, speakers, and the amenities expected from the attendees. The demographics of attendees must also be considered. Meetings and conventions represent enormous economic potential for cities. In the site selection process, the RFP is the announcement of what is required by the meeting/event professional. DMOs and individual hotels must evaluate the potential of the meeting and respond accordingly. Interested properties may invite the meeting/event professional for a fam trip to visit the property.

Education and networking are the most important elements for most meetings. However, people like to be entertained as well as educated, so the meeting/event professional must attend to all the needs of the attendees and provide both. The format of the education sessions and the set up of the meeting space should be appropriate to the objectives of the meeting. Program content should be designed with both a track and level that will target the majority of the attendees. Housing and registration are important components in implementing the plan for a meeting or event. Both paid and voluntary speakers can be utilized—each has positives and negatives. Care must be taken to ensure that speakers are adequately prepared to address the group and are contractually obligated to perform. Finally, ancillary activities like shopping trips, tours, child care, and other services that enhance an attendees' meeting experience should be planned thoughtfully so as not to interfere with the scheduled programming.

Because of the complexity of the meeting planning process, this chapter can only highlight some of the planning activities involved. There are two books that provide more detail on the planning and production aspects of MEEC. They are *Planning and Management of Meetings, Expositions, Events and Conventions* and *Production and Logistics in Meetings, Expositions, Events and Conventions*, both by Fenich.

Key Words and Terms

For definitions, see the Glossary.

annual meetings	housing bureau	rooming list
air lift	keynote address	roundtables
attrition	levels	SMART
break-outs	needs analysis	speaker bureau
cutoff date	plenary session	speaker ready room
early bird rate	poster sessions	stakeholders
fam trip	request for proposal (RFP)	track
general session	room block	workshops
group history	room set	

CASE STUDY

Using Virtual Technology to Enhance a Meeting

The Governance Institute is a member organization serving health care system directors, executives, and physicians. This organization offers annual conferences that provide valuable tools that greatly benefit their members. Members are encouraged to attend, and in the past years these conferences have been a success. This year's conference will take place at the Mountain View Resort and Spa located in Boulder, Colorado. Amy Foote, who is the head meeting planner for The Governance Institute, is experiencing a major decline in attendance for this year's conference. With this challenge Amy and her team of event planners must come up with new ways to market the event and increase attendance.

With the conference being only two months away, Amy decided her team needed to come up with a solution to this problem and increase attendance. The team researched many options and scenarios. With so many new technologies, Amy questions if a virtual component tied into the on-site event could replicate the conference experience. With this in mind, Amy and her team developed a virtual conference to be held during the Boulder conference. This is the first virtual conference Amy has ever planned, and she wants it to be a success. The virtual conference would stream live presentations from all keynote speakers through webcasts and offer online networking with other virtual attendees. There would also be panel discussions featuring question and answers with speakers, and virtual booths from participating sponsors.

A major concern Amy has is how to market this event. She does not want to take away attendance from the actual event. Amy decides only to offer it to members that had declined in advance, and they would not start marketing this event until after most members had registered and booked their travel arrangements. They started to promote the virtual conference two weeks before the live conference took place. Email invitations were sent out that accompanied an online registration. These emails included an introduction to the virtual conference concept, a program of the online sessions, descriptions of the interactive forms, and a link to the website.

With all the planning and research, it was finally time to go live with the conference. On the day of the event Amy and her team monitored online activity through laptops at the Boulder conference. Her virtual team welcomed attendees, announced session schedules, answered questions, and provided feedback while moderating chat sessions. After reviewing surveys and feedback from attendees, the virtual conference was considered a success. It nearly doubled the total attendance with 300 virtual attendees attending the online conference, and 600 prospects registered to attend. Amy and her team will continue to implement virtual conference options when planning future conferences.

1. What do you think of the job Amy did?
2. What else could she have done?
3. What could she have done better?
4. Was it fair to attendees who arranged for and paid to attend in person NOT to be given the opportunity to participate virtually?

Produced by George G. Fenich from East Carolina University

Review and Discussion Questions

1. What is the difference between a meeting goal and a SMART objective?
2. What is the purpose of using program formats, levels, and tracks in designing effective meeting programming?
3. What are the benefits and challenges of using volunteer speakers compared to paid speakers?
4. What are the benefits and limitations of outsourcing components of a meeting, such as housing or registration?
5. How can meeting/event professionals use registration data before, during, and after a convention?
6. How does preregistration assist the meeting/event professional in planning a meeting?
7. Describe the four different methods of housing.
8. Think of a MEEC event you have attended. Who was the target audience? What marketing strategies did the organizer utilize?

About the Chapter Contributor

Amanda Cecil, PhD, is an Associate Professor in the Department of Tourism, Conventions and Event Management at Indiana University. Her teaching and research focus is on event tourism and business travel.

Previous Chapter Contributor

Curtis Love, PhD, Emeritus Professor at the William F. Harrah Hotel College at the University of Nevada Las Vegas.

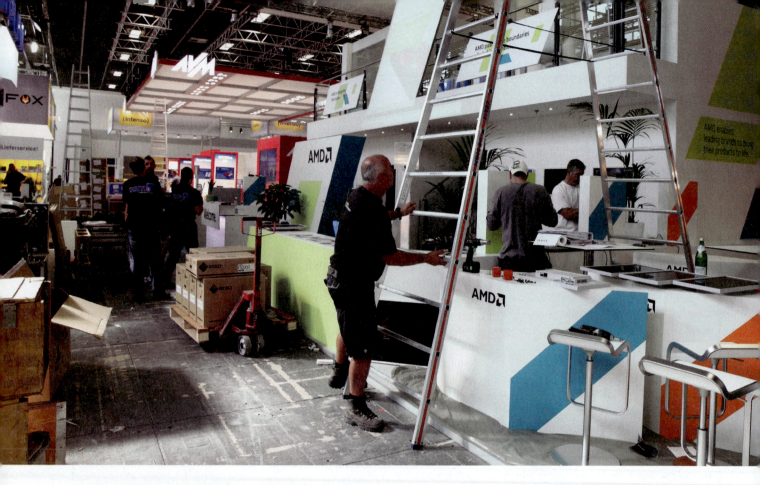

Erecting trade show booths is a major component of the MEEC industry.
Agencja Fotograficzna Caro/Alamy Stock Photo

CHAPTER 14

Producing Meetings and Events

Chapter Objectives

- Discuss the basic requirements of producing an on-site meeting or event.
- Outline strategies and considerations for managing the on-site team.
- Discuss the various considerations and specifics that go into on-site communications.

- Cover the specific considerations to keep in mind when planning and executing on public relations when producing an event.
- Articulate the reasons and important elements of pre-convention meetings.
- Specify the elements needed for a successful post-convention review.

Producing meetings and events is part of the sequential process of planning and staging an event. Producing, or production and logistics, is often thought of as what happens on-site. In large convention hotels, planning is accomplished by the sales team, while production is accomplished by convention services. These are two completely different departments with completely different teams.

On-site Management

There are various areas that must be carefully managed on-site for every event. These include registration, housing, food and beverage, speakers and entertainers, audiovisuals, and ancillary events. Managing each area requires a skillful approach to ensure that the logistics are flawless, costs are contained, and strategic goals and outcomes are being achieved. The following explains each key area.

Registration and Housing

Like the front desk of a hotel, the registration area is the first experience an attendee has with a meeting, convention, or exhibition. A slow or inefficient registration process can set the tone for the entire meeting. The registration area should be heavily staffed the first day and should remain open throughout the event. If international guests are expected, registration materials may need to be translated, and interpreters may be necessary to facilitate a smooth check-in. If an exhibition is involved, having a separate area for exhibitor registration is a good idea.

Registration is one of the areas often outsourced by the meeting/event professional, especially for large events. It is a complex process that requires much training on the part of the registration attendants. Some hotels or convention centers have arrangements with temporary agencies that provide staff that do registration on a regular basis. Some registration management companies handle housing as well.

The registration area should be well-designed and attendees should not have long waits to check-in or ask a question. Electronic kiosks are increasingly being utilized to make registration more efficient. If a significant problem with a person's or an entire group's registration is identified, a full-time staff member should be available to meet with the individual or representative of the group. It is advised that a private meeting room or hospitality area be created near the registration area for this purpose.

Additionally, questions and concerns regarding housing should be addressed at the registration area. If someone there cannot assist, then registration staff should direct attendees to the appropriate resource to solve housing concerns. If the attendee or guest has concerns about accommodations or with the service at the hotel property, he/she should be directed to the key contact at the hotel. If it is not resolved, the meeting planner or third-party representative should intervene.

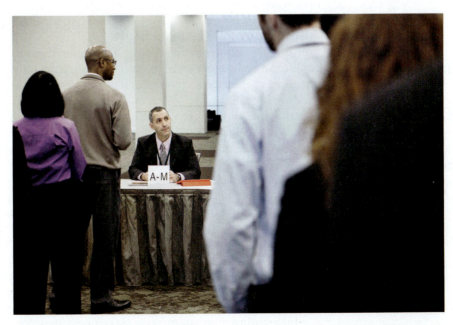

Registration desk at a conference. The sign indicates where registrants should queue up based on the first initial of their last name.
Jetta Productions/Getty images

It is important to note that final registration and housing reports should be requested prior to departing the event location. These reports include critical information needed for future negotiations with hotels, venues, and suppliers. Additionally, these reports should be discussed at all strategic follow-up meetings.

Food and Beverage

At this point, all F&B orders, room location and design, and food providers should have been determined and permits purchased. Most facilities will send a **banquet event order (BEO)** for each individual function in which food and beverage will be provided. This document outlines food and beverage quantities, timing and logistical specifics, staffing needs, and service type. Once on-site, the planner should meet with the catering manager or CSM to review each BEO and ensure anything that is incorrect or needs updating is addressed.

One important consideration that must be finalized is the **guarantee** for each event. This is the contracted number of meals or items that the organization will pay for, regardless of attendance. This process can dramatically affect the budget if the event professional over orders, and can be a source of embarrassment for the host if not enough food and/or beverage is provided. Knowing their event history and projected attendance is imperative to correctly making the guarantee.

Other areas to follow-through with on-site include ensuring all vendors and the organization has the proper permits and licenses to operate, evaluating the space prior to the event to confirm appropriate room set ups, discussing service expectations to the banquet or F&B captain, and reviewing all policies and procedures for food safety and liability issues, especially if serving alcohol.

Chapter 9 goes into detail on food and beverage logistical details and considerations.

Function Room Layouts

A consideration when selecting a venue for an event is how the room will be arranged. Specific factors influence the room layout, such as the number of people, type of meeting, AV and technology needs, speaker tables, refreshment tables, and physical room attributes and/or obstacles. Traditional layouts include auditorium, banquet, reception, theater, classroom, cocktail, boardroom, hallow square, exhibit, classroom style, theater style, conference style, and u-shape. Most venues can give planners a rendering of how each room can be arranged using each layout. Figure 14-1 provides examples of layouts.

Auditorium or Theater Style

Probably the most common seating arrangement in meetings is an auditorium or theater design. An **auditorium style** room set up is particularly useful when there is no need for attendees to interact with one another during the course of the session. In this instance, chairs are arranged in rows facing the same direction. Most commonly, these rows will face the head of the room, which may be designated by a stage, head table, lectern, or screen. A speaker or panel will generally run the meeting, often lecturing to attendees who may be taking notes based on the information the speaker is conveying.

Classroom Style

Sometimes meetings may require tables for attendees to use for completing tests, taking notes, or interacting with other attendees to solve presented problems. **Classroom style** is the most common set up used for these types of meetings. In classroom meeting set ups, chairs are arranged in a similar manner as in an auditorium, but with tables provided for each row of chairs. These tables are generally six or eight feet long and 18 inches deep. If the design is intended for attendees to be sitting on each side of the table, then 30-inch-deep tables (or two 18-inch tables placed back to back) are used to allow sufficient space. In this room set up, the tables are draped, with pads of paper and pencils/pens at each place setting.

Like auditorium room sets, classrooms may be modified as needed. Sometimes classrooms are arranged diagonally toward the head table, or even perpendicular to the front of the room. Perpendicular room sets are challenging because it often necessitates

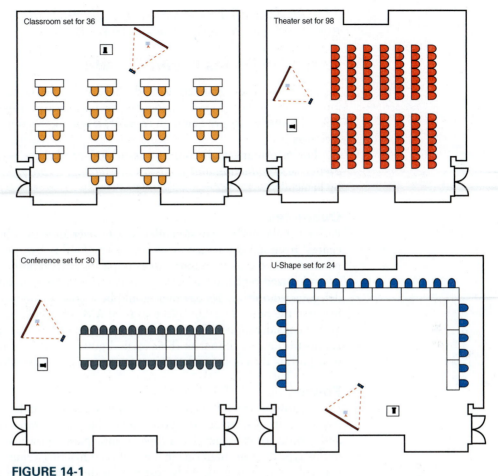

FIGURE 14-1
Traditional venue layouts.

a significant number of attendees to have their backs toward the speaker at the front of the room. If the purpose of the session is to work with table partners, this may not be problematic, but a perpendicular classroom set up is seldom wise when attendees need to be focused on the individual on stage.

Rounds

Round tables are sometimes used for meetings, but are utilized most often for food functions. In smaller break-out sessions, or those meetings requiring a lot of interaction between attendees, round tables facilitate and encourage communication. All the individuals at the table can easily see their table companions and are seated in close enough proximity to one another to allow collaboration.

Many meeting venues use six-foot rounds (i.e., 72 inches in diameter) or less often, five-foot rounds (i.e., 60 inches in diameter). The size of the rounds is important because the diameter dictates how many individuals can comfortably fit. Five-foot rounds can accommodate six to eight individuals, while six-foot rounds may seat eight to ten.

An alternative to full rounds are **crescent rounds**. Crescent rounds may use full-sized round tables, but will not have seats all the way around the table. This is designed so that no one is seated with his or her backs to the head table, and everyone at the table has a clear view of the speaker.

With the changes in expectations for interactive meeting spaces from attendees and meeting planners, multiple new concepts have resulted in creative room layouts. New designs include creating hubs for small groups to be connected. Casual layouts with soft seating like couches, and buffets served at action stations are just the beginning of the future of meetings. Many of these unique set ups require special furniture to be rented, which is available at an additional cost from many venue vendors. Therefore, a venue can be laid out according to the unique vision of the event planner or client.

For information on room set ups, see *Production and Logistics in Meetings, Expositions, Events, and Conventions* by Fenich.

Common Issues Faced On-site

Regardless of where an event is held, there are some issues that all events have in common. Many of these issues are logistic, such as transporting delegates from the airport. The following issues are common to most, if not all, meeting venues, and most, if not all, meetings.

For information on common issues on producing and logistics in meetings and events, see *Production and Logistics in Meeting, Expositions, Events, and Conventions* by Fenich.

Obstacles

Perhaps a planner's greatest challenge is to overcome the obstacles that may hinder delegates' from having a successful event. The facility can present many obstacles that a planner will need to overcome. An example of such an obstacle would be an understaffed or undersized registration desk. Another would be inadequate parking spaces for the delegates who drive. Yet another would be a noise ordinance that prohibits loading out between the hours of 10:00 PM and 6:00 AM. Physical obstacles are not limited to disability considerations. There are also questions of how the delegates will get from their rooms to the gala dinner in their formal gowns if it is raining, and whether the buses transporting the guests to the off-site venue can get to the actual door of the venue.

Power

Most outdoor special events and many events in smaller indoor venues have power requirements that exceed the power available. A generator usually provides this power, and generators are expensive. Properly anticipating power needs is even more important in this type of event than one in a traditional meeting venue. With a generator, the planner will not only pay the daily cost to rent the generator, but a fuel charge as well. Fuel consumption is determined by two factors: how long the generator runs, and how much power is actually drawn from it. The fuel cost will be a multiple of the cost per gallon of the fuel, the time the generator runs, and the power consumption. The planner has control over two of the three elements in this equation.

Any meeting or special event using video or top name entertainment, and more than a few trade show booths or large scenic units will have special power requirements. Power is expensive. The power to run the sound system can be more expensive than the rental of the equipment. Many convention centers offer a discount if the power is requested early. Technical vendors can calculate power requirements fairly easily. If the discount for requesting power early is 30 percent, which is a fairly common discount, it would make sense to order 10 to 15 percent more power than estimated. In this way, ample power is available for less than it would have cost to place the power order after all the detailed requirements had been calculated.

Power charges are not based on consumption, but rather on the maximum amount of power deliverable at any one time. To meter the actual power consumption and charge accordingly is illegal in many states. This would make the facility a utility company and subject to rate regulations. Generator use is charged based on power consumption, but it is based on fuel consumption. A generator that is idling uses fuel even if it is supplying no power. Turning a generator off when it is not needed will save money.

Event professionals involved in events around the globe must be very conscious of local differences. The base voltage may vary: 110 volts in North America versus 220 volts in much of the rest of the world. The style of electrical outlet and corresponding plugs vary widely with over ten different configurations.

Rigging

Plaster ceilings are a production rigger's worst nightmare. Precast concrete roofs with no steel underneath run a close second. Any event involving more than a few hundred people or video image magnification should involve lighting suspended from the ceiling. Unless

A lighting grid suspended from the ceiling.
George G. Fenich

the facility is unusually well equipped for lighting from ceiling positions, lighting must be accomplished by hanging trusses, and hanging trusses involves rigging. Theaters are generally adequately equipped for lighting without hanging trusses, but not necessarily hotels.

The hotel's contracted rigging company will require access to all floor plans not less than two weeks in advance of the event. While two weeks' lead time on a floor plan should be simple for an event contracted a year in advance, generating an accurate floor plan turns out to be a challenge many planners cannot accommodate. In some jurisdictions, the fire marshal, building code inspector, or safety officer can refuse to allow a show to be hung without a detailed hanging plan. Having to cancel a show at the last minute due to failure to submit paperwork can be a career-ending mistake.

Most facilities contract rigging to an outside company for liability protection. This is in addition to the normal reasons one would outsource any task that the facility management may not have enough experience to properly supervise. Given that the rigger's normal job description involves hanging live loads over the heads of the general public, they take their work seriously. This sometimes obstructionist attitude is intended to keep people safe and is not meant to impede the event. Adequate advance notification of schedules and requirements can help ensure that the event venue is hung properly and on schedule.

Floors

It is not safe to assume that just because the building has a ground level loading door big enough to drive a tractor-trailer through, that once it fits through the door, the floor will support it. Even though the floor may be made of four inches of steel-reinforced concrete on the ground, the utility boxes in the floor may not be so well designed. One Orlando area facility dug up and re-poured the concrete around several floor pockets because the constant forklift traffic drove them into the ground. It is also not safe to assume that a certain size scissor lift can fit in the ballroom. For events where these issues are relevant, as part of the site inspection, the planner must ask about the maximum floor load because the information is rarely readily available.

Ballrooms are carpeted, and many hotels insist that plastic sheeting be placed over the ballroom carpet during the move-in and move-out process. If the facility has such a requirement, it is important that the ESC and all technical vendors know about it in advance. The requirement to cover the floor with PolyTack or one of several similar products is becoming more common. Failure to submit a proper floor plan to the people who apply the floor covering, or failure to properly schedule an installation can result in expensive delays.

Many academic theaters have polished wood floors on the stages. Nailing or screwing into them is not recommended, and is generally a fast way to be refused the use of the venue in the future. These floors are not designed for heavy loads such as scissor lifts or forklifts. Staffing and equipment requirements may need to be adjusted to compensate.

Access

Not only must the delegates be able to find the venue and its entrance, but the technical support and catering people need to gain access as well. The design of the loading access can have a significant impact on an event's finances. There is a facility in South Florida where the only loading access to the ballroom is to back a truck along a sea wall for a hundred yards. A 21-foot truck will not make the corner, while a 17-foot truck will. The closest a tractor-trailer can park is a quarter mile away. An event held here, if the technical support equipment were shipped on a tractor-trailer, would need to be unloaded off-site and the equipment trucked into the loading dock using a smaller truck at a considerable additional expense. There is another facility on Florida's west coast where the loading access to the ballrooms is via an open-sided elevator with no top attached on the outside of the building. In this part of Florida, it rains almost every afternoon in the summer. A load scheduled for 4:00 PM in July stands an excellent likelihood of having a problem.

The presence of truck height docks is not enough to guarantee smooth loading. Some facilities, including the WDW Dolphin and the Gaylord Palms, have elevators from the docks to the ballroom. Access to the theater at the Orange County Convention Center involves two elevators, and a push down the hall between them. The number and location of the docks is significant. The Morial Convention Center in New Orleans is all on one level, with loading docks lining one entire side of the building.

Speakers and Entertainers

For a large meeting with multiple speakers and entertainers, keeping track of who is where and what is going on is a monumental task. Recruiting volunteers or hiring temporary staff to assist will make a big difference. The worst thing that can happen is to have a speaker fail to show up for a meeting, and the event professional to not realize it. Likewise, most speakers and entertainers expect some sort of recognition for their time and effort. They may have specialized needs and contractual expectations to be addressed on-site. This is especially true of musicians.

The planner, facility manager, and speaker/entertainer must work together once everyone is on-site for a rehearsal. At this time, the speaker or entertainer should practice his or her presentation on the stage (or in the room) with audiovisual, lighting, music, and so on. Adjustments to the session should be made if appropriate. This is the time for all questions to be answered by the speaker, entertainer, or support personnel.

A new trend is to pre-select sessions or activities with speakers and entertainers of interest, so that attendees come better prepared for a large event. Social media, such as Facebook, Twitter, LinkedIn, Pinterest, Google+, Tumblr, and blogs, can be utilized months in advance for people to begin discussions on a topic. The speaker may facilitate discussion and will design the actual presentation based on what has transpired online. Similarly, some speakers will use this intelligence to assess the attendees' level of knowledge of the topics being discussed. After the session, attendees can be reassessed, and the amount of learning that occurred may be measured.

On-Site Audiovisual

Managing the technology needs and design of a program on-site requires a well-planned approach. Meeting planners are no longer looking for only flip charts and projects, but sophisticated technology options including plasma screens, digital signage, LCD projectors, and intelligent lighting.

A critical piece in planning for and managing the audiovisual needs of the event is selecting a key supplier. The AV provider may or may not be in-house. Some planners opt to travel with their own preferred AV supplier, who is familiar with the event and the organization. The purpose of the partnership is for the supplier to assist the organization in communicating a message(s). Selection of equipment is not the focus; achieving your meeting goals and outcomes is the focus. Sound, lighting, staging, and other equipment needs should be discussed within this context.

During the planning process, key individuals will assemble a **production schedule**. This will provide an overview of the production of each function starting at the installation of equipment to the dismantling of the stage or room set up. This timeline serves as a detailed, step-by-step plan for all parties to follow on-site. It is customary for a production or technical director to be assigned to an event to oversee all technical aspects of the meeting and lead the team of skilled professionals. It is his/her responsibility to ensure that objectives are met, safety and security standards are followed, and the program runs smoothly.

Chapter 11 goes into additional detail on event technology and on-site management.

Ancillary Events

There are a variety of activities that may be incorporated before, during, and after the actual scheduled program. In today's hectic business environment, many people try to squeeze a short vacation into their meeting schedule. More and more, we are seeing husbands, wives, significant others, and children attending meetings as guests. Some meeting attendees tack on a few extra days at the beginning or end of the scheduled meeting to spend some quality time with their family and friends. Likewise, while the meeting attendee is attending workshops and trade shows, the guests want something to keep them occupied. Tours, shopping excursions, cultural events, sport events, dinners, museums, festivals, and theatrical shows are all popular diversions. Every city, no matter how small, has something of interest to explore. The key is not to let these ancillary activities interfere with your overall program objectives. **Ancillary activities** should not be more attractive than the program. However, ancillary activities must be provided, and it is important that they are appropriate to the age, gender, and interests of the guests.

If possible, limit participation in planning ancillary activities for two reasons: additional effort and liability issues. As a meeting/event professional, you need to concentrate on what is going on in the meeting facility. You do not want to worry about whether the bus to the mall is on time. If possible, outsource the management of ancillary activities to a local **destination management company (DMC)**. A DMC is a company that specializes in arranging activities and is an expert on the local area (see Chapter 7 on DMCs, for more information). Likewise, if something should happen and people are injured at an event that you arranged, you do not want to worry about liability issues. A prime example is if child care is offered by the sponsoring organization, additional insurance may be needed to protect the organization from any liability issues. Child care is definitely a service that must be outsourced to a professional child care service. Special licensing is needed to ensure the safety and security of children.

The safest strategy is to provide a list of local activities, and the website address of the DMO. Let the attendees plan their own activities. Be warned: When holding meetings in popular resort locations like Orlando, Florida, or Las Vegas, Nevada, the attractions available can quickly become distractions for the attendees. It is not uncommon to lose a few attendees in Las Vegas when the call of the slot machines is louder than an hour-long workshop on a dry topic.

Meeting and Event Specification Guide

One of the challenges in the meeting and events profession is that, historically, there were few standardized policies, procedures, and terminology. To begin a codification of definitions and standardized practices, an industry-wide task force called the APEX Initiative was created. As mentioned in Chapter 1, APEX stands for Accepted Practices Exchange, and one of its first accomplishments was the development of accepted practices regarding terminology. The committee found that many terms were used interchangeably to describe the document used by a meeting/event professional to communicate specific requirements for a function. Some of these terms included catering event order, meeting résumé, event specifications guide, staging guide operations manual, production schedule, room specs, schedule of services, working agenda, specifications sheet, and group résumé. After a considerable amount of effort and input from all types of meeting/event professionals, hotel convention service managers, DMCs, exhibit managers, and DMOs, the panel created a format that will greatly facilitate the communication between meeting/event professionals and the entities that service their meetings.

The panel developed the **Event Specifications Guide (ESG)**, which is a comprehensive document that outlines the complete requirements and instructions for an event. This document is typically authored by the event/meeting professional and is shared with all appropriate vendors as a vehicle to communicate the expectations of services for a project. The industry-accepted practice is to use the APEX ESG, which can be found on the Events Industry Council website.

The ESG is a three-part document that includes the following:

1. *The Narrative:*   General overview of the meeting or event
2. *Function Schedules:*   Timetable outlining all functions that compose the overall meeting or event
3. *Function Set Up Orders:*   Specifications for each separate function that is part of the overall meeting or event. This is used by the facility to inform set up crews, technicians, catering and banquet staff, and all other staff regarding what is required for each event.

There is also a standardized timetable for communication between the meeting/event professional and the facility and service providers. Although these guidelines may differ depending on the size, timing, and complexity of the individual event, they provide a useful general format.

The ESG contains quite a bit of detailed information. Both the meeting/event professional along with catering/convention services staff and key suppliers will need access to a copy. If any changes are made, they should be recorded in all copies. Fortunately, as technology and connectivity improves, this document will be easier to maintain and update. What was once a five-pound, three-ring binder full of paper forms has been reduced to an app on a mobile device. Changes to the ESG can be made easily and accessed by the appropriate people. What is certain for all meetings is that changes to the ESG are unavoidable. In fact, one of the chief responsibilities of a good meeting/event professional is to react and manage change—often unexpected change.

Size of Event	Submit ESG in Advance	Receive Return From Facility and Vendors
1–500	4 weeks	2 weeks
501–1,000	6 weeks	4 weeks
1,000+	8 weeks	6 weeks

Controlling Costs

In order to stay within budget and reach the financial objectives, it is important to exercise cost control measures. Cost control measures are tools for monitoring the budget. A large event for thousands of people may be managed by only a few meeting planning staff. The opportunities for costly mistakes are rampant. The most important factor is to make sure that the facility understands which person from the sponsoring organization has the authority to make additions or changes to what has been ordered. Typically, the CEO and the meeting planning staff are the only ones who have this **signing authority**. For example, an association board member may have an expensive dinner in the hotel restaurant and say "put it on the association's bill." The restaurant cannot do so without the approval of a person who has signing authority. This helps keep unexpected expenses to a minimum. A review of your expenses should be conducted daily and disputes address each day. Following the event, the invoices or cost projections should be discussed to avoid conflicts after leaving the event destination.

Managing the On-site Team

The organization will need to determine how to staff their meeting/event using full-time employees, temporary staff, and/or volunteers. All staff, regardless of the type, needs to be trained, supervised, motivated, and evaluated. The size of the team will depend on the size and complexity of the event. Again, determining staffing types and service levels should be reflective of the meeting's goals and objectives. It is also important to ensure staffing needs are budgeted, and appropriate resources are allocated to ensure the team is ready on-site. An orientation for employees, temporary staff, and volunteers should take place on-site, followed by a tour of the meeting space, and an opportunity to answer any questions of the team. Additionally, a handbook should be distributed to all team members that details information on the event, the roles and responsibilities of the team, key contact list, answers to frequently asked questions, maps of the facilities, and additional important information.

Employees

The planning team should carefully determine which organizational employees should travel to the event and how they will be utilized on-site. Full-time staff should serve as supervisors to a variety of areas, such as registration, educational sessions, and the exhibition. These individuals are already trained on the needs of the attendees, the type of group and their needs, the culture of the organization, and the expectations set by the leadership of the group. They should serve as a source of information for temporary staff and volunteers, assist with training and supervision, and serve as role models.

The organization will need to budget for the travel of employees. In most cases, air travel, ground transportation, hotel accommodations, and meals must be covered. The organization should have a clear travel policy in place, and clearly communicate whether other expenses such as dry cleaning, phone or internet expenses, parking at the airport, and so on, will be covered. Depending on the location of the event, these expenses can add up quickly, so the organization will need to conduct a cost/benefit analysis to determine employees on-site.

Notably, not all roles can simply be covered by a temporary employee or volunteer. The organization must remember that key on-site positions should be staffed with employees. These areas include overseeing registration, important high-profile functions, production of the general sessions, logistics of the exhibition, and food and beverage guarantees. These areas can affect the outcomes of the meeting and have significant budget implications.

Temporary Staff

Using temporary staff is a good alternative for roles that do not require specialized training (such as registration software, accounting, or security). Facilities may require that organizations use temporary staff for areas focused on safety and security. Medical and security personnel, if required, are typically local, hourly staff or contractors that are familiar with the facility and local services (hospitals, medical clinics, etc.).

During an event, temporary staff will represent the organization and, to attendees and guests, may appear to be employees of the organization hosting the meeting. Therefore, it is imperative that they are trained on the service expectations of the group, briefed on the make-up and needs of the attendees, supervised by employees that share the goals and objectives of the meeting, advised on policies and procedures, and evaluated on their performance. The role of a temporary staff member should be clearly defined to avoid conflicts in different scenarios. For instance, the contracted staff will need to know if they can issue a refund to an attendee (registration), or if they have the authority to remove an exhibitor for inappropriate behavior (security). Communication between temporary staff and key employees is vital to the success of the event.

The DMO or facility can recommend staffing agencies that provide temporary employees. As mentioned previously, these workers should not replace employees in key roles, but provide specialized service roles to support the operations of the event. Planners can contract with agencies or individuals to provide support and save money on travel expenses.

Volunteers

Most events rely heavily on volunteers. A volunteer is someone who is giving his/her time and expertise to assist with the operation of an event at no charge. Again, volunteers should not be used in roles that require specialized services (such as security), nor should they replace employees in key roles at the meeting. However, they can be utilized in many ways, including greeting attendees at the main entry points of the facility, providing directions or destination/facility information to attendees, assisting in the registration area with distribution of badges or materials, or monitoring educational sessions.

It is important to note that volunteers still need to be trained, supervised, and evaluated. Like temporary employees, they will need to be informed on the history, goals, and objectives of the organization; given detailed profile information on attendees and guests; provided clear role expectations; instructed on their level of authority; given a key contact for questions or for directing someone who needs further assistance; and directed on what to wear and the hours they are expected to work. Volunteers can be recruited from many sources, including: (1) members of the association or organization assisting for reduced registration rates or simply to give back, (2) local professionals interested in assisting the specific event, (3) community members who are retired and interested in serving the destination, or even (4) college students looking for professional experience. The DMO or local contacts can provide options for recruiting volunteers.

Volunteers are not paid an hourly wage, but there are expenses associated with volunteers. Planners will need to consider and communicate if they are providing uniforms, meals, reimbursement for parking, or other related expenses. There should be no confusion on what is provided and what is not provided for volunteers. Also, planners should communicate if there is a minimum number of hours volunteers are expected to work. For instance, volunteers may be required to commit to two shifts of four hours each. This will help justify training and providing basic services to volunteers.

Another consideration is motivating volunteers. Organizations want to retain their volunteers for future events, so ensuring they have a meaningful experience is important. There should also be recognition of the volunteers, either during or after the event, to show appreciation of their time and expertise. A simple certificate, small gift, or thank you after the event can go a long way. Some organization host volunteer appreciation events, and even designate a volunteer of the year award.

On-site Communications

Personal Communications

The event professional must bear in mind that they will always be involved in personal types of communication. Personal communication falls under two techniques: formal and informal. While these techniques are self-explanatory, the event professional and their constituents must be aware of when and how to use each. Formal communication occurs in business settings, when interacting with officials and dignitaries, and so on. Informal communication occurs within groups of peers in non-business settings. It is critical that the correct technique be used in the setting where it is demanded.

The two methods used for transmission of information are written and oral. The importance of oral communication skills cannot be stressed enough. Due to the multifaceted nature of the meetings/events industry, the event professional interacts with various stakeholders in order to achieve the desired results.

There are four categories of communication including written, verbal, visual, and behavioral. The following figure provides examples for each category.

Communication Strategies

Written	Verbal	Visual	Behavioral
Training manual	Briefings	Photographs	Videos
Memo	Meetings	Displays	Working practices
Letters	Radio conversations	Models	Role modeling
Email	One-to-one discussions	Demonstrations	Nonverbal communication
Handbooks	Instruction	Printed slogans	Social networking
Staff newsletters	Telephone conversations	Posters	
Reports	Training	Videos	
Information bulletins	Word-of-mouth messages	Internet	
Checklists			

Here are some guidelines for improving communication within the event team.

Establish the Level of Priority: It is important to establish the level of priority immediately. Emergency situations are of course the highest risk for any event, and communication about an incident or potential incident should be given top priority.

Identify the Receiver: By identifying the receiver, the event professional will be able to match their message to the receiver's needs, thus demonstrating empathy. The message will also reach the correct target.

Know the Objective: Clarity in communication is often linked to the development of an action objective. If the event professional knows what they want to achieve, they will be able to express themselves more easily and clearly. Stating a problem and its ramifications is often only the first stage. By indicating what needs to be done, the event professional can more easily achieve the objective and reach an agreed outcome.

Review the Message in Your Head: In preparing to send a message, the event professional should structure the given communication effectively. It is also useful to conceptualize the receiver's likely response.

Communicate in the Language of the Other Person: If examples and illustrations are used that the receiver will understand, the message will be more easily comprehended.

Clarify the Message: If the receiver appears, from his or her nonverbal behavior, not to understand the message, clarification is essential.

Do Not React Defensively to a Critical Response: Asking questions can help the event professional to understand why the receiver has responded defensively. In this way, the event professional can be assured they have reached a common understanding.

Use of Technology

Determine and Acquire Communication Equipment and Resources
The event professional must be knowledgeable about communication equipment and resources: what is needed, where to get it, and who can supply it. This is done while being cognizant of the budget. The event professional must set realistic concepts and expectations and not put forth pipe dreams that the client cannot afford. The event professional must analyze event needs, taking into consideration the type and size of the site/venue along with its users, attendees, staff, and volunteers.

The following strategies can help to develop effective communications between users:

- Identify specific information needs of group members.
- Use simple words in the language of the conference and/or host country.
- Allocate buddies or partners to develop sub-teams.
- Use graphics to impart information.
- Rotate roles.
- Provide all users with opportunities to participate in the group.
- Develop the group's rituals and a group identity.

Emergency personnel—different constituents require different equipment and resources. Emergency personnel need dependable, battery powered communication devices. They may also require non-powered devices such as flag semaphores, reflective batons, and even signs to help them communicate with and direct others during emergencies. The event professional should also assess the adequacy of emergency lighting and illuminated directional signage (battery powered exit signs) in any venue being used. This signage is a form of communication equipment.

Attendees—communication with attendees will most often utilize written and/or digital text such as the event program, list of activities, signs indicating what is happening in a given place and when, and so on. During presentations, AV equipment, such as microphones, amplified sound, and projection equipment, will be used. For more extravagant events, special effects lighting, signage, and so on can be used. Public address systems may also come into play.

Determine Technology Appropriate for Meeting/Convention/Event

Mobile communication—Reducing waste and the focus on sustainability has required event professionals to plan and execute on-site communication in the most efficient and effective way possible. As technology evolves, the primary thrust as well as challenge for the event professional is in moving content onto mobile platforms. With the explosion of smartphones and tablet computers designed for mobility, stakeholders are expecting communication to be available and easily accessible on these devices.

The effectiveness of mobile communication devices comes from an increasing gravitation toward meeting enhancement using online social networking tools such as Twitter.

- More demands from the meeting professional for innovative technology such as polling tools.
- A broadening scope of event technologies such as RFP and bidding software.
- Demands from delegates and speakers, especially younger ones who have grown up in a digital world, for increasing the use of sophisticated multimedia and other technologies that facilitate the flow of ideas between them and their audiences.
- The growing prominence of mobile applications.
- The growing adoption of events that combine in-person and virtual aspects.
- Given the extensive use of the internet, it is critical that the meeting/event professional ascertain that the facility has sufficient *bandwidth* to handle the traffic the event will generate.

Types of Equipment

- *Smartphone*: The primary piece of communication equipment used by event professionals and their attendees is the Smartphone. Most large events will create an app that contains all the critical information about the event. Texting is used regularly. Sometimes people will actually call each other.

- *PA System*: Public address systems are used to communicate with large groups of people. They are usually hard wired, and thus not affected by battery drain. The event professional should ascertain whether the PA systems in the venues have back up power supplies that enable the PA system to be used during emergencies.

- *Walkie Talkies*: These are two-way radios that provide secure, reliable, and instant communication between event professionals.

- *Computer-based*: Computers and their equivalents are the backbone of modern communications. Thus, having a firm grasp of desktop publishing software (e.g. Microsoft Office Suites) is invaluable as an event professional, and essential for good written communication. The event professional should consider where their information is stored, besides on the electronic device itself. One alternative is external storage, which often uses a USB port. A newer alternative is Web storage, often referred to as cloud computing. Here, information is stored on a remote server and accessed via the Internet. The obvious advantage is that the data or information can be accessed from anywhere and by anyone with an access code. The downside is that it is dependent upon Internet access.

Monitor On-Site Communications

The last aspect of on-site communication at meetings and events is to monitor. The event professional must keep track and be up to date on what is being communicated, when it is being communicated, and how it is being communicated. All established policies, protocols, and hierarchies must be adhered to. Equipment must be on hand when needed and in good working order. If any of these things are not correct, the event professional must make adjustments and corrections. The event professional is the one ultimately responsible for every aspect of the meeting/event.

Public Relations

What Is Public Relations?

Public relations is defined as the effective management of relationships and communications, in order to influence behaviors and achieve objectives. As it relates to the meetings/events industry, public relations can be defined as the "presentation of an event via the media or other outlets, stressing the benefits and desirability of such an event" (CIC, 2011). All events involve public relations strategies, some on a small scale and others on a bigger scale.

Public relations activities involve much more than media relations. They include all communications, and the development of relations with all event publics from attendees, to sponsors, speakers, the community where the event will be held, the government, and the organization's members and leadership, among others. It also involves the management of a crisis or unexpected situation in a way that the event image remains positive and, therefore, attractive for constituents.

Professional relationships, just like friendships, grow and strengthen with time and collaboration. In this sense, the relationships built today with the community, the media, organization members, attendees, sponsors, vendors, and other people involved in the execution of the event plan will likely last for years, making the event organization smoother, and probably more successful, each year.

Develop and Manage Media Relations

Media will play a key role in the publicity plan, as they will be responsible for generating the publicity we look for. The catch is that we can't control whether they will support our event or not. Nevertheless, we can help them make the decision of supporting us by developing positive (and hopefully long lasting) relations with them.

The first thing to must know when working with media is that writers and editors specialize in different areas. Therefore, the contact person that is in charge of an event may not be the same as the one that writes about political events and so forth. It is important that we establish a relationship with the right person. In other words, the editor in charge of political events will only cover your event if it is of interest for his audience and if it relates to his/her area of expertise. If you send your communications to any editor, without knowing his/her area of expertise, the communication will likely be ignored. Depending on the event, media may be all over you, wanting to get the latest news minute-by-minute or just not interested at all. Different strategies can be used to keep them informed and interested.

News Releases

A news release or press release is a story, written in third person, that helps communicate important information to the media so that they can write or talk about a particular event. During the event planning process, a series of these releases can be sent to the media to start generating interest and build excitement. The release can be sent alone by email or be distributed as part of a full press kit.

When writing a news release the event professional should do the following.

- *Think Like a Reporter:*   Reporters receive hundreds of these communications and will not pay attention to them unless they are provided with something that can really make their jobs easier, like a story that can attract their audience. Unless this is achieved, reporters will likely ignore the event professional, not return their calls, and will not make the decision to cover the event.

- *Develop the Story from the Reporter's Perspective:*   When we write, sometimes we assume that others know everything we do, but this is not accurate. It is likely that reporters will not recognize the event name when they get the release, and, even if they do, they will not know the details, as they have not been part of the planning process.

- *Make Sure to Include the Important Details:*

     What is the event all about?

     When will the event take place?

     Where will it take place?

     Why is this newsworthy?
     Who will be there?

- *Get to the Point and Provide Unique Information:*   Sometimes including a quote from a well-recognized industry leader can be attractive to the media. Twisting the story to touch people's hearts is almost always a winning formula.

- *Make Sure the Message Sent Is Clear, Easy to Understand, and Accurate*

- *Write Persuasively, but Do Not Lie:*   Lying is not ethical and will put the event professional in a difficult position sooner or later.

- *Make Sure the Communication Does Not Have Grammatical Errors:*   Sending communications with errors make an event professional look unprofessional.

Once the news release is written, it needs to be distributed. To do so, do the following.

- Have a database containing the names and contact information of media outlets that should be approached. The database should contain at a minimum: the name of the reporter or editor, area of expertise, email, phone, and the way each media outlet prefers to receive communications. Obtaining this information can be time consuming and frustrating. Therefore, the event professional should collect this information ahead of time and have it ready when they want to send the communication.

- Send communications soon after writing the release, so that the information contained in them is still new when the media gets it.

- Use the proper way to communicate with media. If they prefer fax, then use it.

- Address communications to the correct person.

- Follow up by phone the day after sending communications to make sure the news release was received. This will give the event professional an idea if the media outlets are interested in covering the event, and will give the event professional an opportunity to answer questions. Reporters are usually very busy and will not necessarily answer all the voice mails they receive. Practice patience and, most importantly, be respectful and professional.

- Check the media outlets to see if they have written an editorial or have announced the event. This is another way to assess the effectiveness of the plan.

Attract and Accommodate Media

Unfortunately, it would be impossible for the media to cover every single event in town. Therefore, the event professional's job is to make enough noise as to get their attention. Doing it requires only one little thing: providing them with something that is newsworthy.

The best way to attract media attention is to build interest by creating a series of stories and events that surround the main event. These activities must be outlined in the plan. For instance, when an event professional is bringing a citywide convention to a city, he or she may calculate the economic impact the congress will have on the local economy, and then communicate it to the local media. This is certainly interesting for the local community, and may be a good way to get their support. If the event is supporting a local charity the event professional could also develop a story based on this fact and this could generate interest among potential attendees or sponsors, and so forth.

Once the event professional has attracted media, they must be ready to answer all their inquiries, and accommodate all their needs. To that end they must have someone on staff assigned to answer media inquiries immediately. Voice mails and emails must be returned within 24 hours, remembering that there is media coverage every day including holidays. Some of the things the media will expect from event professionals on-site are

- A media registration area, separated from attendee registration.

- Someone on staff assigned to accommodate the media's needs; this person should receive members of the media during registration, and introduce him or herself as their facilitator for whatever need they might have.

- Complimentary tickets to enter the event and give them preferential access to special events, speakers, and sponsors.

- A media or press room with access to computers, Internet (Wi-Fi), phone, fax, electric outlets where they can connect their electronic devices, tables and chairs where they can sit and write their stories, and a small table in a quiet place to conduct interviews. It is always nice to provide a refreshment break in the media room.

- Someone ready to provide media with the latest, most accurate news as quickly as possible.

Once the event is over, a news release should be sent to the media communicating the event's most important outcomes. It is a good idea to include some good quality pictures the media can use in their publications. Always remembering that, in order for event professionals to publish an image, they must have permission, not only from the photographer, but also from the individuals portrayed in the picture.

If people have been reading and listening about a specific event for months, it is likely that they are interested in the outcomes. If promoting a fundraising event, the event professional should inform everyone of the amount of money raised and what it will be used for. This will help build credibility, which will, in turn, make the path smoother when pursuing media attention and community support in the future.

Saying thank you is always advised, not only to the media, but also to all constituents. To that end, writing thank you letters or emails may help enhance relationships with supporters, and may even ensure getting their support again in the future.

Table 14-1 provides some tips to accommodate and manage media before, during, and after an event.

TABLE 14-1

Tips to Accommodate and Manage Media Before, During, and After an Event

Before the Event
• Editors and reporters focus on different industries. Make sure to communicate with the right person.
• Use their preferred way of communication.
• Follow up by phone after sending a news release.
• Build interest by creating stories around the event.
• Treat media with respect and professionalism.
• Follow protocols and make media aware of them.
• Appoint someone to be the contact person for all media inquiries.
• Answer media inquiries immediately.
• Invite the media to the event and provide them with complimentary tickets.

During the Event
• Have a media registration area, separated from attendee registration.
• Make sure someone is available on staff to accommodate media needs and to provide the latest news.
• Have a pressroom equipped with Internet, phone, fax, computer access, electric outlets, and so on.
• Have a quiet place available to conduct interviews.
• Provide access to speakers, sponsors, and other VIPs.
• Provide preferential access to special events.

After the Event
• Send a press release with the event's most important outcomes.
• Send pictures to reporters and editors.
• Call supporters and thank them for their help.

Public relations activities involve much more than media relations, they include all communications, and the development of relations with all event publics. Public relations are a fundamental element of the event's marketing plan and will help control people's perceptions regarding an event.

Media Outlets

Various traditional and advanced media, including podcasting, mobile advertising, YouTube, and social media, can reach mass target consumers. The MEEC industries can effortlessly utilize media outlets through Internet technology by broadcasting their messages—as long as the message content is well developed and properly worded in advance. Messages can be created by independent producers and be distributed with an affordable budget, especially when social media is used. For example, a podcast could be downloaded with one click to a mobile device. Messages can be heard and watched through video or audio files, be attached into a blog's file exchange, or generate followers via Facebook's "follow" link. Podcasting can generate a good return on investment by generating a high volume of listeners.

More and more groups use social media to provide daily communications and news announcements. Many companies have benefited from word of mouth when advertising on Facebook and other websites. Blogs are a place where individuals can freely share their thoughts and event activities, with global participation from others. Interactions among members can also stimulate and enhance the visibility of advertisement and promotional activities. Customers also rely on other customers' product or service reviews. However, the validity of reviews has been questioned because fake customers have posted some reviews. Increasingly, online brokers only allow real customers who purchased or booked products and services, or participated in events to review through that particular broker's site (e.g., Expedia).

Selecting and Managing Spokespersons

Not everyone can verbalize a message properly or remain calm and professional during a crisis. To that end, it is important to select a spokesperson who will be responsible for communicating with media on behalf of the event. Some organizations decide to find someone in-house to manage this, while others prefer to outsource it. Depending on the scope of the event, the person selected could be the president of the host organization, or a public relations manager appointed to handle all event communications. In other instances, the organization chooses a celebrity speaker or someone renowned to manage communications, with the hope that this person will become a magnet for people and the media. For example, if the event professional is planning a national culinary fest, they may select a nationally renowned chef to be the spokesperson. The host organization's executive director may also serve as the spokesperson for a nonprofit event, while the president of the Olympic Committee may be appropriate for the Olympic Games. In any case, the person in charge should:

- Be knowledgeable and available to speak about any situation or detail of the event when needed.
- Understand the message that is to be sent and the image it is meant to portray.
- Have a proper image that is aligned with the hosting organization and the event.
- Be a good communicator, capable of communicating an idea clearly, verbally or in writing; controlling his/her facial expressions; and remaining calm in any situation.
- Have the right combination of knowledge and character to establish a healthy relationship with the media.

If the person selected as the spokesperson is not involved in the planning of the event, event professionals must meet with him/her regularly to inform him/her of what has been going on and the way the organization would like to handle it.

Pre-Convention Meetings

A day or two prior to the actual beginning of a meeting, the meeting/event professional should partake in a pre-convention (pre-con) meeting. This is a gathering of all critical people representing all departments within the facility and other outside vendors or suppliers who will be part of the team. In addition to the convention services manager (CSM), who is the primary contact for the meeting/event professional, the following representatives may be requested to attend the meeting: catering or banquet manager or F&B director; audiovisual representative; sales manager; accounting manager; front desk manager; bell staff or concierge; housekeeping manager; security manager; engineering manager; switchboard manager; recreation manager; and all outside service providers, such as transportation, special events, and decorators. Often, the general manager of the facility will stop by, be introduced, and welcome the meeting/event professional. The pre-con meeting allows the meeting/event professional to meet and visually connect with all the various people servicing the event. In most cases, this will be the first time the meeting/event professional meets many of these people. Each representative is introduced, and any changes or additions of duties in their respective departments are reviewed. After the individual departments have been discussed, the meeting/event professional should release the person to return to his or her duties.

The ESG is reviewed page by page with the CSM. All changes are made, guarantees are confirmed, and last-minute instructions are conveyed. The pre-con is basically the last time the meeting/event professional has the opportunity to make any major changes without disrupting the facility. Once an event is in progress, it is very difficult, and potentially costly, to make major changes. If the meeting/event professional decides one hour before a session that the room should be set with only chairs rather than with tables and chairs as listed on the function sheet or banquet event order, it can cause havoc. Additional staff may be needed to remove the tables, and the meeting/event professional may be charged for the labor. Sometimes, the last-minute request of a meeting/event professional cannot be fulfilled. If 50 tables are requested just prior to an event, the hotel may not have them available or may not have scheduled staff for set up.

THE FATHER OF THE BRIDE

A wedding reception was being hosted at a snow skiing resort in the off-season. The sales manager developed the ESG, and everything appeared to be in order as the wedding party and guests arrived. As a special favor for the father of the bride, the event manager made sure a bottle of his favorite liquor was stocked at the bar. Especially since he was paying for the reception. Shortly after the reception began, the father of the bride became irate and approached the event manager. He demanded to know where the popcorn was that should have been on the bar. Popcorn is not usually provided at wedding receptions and was not listed in the ESG. Since the resort was miles from the nearest town, by the time someone went and got it, the reception would be over. This simple omission from the ESG caused a lack of satisfaction for the client.

Post-Convention Review

At the conclusion of a major meeting, the meeting/event professional will create a written document to record all key events of the meeting. This is used for planning the next meeting. It also serves as a report card for the facility and the meeting manager. It will include what went right as well as what went wrong. Then, a post-convention (post-con) meeting is held. It is smaller than the pre-con and may include the planning staff, the CSM, the F&B director, the audiovisual manager, and a representative from the accounting department. This is the time to address any discrepancies in billing, service failures, and problems, or to praise facility staff for a job well done. Most major meetings will have a post-con; smaller meetings may not. If the organization is returning to the destination or venue the following year, it is important to openly discuss lessons learned on both sides to ensure the issues are addressed and corrected. However, if the event will move to a different city, it is a time to re-cap the event and note improvements.

Evaluation

Creating and implementing most meetings is a team effort. Many meeting/event professionals will conduct an evaluation after each meeting to obtain feedback from the attendees, exhibitors, facility staff, outsourced contractors, and anyone else involved in the event. Individual sessions may be evaluated to determine whether speakers did a good job and whether the education was appropriate. Overall, evaluations may collect data on such things as the comfort of the hotel, ease of transportation to the location, desirability of location, quality of F&B, special events and networking opportunities, and the number and quality of exhibitors at a trade show or convention. This information may be collected by a written questionnaire after the event, as well as by telephone, association or corporate website, or by Web-based collection methods. One of the fastest and least expensive is to broadcast an email with a link to the electronic questionnaire. Many software packages are available that will design, distribute, collect data, and tabulate results. The data concerning speakers and logistics will assist the meeting/event professional and program planning committee to improve the programming for subsequent years.

The use of electronic **audience response systems (ARS)** has gained in popularity as costs for renting the equipment or purchasing software have dropped significantly. ARS allows meeting/event professionals to survey a variety of stakeholders via handheld devices, or a smartphone app that transmits information to the meeting/event professional in real time. This allows the meeting/event professional to make adjustments to the meeting while it is still going on and can provide valuable data for future events.

Evaluations can be time-consuming and expensive to design and implement. Unfortunately, some of the data collected by meeting/event professionals are often filed away and not used appropriately—especially if the results are negative toward the event. No board of directors or CEO wants to hear that the site they selected to hold a meeting did not meet attendees' expectations. However, negative comments may ultimately turn into a favorable marketing tool. A good evaluation form is simple, concise, and can be completed in a minimal amount of time. A good source for questions can be to review your event goals and objectives. If the meeting is an annual event, it is important to ask similar questions each year so that data may be collected and analyzed over time.

Timing is also an issue with administering evaluations. If data is collected on-site during or immediately after an event, it may increase the response rate. The meeting/event professional can remind attendees to complete and return evaluations before moving on to the next session. Other meeting/event professionals prefer to wait a few days to ask for feedback. This gives the attendee time to digest what actually occurred at the meeting and form an objective opinion when not clouded by the excitement of the event.

The process of evaluating a meeting should begin in the early stages of meeting planning and tie in with the meeting objectives. Costs for development, dissemination, analysis, and reporting should be included in the meeting budget. The evaluation serves as a valuable component of a meeting's history by recording what worked or did not work for a particular event. It is a cyclical process whereby the evaluation results feed directly into next year's meeting objectives. Committees plan most large meetings. Evaluation results are how information is passed from one committee to the next.

Summary

Producing a meeting or event requires a skilled team to execute the meeting plan. Each area of the event—registration, food and beverage, audiovisual, housing, speakers and entertainers, and ancillary events—must be carefully managed on-site. The event specification guide contains all the details of each function, and important information for the on-site team to review. The event team consisting of staff members, temporary and contracted staff, and volunteers assume many roles to execute the meeting plan. Communicating with the team, the attendees, and the general public requires an intentional strategy, skilled professionals, and dedicated resources. Before, during, and after the meeting, the team should meet to discuss successes, concerns, lessons learned, and improvements to the event plan.

Because of the complexity of the meeting production process, this chapter can only highlight some of the activities involved. The book *Production and Logistics in Meetings, Expositions, Events and Conventions* provides more detail on the production aspects of MEEC.

CASE STUDY

Dilemmas for the New Event Planner

Jack is the meeting and event coordinator at The Almedia in Florida. The beautiful 500-room hotel is located right on the beach and features many luxurious amenities. The property includes three meeting rooms, two ballrooms, and ample amounts of outdoor space for events. The beautiful outdoor area is very popular for weddings and receptions.

Chloe, the new event planner, is getting ready to produce her first event on her own. It will be a reception for V Pharmaceuticals with an estimated 100 attendees. The event is planned outside for 4 P.M. on a Friday. Chloe has been working with V for months and assures Jack that everything will run smoothly.

The event planning process was smooth, but on the day of the event everything seemed to go wrong. Chloe got to work late because she was stuck in traffic. This did not put her in a good mood. When she got there, she checked her email, and saw an email from V Pharmaceuticals. The email was sent last night and they wanted to change their number of attendees to 200. Mr. Vladimir apologized for not letting Chloe know sooner but hoped that she could handle the changes. Frantic, Chloe immediately called the hotel restaurant to let them know of the changes. They planned to serve a lot of seafood and were worried about having enough. Chloe immediately got on the phone with their seafood distributers and inquired about getting more. They informed her they did not have all of the items she needed but they could provide her with some alternatives. Chloe gave them an attitude but eventually agreed to change the menu a little bit.

After the phone calls, Chloe went outside to check on the set up. Mr. Vladimir requested that waiters serve the food, as well as a bar, and a space for socializing, and tables. Chloe was enraged when she saw a buffet style set up for the food. She screamed at the staff to fix it and follow the

(Continued)

directions they were given. Chloe also noticed that the flowers and decorations were not properly set up. She screamed at the staff again. When one of the servers called out of work that was the last straw. Chloe began yelling at everyone, even some guests heard her.

By 3:30 P.M. everything was set up as planned and all the food was almost ready. The guests soon arrived and the event went great and the attendees had no idea about the problems Chloe had earlier in the day. Chloe planned everything for the event, but she did not think of what might go wrong. She was not prepared for any problems, and did not know how to deal with them. Chloe reflected on the day and realized she acted very unprofessional. If she wanted to continue in the event business she would have to learn to prepare for anything and be able to handle the unexpected.

1. How would you have handled each problem?

2. How should Chloe prepare for the future, and the unexpected problems that may arise?

Produced by George G. Fenich from East Carolina University

Key Words and Terms

For definitions, see the Glossary.

ancillary activities
audience response systems (ARS)
auditorium style
banquet event order (BEO)
classroom style

crescent rounds
destination management company (DMC)
Event Specifications Guide (ESG)
guarantee

pre-con
production schedule
signing authority

Review and Discussion Questions

1. What is the difference between the food and beverage projection and the final guarantee?

2. Describe the benefit of the meeting planner managing ancillary events.

3. What roles should volunteers and temporary (paid) staff be assigned to on-site? What critical roles should a full-time staff member perform?

4. How has technology advanced to better communicate with attendees or the public?

5. Articulate the key principles of a good press release.

6. What is the primary purpose of the pre-conference meeting? What is the primary purpose of the post-conference meeting?

About the Chapter Contributors

Amanda Cecil, PhD, is an Associate Professor in the Department of Tourism, Conventions and Event Management at Indiana University. Her teaching and research focus on event tourism and business travel.

Previous Chapter Contributor

Curtis Love, PhD, Emeritus Associate Professor at the William F. Harrah Hotel College at the University of Nevada Las Vegas.

MEEC events are held around the globe.
Markus Mainka/Alamy Stock Photo

CHAPTER 15

International Aspects in MEEC

Chapter Objectives

- Articulate the ways in which MEEC varies around the globe.

- Discuss ownership, sponsorship, and management models important for international meetings and gatherings.

- Recognize important international meeting and trade fair associations.

- Name some specific considerations that are necessary to think through for successful international MEEC events.

The growth of international communications and travel has brought about impressive changes in how the world does business. Thirty years ago, only the largest companies were considered to be international. Today, there are few large companies that do not have an international presence.

Consequently, the meetings, expositions, events, and conventions (MEEC) industries have expanded internationally. In this chapter, we look at how the international scope of MEEC has evolved and how it differs in various parts of the world.

The Union of International Fairs (UFI) publishes regular, and impressive, statistics about the international **trade fair** industry. In their latest figures, UFI estimated that

31,000 exhibitions are held annually, occupying 1.3 billion square feet of total net exhibition space. These events feature 4.4 million exhibitors and welcome 260 million visitors. UFI values the global exhibition industry at USD55 billion.

International meetings also contribute greatly to the economy. For example, in the creation of jobs: 214,000 jobs were created in Australia and up to one million were created in the United Kingdom. Regardless of the location, the purposes of international meetings and exhibitions remain the same—communication, learning, networking, and marketing.

How MEEC Varies around the Globe

Despite similarities of purpose, cultural and business influences have created different models for MEEC happenings in various parts of the world. Chinese incentive travel, for example, can be very large indeed: Tiens Group took 6,400 of their employees on a four-day visit to France to celebrate the twentieth anniversary of their company. Highlights included a private viewing of the Louvre Museum in Paris. They also formed a human-made phrase on Nice beach, which at the time was recorded by the Guinness World of Records as the largest of its kind. It read, "Tiens's Dream is Nice in the Côte d'Azur." The incentive is estimated to have cost USD14.6 million.

THE WORLD'S LARGEST FAIRS

The Canton Fair

China Import and Export Fair, also known as the Canton Fair, has been held in Guangzhou every spring and autumn since 1957. In 2016, the exhibition occupied over 12 million square feet and featured almost 60,000 booths. It attracted 24,500 exhibitors and 188,000 buyers.

Hannover Messe (Fair)

In 2016, 6,500 international exhibitors met over 190,000 visitors. Of these, almost a third were international visitors, especially from the United States and China. The show reported that 5.6 million business contacts were made over the five days of the show. It is important to note that the organizers also held more than 1,700 lectures and panels on topics about industrial technology. Combining exhibition floors and conferences is a growing trend, called the ConFex trend by UFI's CEO, Kai Hattendorf, who points out that attendees come for knowledge acquisition, especially regarding innovation in their industry sector, not just for negotiating the purchase of goods and services.

The fair focuses on core industrial technology in:

- Industrial automation
- Energy
- Digital factory
- Industrial supply
- Research and technology

One of many buildings at the Canton Fair, which is located in Guangzhou, China.
Takatoshi Kurikawa/Alamy Stock Photo

The legendary Stratos brand–activation experience, organized by the Austrian multinational company, RedBull, is another example of a truly global international business event. After five years of planning with a staff of 300, including 70 scientists and engineers, Felix Baumgartner jumped from the stratosphere, at an altitude of 128,100 feet (or four times higher than most passenger jets fly), and set a new speed world record at 833.9 miles per hour. The freefall took place in New Mexico but was televised by 40 TV stations from around the world and, very importantly, it became a live stream sensation on YouTube, watched by eight million followers.

This chapter will focus primarily on conventions and exhibitions as they have experienced exponential and sustained growth over the past decades. This increase has been well documented. The International Congress and Convention Association (ICCA) concluded, in their 50-year study looking at aggregated figures for each five-year period of international association meeting data, that the number of regularly occurring, internationally rotating association meetings was increasing by 100 percent every ten years, and has been consistently doing so for the last half century with no signs of a slowdown. The same picture appears to be true for trade fairs. Kai Hattendorf, Managing Director of UFI, the global association for trade show stakeholders, commented on data from the body's Global Exhibition Barometer by saying that some economists are predicting that the exhibition industry will outperform the global economy in its growth rate.

This section deals with the types of exhibitions and conventions held in Europe, Asia, Australia, Africa, and the Middle East, with a discussion of how they differ in scope and operation; and what areas of the world are embracing such events as a primary method of marketing. Included at the end of this chapter is a short list of international trade fair and meetings organizations.

Europe

The trade fair industry's roots are in Europe. During the Middle Ages, the concept began with farmers and craftsmen bringing their products and wares to the town center to link with their customers. Although the wars of last century devastated European industry, today Europe is the focal point of international trade fairs and exhibitions.

There are two primary reasons for this. First is location—Europe has always been the crossroads of the world. International hub airports in Frankfurt, London, Amsterdam, Paris, and Madrid enable visitors and cargo to arrive easily from all parts of the world. In addition, a superlative network of rail transportation within Europe enables many cities to be within speedy reach of one another. For example, the Eurostar train links London to Paris and Brussels within two hours. The second reason for the growth of trade fairs is Europe's industrial base. With reconstruction help from the United States, Europe recovered its manufacturing and distribution base within a few decades of World War II. With the help of their governments, European industrial centers developed excellent trade fair facilities.

Germany is usually thought of as the center of industry and trade fairs in Europe. Spending by international visitors to Germany on business travel has reached over USD18 billion per year, and four of the world's ten largest exhibition centers can be found here in Hannover, Frankfurt, Cologne, and Dusseldorf.

The Largest Exhibition Venue

Hannover Fairgrounds is the world's largest exhibition site. It features almost 11 million square feet of exhibit space in 27 exhibit halls and an open-air display area. The site includes a Convention Center with 35 conference rooms, 42 restaurants seating 14,000, parking facilities for 50,000, banks, laundry, pharmacy, and Münchner Halle—the world's largest trade fair beer hall. Hannover Fairgrounds offers separate units that provide partitioned areas with their own infrastructure so that several events can run concurrently. More importantly, the regional government and the management company have worked together to establish excellent transportation and lodging facilities.

REPORT FROM CeBIT 2017

CeBIT, the world's biggest high-tech fair in terms of visitors, attracted around 200,000 visitors. Over 3,000 companies from 70 countries participated in CeBIT 2017. Germany's chancellor attended, as did Japan's prime minister. The latter represented the fair's Partner Country for this year.

For 2018, the show has plans to transform itself into "Europe's No. 1 platform and festival for digital technology, innovation and business development for the digital economy," according to a Deutsche Messe spokesperson. It will move to June to enable activities around its theme to take place in the open air in a campus-style set up, and will deliberately aim to appeal to emotions and to Generation Y attendees, with a mixture of entertainment, product demonstrations, dialogue, and party-style-get-togethers.

Italy is another focus of international trade fair activity. Milan is the fashion trade fair center of the world. Other important centers can be found in Bologna and Verona. In Spain, trade fair activity is concentrated around Barcelona, Valencia, and Madrid. While in the United Kingdom, over 13 million visitors attend more than 1,000 exhibitions each year, generating GPD1 billion in spending. Top exhibitions include the:

- Farnborough International Airshow
- International Spring Fair (Birmingham)
- World Travel Market (London)

The Benelux nations also have a strong trade fair program. Excellent facilities exist in Amsterdam, Rotterdam, Brussels, and at Schiphol Airport. Paris, France hosts numerous international events throughout the year as well.

It is probably true to say that the growth of the European Union (its common currency is the Euro) and the removal of trade barriers and tariffs has helped the growth of the European trade fair and exhibition industry.

Perhaps, the greatest growth of trade fairs in Europe is occurring in the countries of Eastern Europe. New facilities have opened in Zagreb, Belgrade, Warsaw, Moscow, and in St. Petersburg, where the new Expoforum center launched in 2014. In recent years, other large Russian cities, such as Kazan, Yekaterinburg, Kaliningrad, and Perm

The Grassmarket has been a focal point in the Old Town for 500 years, and a trading place since the beginning of the City of Edinburgh, Scotland.
StockCube/Shutterstock

have also successfully hosted a variety of international and domestic business events. Work by Mady Keup (2015) highlights the rise of Sochi, a resort town on the Black Sea that has recorded a rapid increase in business travel due to the 2014 Winter Olympic Games. Development for the games not only led to a modern transportation system; the building of new, world class hotels; and investment by the foremost international hotel chains, but it also led to modern facilities for hosting exhibitions, congresses, conferences, and so on. During the Olympics, visitors were also able to buy a 72-hour visa on arrival. Sochi is on the Formula One circuit and one of the host cities for the FIFA World Cup.

Europe also holds many international association meetings. In fact, 15 European cities were featured in the top 20 of the IOCCA annual ranking of cities. Berlin, Germany ranked as the top destination for international association meetings.

The European Society of Cardiology Congress

One of these international association meetings is the European Society of Cardiology (ESC) congress. The ESC is a not-for-profit medical federation of national cardiology associations and individual members from around the world, and represents more than 90,000 cardiology professionals. Its mission, is to reduce the impact of cardiovascular disease. They organize 12 congresses per year on different cardiology topics. Their main event, the ESC Congress, is the world's largest cardiovascular event and it has been held annually since 1962. It takes place over five days in late August or early September, and changes its location every year.

The duration and complexity of their planning cycle can be said to be typical for a large medical convention. It begins with the creation of the request for proposal at about three or four years before the event, and ends with a post conference reporting on the convention just held. The destination selection process usually starts three years before the convention and the format of the event begins to take shape some 18 months before D-day, when the layouts of the lecture and exhibition rooms are sketched out, and the scientific program and abstract policy are determined. Ten months ahead of the event, there is a focus on operational logistics and supplier selection and, a couple of months later, the scientific program and marketing for the event are developed.

In 2016, the congress was held in Rome and the figures were staggering: a record 33,000 health professionals and stakeholders (clinicians, scientists, epidemiologists, nurses, technicians, health care industry executives, opinion leaders, media representatives, and policy makers) from more than 140 countries attended, from Australia to the United States. They discussed topics arranged in themed scientific villages at the Fiera di Roma exhibition and conference center. The Congress also featured an exhibition where over 200 companies displayed their goods and services, spread out over almost 120,000 square feet. The event closed with an historic address by Pope Francis.

The following figures show that international meetings now make increasing use of technological tools to communicate even more widely. The audience was not limited to on-site participants at the ESC Congress, as the events had a virtual reach:

- 1,320,100 plus resources were consulted on ESC Congress 365 (the ESC Congress scientific content platform) between its launch in January 2013 and the event that took place in September 2016 .
- Over 66,000 resources were consulted during the five days of ESC Congress, including more than 35,000 presentation slide sets.

During the ESC Congress 2016, the resources from ESC Congress 365 could be accessed from:

- All mobile devices/computers connected to Internet via www.escardio.org/365
- Computers from the dedicated desk
- ESC Congress 2016 Mobile App

The Congress changes venues within Europe every year: previous destinations have been the Fira Gran Via 2 in Barcelona, the ExCeL center in London, and the RAI in Amsterdam.

Asia

The growth of trade fairs and exhibitions in Asia has been phenomenal over the past 15 years. New facilities and government promotions have taken the industry from its infancy to world class in little more than a decade. Primarily, Asian trade fairs focus on high technology, consumer electronics, and food. However, all types of manufacturing and service industries are well represented. Asian trade fairs and exhibitions are either sponsored by trade organizations, such as the World Trade Centers, or individual governments.

Taiwan and Singapore have been the backbone of Asian trade fairs and exhibitions. Taiwan has excellent facilities and routinely sponsors trade fairs in the semiconductor, consumer electronics, and food industries. Taiwan is also an important exhibitor at trade fairs and exhibitions in North America and Europe.

Singapore is a major destination city and, consequently, attracts many visitors to its textile, fashion, food, and electronics trade fairs. It has multiple facilities all linked to world-class shopping and entertainment complexes. Singapore is also attractive because it provides excellent transportation facilities with a world-class airport. The government of Singapore is very active in promoting exhibitions. International Enterprise Singapore, formerly known as the Singapore Trade Development Board, encourages Singapore's exports, and the Singapore Exhibition and Convention Bureau (SECB) is the lead agency for marketing Singapore as an international exhibition city. It provides financial and marketing support for trade fairs organized by both Singaporean and international organizers.

The growth in Asia's foremost economy, China, is nothing short of phenomenal.

China

Business events in the world's second largest economy, China, have benefited greatly from the impact and stimulus of major sporting events and the Expo hosted here, in terms of both infrastructure development, but also skills enhancement. The Olympics were held in Beijing in 2008, the Expo took place in Shanghai in 2010, and in 2022 China will host both the Winter Olympics (in Beijing) and the Asian Games (in Hangzhou). In addition, the corporate hospitality at these events has brought an increase in corporate meetings, and encouraged the establishment of event service companies in China. The hosting of important political meetings, such as APEC and G20 summits (in 2014 and 2016 respectively), also had an impact.

Exhibitions are very well established in China, as they are an extension of trading. Corporate meetings and incentives are new concepts, and association conventions are less well understood since associations in China are mainly government managed.

Overall, the government plays an important role in Chinese business life. The following is a list of goals that organizers in China want to achieve from hosting international association conferences. While it could be argued that many other international association events share the first objectives, as adapted to their host country, the final two points relate to the standing of government in Chinese society:

- An opportunity for local attendees to see and learn about the latest international advances in their field
- Showcase Chinese achievements and research to international counterparts
- Encourage foreign co-operation, either with individuals, counterpart associations, or academic institutes
- Increase Chinese influence in international organizations by participating on boards and Committees
- Highlight the value of the host's sector with government, media, and other related organizations
- A major event achievement to include in the organization's activity report to the government

In fact, all international congresses held in China must be approved both by the Central Government and the provincial government or the relevant ministry. All large international congresses with a high proportion of international participants have to be approved by the Central Government and the State Council.

The following is a list of recent government policy decisions that have affected the events industry in China. This again illustrates the importance of government in the Chinese MEEC industry:

- In 2012, the Chinese government sent out a very clear directive stating that meetings and major events should be strictly regulated, and efficiency improved. The intention was to eliminate overly expensive and unnecessary frills, and focus more on the educational and scientific elements of the meetings. Therefore, China's associations industry is slowly moving away from lavish, extravagant spending toward a stronger focus on the educational and scientific aspects of meetings and conferences.

- Although China's economy has traditionally relied on manufacturing, the government is encouraging the development of the service economy through tax breaks for companies in tourism, health care, sports, and education, with the result that income from services represented just over 50 percent of GDP in 2015. Growth in events for the service sector is, therefore, to be expected.

- Growth of second tier cities—first-tier cities are full so the government is developing second-tier cities to provide work opportunities for people and encourage them to stay home to reduce migrant workers to first tier cities. Currently, the biggest growth and development in the Chinese hotel sector is in these second-tier cities.

- Since 2012, the government's anti-Corruption Campaign has had a negative impact on hosting international meetings, and the growth of professional city convention bureaus. There is confusion about how to stay compliant with the new directives. International travel, promotion, and hospitality are particularly regulated.

- Cyber economy—Internet connectivity will be improved, and support is given to companies dealing with innovation in business models, product development, supply, and logistics chains for the sector.

- Environmental Protection—the government will promote low-carbon industry and establish a real time, nationwide online environmental monitoring system.

Convention and Exhibition Industries in China   In 1978, only six international conventions and exhibitions were held in China, and it held and took part in twenty-one exhibitions abroad. The first exhibition company, (SIEC), was established in 1985. Today, the quantities and scales of exhibitions in China have been increased by hundred-folds and penetrated into all fields of the national economy. Consequently, each industry had its own international professional exhibitions. There is over 51 million square feet of national indoor exhibition space in China's main venues, about 15 percent of the world's total. In this respect, China is second in the world after the United States.

China is also the second largest business travel market in the world and is on the verge of passing the United States to become Number One, according to the GBTA Foundation (2015). A total of 138.5 million domestic business trips were taken for MEEC purposes in China in 2014 and Meetings, Incentives, Conventions and Events (MICE) business travelers spent a total of USD110 billion (¥680 billion CNY) during those trips.

Shanghai and Beijing hosted the majority of MEEC trips in China in 2014: 52 percent of the total. Other major MICE markets include Guangzhou (24 percent of total trips), Hong Kong (11 percent of total trips), Macau (6 percent of total trips), and Lhasa (4 percent of total trips).

Beijing and Shanghai make up a significant amount of room supply and meeting space in the country with a combined total of some 250,000 rooms. Hotel construction has been robust in secondary markets including Macau, Guangzhou, Shenzhen, Sanya, and Wuhan, and many top-tier hotel offerings are increasingly available to MEEC buyers in these markets. Table 15-1 shows hotel and convention center space in select Chinese cities.

Five convention and exhibition economic belts, the Yangtze River Delta, Zhujiang Delta, Bohai Bay Area, Northeast China, and Central China, have been built in the

TABLE 15-1

Hotel Capacity in Major Chinese Cities

	Beijing	Guangzhou	Hong Kong	Macau	Shanghai
Hotel rooms	12,700	56,000	25,000	29,000	122,000
Convention center space (square feet)	220,000	75,000	753,000	50,000	

Source: CVENT, accessed May 1, 2017

mainland, and many trade shows have reached as far west as Chengdu and Chongqing City in Sichuan Province; and Xi'an, Shaanxi Province. As far as scales and impacts of exhibition projects go, Beijing, Shanghai, and Guangzhou have been the most important three cities of Chinese convention and exhibition industries. As one form of economic concentration, some cities have grown into regional centers, such as Dalian, Shenzhen, Chengdu, Hangzhou, Nanjing, Ningbo, Suzhou, Qingdao, Xiamen, Xi'an, Wuhan, Nanning, Kunming, and Chongqing.

In addition, both Hong Kong and Macau, which are special administrative regions of China, have an important place in international MEEC. As a free port with a major international airport hub, Hong Kong was awarded "Asia's Leading Meetings & Conference Destination" by World Travel Awards in 2016 and "City Destination for Meetings and Events, Greater China" for five years in a row by the MICE publication, *CEI Asia* magazine. Hong Kong's main venues are the Hong Kong Convention and Exhibition Center, the Asia WorldExpo, and the Hong Kong International Trade and Exhibition Center. Macau, on the other hand, is a favorite incentive destination, and its many casinos attract numerous international travelers to the "Vegas of the East." As elsewhere in China, the government also plays an important role, for example, with its visa free scheme: nationals from some 170 countries can visit Hong Kong visa free for periods ranging from seven to 180 days.

It is probably true to say that, even though the Chinese exhibition and meetings industry is developing very rapidly, there are some areas for improvement: The industry is still poorly positioned in many cities, the government gets involved in industry management, domestic exhibition companies are relatively weak in comparison to their international competitors, and professional education and training is still not developed sufficiently. Organizing an event in China is also administratively and legally complex.

The UFI Special Interest Group on China recently identified some key points to consider for international organizers wanting to hold an event in China. These are

- Need to understand local regulations and licensing requirements
- Importance of a local partner
- Rise of e-commerce and online competitors
- Increasing labor costs
- Challenging to find skilled and professional managers

However, Chinese companies and the government are becoming increasingly aware of the need for greater internationalization. For example, the China Convention and Exhibition Society (CCES) and China Association for Exhibition Centers (CAEC) have partnered with international organizations to train and promote their members.

In addition, many Chinese cities began to realize the importance of meetings, which could contribute to the balanced development of the convention and exhibition industry.

Festivals and Special Events in China   With the rapid development of the national economy and the improvement of living standards in China, festivals and special events with various themes are welcomed by more and more local governments, and especially the tourism industry. The Chinese Festivals and Special Events (FSE) industry shows different attributes: The content of events is colorful, including entertainment, sports, and trade shows; the industries of culture, tourism, sports, and manufacturing have been integrated together; there are public service and private products in most festivals and special events. The most important fact is that culture and arts are becoming much more important when developing festivals or special events in China.

But even here, government intervention is prominent, and not just in infrastructure development and policy formulation, but also when marketing to visitors for local hallmark festivals (especially international events). It is common practice for many festivals and special events to be hosted or subcontracted by different levels of Chinese government.

In addition, in a broad sense, many Chinese city governments still manage FSE in a classification and level-oriented manner. It means that the government dismisses its macro-administration, and delegates authority to individual departments such as commerce, domestic trade, science and technology, culture, and trade promotion committees. This kind of administration system could easily lead to political issues.

Incentive Travel in China   Incentive travel is a new kind of business in the Chinese tourism industry, but with a huge potential market. With increasingly more Chinese organizations and companies making use of incentive travel, a lot of traditional travel agencies in China began to change their business model or offer new services. Economic success has generated an increase in incentive travel—Chinese companies hold incentives more frequently and travel to more destinations with a higher number of employees. This trend is expected to increase in the next few years, with small corporate meetings also on the rise, mainly commissioned by pharmaceutical/medical, education, IT, and financial companies.

Some professional trade shows address this sector. The largest and most international are the China Incentive Business Travel & Meetings Exhibition (CIBTM) and the Incentive Travel & Convention Meeting IT & CM China. The first international exhibition in China dedicated to business travel, incentives, and conferences, CIBTM, was launched in 2005. Both shows offer exhibitors the opportunity to meet qualified buyers with an interest in different business travel products and services.

Furthermore, with plenty of tourism resources, competitive prices, and a good tourism image, China is expected to become one of the most popular incentive travel destinations in the world. On the other hand, with its rapid economic prosperity, China is also becoming one of the key incentive travel markets. And many countries, such as Australia, the Netherlands, and Egypt, are enhancing marketing to trade customers and residents in China.

Thailand

Thailand is a major center for clothing and textile trade shows, food and agribusiness, and automotive and engineering fairs. Excellent transportation facilities in Bangkok make it easy for visitors to arrive from around the world. The IMPACT Exhibition and Convention Centre is Thailand's largest, with a total indoor space of over 1.5 million square feet. Since its opening in 1999, IMPACT Exhibition and Convention Center has hosted more than 8,000 events with over 100 million visitors from all over the world. On its website, the company states its ambition to become one of Asia's top five venues. New projects include boosting its on-site bed stock to over 1,000 rooms, with a new one billion baht (about USD29 million) three-star hotel. Its managing company will also invest another 15 million dollars in creating additional meeting, retail, and catering space.

Korea

COEX, Kintex, and Songdo Convensia can be called Korea's three main exhibition centers. All three are situated in or very near the capital Seoul and host a variety of events (exhibitions and meetings). COEX is not just an events venue with almost five million square feet of floor space, but it also hosts Asia's largest underground mall, three five star hotels, office blocks, a department, and a subway station. Kintex (or Korea International Exhibition Center) is in Goyang City. Its exhibition and meeting space was expanded in 2011 to almost 1.2 million square feet of floor space. It is run as a partnership between the Korean national government investment agency and regional and municipal administrations.

Songdo Convensia, situated next to Korea's main international airport, Incheon, offers the largest column-free space in Asia, and is operated by the local tourism organization.

Other Asian Countries

Other countries nurturing trade fair programs with government promotion include Vietnam, Malaysia, and India. In these countries, the facilities are usually owned and operated by the government, and promotional activities are sponsored by various government agencies. Vietnam has taken a strong position in clothing and food trade fairs, while India is at the forefront of Asian information technology and software shows.

Australia

Australia has a long track record of hosting high-profile international events, especially association congresses and incentives. Research by Deloitte on behalf of the Australian Convention Bureaux established that one in five dollars spent by international visitors in Australia was spent by an international visitor attending some form of business event. It is also clear from this study that the MEEC industry in Australia has aligned itself clearly with the government's economic strategy by concentrating on the so-called five pillars: building strengths in manufacturing innovation, advanced services, agriculture exports, education and research, and mining exports. The report goes on to state that convention bureaus have already secured a recorded estimate of 265,316 delegates across 278 international business events (amounting to approximately 1.1 million days) up to 2020. Seventy-eight percent of these participants relate to international business events falling under the five pillars. Australia's major cities, such as Melbourne, Brisbane, Perth, and Adelaide, all have internationally renowned conference and exhibition centers—the Brisbane Convention & Exhibition Centre (BCEC) was awarded the 2016 AIPC APEX Award for the "Best Client Rated Convention Centre." In Sydney, the new ICC (International Convention Centre) opened in Darling Harbour, which is described as Asia Pacific's premier integrated convention, exhibition, and entertainment precinct. It offers exhibition capacity of 376,000 square feet, 86,000 square feet of total meeting space, an external event deck on the waterfront of 54,000 square feet, a theatre with a seating capacity of 8,000, and an adjacent headquarters hotel with 590 rooms.

The image of the Sydney Opera House in Australia is known around the world. It is actually an event center putting on, not only operas, but orchestra recitals, theater, and meeting and special events.
Peter Adams Photography Ltd/Alamy Stock Photo

Africa

Home to 16 percent of the world population, Africa's economy is developing fast. It is estimated that by 2020 there will be 128 million households with discretionary income, by 2025 47 percent of all Africans will live in a city, by 2030 the African middle class will be 300 million, and by 2035 the number of Africans joining the working age population (ages 15 to 64) will exceed that of the rest of the world combined. Already, Nigeria and South Africa in terms of global GDP ranking are at the twenty-second and thirty-third place respectively, according to World Bank statistics from 2015. The Ivory Coast, Tanzania, and Senegal are among the ten fastest growing economies in the world.

The MEEC industry is developing at a fast pace within Africa, both for corporate and association events. In 2015, the African Society of Association Executives (AfSAE) was successfully founded. The following four new convention centers opened their doors in 2016:

- Calabar, Nigeria: Calabar International Convention Centre, 377,000 square feet, total capacity for 5,000 delegates
- Algiers, Algeria: Centre International Conference d'Alger, 2,900,000 square feet, auditorium for 6,000
- Cape Town, South Africa: Century City Conference Centre, on a precinct that combines residential, commercial, and leisure components with a capacity of up to 1,900 participants in 20 spaces. Also, the Cape Town International Convention Centre will now offers an extra 10,000 square meters of multipurpose space in its CTICC East expansion.
- Kigali, Rwanda: Kigali Convention Centre, auditorium for 2,500 and on-site hotel with 292 rooms

Africa is the only growing continent, home to some of the world's fastest growing economies. With its rapidly growing population and continuing urbanization, it expects to achieve a substantial improvement of life expectancy and a serious increase in disposable income per capita. Growth potential is seen for international associations and exhibitions, and a new place for product introductions.

The MEEC industry in Africa has seen significant growth over the past few decades, particularly in South Africa. Since the early 1990s, South Africa has become an increasingly important player, not only on the continent, but also worldwide, culminating in the highly successful hosting of the FIFA World Cup in 2010. The International Congress and Convention Association recently ranked South Africa in the thirty-eighth position worldwide as a meeting destination. In the African context, however, the country is far ahead: The closest African rivals, Morocco and Egypt, occupy the fifty-fifth and sixty-ninth positions, respectively, and South Africa provides 29 percent of Africa's indoor exhibition space. Cape Town is the most popular urban meeting destination in Africa. The city hosted the first Africa Travel Week in April 2014, when three large travel and meeting related fairs were held at the Cape Town International Convention Centre (CTICC). The World Tourism Market Africa, IBTM Africa, and the International Luxury Travel Show Africa attract almost 4,500 leisure, luxury travel, and meeting planning professionals.

Traditionally, the MEEC industry in South Africa has been concentrated around hotel venues and game lodges, but considerable development has taken place in the creation of large multipurpose conference and exhibition facilities. In South Africa, three cities dominate the MEEC industry, namely, Cape Town, Durban, and Johannesburg. To support the development of MEEC in South Africa, the Tourism Grading Council of South Africa launched a star grading system for meetings and exhibition venues; this initiative is considered to be a world first. The FIFA World Cup also left behind a nationwide legacy of improvements in telecommunications and broadcast technology and public transport, as well as a highly positive reputation as a successful destination for major events for the country.

Large numbers of domestic trade fairs and conventions dominate the South African industry, predominantly around Johannesburg, although South Africa as a destination for trade fairs is growing rapidly. A major venue in South Africa includes the Tshwane Events Centre (Pretoria Showgrounds). Upcoming cities in the MEEC industry in South Africa include Bloemfontein, Port Elizabeth, and Pretoria.

The South African Tourism's INDABA is an annual event that has been held in Durban since 1997, one of the largest tourism marketing events on the African continent. The 2016 exhibition attracted more than 7,000 attendees, including over 1,500 international visitors from 67 countries, and hosted 1,049 exhibitors from the Southern African region.

Middle East

Trade fairs and exhibitions in the Middle East are most prominent in Dubai and Abu Dhabi in the United Arab Emirates, due to excellent government promotion, new facilities, and ease of travel access. Both Dubai and Abu Dhabi have international airports with service to every continent. This crossroads concept, as well as the fact that exhibition facilities are located at or near the international airports, is emphasized heavily in promotional materials. For example, both Dubai and Abu Dhabi strongly promote the duty-free zones near their airports and the extensive duty-free shopping available at their facilities. In addition, the regional market for consumer goods is very strong and puts the focus of trade fairs on items like furniture, automobiles, and consumer electronics.

Dubai will hold the World Expo, the first Middle Eastern nation to do so. It is expected that the expo will attract more than 25 million visitors, positively impact UAE's GDP by USD23 billion between 2015 and 2021, and create 277,000 new jobs. A new convention centre in Al Jaddaf near Dubai Creek, to be completed by 2018, is part of the run-up to the Expo. It will provide 592,000 square feet of event space. In 2016, Dubai welcomed three new world-class venues, suitable mostly for corporate conferences, team building, and incentives: Dubai Opera, Dubai Parks and Resorts, and IMG Worlds of Adventure.

It is also fair to say that Qatar has been working very hard to attract both exhibition and meeting planners. The Qatar National Convention Centre, which opened in 2011, was built according to the US Green Building Council's Leadership in Energy and Environment Design (LEED) gold-certification standards. And, in August 2016, the Oman Convention & Exhibition Centre (OCEC) opened its doors with the Oman 2016, one of the largest building and construction exhibitions in the Middle East.

Across the region, new hotel properties are being built. Starwood, Carlson Rezidor, Hilton, and Mövenpick are all active with most new hotels continuing to upscale into luxury categories.

Latin America

The huge population base of Latin America makes it well suited for trade fairs and exhibitions. Until recently, most of the Latin American trade fairs and exhibitions have been regional. However, new facilities and promotional efforts have set the stage for growth in international exhibitions. New facilities in Sao Paulo, Brazil, and Mexico City are hubs for this activity. The Las Americas Exhibition Center in Mexico City provides the latest in technology to support exhibitors and attendees. In addition, the center is built within an entertainment complex that includes a horse racing track, restaurants, hotels, and a shopping center.

Brazil is in the limelight, hosting both the soccer World Cup in 2014 and the Olympic summer games in 2016. It is estimated that the 2014 World Cup contributed over USD60 billion to the country, creating 3.63 million jobs. The event also no doubt helped change Brazil's reputation to that of an innovative country with plenty of research and development, a robust economy, and modern cities.

The following table (Table 15-2) shows a list of international top cities for meetings and events, according to the American Express Meetings & Events Destination Analysis, 2015.

TABLE 15-2
Top International MEEC cities

Top Cities Based on Meetings and Events Activity		
Europe, Middle East Africa	Asia-Pacific	Central/South America
1. London, United Kingdom	Singapore	Rio De Janeiro, Brazil
2. Paris, France	Shanghai, China	Riviera Maya/Cancun, Mexico
3. Amsterdam, The Netherlands	Hong Kong/Macau	Panama City, Panama
4. Brussels, Belgium	Beijing, China	São Paulo, Brazil
5. Frankfurt, Germany	Sydney, Australia	Cartagena/Bogotá, Colombia
6. Munich, Germany	Tokyo, Japan	Punta Cana, Dominican Republic
7. Copenhagen, Denmark	Melbourne, Australia	Buenos Aires/Mendoza, Argentina
8. Barcelona, Spain	Bangkok, Thailand	Cusco/Macchu Pichu/Lima, Peru
9. Riga, Latvia	Bali, Indonesia	Los Cabos, Mexico
10. Berlin, Germany	Taipei, Taiwan	Santiago, Chile

Source: American Express Meetings & Events Destination Analysis, 2015

Ownership, Sponsorship, and Management Models

In the United States, many trade shows are adjuncts to association meetings, and are owned by the association. Others are sponsored by private, entrepreneurial companies and operated on a for-profit basis. Ownership and management are usually accomplished by two companies working toward the success of the show. Other service companies support the industry by helping both the trade show management company and exhibitors.

This model is not always followed for trade fairs and exhibitions in other parts of the world. While there are very important commercial trade show organizing companies (especially in the United Kingdom), in some countries, such as Germany and Italy, it is the venues that do not just rent the space but also organize the fairs. Governments, in collaboration with organizing companies, often plan and operate the trade fairs. For example, the government of China plays a major role in the sponsorship of most trade fairs held in Beijing, Hong Kong, and Shanghai.

Professional Congress Organizer

In the United States, organizers and sponsors of large congresses will typically work with a DMO (CVB) and/or a DMC or third-party planning consultant. Outside the United States, there is an alternative, the professional congress organizer (PCO). The PCO represents the client in dealing with the DMO, DMC, hotel, restaurant, transportation company, and other suppliers. The PCO will negotiate with vendors on behalf of the client. PCOs also tend to be more familiar with international issues like customs, taxation, and government regulations. The PCO may even handle financial transactions, letters of credit, and foreign bank accounts. PCOs are often involved in the content of shows along with speakers, entertainers, and performers (SEPs). PCOs have their own association called the International Association of Professional Congress Organizers (IAPCO).

Global Commercial Exhibition Organizing Companies

There is a leaderboard of five truly global trade fair organizing companies, which operate across the world in all main markets. Here is the list:

1. Reed Exhibitions
2. Messe Frankfurt
3. UBM
4. GL Events
5. Messe Dusseldorf

Important International Meeting and Trade Fair Associations

The International Congress and Convention Association

The International Congress and Convention Association (ICCA) is the global community for the world's meetings industry. It is the only association that comprises a membership representing the main specialists in handling, transporting, and accommodating international events.

ICCA's network of over 1,000 suppliers to the international meetings industry spans the globe, with members in almost 100 countries. ICCA tracks over 17,900 regularly occurring association meetings, which rotate between at least three countries. Access to this data and association clients is the primary reason why companies and organizations belong to ICCA.

International meeting planners can rely on the ICCA network to find solutions for all their event objectives, as ICCA members represent the top destinations worldwide, and the most experienced specialist suppliers.

Speaking on the occasion of ICCA's Fiftieth anniversary, Martin Sirk, CEO, said: "What the long-term data tell us is a story that is dramatic: What is shown is an incredible picture of growth and dynamism, and a trend that justifies even more investment by destinations and suppliers into the international association market, in anticipation of what the future holds."

ICCA has offices in the Netherlands, Malaysia, South Africa, the United Arab Emirates, the United States, and Uruguay.

Adapted from www.iccaworld.com/abouticca.cfm

AIPC

AIPC, which stands for the Association Internationale de Palais de Congrès, represents a global network of more than 175 convention centers in 57 countries. Its mission is to encourage, support, and recognize excellence in convention center management based on the diverse experience and expertise of its international membership through a wide range of educational, research, networking, and standards programs.

AIPC Members operate facilities whose primary purpose is to accommodate and service meetings, conventions, congresses, and exhibitions.

Activities include:

- Conducting industry research and analysis
- Preparing and publishing technical publications
- Carrying out training, educational, and professional development activities
- Maintaining a global marketing and communications presence for members
- Facilitating member networking and information exchange forums
- Maintaining performance standards, including the AIPC Quality Standards program and the AIPC/Ipsos Economic Impact Tool
- Recognizing management excellence through awards programs, such as the AIPC Apex Award, an award made in recognition of the highest client rating received by a convention center; and the AIPC Innovation Award
- Supporting and carrying out advocacy initiatives to promote the value of the industry to key audiences

Adapted from Introducing AIPC, www.aipc.org/index.asp?id=5

UFI—The Global Association of the Exhibition Industry

UFI, which stands for Union des Foires Internationales, is the association of the world's leading trade show organizers and fairground owners. Members also represent the major national and international exhibition associations and selected partners of the exhibition industry. UFI's main goal is to represent, promote, and support the business interests of its members and the exhibition industry. There are 720 member organizations in 84 countries around the world presently signed up as members.

Over 900 international trade fairs bear the UFI approved label, a quality guarantee for visitors and exhibitors alike. UFI members continue to provide the international business community with a unique marketing medium aimed at developing outstanding face-to-face business opportunities.

Adapted from the UFI website, www.ufi.org/about/

International MEEC Considerations

Lessons to Be Learned

It is important for trade fair, event, and exhibition managers to learn the reasons for success in different aspects of the international marketplace. For example, North American trade show managers can learn from their European colleagues in the following three areas.

- *Excellence of Infrastructure:* Public transportation systems in Europe provide excellent support for trade fairs and exhibitions.
- *Logistics:* International trade fair organizers are, by necessity, experts in logistics. Because the lifeblood of many international shows is the international exhibitor, many have specialized departments devoted to helping exhibitors overcome obstacles for exhibiting in their countries. Shipping and storage procedures are simplified and expedited by these agencies to help make exhibiting in their countries as easy as possible.
- *Support Organizations:* In America, many trade shows are sponsored and organized by associations. In other parts of the world, trade fairs and exhibitions are sponsored and organized by trade promotion organizations, such as the world trade centers or government agencies.

Methods of Exhibiting

There are many differences between exhibiting at an American trade show and at an international trade fair or exhibition. These differences need to be a part of the basic research before initiating an international trade fair program.

Typically, companies have choices in how they will exhibit at an international trade fair or exhibition. The US government sponsors US pavilions at many trade fairs, and a US company can work through the government to be part of the US exhibit. If a company does decide to be a part of the exhibit, the US Department of Commerce can provide significant help.

Another option is to exhibit under the auspices of another company that is organizing a pavilion. Like US government sponsorship, a private company may be the main interface, and contractual arrangements are made with it. Companies should fully investigate this type of situation to ensure that the organizing company is reputable, and has experience in the host country and with the desired trade fair.

Joint ventures can also be formed between companies, particularly when one has experience exhibiting at a certain trade fair. In this case, it is important that companies be sure that their products or services do not compete with each other. This type of arrangement works best when the two companies' products complement each other, and it is an excellent way for a company to enter the international trade fair marketplace and gain valuable experience.

Going it alone is another option for companies entering the international trade fair arena. Many large companies choose this route because they have the budget and staff to support the complexities of international exhibiting. Smaller companies must ensure that they have a clear understanding of all the requirements, costs, and scheduling before committing to this route. For example, smaller companies must factor in all the personnel time and costs involved in verifying that all tasks are completed. Assuming that the preparation time for an international trade show is the same as that for a domestic trade show can be a very costly mistake.

Terminology

In many parts of the world, an exhibit is not called an exhibit, or even a booth, but rather, it is called a **stand**. And this is only the beginning of the differences in terminology. Depending on where the trade fair is being held, and who is managing it, participating companies must be familiar with these differences.

For example, in Germany the following terms must be understood:

- **Ausstellung:**   Consumer show
- **Kongress:**   Meeting or convention
- **Gesellschaft:**   Company or society
- **GmbH:**   Limited liability company
- **Messe:**   Trade fair
- **Messegelande:**   Fair site

And in the United Kingdom:

- **PLC:**   Public limited company
- **Trade exhibition:**   Trade show
- **Delegate:**   Attendee at conference
- **Accommodation:**   Housing

Contractual and Procedural Issues

In addition to terminology differences, contractual and procedural differences abound. Labor rules in the United States are very different from those in Europe or Asia. In Asia, there are few unions and no jurisdictional issues. Exhibitors have much more freedom in what they can do within their exhibit. In Europe, although there are unions, they are much more flexible than many in the United States.

Companies should not assume that set up or logistical contracts read the same as those in their home country. Substantial differences exist from country to country, and from trade fair to trade fair. Companies should read each contract closely and adhere to all the requirements. If something is not understood, it should be brought to the attention of show management immediately.

Customs Clearance

Exhibition organizers at international shows provide access to experienced international freight forwarders, who also act as custom brokers, to ensure that everything is in order and arrives on time. The freight forwarders are knowledgeable about the customs regulations for the host country and take action to ensure that exhibitors know of every requirement and deadline.

Typically, goods can be temporarily imported to an international show site without having to pay duties or taxes, using either a **carnet** or a **trade fair bond**. A carnet can be very complicated to obtain, and a hefty bond must often be established. However, most trade fair venues offer trade fair bonds, which are simple to arrange. Again, the international freight forwarders are the point of contact for trade fair bonds. Be sure to inquire about host country rules on giveaways and promotional materials. In some countries, a duty is charged when the value is above a certain limit, in others, it is not.

Protocol

Business etiquette refers to the rules that allow people to comprehend what is suitable in any situation. It is the responsibility of an event organizer working internationally to research the business customs of the host country in which they are holding their event. Staff should then be thoroughly trained on these differences before departing for the trade fair or other events. Always remember that what is acceptable in one country may very well be offensive in the next country or at another trade fair. Language is of course one of the most obvious differences: although English is normally the official language of international business, it is not safe to assume that all attendees or suppliers speak English. The wise company will ensure that at least some of the staff are bilingual, particularly in the host country's language. In addition, different cultures are more, or less, direct when passing on information: Hall (1976), categorized communication behavior as low-context when, as in Scandinavia and North America, people spell out information explicitly. In contrast, information may have to be deduced from the context and nonverbal clues, as in Chinese and Arabic, which are high-context cultures.

Staff members will be greeting people from many countries to their international event. It is imperative that they be familiar with the appropriate greetings and forms of address for different cultures. Although most event stakeholders will not be offended if protocol is not strictly followed, it does give them a positive impression if their cultural standards are observed.

Culture can be defined as the collective programming of the mind that distinguishes the members of one group or category of people from others. There are six dimensions regarding culture that are particularly important for conducting international business. They are explained in the following with examples of how business etiquette should be adapted accordingly.

Identity (Individualism versus Collectivism)

This dimension deals with the position of the individual in society. While collectivist countries see themselves primarily as belonging to powerful groups (such as an extended family) and work hard to maintain group harmony, individualist societies value independence and individuals are expected to speak their own minds.

In collectivist countries, such as China, it is, therefore, very important to invest time to build strong, mutually beneficial relationships, also known as guanxi. In addition, it is rude to say a blunt "no" in negotiations, since this will hurt the group harmony. When negotiating in China, always give many alternatives so that the Chinese negotiators have room to negate several options with dignity. Also, always keep the same negotiating team throughout the process.

Hierarchy (Power Distance)

This refers to the degree in which less powerful members of a society or an institution (like the family) are happy to accept inequalities in the distribution of authority. A high level of power distance indicates that a particular society expects top down authority as their norm.

In the Netherlands, a country with low power distance, avoid giving an impression of superiority. Egalitarianism is a central tenet of Dutch society. Everyone in a Dutch company, from the boss to menial laborers, is considered valuable and worthy of respect.

When interacting with French business contacts, never use first names or the informal "tu" until you are told to do so. France is a country with relatively high power distance and it is important that you respect the hierarchy of employees within the same company.

Age and rank are very important in Korea, so it is usually easiest to establish a relationship with a businessperson of your own age.

Truth (Uncertainty Avoidance)

This factor refers to the degree in which a society can tolerate ambiguity. Are people looking for the one, absolute truth (high uncertainty avoidance) or are they happy to live in a less structured, or even unstructured, environment (low uncertainty avoidance)?

Meetings in high uncertainty avoidance countries, such as Germany, should be planned well in advance. These countries also tend to have a large number of official rules and legal regulations regarding contracts and import/export barriers.

In addition to the dimensions listed previously, other elements should be considered when doing business internationally. Food and drink often plays a more important role than in the United States. In many parts of Asia, lengthy business dinners with many toasts to the hosts and VIP guests are a vital part in forming a lasting business relationship. In Japan, the host will always treat when you are taken out. Allow your host to order for you. Be enthusiastic while eating, and show great thanks afterward. In Russia, everyone at a dinner is expected to consume vodka—by the shot and not sipped. Furthermore, with each shot a different guest gives a toast, with toasts becoming more and more lengthy with every drink. At a business meeting in Saudi Arabia, coffee is often served toward the end of the meeting as an indication that the meeting is about to end.

Differences in the perception of punctuality also exist. Therefore, a meeting should absolutely start on time in Switzerland or Germany, but people in India or Nigeria may see event project milestones as flexible.

There are also marked differences in how much personal space people from different cultures might expect—how close people can be to each other before feeling uncomfortable. Anglo Saxons tend to occupy the largest area of personal space, followed by Asians, whereas Mediterranean people and Latin Americans use the shortest distance. In many countries, there is little public contact between the sexes, apart from handshakes. Do not kiss or hug a person of the opposite sex in public—even if it is your spouse. On the other hand, in some countries contact is permitted between people of the same sex. Men may hold hands with men and even walk with arms around each other; this is interpreted as nothing but friendship.

Lastly, there are some symbols/colors/numbers and gestures that are best avoid.

These are simply a few of the cultural issues that foreign businesspeople must face. Before traveling to any country, it is wise to consult as many sources as possible to learn the appropriate business and social behaviors for the culture. Take the time to learn the appropriate behavior in the host country and the greeting expectations for potential visitors to the trade fair.

The following are aspects of international trade fairs that are different from US exhibitions. Keep in mind that these are generalizations and do not apply to all situations.

- Hospitality events are generally held on the exhibit floor, with many companies providing food and beverages as a matter of course in their exhibit.
- Height restrictions may be nonexistent. Many large exhibits may be two or three levels.
- Rules on smoking in the exhibit hall may not exist, and many exhibitors and attendees may smoke in the exhibits.
- Some trade fair organizing companies may not offer lead retrieval systems that US companies are accustomed to. It is always wise for a company to bring its own method of capturing leads.
- International trade fairs are often longer in duration than US trade shows and are often open on weekends as well. Although, in Europe, the show may run from 9 AM to 6 PM, in Brazil or other Latin American countries it is common for trade fairs to open at 2 PM and run until 10 PM or 11 PM.
- Be aware that most of the world outside the United States uses the metric system. Voltages may differ, and exhibitors may need plug-in adaptors or transformers.

Other Considerations

- Visas may be required for entry and exit.
- Items that Americans take for granted may have to be declared upon entry to a country. For example, brochures and written materials must be declared and taxes paid on them.
- Many international destinations require payment of departure taxes.
- Most countries require that payment be made to ensure that goods exhibited at a trade show are exported and not sold within the country. A freight handling company can arrange a bond as security.
- And many more, when in doubt, ask.

The exchange of business cards with Asians is very formal.
Tomohiro Ohsumi/Bloomberg/Getty Images

TIPS FOR ETIQUETTE AROUND THE WORLD

- When giving away gifts in Switzerland, avoid giving away knives—it is considered bad luck.
- In many Asian countries, it is not appreciated to pat people on the shoulder or initiate any physical contact.
- In China avoid the colors blue, black, and white for gift wraps, as they are associated with funerals and death respectively.
- You should not give chrysanthemums in Spain or France, or heather in Germany, where they are used for funerals.
- In most Arabic countries, the left hand is considered dirty, so you should never eat or accept anything with this hand. Be sure when giving gifts or promotional materials that you do so with the right hand.
- The number eight is the luckiest number in China, as its pronunciation is close to a word meaning to make a fortune, whereas the pronunciation for the number four sounds like death.
- In Japan, business cards are presented after a bow or handshake. Present your card, using both hands, with the Japanese side facing your colleague in such a manner that it can be read immediately. Handle cards very carefully, and do not put them in your pocket or wallet. Never write on a person's business card in his or her presence.
- In the United States, the hand gesture where the thumb and forefinger are forming a circle with the other three fingers raised is considered the "OK" sign, whereas:
  - In Brazil, it is considered a vulgar or obscene gesture.
  - In Greece and Russia, it is considered impolite.
  - In Japan, it signifies money.
  - In southern France, it means zero or worthless.
- In the United States, waving the hand back and forth is a means of saying hello, whereas:
  - In Greece, it is called the *moutza* and is a serious insult: The closer the hand is to the face of the other, the more threatening it is.
  - In Peru, waving the whole hand back and forth can signal "no."
- In most of the world, making a fist with the thumb raised means "OK." In Australia, it is a rude gesture.

Summary

The growth of international trade fairs and exhibitions and international meetings has been phenomenal over the past fifteen years. Europe, the historical home of trade fairs, continues to strengthen its hold on the world's largest trade fairs and those with the most significant economic impact. Asia has made great strides by building state-of-the-art facilities and promoting its efforts throughout the world. The Middle East, Africa, and Latin America all have strong efforts under way to capture a larger piece of the international trade fair, exhibition, and convention market.

Worldwide communications, easy travel access, and open markets have been a boon to the international event industry. Few large companies can afford to *not* be in the international marketplace today. What was once the playground of only the world's largest companies is now a necessity for most companies of any size. Trade fairs and exhibitions are the easiest method for these companies to enter the marketplace and meet their potential customers.

Exhibiting at international trade fairs is not easy. Cultural and business differences present a new set of challenges for the exhibitor, along with more complex logistics and travel procedures. Companies must seriously analyze all factors before committing to an international trade fair program.

CASE STUDY

Making Alternate Plans because of a Volcano

Steve has worked for the Courier Hotel in London as a meeting planner for four years. During his time there he has brought in a lot of business to the hotel and is seen as being great with potential clients. After many years of negotiation, he finally brings in Contech Financial for their yearly convention of all their sales reps from around the world. During this convention, Contech will use all the meeting space located at the Courier, as well as use the in-house bar and catering for all meals, so Steve is looking for a rather large profit from this event.

One week prior to the event a volcano in Iceland erupts, putting ash into the sky and grounding all air traffic across much of Europe. With there being so little time before the conference starts, Steve is worried about the event canceling. Usually Steve would not worry too much because he would still get money from the group if they canceled. However, in talking with Contech, he was reminded of the Act of God clause that was put into the contract, meaning that if this volcano caused air travel to be stopped, the meeting could be canceled at no charge.

After several calls to local airports, Steve finds out that every airport near London expects to not resume any flights for at least a week— after the dates of the Contech meeting—and probably more. Steve finally finds out that an airport across the English Channel expects to resume international flights in two days since it was not being affected by the ash as much as England. Steve comes up with a plan to shuttle people across the English Channel from this airport in order to still accommodate their meeting.

Steve contacts Contech and lets them know of the new plan, and tells them exactly how much extra the shuttle will cost. The company grows angry over the fact that Steve is requiring them to pay for the shuttle, which will add a few thousand more pounds onto their already large bill for the meeting. Contech tells Steve that unless the Courier Hotel picks up the bill for the shuttle the company will have to cancel the meeting as they are already at budget.

1. Should Steve agree to have the Courier pick up the bill for the shuttle?
2. Was it wrong of Steve to suggest that Contech should pick up the bill for the shuttle in the first place, considering that the company already had an out in their contract?
3. Steve has obviously gotten Contech upset about the shuttle. What could Steve do to assure that they that they not only keep the event scheduled as planned, but also make sure that they return for future events?
4. Is the attrition clause in the contract enforceable since many of Contechs employees may not be able to change their flight plans?
5. Will the extra cost for the shuttle offset airline costs that attendees would incur if the meeting was cancelled?

Produced by George G. Fenich from East Carolina University

Key Words and Terms

For definitions, see the Glossary.

Ausstellung
carnet
Gesellschaft
GmbH
International Congress and
  Convention Association (ICCA)

Kongress
Messe
Messegelande
PLC
trade exhibition
trade fair

trade fair bond
stand

Review and Discussion Questions

1. List some ways that international trade fairs may differ from US trade shows.

2. What are two reasons for Europe's strength in the international trade fair industry?

3. What are the purposes of UFI, AIPC, or ICCA?

4. What are some of the complexities that a company must consider before taking part in an international event in China?

5. Before proceeding with your exhibition or conference outside of North America, list at least five pieces of knowledge you will require before moving ahead. Where will you get the information?

About the Chapter Contributors

Mady Keup is Course Director for the Master of Science programs in Strategic Event Management, Tourism Management, and International Hospitality Management at SKEMA Business School in France. Mady was Head of the London Convention Bureau (now London & Partners) for five years, and she is an MPI (Meeting Professionals International) accredited trainer and an instructor for Destination Sales Training in Europe and the Middle East on behalf of Destination Marketing Association International (DMAI). Mady travels extensively for consultancy and training in Europe, the Middle East, and North America.

The section on China was provided, in part by:

Jenny Salsbury, CEO at IMC Convention Solutions, formerly Senior Director, International, China National Convention Centre.

Dr. Chunlei Wang, Associate Professor in the Department of Event Management, School of Tourism and Event Management, Shanghai University of International Business and Economics, Shanghai.

The section on South Africa is largely based on the contribution by:

Uwe P. Hermann, a faculty member and researcher in the Department of Tourism Management, Tshwane University of Technology, Pretoria, South Africa.

Previous Edition Chapter Contributor

Sandy Biback, CMP, CMM, lecturer of Meetings and Conventions.

MEEC events are like puzzles- eventually they must be put together.
Maksim Kabakou/Alamy Stock Photo

CHAPTER 16

Putting It All Together

Chapter Objectives

- List items needed to understand the event's organizing association.

- Articulate the event's goals.

- Articulate specific items to consider when determining the event's budget.

- Discuss the elements to keep in mind when considering the event's income.

- Specify the necessary components involved in the request for proposal.

- Discuss the main considerations for conducting the first site inspection.

- Outline the important steps in the destination selection.

- Articulate the importance and the considerations necessary for the second site inspection.

- Discuss the part played by the marketing committee.

- Cover the steps involved in the creation of a conference program.

- Outline the importance of partnerships.

- Clarify the considerations involved in handling the event's contract.

- Specify the events and sequencing determined by the meeting timeline.

- Discuss the important items to consider after the meeting.

Many books contain a concluding chapter that repeats and summarizes the elements of earlier chapters. In this textbook, a fictitious case study of a citywide convention serves the same purpose. The goal of this case study is to bring together all the previous chapters. Throughout this text, you have read about the tasks associated with meeting/event planning. Through this case study, you will learn more about topics from the previous chapters, and how they apply to a citywide annual conference for 3,000 attendees. The objective of this case study is to help you understand the various tasks a planner or event professional (these terms will be used interchangeably throughout this chapter) must complete for a meeting, exposition, event, or convention (MEEC) to be successful. In addition, this case study will help the reader understand the complexities of the budget and timetable, as well as the many people with whom an event professional must communicate.

This case study uses a three-year planning timetable for one citywide conference. The meeting planning cycle is continuous, and it is important to understand that two of the key skills an event professional must possess are the abilities to organize and to multitask. Event professionals typically work on three to five meetings or events simultaneously, each in different stages of development.

As you review the budget portion of the case study, it is important to understand that many variables, including the time of year the meeting is held, the planner's ability to negotiate, the value of the business to the facility, and the trade-offs, will affect the budget. This budget is broad and was created to highlight the many details the planner must consider.

MORE SHAMPOO PLEASE

The Hilton New Orleans Riverside is a large convention hotel. The hotel contains over 1,600 guest rooms and suites, 130,000 square feet of meeting space, and a 90,000-square-foot health and fitness center. Needless to say, it hosts countless meetings and conventions. Whenever a convention attended predominantly by females is booked into the hotel, the housekeeping staff is instructed to double the amount of shampoo and towels in each guest room: women use more of each. The hotel also increases the strength of their linen laundry department: Makeup is more difficult to remove from linens.

The Association

As a meeting or event planner, it is important to understand your audience—the attendees of the event. For association meeting planners, this is critical as they market the conference to association members and to potential members. The meeting planner must also communicate information about members of his or her association to suppliers for the convention. The better a supplier understands the audience of the meeting planner, the better the supplier can serve them. For example, if a hotel knows that most of the people attending a meeting are women, the hotel might add products that women use, such as hand cream or shower caps, to the room amenities.

The American Small Animal Association (ASAA) is an example of a (fictitious) typical association in the United States. The ASAA is an 8,000-member nonprofit association whose members are veterinarians from throughout the United States who specialize in care for small animals. The ASAA was founded ten years ago by a group of veterinarians who saw the need to update research, and to network with other veterinarians specializing in small animal care. Over 60 percent of the organization's membership operates independently owned veterinary clinics; the remainder of the association members is suppliers to the veterinary industry. The suppliers include pharmaceutical companies, prescription food companies, and product suppliers. Although the number of women members is increasing, 60 percent of the members are male; 55 percent Caucasian; 30 percent African American; and 15 percent a mix of Latino, Asian, and Native American. It is important to know the makeup of the organization

Logo for the (fictitious) American Small Animal Association.
George G. Fenich

so that the event can meet its wants and needs. The planner or organizer must ask two questions: Who is the group? Why are its members here?

An executive committee and a board of directors operate the ASAA, while the executive director and seven committee members oversee the day-to-day operations of the association. Members of the board of directors are elected from seven established regions and serve two-year terms. All board elections take place during the annual meeting and are announced during the final night. Sue Rodriguez is the director of meetings for the ASAA and is a full-time employee. Sue is one of five full-time employees and is responsible for coordinating the seven regional meetings and the annual conference; she reports directly to the executive director. Planning for the annual conference begins three years in advance of the meeting date. For the past five years, attendance at the annual conference has increased five percent per year; and last year, 37 percent of the membership attended the meeting. This increase is attributed to the success of the trade show portion of the conference that was added five years ago.

Goals

To begin preparation for the annual conference, Sue reviews past annual conference evaluations from attendees and members of the board of directors. The board of directors wanted to save money by cutting down on the cost related to networking activities, but the members indicated how important it is to have time to meet other professionals from around the country. The board would also like to see a 10 percent increase in revenues over expenses because, other than membership dues, the annual conference is the largest revenue source for the association. Last year, the ASAA created the Small Animal Preventive Disease Certificate (SAPDC). During the annual convention, veterinarians can earn five continuing education units (CEUs) and learn about the preventive medicines that can be used to save the lives of small animals. Additionally, the board of directors requested that a **corporate social responsibility (CSR)** segment be included in the annual conference. Once a destination is selected for the annual meeting, Sue will work with the local community to identify not-for-profit organizations that need help.

To help focus her thoughts, Sue reads the ASAA mission statement: The mission of ASAA is to provide an educational forum for members to exchange ideas and develop ways to ensure the health of small animals. This mission is accomplished by providing quality education for its members, offering assistance to new veterinarian clinics, and providing a forum for members to meet and to assist each other with emerging technologies.

To help Sue measure the **return on investment (ROI)**, she creates operational and educational objectives. The operational objective for this conference is to increase meeting profits by five percent over last year's conference. Sue works with the program committee to create the educational objectives for this meeting, which is to increase the number of attendees enrolled in SAPDC classes by ten percent, and to provide additional networking opportunities. Sue hopes to meet these objectives by offering a four-day conference focused on education and networking that will result in an increase of conference profits by five percent.

Budget

To create the budget (see Tables 16-1 and 16-2), Sue reviews the past meeting budgets. For her expenses, she includes the cost of marketing materials, the convention center, host hotel, decorator, audiovisual equipment, speakers, entertainment, and staff. In addition, Sue must consider operational objectives for the meeting. To locate income sources, Sue looks at past meeting **sponsors** and exhibitors. This year, marketing will include increased social media and solicitation of technology sponsors to offset the cost of Wi-Fi.

The hotel budget will include meeting room rentals, food and beverage, staff sleeping rooms, and service charges and gratuities. In creating the budget, Sue knows that she will have some negotiation opportunities based on the ASAA sleeping and meeting room usage ratios. The better that the ASAA's use of meeting rooms to sleeping rooms will match the hotel's ideal sleeping room to meeting room ratio, the better the rate that can be negotiated. To assist in managing the hotel blocks, Sue uses a housing bureau.

The convention center expenses will include the cost of space for meeting rooms, the exhibit hall, electricity, Internet connection, garbage pickup, security, and staffing for coffee and food stations. To maximize dollars, Sue plans the majority of her educational events at the convention center. This not only enables her to use the daily rate for the rooms at the convention center, but it is also a selling point for the exhibitors who want attendees near the trade show.

Sue will need to identify a **general services contractor (GSC)** to provide decorations and to set up the trade show. She will also need to assess audiovisual needs for both the hotel

TABLE 16-1
Budget Income

Budget	Income	Registration
		3,000 attendees
Members		1,680 attendees
early (at 60% = 1,008 people)	$600 p/p	$604,800
late (at 40% = 672 people)	$800 p/p	$537,600
Nonmembers		600 attendees
early (at 50% = 300 people)	$700 p/p	$210,000
late (at 50% = 300 people)	$900 p/p	$270,000
Student (at 5% = 120 people)	$200 p/p	$24,000
Speakers (100 people)	$300 p/p	$30,000
Exhibitors	Included in exhibit fee	
Registration Total		**$1,676,400**
SAPDC (500 people)	$200 p/p	100,000
Exhibitors	$3,500 p/exhibit	$1,750,000
Sponsors (500 exhibitions)		$150,000
Bookstore		$10,000
Other		$5,000
Total Income		**$3,691,400**
Expenses		$2,081,188
Net Income		**$1,610,212**

TABLE 16-2

Budget Expenses

Budget	Expenses
Convention Center	$450,000
Host Hotel	$312,643
GSC	$102,245
Signage	$80,000
Audiovisual Equipment	$200,000
Webcasting	$60,000
Pressroom	$30,000
Transportation	$50,000
Off-Site Venue	$75,000
Golf Event	$20,000
Marketing Committee	$190,000
Program Committee	$20,000
Speakers	$72,000
Entertainment	$30,000
Security	$180,000
Insurance	$100,000
Special Services	$5,000
Printing	$10,000
Temporary Staff	$67,200
Gifts	$20,000
Site Visits	$2,100
Other	$5,000
Total Expenses	**$2,081,188**

and convention center. The GSC will provide staging for the reception, general session, trade show, and awards night, and the **audiovisual (AV) company** will provide sound and light. To provide an accurate quote, the GSC must be given information on carpeting requests, number of trade show booths, estimated freight use, and types of staging needed for the opening session, general session, and awards dinner. The AV company will need to know the sound and lighting needs for each venue and the type of production for the general session, opening reception, and awards dinner. The general session will be sent via webcast to members who are unable to attend, so Sue lists this as a separate expense (see Table 16-2).

To budget transportation, Sue looks at past budgets to determine how many attendees used the shuttle service for airport transfers, but she knows this expense will vary greatly depending on the existing transportation options in a given city. At this point, she includes full shuttle service for each day of the conference, VIP transportation, and transportation to the off-site events and the golf tournament. In addition to ground transportation, Sue's transportation budget includes air transportation for staff and VIPs, as well as freight shipping.

Reviewing the budget history is also a good starting place when Sue allocates funds for marketing. This year she will spend less on hard items, like brochures and direct mail pieces, and more on electronic marketing, social media, and bloggers

Of the speakers for the ASAA, 75 percent are members presenting research papers. To encourage members to make presentations, the ASAA offers presenters a 50 percent discount on the early registration fee. Most of the money allocated for speakers is actually used for entertainment and a keynote speaker. To locate the keynote speaker and entertainment, Sue uses a speaker's bureau; the speaker's bureau's fee is included in this expense item.

In order to have a smooth meeting, Sue will need to hire temporary staff. This budget item includes the cost for registration personnel, staff for on-site assembly of attendee packets, room monitors, and staff to distribute evaluations and carry out other duties.

Sue will need to bring in temporary staff one day prior to the meeting for training and will pay staff for their time.

Security is an ongoing expense that the ASAA must include in its budget. Because the ASAA is increasing its involvement in new research for small animals, and this new research is both confidential and controversial, more security will be needed.

Insurance is another expense that is increasing. Sue includes insurance to cover attrition and loss of revenue due to acts of God, terrorism, and liability. To cover expenses for attendees with special needs, Sue includes a special services item in the budget, which will be used for members who identify themselves as needing translators, written material to be published in Braille, sign language interpreters, special accommodations for seeing eye dogs, and so on.

When Sue creates the budgets, she contacts city officials where the meeting will be held. As a nonprofit organization, the ASAA is exempt from most city and state taxes, but she must file the documents to ensure the exemption. Furthermore, Sue will need to bring forms proving that the ASAA is a nonprofit organization; the forms will also be filed with suppliers.

Sue includes some expenses in the budget even though she knows that these expenses will be picked up by sponsors. Each year, Sue has no problem finding a company to sponsor the tote bags given to all the attendees, transportation, the meal for the opening reception, and the entertainment for the VIP dinner. It is important that Sue includes these items in the budget to document these expenses.

To allow for unexpected expenses, Sue creates an "other" expense category, which is used to cover additional expenses that do not occur every year, or that are not planned for. For example, if the cost of shipping increases, this contingency would be covered.

Income

The income (see Table 16-1) will offset the expenses for the meeting. Estimated expenses for this meeting are $2,081,188. To reach the financial objectives, Sue must not only pay all expenses, but also build in an excess of revenues over expenses.

In determining the income, Sue starts with income generated from the registration fees. She first takes the expected attendance of 3,000 and subtracts 500 exhibitors whose registration fee is included in the exhibitor fee, and then subtracts the 100 speakers who will pay a reduced registration. The ASAA has three registration fee categories: members, nonmembers, and students. Convention history shows that 70 percent are members, 25 percent are nonmembers, and 5 percent are students. To reduce attrition fees, Sue creates an early registration fee and a late fee for members and nonmembers. Typically, 60 percent of the members and 50 percent of the nonmembers will register early. Sue estimates that if registration alone will cover expenses, she must charge $629 per person. With this in mind, Sue's registration fee structure is $600 for an early member, $700 for an early nonmember, $800 for a late member, and $900 for a late nonmember. Students only pay $200, thus encouraging them to join when they are employed in the field. Sue estimates her registration income to be $1,676,400.

Following the income generated from registration fees, the exhibitors are the largest single source of income for the ASAA. It will cost the ASAA approximately $15 per square foot to rent the convention space, GSC, and audiovisual equipment. The ASAA will sell this trade show space for $35 per square foot. History shows a steady 10 percent increase in exhibitors per year; at the last conference, about 450 companies ordered booths. Sue estimates exhibitor income for this year to be $1,750,000 (500 exhibitors spending $3,500 each for a ten-foot by ten-foot booth).

Other sources of income that Sue includes in the budget are rebates generated from hotel rooms, the transportation company, and the GSC. Rather than accept commissions for these items, the ASAA negotiates a rebate per room night that becomes an income stream. There is a small amount of money raised by the sale of the bookstore products, including books, shirts, and branded products.

Income from the SAPDC is $200 per person, in addition to the registration. Last year, the ASAA charged $300 per person—the cost is low to encourage attendees to take classes toward certification.

Request for Proposal

Once the meeting objectives are laid out and a budget determined, Sue creates a **request for proposal (RFP)**. In creating the RFP, Sue wants to include accurate information to help hotels and cities submit good proposals. She includes meeting specifications on the ASAA and explains that the RFP is sent three years prior to the annual conference date. Although most RFP's are submitted electronically, Sue creates a hard copy and uses it as a guide to help her send consistent information to vendors. After the venues and destinations respond to the RFP, Sue reviews the information with Dave Rogers, executive director, and Elizabeth Rice, a board member serving as the convention chair. Sue, Dave, and Elizabeth will choose two cities to visit to conduct an initial site inspection. After the initial site inspections to all selected cities are complete, a decision will be made, and Sue and Dave will conduct a second site inspection to the chosen city to begin contract negotiations. To avoid any bias, the ASAA will pick up the cost of the site inspection with the understanding that, when a city is selected, the host city will rebate the cost of the site inspection.

The RFP will include a list of cities under consideration and the preferred dates. Although the dates may vary between the months of March and April, the days of the week must be Thursday to Sunday. The annual conference is held around the country, primarily in large cities near places where members of the board of directors reside.

Sue's RFP includes a detailed grid of her meeting room needs. She includes special requests; for example, her classroom sets require two chairs per six-foot table and a water station with recyclable water cups set in the back of the room. She also includes a food and beverage summary that notes special dietary needs of attendees. Her meeting room grid includes the event, number of attendees, and room set.

The ASAA prefers to use no more than five hotels in a given city. A grid is created requesting the number of suites, single rooms, and double rooms that the ASAA anticipates using at each hotel. When considering a city, Sue looks for downtown hotel properties that offer a wide range of room prices, but the hotels need to be in close proximity to each other. The host hotel must be willing to block a minimum of 900 rooms. In addition to the sleeping room block, the host hotel will be the site of the opening night reception and break-out rooms for special-interest groups. A detailed history, in the form of a grid, of the last three years, is included in the RFP. The history grid shows the peak room nights, meeting room block, sleeping room block, pickup for the host hotel and the room block, and pickup at each of the non-host hotels. She also includes a food and beverage section showing reported use. The ASAA reports a ten percent increase in meeting attendees per year over the last two years and has an attrition rate of only two percent.

The final portion of the RFP is a two-page questionnaire for the hotel to complete and submit with the proposal. Questions include green initiatives, comp room policy, deposit policy, definition of sold out, attrition policy, master accounts, split folios, shuttle service availability, tax rate, nonprofit tax policy, service charges, gratuity distribution, Internet connection and fees, phone charges, and fitness facilities fees. Sue also includes questions about how the hotel handles in conjunction with (ICWs) and exhibitor room blocks, and whether the hotel will work to create priority housing for members over non-members. Sue found that this form provides a quick way for her to compare hotels.

Using the RFP link on the destination marketing organization (DMO)/**convention and visitor bureau (CVB)** website, Sue enters meeting information and attaches a questionnaire for the DMO to complete. The questionnaire includes questions regarding state, local, and hotel room taxes, as well as holidays, union contracts, special venues, DMO services, and citywide events or holidays that take place during the ASAA meeting dates.

First Site Inspection

Sue, Dave, and Elizabeth have reviewed the proposals and identified two cities with available dates to host the ASAA citywide: Chicago and Dallas. Sue calls the DMOs in those cities to arrange to spend three days in each city and explains to them that the team plans to conduct a detailed site inspection to look for hotels, off-site venues, and golf courses. She sends the site inspection form that the team will use to evaluate the city and properties, explaining that the team will stay at the hotels under consideration as host properties, and will conduct short tours of non-host hotels under consideration. For the non-host properties, the team only needs to meet with the hotel sales contact, see a standard room, and tour the outlets.

Day One

Mark Tester, vice president of sales, Chicago CVB, meets Sue, Dave, and Elizabeth at Chicago's O'Hare airport. On arrival, Mark gives a driving tour of downtown, passing by all the hotels under consideration. They have lunch at the Chicago Museum of Art, where they are joined by Kesha Evans, owner of Windy City, a destination management company (DMC). Kesha explains the various services she can provide, including transportation and arrangements for off-site events, spouse tours, and private dining. Tom Delaney, catering manager at the Chicago Museum of Art, introduces himself and takes the group on a tour of the private function areas of the museum, and recommends the best area for an off-site event. He opens his tablet to show visuals of the many meeting set-up and décor options. He gives Sue a sales packet with sample menus and pricing, and says that he will send an email with a link with more detailed information.

After lunch, Mark takes the inspection team to the Hyatt Regency McCormick Place to meet with its sales manager, Bob Taylor, and its general manager, Larry Rose. They tour the property, looking at sleeping rooms, suites, singles, and doubles, as well as the meeting rooms and ballrooms for possible locations for the opening reception, special-interest group meetings, and available outlets. After the tour, they meet in one of the conference rooms to discuss available dates, rates, and Internet options.

Then Sue, Dave, and Elizabeth meet at 6:00 PM in the hotel restaurant for dinner. During dinner, they make observations, noting how the guests are treated, what the quality of the food is, the time food is served, and whether the wait staff is attentive. They order different entrées to sample the many types of food their attendees might order if they stay at this hotel. After dinner, Sue walks to the meeting space, looking into the meeting rooms to see how the rooms are set.

Day Two

At 8:30 AM, Mark meets the team members who have already eaten breakfast and checked out of the hotel. Mark has arranged for a 9:00 AM meeting with Randy Moses, senior sales manager of McCormick Place Convention Center. Randy gives a tour of the facility, taking time to show them what he sees as the best locations for their functions, loading docks, and shuttle drop-off and pickup, as well as the areas where sponsored items such as banners are allowed. Sue asks about available dates, food and beverage concession hours, Internet/Wi-Fi charges, taxes, union rules, and contract renewal dates. Randy provides this information and discusses the security, and the medical and emergency procedure guidelines. Both Mark and Randy explain to Sue, Dave, and Elizabeth how the DMO and convention center work as a team to help market the Chicago meeting to attendees. They discuss marketing options, including pre-mailers, email, social media, and on-site promotions the year prior to coming to the host city.

For lunch, Mark takes the group to the Golden Princess, a luxury yacht owned by ABC Charters, a company that provides dinner tours of Lake Michigan. Rich Cunningham, general manager of ABC Charters, meets with them. Today, they are having a special lunch for the meeting planners to sample the menu and enjoy a mini-charter experience. The president of Chicago DMC Services, Deborah Adams, explains her services and has videos on her tablet that show other off-site locations Sue may want to consider.

The afternoon is spent making contacts and touring the hotels under consideration. Mark arranges 30-minute tours of each non-host hotel and explains to the hotel sales contact that they only want to see sleeping rooms and restaurant areas. By 4:00 PM, Sue, Dave, and Elizabeth are ready to check into the Hyatt Regency Chicago, the second hotel under consideration as the headquarters hotel. Rachel Monroe introduces herself as the association sales manager and begins the tour. She is excited about a new ballroom that was recently added and explains how the ballroom could be used for the opening reception. After the tour, Richard Moore, the general manager, joins the group to look at available dates and rates. Sue, Dave, and Elizabeth take an hour break and meet in the restaurant for dinner. During dinner, they review all notes from the past two days. After dinner, Sue takes her tour of the meeting rooms.

Day Three

The team checks out early and waits in the hotel lobby. As they check email, they notice a line forming as people check out of the hotel. They take mental notes, observing how long the checkout time is and how courteous the employees are at the front desk and bell stand. Mark arrives at the hotel and takes the group to the first stop, Harborside International Golf Center, a four-star course only 12 miles from downtown Chicago. The group meets with the special events manager of the Harborside to discuss the optional golf outing that is part of the ASAA event. The tournament is held Thursday afternoon, prior to the opening reception. Mark takes the group to one more golf course and on two more hotel site inspections before they depart for the airport. Sue, Dave, and Elizabeth thank Mark for his time, and inform him that they will be touring Dallas next month and plan to make a decision in two months. After the Dallas site inspection, the ASAA will make its decision and will contact the bureau regarding this decision.

Destination Selection

One month later, Sue, Dave, and Elizabeth go to Dallas for another three-day site inspection. Patty Brown, the sales manager of Visit Dallas DMO, arranges for the group to meet with staff from the hotels, the convention center, and the off-site locations. Patty points out all the changes in Dallas, including the Omni Dallas Hotel that is attached to the Dallas Convention Center.

After both site inspections conclude, the inspection team reviews their notes. Due to the conflict of dates with other industry meetings, they decide to meet on St. Patrick's Day. When evaluating Chicago, they are concerned about room availability, the renewal dates for some union contracts, and the fact that the cost to hold the meeting in Chicago is 25 percent more than in Dallas. This increase in cost might be offset by the number of attendees who prefer to meet in Chicago over Dallas, but this meeting will attract more attendees seeking the SAPDC—thus location will not be as much of an issue. Dallas is selected for the annual conference. Sue calls Mark from the Chicago CVB and expresses their concerns, and explains why Dallas was selected. Sue reminds Mark that they have not held a meeting in Chicago in five years and would like to look there again in the future.

Second Site Inspection

Day One

Sue sends Patty Brown, at the Visit Dallas DMO, a letter of intent to hold the conference in Dallas and contacts her to help arrange a second site inspection. This second site inspection will include only Sue and Dave, and will be for three days. The goal is to finalize non-host properties, select off-site venues and a golf course, select the DMC and transportation company, begin contract negotiations, and select an organization for the CSR project. When Sue and Dave arrive in Dallas, they rent a car and take a self-guided tour of the city. They check in at the Omni Hotel Dallas, the location of the headquarters hotel for the meeting.

At the Omni Hotel Dallas in downtown Dallas, Sue and Dave meet with Loretta Jones, global director of sales, and Vicki Wall, the **convention services manager (CSM)**. Once the contract is signed, Sue will work with the CSM for the remainder of the meeting. During this meeting, Sue and Loretta will begin negotiations for sleeping rooms, meeting rooms, shuttle service, and so on.

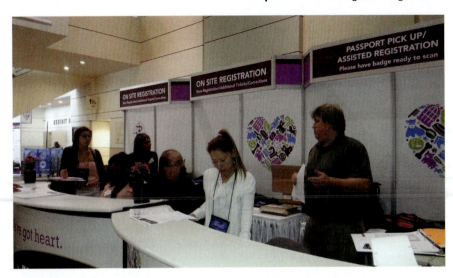

Registration company trains temporary staff prior to the opening of the conference.
M.T. Hickman

After the meeting with the hotel staff, Sue meets Sonja Miller, sales manager of the Dallas Convention Center; Erika Bondy, CMP, senior event coordinator; and Bill Baker, director of catering. Once the contract is signed, Sue will work with Erika on all her meeting details, and with Bill on meeting food and beverage requirements. Today, Sue begins negotiating rates with the Dallas Convention Center. At the meeting, she will review her needs and see what is the best win–win situation for her attendees and the convention center.

Sue and Dave have lunch at the Dallas Museum of Art and meet with the catering sales manager, Cindy Hartman, to review rates for having the VIP dinner in the restaurant. Carolyn Petty, president of EMC (a DMC), joins Sue and Dave for lunch to discuss what the DMC can provide for the ASAA meeting, including gift baskets and general transportation needs.

In the afternoon, Patty has arranged for Sue to meet with two of the non-host hotels under consideration in the city for sleeping room space. At each hotel, Sue meets the sales manager to negotiate the rates and amenities. For dinner, Patty takes Sue and Dave to a small Mexican restaurant that is a favorite of the locals. At dinner, Patty discusses the services that Visit Dallas can assist with, including registration personnel, marketing, social media packages to promote the meeting, leads for suppliers, transportation, Internet services, and on-site concierge to help attendees with local dining and sightseeing activities. She will staff a promotional booth at the meeting prior to the one in Dallas.

Day Two

The morning is spent touring and re-establishing contact with the remainder of the hotels that will provide sleeping rooms. Sue and Dave have lunch at the Perot Museum of Nature because they are looking for a fun site for the VIP meeting. They meet with Nicole Benson, event sales manager, for a tour and a discussion of possible dining options. Although this is an option, it might be too casual for the group. Nicole brings her tablet to show pictures of events held at the museum, and Sue's concerns dissipate.

In the afternoon, Sue and Dave tour two golf courses. For each course, Sue makes contacts, has the event sales manager take them on a nine-hole tour, and begins discussing rates. Sue pays attention to where the group might meet before and after the tournament.

Day Three

Sue and Dave begin the day meeting the GSC contact, Jack Boyd, account executive for the Freeman Companies, the GSC, and Mark Lee, director of sales, PSAV, Dallas, an AV company. Jack, Mark, Dave, and Sue meet first at the Dallas Convention Center and then at the Omni Dallas Hotel to discuss GSC and audiovisual equipment needs. They tour each venue, discussing specific staging, set up, Wi-Fi, and other needs for each event.

The last stop of the day is to the Dallas SPCA to meet with Iris Henderson, volunteer coordinator. While researching a site for the meeting's CSR, Sue learned about the Dallas SPCA and their program for groups to donate time sanitizing the animal shelter.

Marketing Committee

ASAA has both an in-house marketing department and an outside advertising agency, and they work together to create the marketing campaign for the annual conference. After Sue returns home from the second site inspection, she meets with George Day, the ASAA director of marketing, and Julie Love, the account manager for Idea Maker, Inc., an advertising company. George and Julie share the results of a member survey, which reported that members are using Facebook, LinkedIn, and Twitter. They explain to Sue the importance of increasing social media in the marketing plan. Sue discusses the convention location and the meeting objectives, and also explains how important promoting the new SAPDC is for this conference. After two weeks, Sue meets with George and Julie again. Julie brings theme ideas and visuals for the marketing pieces. After reviewing several themes, "Power of Prevention" is selected. It is decided that three marketing tools will be used. A four-color, postcard-size mailer will be developed as a teaser, and will be mailed to all past conference attendees and targeted to potential members. This teaser will also be used as an advertisement that will be placed in industry newsletters' digital magazines. The second piece will be an email announcement sent to all association members with a link to the convention Web page, which will include a convention agenda giving dates, times, and speakers; a program-at-a-glance grid; current sponsors; and convention and housing registration forms. The final approach is the social media campaign that will include posts on Facebook, LinkedIn, Snapchat, and Twitter. Working with popular convention speakers, the marketing committee will post information on Facebook and LinkedIn, and will Tweet about the conference activities. In addition, YouTube videos will be added to the conference website to generate excitement and encourage early registration, and bloggers will be hired to write about and post their conference experiences. This year, in an effort to use less paper, a one-sheet program will be created with the location of exhibitors in the trade show and a summary of the conference activities. After registering for the conference, attendees will download the conference app, which will include information on the program, speakers, educational sessions, location of exhibitors, and detailed information on their products. Additionally, the app will have a section for attendees to interact with each other, and will include an electronic game that will encourage attendees to network and meet exhibitors.

George is excited about the app and explains to Sue and David that the game developed for the app will be used to highlight key sponsors, thus adding a new revenue source to the conference.

During each conference, a new board of directors is introduced, awards are given, and important announcements must be made. Sue, George, and Dave meet to discuss the types of presentations that will be made and the scripts that George and his team will write. Sue is responsible for arranging rehearsal time for each presentation.

The marketing committee is responsible for creating press releases, which will be sent to professional publications. For each conference, a new piece of research is featured, and the marketing committee works to promote this research to the public.

Creation of the Conference Program

When Sue returns from the Dallas site inspection, she meets with the program committee to begin creating the educational content of the meeting. Serving on the program committee is Doug Walker, board member and chair of the SAPDC; Dan Dearing, chairman of the board of directors of the Program Committee for the Power of Prevention annual convention; and his appointed committee members, Liz Stewart and Mark Collins, along with Donna Smith, ASAA administrative assistant. These five people and Sue will work together to create the content of the meeting.

Sue begins the meeting by giving each committee member an option to receive a hard copy or electronic notebook with responsibilities of the committee members, past convention notes, and the meeting theme, the "Power of Prevention." Sue wants to make sure that the committee members understand the objective of the meeting: to increase the number of member attendees taking the SAPDC by ten percent by offering a four-day conference that is focused on education that will increase meeting revenues over expenses by five percent. The committee agrees to follow the same meeting agenda as in the past: opening reception, general session, concurrent sessions, awards dinner, and a **poster session** located in the middle of the trade show. The conference will include an ASAA VIP dinner, a golf tournament, and a total of 120, 90-minute education sessions in two days. The one change to the schedule was to add two, four-hour segments for the SAPDC class. The committee will locate speakers for SAPDC classes and all break-out sessions. ASAA members will present 100 of the 120 educational sessions. To help the program committee, a separate committee—called the paper review committee—is created that will issue the call for papers, will grade and evaluate papers, and inform the program committee of its final selection for presentations and **poster sessions**. Sue will use a speaker's bureau for the opening reception, general session, awards dinner, ASAA VIP dinner, and all entertainment.

Sue reviews the time line with the committee. Using abstract management software, the paper review committee will begin the call for papers one year prior to the meeting; six months prior, the paper review committee will provide the program committee with the final selection, and the program committee will make initial contact with presenters and speakers. The committee will recommend speakers for all sessions. Once speakers and backup speakers have been identified, Sue will send out invitation letters in which she will outline the audiovisual options, and ask the speaker to sign a commitment sheet and provide an abstract of the presentation, as well as his or her biography and photo.

The committee will be responsible for contacting all the speakers and following up with those not responding. There will also be a point person for all speaker questions. Once speakers have been selected, Sue's role is to collect information, assign time slots, and correspond with the speakers, including letters of acceptance and a reminder letter.

One key feature in the conference is the exhibitors. Jill Kochan, ASAA staff, is the ASAA trade show manager for the conference. Jill is responsible for all communications with the exhibitors and the GSC as they set up the trade show. Jill will work closely with Sue to communicate exhibitor needs and will meet with the GSC to create specifications for the exhibitor prospectus.

The newly formed CSR Committee will work with the Dallas SPCA on a program that will give attendees an opportunity to volunteer at the new shelter during the conference. In addition, the committee will work with marketing to create an announcement to encourage attendees to bring items to the conference that will be donated to the SPCA. To thank ASAA for their help, the SPCA will put on a "puppy pet" in the lobby on the first day of the conference.

Partnerships

As Sue prepares for this meeting, she knows the importance of her meeting partners. Throughout the conference, Sue depends on many companies to provide excellent service and to create a memorable experience for the ASAA members. She reviews her contact list, looking at the many companies she will partner with for the upcoming conference.

Although most housing bureaus can provide a complete housing package, including hotel selection, negotiation, and contract, Sue prefers to work with the housing bureau after she has selected the hotels. Once the selections have been made, the housing bureau will manage the hotel room block. The housing bureau will create a Web link for attendees to book rooms online, and a downloadable form for attendees to complete, scan, and email. Once an attendee selects a hotel, the housing bureau will send a confirmation letter. One of the best aspects about Sue's partnership with the housing bureau is room block management: Rather than call all the hotels being used, Sue calls the housing bureau for monthly, weekly, and daily rooming reports as needed and depends on the housing bureau to manage the exhibitor room block.

Sue likes to partner with a local DMC for the annual conference. For this conference, Sue uses the DMC for arranging the airport meet and greet, hotel transfers, VIP transportation, and shuttle service from hotels to the convention center. The DMC makes all logistical arrangements for the VIP dinner, which allows Sue to concentrate on VIP invitations and the content of the event. Sue also appreciates the fact that a DMC normally has access to many motor coach suppliers because transportation is always an area of concern for Sue. Once, in Washington, DC, Sue contracted with a motor coach company, and one of the motor coaches broke down with all her attendees in it. The company had no backup motor coaches, so her attendees waited almost an hour to be rescued and taken to the event.

For key speakers and entertainment, Sue uses a speaker's bureau because she does not have the time to research the many speakers and entertainers who could speak to ASAA members. The speaker's bureau will make recommendations on the best speakers and entertainers; and, once Sue makes her selection, the speaker's bureau will handle all arrangements. It will ensure that the speakers are at the meeting on time and, if something happens, the speaker's bureau can quickly arrange for a backup speaker.

Sue selects an online registration company to create the meeting registration site and collect registration fees. The designated registration company will accept registrations electronically, automatically send attendees a confirmation letter that contains a link to the housing bureau, and stores the registrations for easy retrieval to create name badges. The company that Sue selects offers on-site registration services, staffing, and financial reports. This provides attendees with a consistent registration experience, and the meeting planner with quick access to reports to monitor registration activity and income.

Sponsors are important partners for the ASAA conference. Sue will work with all the sponsors to ensure that they receive exposure to members in exchange for their financial and/or in-kind support. Sue realizes that without annual conference sponsors, the ASAA would not reach its financial objectives for the convention.

The ASAA has always included meeting security for the safety of attendees and exhibitor products, but for this conference Sue will increase security. An animal rights association contacted the ASAA and plans to protest a new test being conducted on laboratory rats. Sue realized that she must allow this group to protest, but she wants to ensure that they protest peacefully and do not disturb meeting attendees.

Key partners in making the conference a success are the GSC providing the decorations, and the AV company supplying the electronic equipment. Sue considers the GSC as the partner that brings the theme to life, so the decorations must wow attendees visually. Sue recognizes the important role the GSC plays in keeping the exhibitors happy in addition to pleasing the conference attendees. This is important to the ASAA, as the exhibitors generate 44 percent of the revenue for the conference.

Sue loves to work with the AV company because this partner is crucial for every meeting event. Without proper projection and sound, the attendees would not be able to learn. Sue works closely with its staff during the meeting. One burned-out light bulb or malfunctioning microphone can ruin a break-out session.

To keep things running efficiently at the conference, Sue hires temporary staff and builds a partnership early with these people. They will be part of the team and will represent the ASAA during the conference.

Contracts

Sue has a contract for each convention partner and every service provider. Each contract specifies the exact services that are expected and the penalties if the expectations are not met. Early in Sue's career, she worked with an association that signed a contract that did not include a realistic attrition clause. The association did not meet its room block and paid the hotel over $50,000 for unused rooms. At least one year out, Sue reviews each contract carefully. Long before the meeting begins, Sue will have contracts finalized with the host hotel, housing bureau, registration company, airlines, off-site venue, golf course, speaker's bureau, security, AV company, DMC, GSC, and many others.

Meeting Timeline

One Year to Six-Month Countdown

Sue looks at her **meeting time line** and realizes that she is 18 months away from the Power of Prevention annual conference. She takes out her meeting resume and reviews all contracts. She meets with George and Julie from the marketing committee to review electronic and hard copy marketing pieces. If Sue and her team miss an educational session or a grammatical error, then then it will be printed with the omission or error. If the mistake is important enough, the marketing piece will be reprinted and the expenses added to the cost of the conference. Fortunately, with electronic pieces changes can quickly be made with minimal expense.

She arranges a meeting with Doug and Dan from the program committee to select the speakers for the convention. On selection, Sue sends out the acceptance letter to the speakers. In her letter, Sue requests that the speaker confirm his or her commitment by sending an electronic speaker biography, digital photo, presentation abstract, and audiovisual needs form. Sue makes a point to contact the speaker's bureau to check the status of the motivational speaker and entertainment. She requests that all electronic equipment needs are identified one year prior to the meeting. By doing this, Sue is able to have a more accurate budget item for the equipment.

Sue secures ten sponsors for the meeting, including Small Vets Plus, a company that supplies the vaccines for small animals, for the tote bags; Houver Pharmaceutical, a small-animal antibiotic producer, for transportation; LabSmlab, a provider of medical instruments used in animal surgery, for the opening night reception; Mix-a-Vet, a developer of special food for small animals, to sponsor the conference app; and Smalco, a pet store featuring small-animal products to sponsor the closing night dinner. Small Vets Plus will cosponsor the VIP entertainment and the awards dinner. Sue will contact each sponsor to confirm the commitment and sign the contract. In her conversation, Sue reminds sponsors that she needs to have them return a form with the exact spelling of their company name and the design of their signage or logo in a form that can be used on mobile applications.

The trade show floor plan for the Dallas conference was created and approved 14 months prior to the Dallas meeting. Exhibit space for the Power of Prevention conference was sold on-site at the ASAA conference prior to Dallas—the ASAA has an 87 percent exhibitor retention. Nine months out, the GSC updates the floor plan and emails electronic exhibitor links to potential exhibitors. The ASAA uses exhibition software to create an electronic floor plan, manage booth sales, exhibitor registration, and provide financial reports to monitor sales.

In addition to the trade show, Sue works with the GSC in finalizing the set up for the opening reception, general session, and awards dinner. She determines where the media center and the registration area will be located. Sue depends on the GSC to recommend the best location to place sponsor banners, gobos, and signage. Most convention centers have strict rules regarding banner and signage placement; and GSCs that work with convention centers frequently know the rules and have great ideas on how sponsors can be recognized.

Six Months to the Day of the Meeting

Fast forward to the six-month countdown for the Power of Prevention conference. The marketing committee writes and sends press releases and increases Facebook posts and social media promotions.

Early registration forms begin to arrive within weeks after being sent. In reviewing the registration forms, Sue notices that three of the attendees indicated that they have mobility disabilities and will need special accommodations. In compliance with the Americans with Disabilities Act (ADA), Sue will work with all meeting partners to ensure that these attendees are able to fully participate in the conference. She needs to arrange for handicapped rooms and notes that the meeting rooms will need to be set with aisles to accommodate these attendees.

Sue receives the menus from the hotel catering manager and selects the meals. She focuses on selecting menus that will appeal to all the attendees. The evaluations from last years' conference indicate that attendees wanted more healthy and vegetarian options.

She contacts the host hotel and convention center to get the names of the meeting rooms that will be used for the Power of Prevention conference. It is important for Sue to get the name of the location of the meeting rooms so that this information can be added to the convention program and app. Hotels and convention centers rarely want to give this information out early, as they do not want to commit to a particular meeting room that might be sold to another planner, so good communication and flexibility are important.

Sue works with the DMC to review the menu, as well as the GSC for the VIP dinner at the Perot Museum of Nature and Science. The dinner will be in a room that overlooks downtown Dallas and the evening will include a private tour of the museum and the opportunity to create a new virtual species of bird and test its ability to fly. Sue contacts Larry Grant, the event organizer at Tennyson Golf Course, to finalize tournament rules. It looks like this will be a great year for this event—30 people are already registered for this event. Sue gives Larry the names and their handicaps.

During this time, Sue will also contact the DMC to finalize shuttle routes to all events, enabling her to begin ordering signage for transportation. Sue learns each year how even highly educated people get lost at meetings—it baffles her that veterinarians cannot read the location material in their program and on the app. Sue must clearly list all the events, their locations, and the shuttle service times. Signage is very important in the total conference experience.

Month Five

Five months prior to the meeting, Sue sends out reminders to all speakers, and she works with the marketing committee to finalize and send the marketing brochure and update social media promotions. After some quiet time to proofread the meeting material, she creates a detailed work schedule for staff, temporary employees, and volunteers. Sue orders meeting name badges and meeting supplies, and then calls the security company to review her needs.

Months Four and Three

During the fourth and third months prior to the meeting, Sue monitors registration on a weekly basis. At the third month, Sue reviews registration and makes adjustments to her room block (she negotiated this option in her hotel contract as a way to control attrition).

Sue looks at her initial room block (see Table 16-3) and compares it with current hotel registrations. Convention history shows that 60 percent of the people register early, indicating that, in a perfect world, the host property would have 600 rooms reserved and the remaining properties would have 300 each. In looking at the actual hotel registrations, Sue notices that all rooms have been filled at the Hyatt Regency Downtown Dallas, but she is unable to get additional rooms so will need to close reservations for the Hyatt Regency. The Hilton Anatole and W Hotel are right on schedule and will require no changes. The Holiday Inn is 200 rooms less than what it should be; Sue reduces the block by 40 percent and is now obligated for 300 rooms rather than 500. She has the opposite

TABLE 16-3

ASAA Hotel Room Blocks

Hotel	Omni Hotel Dallas	Hyatt Regency Downtown Dallas	Hilton Anatole	W Hotel	Holiday Inn
Initial Room Block	1,000	500	500	500	500
90-Day Room Block Review	700	500	300	300	100
Room Block Adjustment	Over—will add 50 rooms	No change	On schedule	On schedule	Under—will remove 200 rooms
New Room Block	1,050	500	500	500	300

problem with the Omni Dallas Hotel, the host hotel—the host property is 100 rooms over what she expects, so she conservatively increases the block by five percent and is obligated for 1,050 rooms.

In addition to the room block adjustments, she has received calls from the convention center to move the location of meeting rooms and from speakers needing to cancel. These changes affect the information in the one-page program and the conference app, so it must be revised. She sees this as a time of many changes, but these changes are all part of Sue's job. The work she did a year ago is paying off. A speaker cancels, so she contacts the program committee to see whom they have planned as a backup.

Month Two

At two months out, Sue arranges another trip to Dallas. Patty, CSM of the Dallas CVB, arranges for Sue to meet with all the key contacts to make the Power of Prevention conference a success. Vicki, the director of CSM at the Omni Hotel Dallas, meets with Sue to conduct a property walk-through, and she introduces Sue to the catering manager to review the menu, the accounts receivable contract to explain the bill review process, the front desk manager to confirm pre-key guests and the check-in and checkout process, and the director of security and medical staff to review emergency procedures. The CSM explains that she is the hotel contact and will assist Sue in providing information needed from the hotel, from room pickup to bill review. Vicki and Sue will work closely together.

At the Dallas Convention Center, Sue meets with Erika Bondy, Senior Event Coordinator, to conduct a walk-through, and invites the GSC and the AV contacts to join her. By doing this, Sue has many eyes looking for potential problems that might occur. She will also spend time with the catering manager to review the menu for the lunch and awards dinner.

Sue meets with the DMC representative to walk through hotel transportation routes and finalize menus, decorations, and entertainment for the VIP dinner at the Perot Museum of Nature and Science. Sue then meets with the event coordinator at the Tennison Golf Course to update the player list and review pairings.

When Sue returns from Dallas, she works with marketing to make updates to the app and sends the one-page paper program to the printer. She also ships materials to the convention site; works with the marketing committee on the final scripts; and reviews her staging guide that has all her contacts, contracts, menus, and notes for her to review, as well as the time-line.

Month One

One month prior to the meeting, Sue continues weekly monitoring of the registrations and sends reminder emails to all the speakers. She works with the advertising firm to approve press releases to announce the research findings that will be presented at the Power of Prevention conference; she also works with the staff to finalize work schedules, marketing, scripts, and rehearsal times. Sue will create a checklist and pack her convention material. She is a good planner and has thought about backup plans for her activities. For example, if the golf tournament is rained out, the group will spend the morning on a sports tour of Dallas.

Sue likens the month before the meeting to a tennis match. Emergencies—which feel like five to ten tennis balls coming across the net at her at the same time—can hit her, so Sue knows she must be ready with her racket in hand to successfully hit those balls back over the net and be ready for the next barrage of balls.

Pre-meeting Activities

Three days prior to the meeting, Sue and her staff arrive in Dallas to set up the meeting headquarters. She is happy to see that all her convention material has arrived safely. Sue meets all contacts to finalize meeting plans and arranges a walk-through of the host hotel and the convention center with her staff, temporary employees, and volunteers. The host hotel arranges a pre-con meeting where everyone working on the meeting gets together and reviews the meeting resume for any changes or concerns.

Sue monitors the set up of all meeting events and conducts on-site troubleshooting. Something always needs to be changed; it might be a sponsor sign with an error that needs to be redone by calling the GSC or a more complicated situation like the space for the registration being too small. This is a time of constant problem solving.

Sue joins George and the marketing staff as they rehearse for the general session, set up the pressroom, and conduct a press conference. George takes time to review the press list with Sue because she needs to know the names of press attendees to ensure that, when they arrive, someone from the ASAA staff can quickly assist them. Good publicity can ensure the success of future conferences.

Meeting Day Activities

The meeting begins, and Sue is busy working with the staff to ensure all meeting rooms are set up properly, and that all speaker materials and evaluations are ready. Her role is to work behind the scenes to make the attendees' experience perfect. She is the first one to arrive on-site and will be the last person to leave. The day is filled with questions that she must clarify or problems that need to be solved. This is the time that excites Sue—the time when she sees all her hard work become a reality. She uses the contacts she made to quickly solve problems. For example, the equipment in one of the rooms is not working, so she calls the AV company and the problem is quickly solved. At the beginning of each day, Sue meets with the hotel CSM and the accounts receivable department to conduct a bill review. She also checks with the housing bureau to follow up on a comparison of the ASAA registration with the in-house guest list to ensure that ASAA attendees are properly coded to the ASAA block, which helps with future event accommodations.

A special ASAA exhibitor headquarters office opens at the convention center. Jill, the ASAA's trade show manager, will remain in this office to handle any problems that might occur during the trade show and to accept exhibitor bookings for next year's ASAA conference.

After the Meeting

Immediate Post-meeting Activities

A tired Sue sips coffee and takes a moment to review the successes of and the areas of opportunity for the Power of Prevention conference. Before leaving Dallas, Sue will facilitate a post-con meeting to evaluate this year's conference, where people who attended the pre-con meeting will be present to discuss the conference and answer

Since Sue works with small animals, she often jokes that her job is like "pulling a rabbit out of a hat."
Olinchuk/Shuterstock

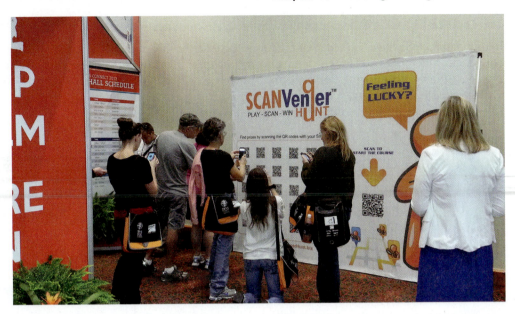

Attendees participate in a scavenger hunt
M.T. Hickman

questions: What were the problems? What could be done to improve this situation for future conventions? She will work with the hotel and vendors to reconcile registration numbers, review all pickups, and estimate ancillary business.

Planning a convention is a team event. Sue takes time to thank all speakers, sponsors, committee members, and facilitators for helping with the conference—she also rewards her staff by giving them a free day in Dallas to relax.

Two-Month Post-meeting Activities

After the statistics and evaluations have been reviewed, Sue begins her report to the executive director and to the board of directors regarding conference ROI. It is import-ant after each conference that an evaluation is conducted. In creating this conference, Sue and her team set the convention objectives: to increase the number of attendees taking the SAPDC by ten percent by offering a four-day conference that is focused on education and networking, which will increase conference profits by five percent. What is the point of having a convention if the success is not measured? Part of the meeting planner's job is to demonstrate how a convention or meeting helps achieve organiza-tional goals. By establishing objectives and reviewing ROI, a planner can show his or her role in supporting company objectives and the bottom line.

Sue is excited about the Power of Prevention convention. The industry press gave excellent pre-meeting coverage, with over $50,000 tracked as nonpaid advertising. The marketing committee's decision to purchase push-ads on Facebook and hire blog-gers for the meeting also contributed to the success of the meeting. Sue believes this third-party endorsement definitely increased attendance. She also credits the market-ing committee for adding the Exhibitor Scavenger Hunt to the conference app. Ten sponsorships were sold to exhibitors at $1,000 each resulting in $10,000 additional sponsorship revenue, and both the attendees and exhibitors enjoyed the experience. The attendees loved playing the game and competing with each other, and the exhibi-tors who purchased the Scavenger Hunt sponsorship enjoyed increased traffic to their booth. The meeting objectives were met: 500 people took the classes for SAPDC (a ten percent increase from the 454 who took SAPDC classes last year), and meeting profits grew from $1,598,512 to 1,678,437 (a five percent increase).

Sue finishes her report and takes a call from the Orlando Convention Center, the location for next year's annual conference. She is 12 months away from the conference and is receiving the names of the meeting rooms that will be used . . . and the meeting cycle continues.

Summary

In this chapter, you have learned about the process of creating a citywide meeting. This is a large task for one person and requires many partners to make the conference or event successful. Through this case study, you have been able to see the life of a meeting planner and have looked at the many tasks leading up to the conference. The chapter began with creating conference objectives and budgets, and it ended with evaluating ROI to determine the success of the meeting.

Key Words and Terms

For definitions, see the Glossary.

audiovisual (AV) company

convention services manager (CSM)

convention and visitor bureau (CVB)

corporate social responsibility (CSR)

general services contractor (GSC)

meeting time line

poster session

Review and Discussion Questions

1. Who is the group in this chapter? Why are they here?
2. Where else has the group met?
3. What are the steps Sue goes through to plan this meeting?
4. Whom does Sue work with on her staff?
5. Whom does Sue work with in the city where the meeting is being held? Which suppliers or vendors?
6. What does Sue do after the meeting is over?

About the Chapter Contributor

M. T. Hickman, CMP, CSECP, is the lead faculty and head of the Travel, Exposition, and Meeting Management program at Richland College in Dallas, Texas. She began her career at the Irving, Texas, CVB, where she worked in many departments, including tourism sales, convention sales, and special events. Over the years, she has worked as director of marketing for the National Business Association and as a proposal writer for WorldTravel Partners. She is active in meeting and exposition planning associations, including MPI, PCMA, IMEX, and IAEE.

Previous Edition Chapter Contributors

David Gisler, (Retired) Director of Sales and Training, Total Show University, Freeman Companies

Bitsy Burns, CMP, Director of Operations, Southwest Veterinary Symposium

Erin Donahue, Director Global Sales, Omni Hotel Dallas

Patty Towell, Sales Manager, San Antonio Convention and Visitor Bureau

Dana Rhoden, CMP, CMM, Marketing and Recruitment at CityVet

APPENDIX

This appendix includes a detailed example of a Site Selection Sample Request for Proposal (RFP).

Forms for use in Requesting a Proposal and On-Site Selection

The sections that follow provide a number of forms, or frameworks, that are used by meeting professionals. Studying and reviewing these documents will help provide the reader with a better understanding of the myriad of details that a meeting professional must deal with.

Site Selection—Sample Request for Proposal (RFP) (v. 18b)

Group or Meeting Sponsor: Full name of organization (acronym in parentheses)

Contact Information: Name(s) including alternate contacts, title(s), address(es), communication numbers (phones, fax, email, tdd/tty), and contact times and time zones.

Organization: Provide brief organizational description—structure, mission, and purpose.

The Meeting: Provide brief description—purpose, goals and objectives, general format, and audience profile.

History: Provide up to two years of meeting history—dates, attendance, hotel(s) used, rooms blocked and picked up, and range of rates.

Schedule for Future Meetings; Future Years for Meeting

Considerations for This Meeting:

Destination(s) and site(s)

Dates (acceptable and unacceptable)

Rates

Special requirements/information (transportation, attractions/restaurants, quirks)

References: Request for meetings of similar size, focus/scope, held in last 6 to 12 months.

Proposals Due/Decision Process: Provide date by which proposal must be received and what collateral materials should be included. Describe decision process and date by which decision is expected.

Meeting Specifications:

Sleeping Room Block: Describe day-by-day, including early arrivals/late departures; bed and room types; suites.

Meeting Space: Provide day-by-day description of the program, including meeting/conference office space, speaker ready room, lounges, and times needed.

Exhibit/Display Space: For literature tables, other displays or exhibits and the times the space is needed. Include move-in and move-out times.

Site Selection
Request for Proposal
Organization Name
Attachment A

If you plan to submit a proposal, please keyboard all information and upload these forms to (*email address*).

Property name _____ **City/State** _____

Property contact name/title/email and phone _____

Year property built _____   Last building inspection and results _____

Number of floors _____   Total number of rooms _____ suites _____

Single/one-bedded rooms _____   Double/two-bedded rooms _____

Number of nonsmoking rooms _____   Number of disability-accessible rooms _____

Year of last guest room renovation _____   Year of last public space renovation _____

Scope of Planned Renovation and Schedule:

Type of property

☐ *meeting/convention*   ☐ *resort*   ☐ *full service*   ☐ *limited service*
Market tier: ☐ *luxury*   ☐ *upscale*   ☐ *moderate*
Property location: ☐ *suburban*   ☐ *downtown/city center*

Property Ownership and Management

Chain owned? (Y/N) _____ If no, name of owners. _____

Management Company _____

Franchise? (Y/N) _____

Owner's company is at least 51 percent owned, controlled, and operated by an American citizen minority? (Y/N) _____

Owner's company is at least 51 percent owned, controlled, and operated by an American citizen nonminority woman? (Y/N) _____

**Site Selection
Request for Proposal**
Organization Name
Attachment A

If you plan to submit a proposal, please keyboard all information and upload these forms to (*email address*).

Property name _____ *City/State*_____

Property contact name/title/email and phone _____

Rating
AAA Diamonds   1   2   3   4   5   not rated
Mobil Stars   1   2   3   4   5   not rated
Other rating(s) (specify) _____

Outlets
Name _____ Location _____ Hours _____
Full or Ltd. Service _____ Nonsmoking?_____

Transportation and Parking
Airport One
Name _____ 3-Letter code _____
Distance from property _____ miles
     Minutes/rush hour _____ Minutes/nonrush hour_____
Complimentary shuttle (Y/N) _____
Estimated taxi charge (each way) _____
Alternate mode of transportation _____ Cost each way _____
Driving directions (attach)

Airport Two
Name _____ 3-Letter code _____
Distance from property _____ miles
     Minutes/rush hour _____ Minutes/nonrush hour _____
Complimentary shuttle (Y/N) _____
Estimated taxi charge (each way) _____
Alternate mode of transportation _____ Cost each way _____
Driving Directions (attach)

Number of parking spaces at property _____ Charge for self-park _____
Charge for valet park _____
Identify facility's parking capacity for large trucks, semitrailers, and so on: _____

Taxes, service, and/or gratuity charges
The current rooms tax is ____percent plus $____ occupancy tax.
There is ___ is not ___ a ballot initiative in the next election to raise those taxes.
There is a ____ gratuity or a ____ service charge of ____percent on group food and beverage.
This is taxed at _____percent.

Site Selection
Request for Proposal
Organization Name
Attachment A

If you plan to submit a proposal, please keyboard all information and upload these forms to (*email address*).

Property name _____ **City/State** _____

Property contact name/title/email and phone _____

Facilities/Services on Property (check all that apply)

- ☐ Cocktail lounge
- ☐ 24-hour room service OR
- ☐ Room service Start time _____ End time _____
- ☐ Safety deposit boxes/lobby area
- ☐ Express check in and out   ☐ Video review/check out
- ☐ Full business center   Hours _____ A.M. to _____ P.M.   Days of the week _____
- ☐ Gift/newsstand   Hours _____ A.M. to _____ P.M.   Days of the week: _____
- ☐ Full-service health club   Hours _____ A.M. to _____ P.M.   Days of the week: _____
- ☐ Laundry/valet service (circle applicable responses)

Circle one: On property or Sent out

  Circle service: *5 days/week*   *6 days/week*   *7 days/week*   *overnight service*
- ☐ Shoe shine service
- ☐ Indoor pool   ☐ Outdoor pool
- ☐ Airline desk(s)   (specify) _____, _____
- ☐ ATM (Current use fee is $ ____.____.)
- ☐ Car rental desk(s)   (specify) _____, _____
- ☐ Evening turndown service   ☐ All guests   ☐ VIPs only
- ☐ Golf course
- ☐ Tennis court(s)
- ☐ Racquetball courts
- ☐ Other (specify) _____

Guest Rooms

- ☐ In-room safe   ☐ No charge   ☐ Charge to use ($_____/day)
- ☐ Working desks with outlets above floor
- ☐ Voice mail   ☐ Personalized voice mail
- ☐ Two line phones/all rooms   ☐ Two line phones/concierge/specialized rooms only
- ☐ Data ports on all phones   ☐ Digital or analog phone lines
- ☐ Phone in bathroom   ☐ Bathroom phone/concierge or specialty rooms only
- ☐ Access charge for local phone calls _____ ☐ Access charge for toll-free calls _____
- ☐ AM/FM radio   ☐ With cassette player   ☐ With CD player
- ☐ Color TV
- ☐ Remote control TV   ☐ Cable TV   ☐ Satellite TV
- ☐ All news cable channel   ☐ Weather channel
- ☐ Other special channels (specify) _____
- ☐ In-room movies on demand
- ☐ Closed-circuit television (CCTV)

```
┌─────────────────────────────────────────────────────────────────┐
│                        Site Selection                             │
│                     Request for Proposal                          │
│                       Organization Name                           │
│                         Attachment A                              │
└─────────────────────────────────────────────────────────────────┘
```

If you plan to submit a proposal, please keyboard all information and upload these forms to (*email address*).

Property name _____ *City/State* _____

Property contact name/title/email and phone _____

Guest Rooms (cont.)

☐ In-room video players
☐ Iron/ironing board
☐ Mini-bar   ☐ Refrigerator on request
☐ Coffee/Tea maker   ☐ Daily complimentary coffee/tea
☐ Working desk/desk lamp
☐ Free **daily** paper delivered to room ☐ Paper/**weekdays only**

Reservations and Check-in/out

☐ Reservations may be made through a toll-free number.
    ☐ That number is _____   ☐ Number is accessible throughout United States.
    ☐ A number that can be used for those residing in the state in which the reservations department is located:
    ☐ A reservation number for those outside the United States is ( ) _____.
    ☐ The TTY/TDD number is ( ) _____.
    ☐ The fax number for reservations is ( ) _____.
    ☐ Reservations may be made on line at http://www._____,
    ☐ or by email to _____.
☐ All rooms in a group's block are released to the toll-free number.
☐ The property has an in-house reservations department.
☐ The reservations department is located off-site.

☐ Check-in time is _____. Check-out time is _____.

☐ The facility will audit the room reservations using a group's registration list.

Site Selection
Request for Proposal
Organization Name
Attachment A

If you plan to submit a proposal, please keyboard all information and upload these forms to (*email address*).

Property name _____ **City/State** _____

Property contact name/title/email and phone _____

Safety and Security (check all that apply)

☐ Smoke detectors in all guest rooms   Hardwired?   Y/N _____
☐ Smoke detectors in hallways   Hardwired?   Y/N _____
☐ Smoke detectors in public areas   Hardwired?   Y/N _____
☐ Audible smoke detectors   ☐ Visual alarms for people with hearing impairments
☐ Sprinklers in all guest rooms   ☐ Sprinklers in hallways
☐ Sprinklers in public areas
☐ Fire extinguishers in hallways
☐ Automatic fire doors
☐ Auto link to fire station
☐ Auto recall elevators
☐ Ventilated stairwells
☐ Emergency maps in guest rooms/hallways
☐ Emergency information in all guest rooms
☐ Emergency lighting
☐ Safety chain on door   ☐ Doors with viewports ("peep holes")
☐ Deadbolts on all guest room doors
☐ Restricted access to guest floors
☐ Property has AEDs (automatic external defibrillators)
    ☐ Staff has been trained to use defibrillators   *Per shift* _____
☐ Staff trained in CPR   *Per shift* _____
☐ Staff trained in first aid   *Per shift* _____
☐ Secondary locks on guest room glass doors
☐ Room balconies accessible by adjoining rooms/balconies
☐ Primary guest room entrance accessible by interior corridor/atrium
☐ Guest room accessible by exterior entrance only
☐ Guest room windows open
☐ Uniformed security
☐ 24-hour security throughout facility   Number of staff ___
☐ Public address system
☐ Video surveillance in public areas/elevators
☐ Video surveillance at entrances
☐ Video surveillance in hallways
☐ Staff trained in issuance of duplicate keys/cards
☐ Emergency power source: _____
    ☐ SOPs for power outages _____

Food Safety:
Detail the frequency of inspection by county or city health inspectors and the results of the last three (3) inspections.

Site Selection
Request for Proposal
Organization Name
Attachment A

If you plan to submit a proposal, please keyboard all information and upload these forms to (*email address*).

Property name _____ *City/State* _____

Property contact name/title/email and phone _____

Emergency call response time (for fire, police, EMTs) in minutes to your property _____
Does property have an emergency evacuation plan? (Y/N) _____
How often does property conduct emergency evacuation drills? _____
Nearest police station (blocks/miles) _____ Nearest hospital (blocks/miles) _____
Does facility comply with all country/state/local fire laws? (Y/N) _____

Please describe

• The actions your facility took beginning 9/11/01 for the safety and comfort of your guests:

• Any change of policies governing safety/security instituted or reinstituted since 9/11/01.

• The communication tree among your property and local/state/federal emergency management officials.

• Any policies in effect that govern "containment" of guests in the property for issues of bioterrorism? Inability to travel because of airport closures?

"Oversold/Underdeparted" ("Walk") Policies or Guidelines

☐ Property will arrange accommodations at comparable or superior property within ten minutes of this property.
☐ Property will pay directly for one room night and tax at comparable property.
☐ Traveler will be provided with transportation.
☐ Traveler will be reimbursed for (number) _____ of phone calls to home and/or office.
☐ Other (specify) _____

Site Selection
Request for Proposal
Organization Name
Attachment A

If you plan to submit a proposal, please keyboard all information and upload these forms to (*email address*).

Property name _____ City/State _____

Property contact name/title/email and phone _____

Staff and Staffing

☐ Average length of employment at this property:
   Management staff _____ years   line staff _____ years
☐ Staff organized for the purpose of collective bargaining (List unions and staff positions, contract renewal dates on separate sheet.)

Policies and Miscellaneous Charges

☐ Credit cards are charged when reservation is made.
   ☐ If charged, is it for _____ first night _____ last night _____ all nights
☐ Guest may cancel guaranteed reservations without penalty/charge
      _____ to 4 P.M./day of arrival   _____ to 6 P.M./day of arrival   _____ 24 hours
      _____ 48 hours   _____ 72 hours   _____ other
☐ Guest substitutions are allowed, at any time, without penalty or charge to group and/or individual.
☐ Guest substitutions are not allowed without a charge to group and/or individual.
☐ Extended stays (based on availability) are allowed at no charge.
☐ Early checkouts incur a charge of $_____ if the front desk is not notified at check-in.
☐ The property charges $_____/page for receipt of faxes.
☐ The property charges $_____/page to send faxes.
☐ There is a charge of $_____ for receipt of packages.
☐ There is a charge of $_____ for property to send packages.
☐ There is a charge of $_____ to deliver packages to individual or group.

Site Selection
Request for Proposal
Organization Name
Attachment A

If you plan to submit a proposal, please keyboard all information and upload these forms to (*email address*).

Property name _____ *City/State* _____

Property contact name/title/email and phone _____

Policies and Miscellaneous Charges (cont.)
☐ Is a resort or hotel or other fee added to the room rate? Y/N _____
   ☐ If so, the current amount per room (or per guest) per night is $_____ which is/is not taxed.
      ☐ This covers:
         ☐ Contractual issues that must be included in our contract are attached to this document.

Energy Issues
☐ The property does charge an energy surcharge of $_____ per room per night. This charge is or is not taxed. (Is ____ Is not ____) If taxed, it is at _____percent.
☐ The power supply for the property is from _____.
☐ Describe the property's backup power source(s):
☐ Describe the property's emergency procedures for brownouts and blackouts:
☐ Describe the property's backup systems for water and phones:
☐ Define any charges for use of electrical outlets for meetings and/or in public space and/or in guestrooms:

Environmental Issues
☐ Our property recycles the following materials:
    _____ paper   _____ plastic   _____metal/tin/aluminum
☐ The method by which guests may recycle is:
☐ We ask guests to advise us by use of a card if they want their towels and/or bed linens changed every day.
☐ Other areas we protect the environment are:

Site Selection
Request for Proposal
Organization Name
Attachment A

If you plan to submit a proposal, please keyboard all information and upload these forms to (*email address*).

Property name _____ *City/State* _____

Property contact name/title/email and phone _____

Other Groups
During the group's preferred dates, the other events confirmed in the city, including conventions, festivals, other public and private events that are known to the bureau or the facility, are:

During the group's preferred dates, the other events confirmed in the facility are:

City/County Labor Issues
Note any groups organized for the purpose of collective bargaining in the city or county whose contract deadlines are 2 months on both side of preferred dates, and their history of labor actions:

Audiovisual Equipment
☐ The in-house or recommended company is _____.

☐ The facility has the ability to negotiate prices on behalf of the AV company. (Y/N) _____

☐ A discount of _____ percent off list prices can be offered for AV equipment for the meeting.

☐ The service charge is _____ percent. It is taxed at _____ percent. It is not taxed. _____

☐ If an outside AV company is brought in by our organization, there is _____ is not _____ a fee.
   ☐ If there is a fee, it is _____.

Electricity Supply/Vendor
☐ Electricity (for exhibits and meeting space) is provided to the facility by _____ in-house or _____ external vendor. (If external, specify _____.)

☐ The facility has the ability to negotiate prices for meeting and exhibit electrical service.
   (Y/N) _____

☐ Electricity is available to the outdoor portions of the facility (for outside exhibits).
   (Y/N) _____

☐ A discount of _____ percent off list prices can be offered for meeting room and exhibit electricity for the meeting.

Site Selection
Request for Proposal
Organization Name
Attachment A

If you plan to submit a proposal, please keyboard all information and upload these forms to (*email address*).

Property name _____ *City/State* _____

Property contact name/title/email and phone _____

Operations and Technology

☐ Our sales/convention services staff use _____ word processing software, version
_____.

☐ Sales and convention services personnel use e-mail. _____ yes _____ no
   Email addresses are:
   ☐ Sales _____
   ☐ Convention/Catering services _____
   ☐ Reservations _____
☐ Sales and convention services have Web access. ___ yes ___ no
☐ Reservations is fully automated and can respond by e-mail. ___ yes ___ no
☐ Our Web site address is _____.
☐ Group/Meeting reservations can be made on line.
   ☐ If reservations may be made on line, please specify information that must be included in any
      published URLs and any restrictions and/or policies.

NATIONAL SALES RESPONSE FORM
(Year/Meeting) Site Selection
Request for Proposal: (Name of Organization)

Please complete and return this form after reading the RFP. To allow us to track proposals, please advise to which properties in which cities you will send the RFP. **Please upload this to (*email address*), or fax this form to (*name, fax number*) to be received by (*day, date, time/time zone*).**

Please print or type in black:

Company _____

Contact name/title _____

Direct phone no. _____

Direct fax no. _____

Email address _____

The RFP is being sent to the following properties:

_____/City _____

_____/City _____

_____/City _____

_____/City _____

_____/City _____

_____/City _____

Comments:

DMO RESPONSE FORM
(Year/Meeting) Site Selection
Request for Proposal: (Organization/Meeting Name)

Please complete and return this form after reading the RFP. To allow us to track proposals, please advise to which properties you will send the RFP, keeping in mind that it should only be sent to properties not represented by the companies noted in the cover note and only to those that meet the criteria. If responses are received by properties that do not meet the criteria, or by vendors for whom we do not need services, we will reject the proposals.

Please upload this to (*email address*), or fax this form to (*name, fax number*) by(*day/date/time/time zone*).

Please print or type in black:

DMO _____

Contact name/Title _____

Direct phone no. _____

Direct fax no. _____

Email address _____

The RFP is being sent to the following properties:

                         _____

                         _____

                         _____

                         _____

                         _____

                         _____

Comments:

Property RESPONSE FORM
(Year/Meeting) Site Selection
Request for Proposal: (Organization/Meeting)

Please complete and return this form after reading the RFP but before sending a proposal. There is no need to send a follow-up letter or e-mail, or to call once this form has been sent. **Please upload this to (***email address***), or fax to (***organization/fax number***) to be received by (***day/date/time/time zone***).**

Full proposals and collateral are due by (day/date/time/time zone).

Please complete and return this information whether or not a proposal is being submitted. If completing by hand, please use black ink.

Property name/City _____

Contact name/Title _____

Direct phone no. (_____)_____

Direct fax no. (_____)_____

Email address _____

URL http://www. _____

Check/complete all applicable responses:

_____ We will send proposal and collateral to be received by (*due date*).
_____ Dates noted on first option basis are being held for this group.
_____ Dates will *not* be held until a contract is signed.

Dates available/First option　　　　**Dates available/Second option**

_____　　　_____
_____　　　_____
_____　　　_____
_____　　　_____

_____ We regret we are *unable to send a proposal* for the following reason(s):
　　_____ None of preferred dates available.
　　_____ Meeting space and/or sleeping rooms not appropriate for meeting.
　　_____ Unable to meet rate parameters.
　　_____ Other (specify):
　　　　_____
　　　　_____

Comments:

GLOSSARY

Accepted Practices Exchange (APEX)   Initiative of the meetings, expositions, events, and conventions industry managed by the Event Industry Council (EIC). APEX develops and manages the implementation of accepted practices (voluntary standards) for the industry.

Act of God   Extraordinary natural event, such as extreme weather, flood, hurricane, tornado, earthquake, or similar natural disaster, that cannot be reasonably foreseen or prevented and over which a contracting party has no reasonable control. It makes performance of the contract illegal, impracticable, or impossible; thus the parties have no legal responsibility to continue performance of the contract.

Action station   Place where chef prepares foods to order and serves them fresh to guests. Popular items for action stations include pasta, grilled meat or shrimp, carved meats, sushi, crepes, omelets, flaming desserts, Caesar salad, and so on. Also called performance stations or exhibition cooking.

Advancing of a venue   confirming in "advance" all of the details surrounding a meeting or event with a venue contact.

Agenda   List, outline, or plan of items to be done or considered at an event or during a specific time block and may include a time schedule.

Air lift   The capacity of airlines flying into a destination in terms of the number of flights and numbers of seats available.

American service   Serving style where guests are seated and served food that has been preportioned and plated in the kitchen.

American Society of Composers, Authors, and Publishers (ASCAP)   Membership organization that represents individuals who hold the copyrights to music written in the United States and grants licensing agreements for the performance of that music.

Americans with Disabilities Act (ADA)   US legislation passed in 1992 requiring public buildings (offices, hotels, restaurants, etc.) to make adjustments meeting minimum standards to make their facilities accessible to individuals with physical disabilities.

Amphitheater   Outdoor facility with a flat performance area surrounded by rising rows of seats or a grassy slope that allows the audience to view the performance. The seating area is usually a semi-circular shape or adapted to the surrounding landscape.

Ancillary activity   Event-related support services within a facility that generate revenue.

Annual meeting   Meeting that takes place once a year.

Artificial intelligence (AI)   The theory and development of computer systems able to perform tasks that normally require human intelligence, such as visual perception, speech recognition, decision-making, and translation between languages.

Association   Organized group of individuals and/or companies that band together to accomplish a common purpose, usually to provide for the needs of its members. It is usually a nonprofit organization.

Association of Destination Management Executives (ADMEI)   Association of Destination Management Executives International.

Attrition   Difference between the actual number of sleeping rooms picked up (or food and beverage covers or revenue projections) and the number or formula agreed to in the terms of the facility's contract. Usually there is an allowable shortfall before damages are assessed.

Audience response system (ARS)   System in which the audience is outfitted with small keypads that allow them to answer questions quickly and have their data tallied immediately.

Audiovisual (AV) company   Supplier of technical staff and audiovisual equipment (e.g., projectors, screens, sound systems, video, and staging).

Auditorium style   Seating arrangement where chairs are arranged in rows facing head table, stage, or speaker. Variations are semicircular and V-shaped.

Augmented reality   A live direct or indirect view of a physical, real-world environment whose elements are augmented, or supplemented, by computer-generated sensory input such as sound, video, graphics, or GPS data.

Ausstellung   German term for consumer show.

B2B   An event at which products, services, or promotional materials are displayed to attendees visiting exhibits on the show floor. These events focus primarily on business-to-business (B2B) relationships.

B2C   An event at which products, services, or promotional materials are displayed to attendees visiting exhibits on the show floor. These events focus primarily on business-to-consumer (B2C) relationships.

Banquet Event Order (BEO)   Form most often used by hotels to provide details to personnel concerned with a specific food and beverage function or event room set up.

Bar back   Cabinets and work space behind a bar where alcoholic beverages are served.

Blog   Online diary that is posted to the web.

Boardroom   Room set permanently with a fixed table and suitable seating.

Break-out room   Small function room set up for a group within an event as opposed to a plenary or general session.

break-outs   Small-group session, panel, workshop, or presentation offered concurrently within the event, formed to focus on specific subjects. The event is separate from the general session but is held within the event format. The sessions can be arranged by basic, intermediate, and advanced levels or divided by interest areas or industry segments.

Broadcast Music, Inc. (BMI)   Music licensing organization that represents individuals who hold the copyrights to music written in the United States. It grants licensing agreements for the performance of music.

Butler service (1) Style of service that offers a variety of both hot and cold hors d'oeuvres on platters to guests at receptions. (2) Style of table service where guests serve themselves from platters presented by the server. (3) Specialized in-room service offered by a hotel.

Carbon offset A reduction in emissions of carbon dioxide or green-house gases made in order to compensate for, or to offset, an emission made elsewhere.

Carnet Customs document permitting the holder to carry or send merchandise temporarily into certain foreign countries (for display, demonstration, or similar purposes) without paying duties or posting bonds. *Also called* trade fair bond.

Catered event Event that generally has one host and one bill. Most attendees eat the same meal.

Certified Meeting Professional (CMP) The foremost certification program of today's meetings, conventions, and exhibitions industry. The CMP program recognizes individuals who have achieved the industry's highest standard of professionalism.

Classroom style A meeting room setup where participants sit at desks much like in a classroom.

Clear span tent Tent that has a strong roof structure so it is possible to hang lighting from the beams by using special clamps.

Community infrastructure Those facilities and companies in a locale that support the MEEC industry.

Complete meeting package (CMP) All-inclusive plan offered by conference centers that includes lodging, all food and beverage, and support services, including audiovisual equipment, room rental, and so on.

Concessionaire Person or company that operates the concessions.

Conference (1) Participatory meeting designed for discussion, fact-finding, problem solving, and consultation. (2) Event used by any organization to meet and exchange views, convey a message, open a debate, or give publicity to some area of opinion on a specific issue. No tradition, continuity, or periodicity is required to convene a conference. Although not generally limited in time, conferences are usually of short duration with specific objectives.

Conference center Facility that provides a dedicated environment for events, especially small events. It may be certified by the International Association of Conference Centers (IACC).

Consideration Cause, motive, price, or impelling influence that induces a contracting party to enter a contract.

Continuing education unit (CEU) Requirement of many professional groups by which members must certify participation in formal educational programs designed to maintain their level of ability beyond their original certification date. CEUs are nonacademic credit. One CEU is awarded every ten contact hours in an accredited program.

Contract Agreement between two or more parties that creates, for each party, a duty to do or not do something, and a right to performance of the other's duty or a remedy for the breach of the other's duty.

Convention Event where the primary activity of the attendees is to attend educational sessions, participate in meetings/discussions, socialize, or attend other organized events. There is a secondary exhibit component.

Convention and visitor bureau (CVB) Not-for-profit organization charged with representing a specific destination and helping the long- term development of communities through a travel and tourism strategy. CVBs are usually membership organizations bringing together businesses that rely on tourism and events for revenue. For visitors, CVBs are like a key to the city. As an unbiased resource, CVBs can serve as a broker or an official point of contact for convention and event planners, tour operators, and visitors; they assist planners with event preparation and encourage business travelers and visitors alike to visit local historic, cultural, and recreational sites.

Convention services manager (CSM) Person whose job is to oversee and arrange every aspect of an event. The CSM can be an employee or hired ad hoc to plan, organize, implement, and control meetings, conventions, and other events.

Copyright Federal law that allows for the ownership of intellectual property (writings, art, music). Copy-written material cannot be used without the owner's permission or the payment of royalty fees.

Corkage Charge placed on beer, liquor, and wine brought into the facility but purchased elsewhere. The charge sometimes includes glassware, ice, and mixers.

Corporate social responsibility (CSR) Corporate initiative to assess and take responsibility for the company's effects on the environment and impact on social welfare.

Corporation A group of people who obtain a charter granting them (as a body) the legal power, rights, privileges, and liabilities of an individual, but are distinct from those individuals making up the group.

Crescent rounds Seating at round tables with chairs placed at two-thirds to three-quarters of the table and no seating facing the speaker.

Cutoff date Designated date when the facility will release a block of sleeping rooms to the general public. The date is typically three to four weeks before the event.

Dates, rates, and space Words that begin the maxim "Dates, rates, and space–you can only have two," which is used by hoteliers to sum up meeting negotiations. The meaning is that the planner can get two out of the three things wanted for a meeting: the wanted dates and rates, but not the space; the wanted dates and meeting space, but not the rate; or the space and rates, but not the dates.

Destination management company (DMC) Professional services company possessing extensive local knowledge, expertise, and resources; and specializing in the design and implementation of events, activities, tours, transportation, and program logistics. Depending on the company and the staff specialists in the company, a DMC offers, but is not limited to, the following: creative proposals for special events within the meeting; guest tours; VIP amenities and transportation; shuttle services; staffing within convention centers and hotels; team building, golf outings, and other activities; entertainment, including sound and lighting; décor and theme development; ancillary meetings for management professionals; and advance meetings and on-site registration services and housing.

Destination International (DI) World's largest resource for official destination marketing organizations (DMOs) dedicated to improving the effectiveness of DMOs in more than 25 countries. DMAI provides members with educational resources, networking opportunities, and marketing benefits worldwide.

Destination marketing organization (DMO) *See* CVB.

Disability The consequence of an impairment that may be physical, cognitive, mental, sensory, emotional, developmental, or some combination of these.

Drayage Delivery of exhibit materials from the dock to an assigned exhibit space, removal of empty crates, return of crates at the end of the event for recrating, and delivery of materials back to the dock for carrier loading.

Early bird rate Lowered rate offered as an incentive for attendees to send in registration before a predefinite date. *Also called* early bird discount.

Events Industry Council (EIC) Federation of national and international organizations representing individuals, firms, or properties involved in the meetings, conventions, exhibitions, and travel and tourism industries. Formerly the Convention Liaison Council.

Exclusive service Service that is provided only by the official service contractor.

Exhibit hall Area within a facility where the exhibition is located.

Exhibition (1) Event at which products and services are displayed. The primary activity of attendees is visiting exhibits on the show floor. These events focus primarily on business-to-business (B2B) relation- ships. (2) Display of products or promotional materials for the purposes of public relations, sales, and/or marketing.

Exhibition management company Company or individual who designs and/or builds exhibits. The EMC may also provide other services.

Exhibition service contractor (ESC) Organizer or promoter of an exhibition responsible for the rental of space, as well as financial control and management of the exhibition. Sometimes an agent can act in this capacity.

Exhibitor-appointed contractor (EAC) Company other than the designated "official" contractor providing a service to an exhibitor. EACs are a subset of service contractors that work for the exhibiting company, and travel throughout the country setting up and dismantling their booths, rather than working from one city or location.

Exhibitor service manual Manual or kit, usually developed by the service contractor for an event, containing general event information, labor/ service order forms, rules and regulations, and other information pertinent to an exhibitor's participation in an exhibition.

Exposition (1) Event at which products and services are displayed. The primary activity of attendees is visiting exhibits on the show floor. These events focus primarily on business-to-business (B2B) relationships. (2) Display of products or promotional material for the purposes of public relations, sales, and/or marketing.

Fam trip Familiarization trips. Method of promoting a destination or particular facility to a meeting planner. Fam trips are a no- or low-cost trip for planners to personally review sites for their suitability for a meeting. These trips may be arranged by a local community or by a hotel directly.

Food and beverage minimum A lower limit or threshold above which a group agrees to spend on food and beverage during their event.

Force majeure Event (e.g., war, labor strike, extreme weather, or other disruptive circumstances) or effect that cannot be reasonably anticipated or controlled. *Also called* fortuitous event. *See* Act of God.

Frame tent Tent that is set up on the grass. It is one of the simplest of all meeting venues and requires little advance planning beyond making sure the tent rental people can get set up in time. *Also called* open-sided tent.

Gamification The use of game thinking and game mechanics in nongame contexts to engage users in solving problems. It is often incorporated into MEEC programming.

Gantt Charts A type of bar chart, developed by Henry Gantt in the 1910s, that illustrates a project schedule.

General service contractor (GSC) Organization hired by the show manager to handle the general duties necessary to produce the show on-site, providing a wide range of services. *Also called* official show contractor.

General session Meeting open to all those in attendance at an event. *See* Plenary Session.

Gesellschaft German term for company or society.

GmBH German term for a limited liability company.

Government agencies Subdivisions of federal, state, or local government.

Green meeting Incorporating sustainable practices.

Greenwashing Refers to any misrepresentation by a company that leads the consumer to believe that their policies and products are environmentally responsible, when their claims are false, misleading, or cannot be verified. Greenwashing is also used to identify the practice of companies spending more money on the campaign to notify customers of their environmentally friendly efforts, than the efforts themselves.

Group history Document that provides detailed information regarding previous events an entity has held.

Guarantee Amount of food that the planner has instructed the facility to prepare and that will be paid for.

Hosted buyer The business practice whereby a potential "buyer" of convention products or services has their travel expenses paid by exhibitors at a convention in return for agreeing to meet with exhibitors. The concept was originated by Ray Bloom of the IMEX group in the United Kingdom.

Hotel A type of accommodation where one pays for the service.

Housing bureau Third-party outsourced company that handles all hotel arrangements for a fee (may be paid by the local convention and visitor bureau).

Hybrid meetings Events that combine face-to-face interaction with virtual interaction utilizing technology.

Incentive trip Travel reward given by companies to employees to stimulate productivity.

Incentive travel programs A reward system for performance where travel, rather than cash or products, is given as the reward.

In-line exhibit Exhibit space with exhibit booths on either side and back.

Interactive nametag Radio frequency identification (RFID) either attached to a slim piece of paper behind a badge or made part of a slightly larger wearable nametag device. The RFID-based service offers better networking and interactivity between conference attendees as well as between attendees, and vendors.

International Association of Conference Centers (IACC) Association in which member facilities must meet a list of over 30 criteria to be considered an approved conference center.

International Congress and Convention Association (ICCA) Large international association.

Island booth Booth/stand space with aisles on all four sides.

Keynote address Session that opens or highlights the show, meeting, or event.

Kongress The German spelling for a congress—a convention.

KSAs Knowledge, skills, and abilities.

Lead retrieval Process used to capture customer information. The process begins with the meeting organizer asking questions during the registration process that will identify information of importance to the exhibitor.

Level   (1) Level of audio volume. Level refers to the power magnitude in either electrical watt or acoustic watts, but is often incorrectly used to denote voltage. (2) The relative depth of knowledge of attendees.

Local event   Event, such as a graduation ceremony or a local festival, that draws its audience primarily from the local market. Typically 80 percent of attendees reside within a 50-mile (80-km) radius of the event site. Local audiences typically do not require overnight accommodations.

Material handling   Services performed by a general service contractor (GSC) that include delivery of exhibit materials from the dock to an assigned space, removal of empty crates, return of crates at the end of the event for recrating, and delivery of materials back to the dock for carrier loading. It is a two-way charge, incoming and outgoing. *See* Drayage.

MBECS   Meeting and Business Event Competency Standards.

MEEC   Meetings, Expositions, Events, and Conventions.

Meet and greet   System of deploying individuals at critical points of arrival for meeting or event attendees with the purpose of greeting them and providing information.

Meeting   Event where the primary activity of the attendees is to attend educational sessions, participate in meetings/discussions, socialize, or attend other organized events. There is no exhibit component to this event.

Meeting history   A record of what transpired when a meeting or event was held in the past.

Meeting time line   Schedule that includes each task to be accomplished. It is the core of the program plan.

Messe   German term for trade fair.

Messegelande   German term for fair site.

Multilevel exhibit   System often used by large companies to expand their exhibit space without taking up more floor space. The upper floor may be used for special purposes, such as meeting areas, private demonstration areas, or hospitality stations.

Needs analysis   Planning tool used to determine the client's needs and expectations for a meeting.

Negotiation   Process by which a meeting planner and a hotel representative (or other supplier) reach an agreement on the terms and conditions that will govern their relationship before, during, and after a meeting, convention, exposition, or event.

NFC   The abbreviation for near field communication. It is a set of standards for smartphones and other mobile devices to establish radio communication with each other by touching them together or bringing them into close proximity, usually no more than a few centimeters.

Off-premises catering   Foods that are usually prepared in a central kitchen and transported for service to an off-site location.

On-premise catering   Meals that are catered on-site during an event.

Parol evidence   Evidence of an oral agreement that can be used in limited instances, especially where the plain meaning of words in the written document may be in doubt. A court will generally construe a contract most strongly against the party that prepared the written document; if there is a conflict between printed and handwritten words or phrases, the latter will prevail.

Peninsula booth   Exhibit with aisles on three sides.

Per diem rate   Rate paid per day. Some event attendees, such as government employees, have a limited amount of money (a daily allowance) they can spend per day on food, lodging, and other expenses.

Permit   License required by many local governments to use parks or even private property for special events. The police, the fire department, and (in many places) the building code officer must be notified when a permit is desired.

Pickup   Of the hotel rooms set aside for a group, the number actually used by event participants or "picked up."

PLC   German term for public limited company.

Plenary session   General assembly for all participants.

Podcasting   Method of distributing multimedia files, such as audio or video programs, for playback on mobile devices and personal computers.

Pole tent   A temporary fabric-covered shelter that is supported by one or more poles in the middle of the area.

Poster session   (1) Display of reports and papers, usually scientific, accompanied by authors or researchers. (2) Session dedicated to the discussion of the posters shown inside the meeting area. When this discussion is not held in a special session, it can take place directly between the person presenting the poster and interested delegate(s).

Pre-con   A pre-conference meeting at the primary facility at which an event will take place just prior to the event beginning. Attendees generally include the primary event organizer, representatives of the event organizer/host organization, department heads at the facility, other facility staff as appropriate, and contractors. The agenda focuses on reviewing the purpose and details of the event and making final adjustments as needed. Compare with post-con meeting.

Pre-function space   Area adjacent to the main event location often used for receptions prior to a meal or coffee breaks during an event.

Production schedule   A project plan or of how the production budget will be spent over a given timescale, for every phase of a business project.

Professional congress organizers (PCO)   A company which specialises in the organisation and management of congresses, conferences, seminars and similar events.

Promotional mix model   Mix that includes four elements: advertising, sales promotion, publicity and/or public relations, and personal selling. However, this author views direct marketing as well as interactive media as additional major elements in a promotional mix model.

Public relations   The profession or practice of creating and maintaining goodwill of an organization's various publics (customers, employees, investors, suppliers, etc.), usually through publicity and other nonpaid forms of communication.

Public show   Exhibition that is open to the public, usually requiring an entrance fee. The attendees are basically defined by their interests and geographic proximity to the show location.

Rack rate   Facility's standard preestablished guest room rates.

Radio frequency identification device (RFID)   Tag attached to a product or device that emits a short-distance signal that allows the user to accurately track information.

Request for proposal (RFP)   Document that stipulates what services the organization wants from an outside contractor and requests a bid to perform such services.

Return on investment (ROI)   Net profit divided by net worth. This financial ratio indicates the degree of profitability.

Risk   The potential of losing something of value.

Room block   Number of rooms guaranteed by the event planner. These rooms are subtracted from the hotel inventory as attendees make reservations.

Room set up   Physical arrangement of a room, including the layout of tables, chairs, and other furniture.

Rooming list   A list, whether printed or electronic, by which an event organizer and/or their designates (e.g., a housing bureau) delivers multiple reservations to a hotel or other housing facility. Often the information contained in a rooming list is originally gathered through attendees' completed Housing Forms.

Room set   How a room is laid out including the location of tables, chairs, etc.

Roundtable   Group of experts who meet on an equal basis to review and discuss specialized professional matters, either in closed session or (more frequently) before an audience.

Schedule   Listing of times and locations for all functions related to an event. This information should be included in the specifications guide for an event.

Seasonality   Period of time when the demand for a certain supplier's product or service is usually high, low, or neither. For example, winter in Florida is high season, while summer is low season.

Service contractor   Outside company used by clients to provide specific products or services (e.g., pipe and drape, exhibitor manuals, floor plans, dance floors, or flags).

Set Over Guarantee   The number of seats or places a facility sets up over and above the minimum number assured by the host.

Shoulder   Beginning and ending days of a room block when fewer rooms are contracted.

Signing authority   Person from the sponsoring organization who has the authority to make additions or changes to what has been ordered.

SMART   Acronym for the critical components of a well-written objective: Specific, Measurable, Achievable, Relevant, and Time constrained.

Social media   The social interaction among people in which they create, share, or exchange information and ideas in virtual communities and networks.

Sourcing   Refers to a number of procurement practices aimed at finding, evaluating, and engaging suppliers of goods and services.

Speaker bureau   Professional talent broker who can help find the perfect speaker to match the event objectives as well as the budget.

Speaker ready room   Area set aside for speakers to meet, relax, test audiovisual equipment, or prepare prior to or between speeches. *Also called* ready room and try-out room.

Specialty service contractor   Supplier that deals with a specific area of show production or event service, such as photography, furniture rental, audiovisual equipment, or floral decoration.

Sponsor   (1) Person or company underwriting all or part of the costs of an event. Sponsors may or may not participate in any of the profit from the event. (2) Individual who assumes all or part of the financial responsibility for an event or commercial sponsor that provides financial backing for an aspect of an event and in return receives visibility, advertising, or other remuneration in lieu of cash.

Sports facilities   Venues in which sporting events are held.

Stadium   Facility that is usually designed for baseball or football as a primary function and that may be domed or open. It is sometimes difficult to distinguish a stadium from a large arena.

Stakeholders   Anyone who has a stake in an event. This includes organizers, attendees, speakers, planners, vendors, exhibitors, the community, and more.

Stand   European term for booth or exhibit. *See* Standard Booth.

Standard booth   One or more standard units of exhibit space. In the United States, a standard unit is generally known to be a ten-foot by ten-foot space (one standard booth/stand unit equals 100 square feet). However, if an exhibitor purchases multiple units side by side or back to back, the combined space is also still referred to as a booth or a stand. It is a specific area assigned by management to an exhibitor under contractual agreement. *See* Stand.

Sustainability   Practices and development that can continue indefinitely without degrading the environment.

Tablescapes   Décor and decoration placed on top of tables, such as flower arrangements.

Theater   Facility with fixed seats, usually on a sloped floor, with sight lines focused on a permanent stage. Typically, a stage box is located behind the proscenium, which contains the performance area and the fly loft.

Third Parties   Intermediaries in the sales process, such as Hotels.com for hotel rooms, or Experient for meeting and convention venues.

Track   Separation of programming into specific genres, such as computer skills, professional development, marketing, personal growth, legal issues, certification courses, and financial issues.

Trade exhibition   *See* Trade show.

Trade fair   International term for an exhibition.

Trade fair bond   When exhibiting tangible products outside the home country of the organization, a Temporary Importation Bond (TIB) or Carnet must be posted. This is usually equivalent to the sales tax of VAT generated by that product and is meant to ensure that the product is "exported" after the trade show or exhibition.

Trade show   Exhibition of products and/or services held for members of a common or related industry that is not open to the general public.

Triple bottom line   Taking into account of the social, environmental (or ecological) and financial impacts of a meeting or event.

Venue   (1) Site or destination of meeting, event, or show. (2) Location of a performance, such as a hall, a ballroom, or an auditorium.

Virtual reality   Computer-generated simulation of a three-dimensional image or environment that can be interacted with in a seemingly real or physical way by a person using special electronic equipment, such as a helmet with a screen inside or gloves fitted with sensors.

Virtual trade show   Attendee-based trade show that is an online experience where the individual can walk the floor and visit booths without leaving his or her home or office. Varying styles of interactivity and graphics are used in this approach.

Workshop   (1) Meeting of several persons for intensive discussion. The workshop concept has been developed to compensate for diverging views in a particular discipline or on a particular subject. (2) Informal and public session of free discussion organized to take place between formal plenary sessions or commissions of a congress or of a conference, either on a subject chosen by the participants themselves or on a special problem suggested by the organizers. (3) Training session in which participants, often through exercises, develop skills and knowledge in a given field.

Yield management: Computer program that uses variable pricing models to maximize the return on a fixed (perishable) inventory, such as hotel rooms, based on supply-and-demand theory.

INDEX